COMEDY AND TRAGEDY ON THE MOUNTAIN:

70 Years of Summer Theatre on Mt. Tom, Holyoke, Massachusetts

JACQUELINE T. LYNCH

Published by Jacqueline T. Lynch
P.O. Box 1394
Chicopee, Massachusetts 01021
www.JacquelineTLynch.com

ISBN-13: 978-1540532459
ISBN-10: 1540532453

This is dedicated to the all the actors, actresses, and technical crew
who gave their all at every performance, and for the audience who supported them...
and for the theatre critics and press who left us a permanent record.

CONTENTS

ACKNOWLEDGMENTS

Many years after The Valley Players ended their run, business manager Carlton Guild donated several boxes of their accounts, programs, and scrapbooks to the Holyoke Public Library. He wrote to librarian Mrs. Mary Kates in 1983 at the time of his donation,

I'm sure that no lines are going to form down to the sidewalk and around the block waiting to see them or other Valley Players material.

Perhaps there were no lines around the block to view the material he generously left to Holyokers and future historians, but I have treasured my time looking through his scrapbooks (which included, among many newspaper clippings, a feather quill used in a play set in the Revolutionary War, letters from staunch supporter Mrs. William Dwight, "Minnie," of the *Holyoke Transcript-Telegram* and her subsequent obituary, a black-edged obituary notice for actress Anne Follmann, an invitation to funeral services for Joe Foley, and always news of actors and former members of the company when they played elsewhere. Reading his notes and play programs, I enjoyed that thrill perhaps unique to writers and historians when long ago voices speak to them and are alive again: the actors like Jackson Perkins and Lauren Gilbert, Joseph Foley, Ted Tiller; the theatre critics like W. Harley Rudkin, the audience and the Pioneer Valley as it was.

I cannot thank the late Carlton Guild enough for his legacy that was my guide on this journey.

My thanks as well to Eileen Crosby, Archivist at the Holyoke History Room and Archives, Holyoke Public Library for her great assistance in utilizing the excellent resources of the History Room, and for her support on this project.

I'm very grateful to all those involved in various capacities with theatre on Mt. Tom who supplied interviews, comments, or correspondence for this book: among them Barbara Bernard, Margaret "Peggy" Bowe, Dan Brunelle, Hugh Fordin, Marc Gonneville (and to Joanne Purcell for helping to set up the interview with Mr. Gonneville), to Don Grigware, Sheryl Mardeusz, George Murphy, Paul Rohan, and Dan Brunelle. Thanks to William Guild for sharing his memories of growing up with The Valley Players, and to his son Ethan for arranging my interview.

My thanks to Mrs. Gail Watson, from whom I got the first Valley Players programs many years ago that started me on this journey.

Thank you to James Gleason of *The Republican* (Springfield, Massachusetts) for granting permission to use the photo of Barbara Bernard and Van Johnson on WHYN TV-40 set.

Thanks to John T. Lynch for drawing the comedy/tragedy logo for the front cover, and to John Hayes for proofreading the manuscript. Author photo by Gretje Fergusson.

FOREWORD

By Barbara C. Bernard

When Jacqueline Lynch interviewed me in 2015 about my memories of Holyoke's Valley Players, I told her "the Valley Players was such a vital part of my life I died a little when it finally closed." That may have sounded a little dramatic but I really did lose something so special.

My enjoyment of live performances began as a child in North Adams with parents, aunts and uncles, all theatre and concert enthusiasts. Not only did I get to see Broadway shows at an age where I probably didn't understand what was going on in the cabin in *Tobacco Road*, but live theatre was in full swing in nearby Pittsfield and Stockbridge with the Berkshire Theatre Group, the Colonial Theater and Fitzpatrick Main Stage. As a college student at Mount Holyoke, I had heard in nearby Holyoke, an industrial city much like my hometown, there was a summer theater called The Valley Players. I was at home working during summers so during those years I never saw a production there.

Knowing there was The Valley Players in Holyoke probably saved my life in 1950. There I go being dramatic again, but my husband and I, married in 1948 after my college graduation, lived in a suburb of Pittsfield where we both worked and we were in an area where live performances prevailed. I still recall seeing Mady Christians in a play and Koussevitzky conducting at Tanglewood. Our life was absolutely perfect and when we bought a business which required us to move to Holyoke, the one bright spot was remembering there was a great summer theater, The Valley Players.

We began to go to the plays our first summer and never once missed a performance. In a short time my Pittsfield career in radio brought me into the same one in the Paper City and eventually into television. At one time or another all the actors and actresses, as well as Jean and Carlton Guild, the founders of The Valley Players, were guests on my programs. Interviews were delightful and because all of the actors lived in various rented rooms in private homes in Holyoke they appreciated visiting with us in our air conditioned house, with our little girls and our dog giving them a sense of home away from home.

Our wardrobes were available to the players to borrow if they needed specific outfits for specific parts, and when Ruby Holbrook, then the wife of Hal, was pregnant she borrowed my maternity clothes. Many summer players brought fame to this area perhaps, with Hal Holbrook who created *Mark Twain Tonight!* There was not a member of the audience that opening who did not acknowledge that we had seen something which would take the world of theatre by storm. Hal reprised the role many times through the years, updating it a little, and once again bringing a full audience to its feet with applause when he returned to Holyoke to present it as a fundraiser for the efforts to bring live theatre back to Holyoke with the Victory Theater project.

Fortunately, our area abounds in excellent all-season live theatre, but for those who love it so, there is never enough. Of course as a resident of Holyoke I feel a city is that much richer if it has its own live summer theatre and The Valley Players truly made Holyoke a more exciting city. There are so many memories, such as Mountain Park always saving its fireworks display to coincide with intermission of the plays, and the refreshment stand serving crispy clear-cold "birch beer," and never a play produced to which one would feel uncomfortable bringing one's grandmother, teenage child, or minister.

I personally am, and I feel confident all readers of this wonderful book Jacqueline has produced are grateful for her considerable research and her ability to make our memories come alive again. The Valley Players was a unique part of Holyoke history and certainly in my life, which makes being elderly not as unpleasant as it would have been without seventy years of remarkable summer theatre.

INTRODUCTION BY THE AUTHOR

A playwright usually begins a script with the only stage directions that will be reprinted in the play program for the audience to see:

The Time: …

and

Setting: …

These notations will drop the audience instantly into the world they are about to see on stage. Theatre is always present time because it is live. Film and television (even live television in a sense) is always filtered by the camera viewpoint, by the editor, and by the very passage of time between when it was produced until the time the audience gets to see it. But live theatre has no filters between actors and audience. As such, it is the most intimate art form.

A book on theatre can relate facts and stories, and to be sure, you will find plenty here, but it cannot hope to achieve the same excitement of intimacy. However, we will start on the right foot by leading off like a playwright's script…

The time: 1895 to 1965.

Setting: A wooden, barn-like summer playhouse…in an amusement park…on a mountain…in a New England factory town.

As unlikely a place as you will find for stage plays, but as much a part of the community as the stores and businesses, and the red brick maze of factories and canals down below the mountain, in the so-called "Flats" by the Connecticut River. The place was Holyoke, Massachusetts. For some seventy years live theatre created magic on the lush green mountain above the city.

Though a summer playhouse, any theater, any stage, may seem like a world unto itself, it is not; not entirely. It reflects its era and its location, that larger world outside its wooden walls; therefore this story is as much about Holyoke, the tri-city area of Holyoke-Chicopee-Springfield, and the Pioneer Valley of western Massachusetts, because this was the audience for the little playhouse on Mt. Tom. If you are familiar with these towns, then you will find much in this book to jog your memories, for this is *your* story. If you are a stranger to this part of the world, then you will be introduced to a unique spot of 400 years of history with a mosaic of images of colonial settlement along the Connecticut River, the heartland of New England, where a planned city created by the Industrial Revolution became part of an urban corridor made broader still by the suburban spread of the 1950s. This valley enjoyed a long and unique relationship with live theatre, both in the great downtown brick and mortar theaters of "winter stock" and the barns and tents of summer stock. At one time or another, all the greats of the American stage came to the Valley.

There is a special ambience to *summer* theatre. We do not travel to the grand palaces of urban downtowns; the stars come to us. They are close enough to touch, not only on stage, but in the local grocery store or coffee shop. We do not need to hang around the stage door to see them; they may have arrived in the car parked next to ours in the dirt lot.

It was called "the barn circuit" because most summer theaters were originally barns, or called "the straw hat circuit" because the ladies and gentlemen of the audience wore straw hats to the theater in summer. The theater may be a wood frame structure with screens to let in a cool breeze (or the heat and humidity), or it may be a tent temporarily constructed. Both will be closed in September, to be shuttered for the winter, or the tents dismantled, as if they had never existed. For those with cherished memories of their performances, their ghosts linger today.

Bosley Crowther, theatre and film critic for *The New York Times* described in the 1930s the atmosphere of summer theatre on the Maine shore in Ogunquit and in Lakewood and what it did for the actor:

…audiences largely made up largely of urban vacationists…no child of the sock and buckskin, who has been able to spend a month or six weeks on the edge of a clear blue lake, where the sun sparkles brightly by day and the loons cry mournfully by night, or within the sound and smell of the long rolling ocean, can return in the fall to Broadway anything but a better man—if not a better actor.

Walter Hartwig, founder of the Ogunquit Playhouse recounted the charm for the audience in an article for *The New York Times* in August 1935:

There is glamour, romance and adventure sold with a ticket to a summer theatre. Most of the summer theatres are situated in romantic settings. The surprise of the unexpected helps. There is a thrill in the experience of getting good or well-known actors in popular plays and under conditions and surroundings that hardly suggest such an experience. The summer theatre is intimate with its audience from the time the purchaser of a ticket steps up to the box office until the show is over.

A New England tradition born of the resort era, summer theaters gave actors a chance to earn a living year-round when the theatre season in the cities ended in May. They followed their audience to the shore and the mountains, getting out of the city. In Holyoke, Massachusetts, however, they came *to a city*, a mill town, and an idyllic park on the mountainside above it. The theater was called the Casino, built in 1901, and remained here as a showcase for live theatre until 1965. It held an audience of about 2,500 at its greatest capacity early in the century.

There was not one company of players, but many, as entertainment evolved from vaudeville,

operetta, WPA-sponsored shows in the Great Depression, and then its heyday from 1941 to 1962 with a resident repertory company called The Valley Players. In the early 1960s, two new incarnations: The Casino-in-the-Park, and finally, the Mt. Tom Playhouse with touring packaged shows featuring well-known stars from television and the movies. Many stars of stage and screen, and many newcomers who would one day become stars, performed over six decades at the Casino.

The voices emanating from the stage were joined by voices from the audience, from the newspaper reviews, from local television and radio, all echoing down the thickly wooded mountain to the broad open valley below. Here are a few:

The *Holyoke Transcript-Telegram* daily newspaper from 1953:

The Valley Players have made this community a richer place in which to live during the summer season. They've made for us a happy feeling that they belong to us.

Jim Othuse, who went on to a career in designing sets and lighting for the theatre, began as an apprentice with The Valley Players:

I remember loving every day that summer of 1962 when I was eighteen. I am so glad I got to experience a technical apprenticeship with the company. I am still designing sets and lighting for theatre and loving it. I cherish those days at the Casino that led to my career.

Don Grigware was a young boy tagging along with his father, who worked weekends at the Mountain Park amusement park where the theater was situated, and also ran concessions for The Casino. Don would one day work as teacher, an actor and reviewer:

I would peek into the parking lot and watch the actors arrive about an hour before curtain and then when the performance began, I would sneak into the theater, crouch down behind the seats and watch the play. I think I was so infatuated by watching the actors strut around onstage and speak with perfect diction…Years later when I studied with Stella Adler and Jose Quintero and they spoke of total commitment to the craft, my mind would always flash back to watching the Valley Players portray a myriad of characters week after week…whatever I have accomplished in my acting and writing, however small, has made my life richer. What a background; I wouldn't trade it for anything.

Brad Russell, who later worked as an actor in New York, worked at the Casino as a young man when he was called Bob. He cleaned the theater and worked in the box office. He recalls the couple who served as managers of the company, Jean and Carlton Guild:

Jean and Carlton were very sweet to me and we remained friends for years. I can honestly say it was the happiest summer of my life.

Margaret "Peggy" Bowe, who took speech and drama lessons as a child from Jean Guild and went on to major in Theatre at Emerson College and eventually retire from the U.S. Army as a Signal Corps Lieutenant Colonel, says of her:

I am the person I am today, in strong measure, because of Jean Guild.

George Murphy, actor, local radio and television personality, who worked as an apprentice for the Mt. Tom Playhouse when he was a teenager:

There were times I really didn't want to leave. But I'd always dream of that place…and there is a smell that I loved about backstage. I can't liken it to anything. I just know that there's a smell that it's—it's almost euphoric at times. And I miss that so much.

Dan Brunelle, another apprentice at the Mt. Tom Playhouse:

There were great productions done and I met a number of well-known actors over the two seasons that I was involved at Mt. Tom, and apprenticing is a splendid way to introduce a dopey kid to a wider world…an invaluable learning experience that I thoroughly enjoyed.

Barbara Bernard, local radio and television personality, and newspaper columnist:

Those were such good plays. It just brought this whole community to be alive.

Columnist Anabel B. Murphy for the *Holyoke*

Transcript-Telegram noted of the 1963 season at The Casino-in-the-Park:

Our judgment is that if you saw any five plays now on Broadway, or on Broadway last winter, you would not have spent your money as well as you would have if you bought tickets for the five shows that have been put on at Mountain Park so far this summer.

Hal Holbrook, who was a member of The Valley Players in the 1950s, and who went on to a distinguished career on stage, screen and television, winning numerous awards, including Broadway's Tony Award®, remarked in his memoir about summer theatre and the appreciation by the audience:

It was a different breed of actors then. There were stars. Not the 'movie stars' we idolize today, created by the enormous cinema screen and advertising. Those leading actors of yesteryear were stars because when they stepped on a stage, something happened. A presence arrived. Stakes rose and the ante went up. They did not alter or distort the reality taking place on the stage—they increased it.

Carlton and Jean Guild, producers of The Valley Players, noted in a 1954 program:

At best, (and we're convinced that here in the Pioneer Valley is the best), summer-theater operation is not a lucrative business. Its greatest rewards are not monetary. They are personal.

The Guild's son, William, who grew up with The Valley Players:

I just remember loving the whole experience. I would cry every year when the actors got on the train in Holyoke to go back to New York, and I would cry for a couple of days afterwards. Then it was back to Holyoke High School; that's enough to make you cry even more.

Theatre, for those towns lucky enough to have it, has a special impact on a community, and enriches it on so many levels. The people in the audience are not customers so much as they are collaborators, and in no other business does this happen.

Samuel Johnson, the lexicographer of the Age of

Reason remarked in one of his famous epigrams:

The drama's laws the drama's patrons give,
For we that live to please must please to live.

The house lights are going down now, and the stage lights are coming up. The actors are making their entrance...

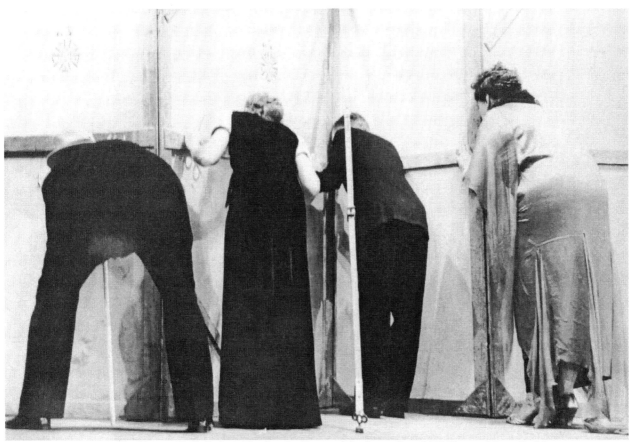

Torchbearers 1945: Robert Ermhardt, Carmen Matthews, Ronald Telfer, and Jean Guild
peeking at the audience

1895-1930s: Vaudeville and operetta
1930s WPA Theatre
The Pioneer Valley Drama Festival – 1940
The Valley Players – 1941 – 1962
Casino-in-the-Park 1963
Mt. Tom Playhouse – 1964-1965

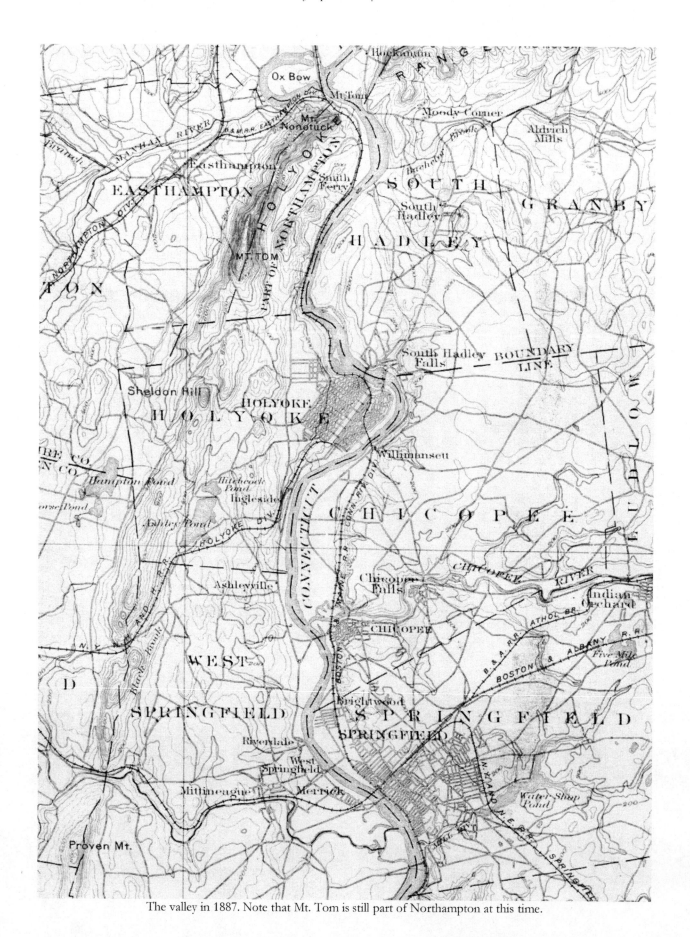

The valley in 1887. Note that Mt. Tom is still part of Northampton at this time.

CHAPTER 1

You Are Here: A Brief History of the Pioneer Valley

New England is famous for its summer theaters: Ogunquit, The Cape Playhouse, Lakewood—from the Berkshires to the Connecticut shore, for generations summer playhouses have provided big-name entertainment to small towns and have been a training ground for future greats of the stage and screen. In the 1950s, the so-called heyday of summer theatre, it was reported that half of all summer stock theaters in the country were located in New England.

Humphrey Bogart played at Lakewood in the Maine woods. Bette Davis started as an usher on Cape Cod at the Cape Playhouse. There is still a bust of Katharine Hepburn at the Ivoryton Playhouse in Ivoryton, Connecticut, where she performed as a young actress. James Stewart, Henry Fonda, and Margaret Sullavan, among other future Hollywood icons, got their start at the Falmouth Playhouse in Falmouth, Mass. Most great actors and actresses of the nineteenth and twentieth centuries passed through New England's straw hat circuit, from Booths to Barrymores. These theaters are humble, but there is greatness in them. The most ramshackle wood frame playhouse may have, as regards the history of American theatre, a most exalted pedigree.

Where does Holyoke, Massachusetts, fit in? It is the quintessential factory town. There are no summer vacationers here. It is not the Cape – Dennis or Falmouth, not the mountains – not Lakewood, not the shore – not Ogunquit. It does not have wealthy roots like the Westport Country Playhouse in Connecticut.

Yet it had a robust life, including theatre, from the late nineteenth century through the 1960s – until the factory town itself began to experience recession, when its mighty industries went out of business, or moved to the South to leave decaying brick shells and firetrap tenements, when the city started its economic decline – and this led, for a time, to its cultural decline.

No one could have foreseen this city's urban blight of the 1960s and 1970s back in the 1800s when the paternalistic factory owners built their grand mansions on the hill above the kingdoms they created of textile and paper mills, workers' tenement housing, and three levels of canals that brought energy from the river to the factories.

The river was there long before, curling around the mountain: Mt. Tom. With an elevation at just over 1,200 feet, its long, horizontal silhouette is visible for miles: resembling the humped back of a recumbent, shaggy beast. In 1939, this broad section of the Connecticut River Valley from northern Connecticut to southern Vermont was christened "The Pioneer Valley" by business and tourism concerns to promote the area.

A view of the valley from a book of essays by local writers called *The Pioneer Valley Reader*:

The themes that have emerged in the Pioneer Valley are big ones. The Valley was the first inland frontier, a place distinct from Boston and the Atlantic coast…throughout its history, the Pioneer Valley has been a seedbed of such reform initiatives as Jonathan Edwards's Great Awakening, Shays's Rebellion, abolitionism, women's education, Edward Bellamy's utopian critique of industrial society…The region's Puritan seriousness, higher education, scenic beauty, and remoteness have nourished writers and thinkers of all kinds. The Valley has been a place to pursue one's unique voice out of the mainstream of   *American life.*

***

Explorers to western Massachusetts in the 1630s, a band of that curious combination of Puritan Capitalists, came up the river – a much easier effort than traversing the thick woodlands between the river and Boston – and established their first settlement in Springfield. The Springfield Plantation covered a much wider range then than its current modern city; across the river, and northwards in a great swath of unexplored territory. In 1651, Springfield, over forty years before Salem, was the first settlement in the colony to have a witchcraft scare over a murder, with the accused being sent to Boston for trial. Charges were dropped against a man because his wife, the actual murderer, confessed, but she died in prison before her execution.

The northern part of the settlement around present-day Northampton, "Nonotuck," was purchased from the native tribes in the area. Hampshire County was carved out of Nonotuck, and encompassed all of the English-inhabited areas of western Massachusetts. Elizur Holyoke

was a planter in the 1660s, a surveyor, born in England, who lived in the Springfield settlement with his wife (Mary, the daughter of Springfield founder William Pynchon) and children. He later became an associate judge. Both the future city of Holyoke, and the small mountain situated across the river in future South Hadley, would take his name.

He was present the year of the burning of Springfield in 1675 during King Philip's War, when the Wampanoag tribe engaged in a series of fierce battles with white settlers. Some sources say Elizur Holyoke died in this year, or 1676, as Captain in defense of the town. His son Elizur Jr. moved to Boston. Holyoke's grandson Edward became president of Harvard University. In the 1880s, a descendent, Dr. Frank Holyoke, moved to the city named for his ancestor. There are no monuments today to Elizur Holyoke, except for the mountain on one side of the river and the city on the other side of the river that bear his name.

Throughout the colonial period, Queen Anne's War, the French and Indian Wars, the settlers encountered sickness, struggle for survival, culture clash, occasional attack, as again with the 1704 Deerfield Massacre, with those not killed taken captive to Canada. The commercial enterprise of their settlement, which it most certainly was founded on as much as it was a Puritan escape for religious freedom from the reign of King Charles I, managed to thrive on the friction. However, the area that would come to be future Holyoke was still unnamed, and was still a part of the Plantation, only a small agricultural dot in the wilderness marked by a tavern that marked the halfway stop on the stagecoach route between Springfield town and the new county seat of the area, Northampton.

The American Revolution weeded out Tories, who adapted or emigrated, and business went on as usual with no actual battles taking place in the valley. The spectacular effort of General Henry Knox's crew dragging cannon on sledges pulled by oxen in the winter snow from Fort Ticonderoga in upstate New York to Boston that came through the area in January 1776 was perhaps the valley's strongest link to the war, as well as the men who fought in the war. Colonial graveyards in the area today are the final resting place of many locals who left home and farm to fight the British.

Shays' Rebellion was violent but short-lived, from late 1786 to February 1787, a home-grown rebellion against the new American government in Boston by farmers protesting taxes. The rebels were chased from their clash with authorities at the Springfield courthouse, up through future Chicopee and dispersed in the wilds of Hampshire County.

***

The next decade brought a serious buckling down to commerce and exploitation of the valley's natural resources now that the dust had settled over outside conflicts and forces beyond the valley. It began with the river, which was the mother of settlement here, and from which feeder canals would generate massive power. In 1794, the first canal in the United States was built in South Hadley, two and a half miles long; the shape of things to come to harness water power for manufacturing.

Southward in Springfield, the area to be known as Court Square, where Shays' men had been defeated at the courthouse and where a new one was built, became the hub of a community that expanded from the river's edge to the eastern heights, where the Arsenal that George Washington had established (and Shays' men failed to sack), sat above all. Taverns, shops, and banks popped up overnight, and the formation of Hampden County, carved from the southern part of old Hampshire County in 1812, returned Springfield to a county seat. It would quickly surpass Northampton in population and wealth, but the two towns would always share an equal importance in the culture of the valley.

In between them, on the same side of the river as Northampton, was the stagecoach stop between Northampton and Springfield that had developed into an area familiarly called Ireland Parish. It had been deeded to John Riley, a farmer who had owned the land in the late 1700s. Boston entrepreneurs saw the area as a potential spot for manufacturing and they purchased a large section of Riley's land along the river. Most of this was not developed until 1848, when capital from investors secured the rights of the Hadley Falls Company, which had made such inspired use of their experimental canal.

Ireland Parish became the new home of immigrants from Ireland who built the dam, the canals, and the factories. Historian Peter Loughran wrote:

The immigrant mill-hands found in Holyoke reminders of

"home" – green hills and miserable living conditions. On a pay of 75 cents a day, a laborer could not afford to live in the tenements he had helped to build. He called a poorly built riverside shanty home.

Shacks in "the Patch" were eventually abandoned for an apartment in a tenement in "the Flats," where some 105 persons lived in a seventeen-room tenement. There were no adequate toilet facilities, and sickness was rampant, notably in an 1849 cholera epidemic that decimated the Irish population. Another epidemic of smallpox hit in 1850 and left hundreds dead. It was not until the passage of health laws and bringing clean drinking water from reservoirs in the hills above the town that this dire situation was alleviated.

When Holyoke became a town in 1850 it was still mostly farmland, with the addition of one small cotton mill, and as the name Ireland Parish suggests, was largely settled by Irish, as far back as the 1740s. In another hundred years, it became a completely different world of water power, factories, and the enormous dam across the Connecticut River that transformed the area. The dam in the autumn of 1848 began modern Holyoke, but it wasn't until March 1850 that the town incorporated and took Holyoke for its new name, after Elizur, who on a surveying expedition may or may not have named Mt. Holyoke on the other side of the river in South Hadley for himself. Within the next few years, several cotton mills were built, and then the first paper mills.

It has been called "the first planned industrial city in the nation," though other industrial experiments occurred on a grander scale in Lowell, Massachusetts, whose investors also helped to establish a manufacturing base in northern Springfield, which in 1848 separated and formed the town of Chicopee. Chicopee, which had been a farming community for some two hundred years, suddenly found itself a burgeoning manufacturing center, with an enormous diversity in products made, leading to the future city's motto, *Industriae Variae*, or varied industries. As with Holyoke, the first builders of the mills were Irish, and the Yankee mill girls who manned the looms were in turn replaced, generation after generation, with Irish, French, and Polish, a stream of immigrants from Europe.

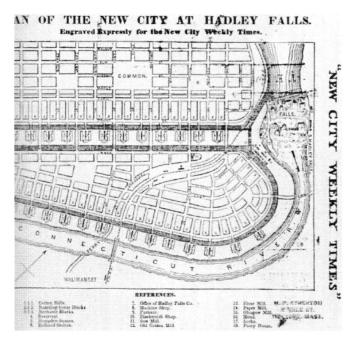

With manufacturing came a transportation hub, as in 1839 a railroad from the east reached Springfield, linking it with the town of Worcester. Two years later the Western Rail Road bridge spanned the Connecticut River, and the tracks crawled further west to the Berkshires. In 1842, the Connecticut River Rail Road was chartered to build a rail line from Springfield to Northampton, linked through Holyoke.

Holyoke was undergoing its own internal transformation, and a series of three canals on levels stepping up the hill from the river to the commercial district was built in stages from 1847 to 1893.

Across the river in South Hadley, their little Mt. Holyoke enjoyed its own infusion of visitors just

by the addition of road carved out to the top as early as the 1820s where stage coaches, and eventually a funicular, led the way to a pleasant view of gentle rolling farmland. Famous visitors to the Mt. Holyoke Summit House throughout the nineteenth century included Ralph Waldo Emerson, Nathaniel Hawthorne, and Jenny Lind. Civil War general and Hadley hometown boy Joseph Hooker visited in 1875.

A flurry of building activity continued across the river in Holyoke in the early 1870s, but increasing numbers of immigrants and workers for the factories were living in crowded conditions. According to *Holyoke Transcript-Telegram* columnist and author Ella Merkel DiCarlo, "Several families packed themselves into rooms intended for only a few. Slops ran all over the yards. The *Transcript* reported, 'It is no wonder that the death toll in 1872 was greater in Holyoke than in any large town in Massachusetts.'" When the Sisters of Providence opened a hospital in Holyoke in 1873, their subsidiary orphanage was created in part as a response to the huge numbers of children left without parents after frequent epidemics.

Author and Pulitzer Prize winner Tracy Kidder, who wrote of Holyoke in his book *Among Schoolchildren*, mused that Yankees "invented" Holyoke, but that Irish laborers built it. The Connecticut River, which gave life to the industries in the valley towns along its shores, would also suffer consequences, as "...Holyoke produced more paper than any other city in the world, staining the wide Connecticut a variety of colors all the way down to the city of Springfield."

Author Edwin M. Bacon described the canals that siphoned off the river water and shot it to the mills for power in this passage from 1906:

...the first or upper level canal, extending through the heart of the city for a mile and a quarter; the second level, paralleling the first, then sweeping around, following generally the River bend; and the third level, carrying its water to the many mills in the south part of the city along the River Bank. The city's streets are laid out in relation to the canal system.

The Germania Mills were located on the first level canal in 1865, a wooden building, later enlarged in 1870. On the second level, Parson's Paper was the first paper mill in Holyoke in 1853, joined later by Whiting Paper in 1865, the Valley Paper Company and Riverside Paper Company in 1866, the Albion Paper Company in 1878 and the Nonotuck Paper Company in 1880. These were only a part of Holyoke's huge manufacturing base.

In 1873, the Connecticut River swarmed with timber from log drives down from Vermont when Titus and Erastus Morgan started their sawmill. The logs had floated some 300 miles to cut for market from spring to fall. Men worked some sixteen hours a day, seven days a week battling log jams and guiding the timber on the river. At Holyoke, where they arrived at the massive dam, the rustic logging operation met head-on the new technology of the Industrial Revolution. Steps away on the shore were factory workers, including children, toiling upwards of seventy hours a week,

beginning their workday in the dark at 5:00 a.m. and ending at 6:30 p.m., six days per week.

Opportunity is relative. Paul Rohan, Holyoke native, mused in an interview for this book:

The idea that someone could go and have a job working on building a dam, then building canals, then building buildings, and then mill jobs in those buildings—you know, for people in Ireland, that was like beyond belief. How could it possibly be so good?

Probably the most famous of the mills in what would be called the Paper City was not a paper mill at all, but a silk mill. Skinner's Silks were synonymous with high fashion in the nineteenth century, from a factory begun by an English immigrant. William Skinner had emigrated from England at the age of nineteen. He had been apprenticed to his father while in England, then he and his brother established their own mill, and in 1868 in the village of Williamsburg, part of Northampton, William Skinner began his grand operations, the Unquomonk Silk Mills, named for a local Native American tribe. However, all was destroyed in the devastating Great Mill River Flood of May 16, 1874, and Skinner set his sights on Holyoke. He explained in a letter to the *Springfield Republican*, "I have fixed upon Holyoke as my future place of business...cheap and reliable waterpower is to a manufacturer what good rich land is to a farmer..."

He dismantled his home and reassembled it on the corner of Cabot and Beech streets. He called it Wistariahurst. It was a twenty-six-room mansion, of parquet floors and vaulted ceilings, its exterior decorated with flowering wisteria vines that gripped and cuddled the home. Iconic stone lion figures were brought over from Rome in the 1880s. It had electricity before most towns in the area did.

Holyoke had been called the Brick City before 1880, but became the Paper City as most of the industries were devoted to the manufacture of paper, additionally the Wauregan Paper Company, Chemical, Dickinson & Clark, Winona Paper, and National Blank Book.

City Hall and its elegant tower, however, were granite. In 1876 the city's first hotel, thirty beds, was established on Dwight Street. Holyoke had a later start than the other towns, but it caught up with impressive vigor.

Holyoke Transcript building

With increasing population came several newspapers to serve the community. William Loomis ran the *Holyoke Daily Transcript*, then was joined by William G. Dwight in the 1880s. Another paper started in 1886 – the *Holyoke Daily Democrat*, by Charles Bellamy, brother to famed Edward Bellamy, who was a Chicopee native,

High Street, 1908 postcard

editor for the *Springfield Daily News* and author of the groundbreaking utopian novel, *Looking Backward 2000-1875*. In 1900, the *Holyoke Democrat* changed hands and became the *Holyoke Telegram*. The populations these newspapers served were, in the tri-city area, at least 50-percent foreign born and more at any given time in the late 1800s, and of that immigrant population, at least half were Irish. A wave of German and French-Canadian immigration would follow in the late nineteenth century.

The factories and the newspapers are such an important factor in this story because these create the fabric of the community and had a direct correlation to the establishment of theatre in the area. Of course, there were more than factories here in the tri-city area; there were bustling downtowns by this time around the turn of the

twentieth century with scores of shops and businesses, there were hospitals, schools and colleges, and all manner of commerce that enabled a wider community to flourish. But it was the factories and the newspapers that made up two of the points on the triangle to enable a promising environment for theatre: the factories brought workers to the area from outside, who were the audience and who, by their employment, had money to spend on the theatre. By 1897, there were *eleven* newspapers in Holyoke. The newspapers provided a way for the theater managers to advertise and communicate with their prospective audience – and also provided the theatre critics a forum to publish their opinions on the plays. Through their articles, they created a fan base, making unknown stage players famous.

The critic, often parodied as the enemy of the

actor, is really one of the most important components in allowing the transformation of stagecraft from art to business. Hopefully, to profitable business, but that is the capricious nature of art and commerce. In the next fifty years to the mid-twentieth century, it is remarkable how many newspapers there were in the valley, and how many of these had a person on staff solely to write theatre reviews. Even small-town weeklies regularly sent writers to the latest opening night in neighboring towns and cities. This is something we rarely see today – not only are there fewer newspapers, but the weeklies that exist carry a lot of press releases for business openings, club notes, and community calendars, and otherwise do not attempt to emulate the news and features of the dailies (most of which no longer employ regular theatre critics, either).

The factories and the newspapers were two points on the triangle, but the third necessary aspect to provide a flourishing environment for theatre was transportation. The summer playhouse on Mt. Tom began as only a gimmick: an added attraction for the local trolley company as a destination that encouraged riders to stay until the end of the line.

In Holyoke, William Loomis was one of the directors of the Holyoke Street Railway Company, incorporated in 1884, which had a fleet of horse-drawn carriages. He took over complete control of the company in 1888, and in the early 1890s transformed the railway into a series of electric trolley lines. He bought 365 acres on Mt. Tom. There he established a picnic grounds with a mini-zoo and provided a pleasant park for the factory workers down below in the Flats to escape the summer heat.

Piece by piece, the park became a pleasure center as a tintypes booth was placed there, along with an open-air restaurant and dance pavilion, and in 1895, an open-air stage on raised platform. It was a simple beginning to an amusement park that became a Holyoke signature and beloved by generations, and a simple beginning to one of the best summer theaters that ever existed in New England. That same year, the Duryea brothers who built their prototype gasoline powered automobile in a garage in Chicopee, test ran it in Springfield. Cars would bring thousands to remote summer theaters in the future.

In 1897, Loomis sold the park to the Holyoke Street Railway, and the state granted a charter for the construction of a pleasure park here. Over time, the park grew in popularity with the addition of walking paths and observation towers. From the towers looking southward, they could see the broad valley below, following the ribbon of river down to Springfield, and all the pleasant rolling land in between.

An economic recession in the 1890s led to hard times for some of the then twenty-six paper mills in town. Holyoke continued to evolve as earlier immigrants left the tenements and moved to better apartments and houses away from the Flats. Churches followed their congregations up the hill. Factory owner William Skinner and newspaper owner William Whiting pushed the drive for Holyoke Hospital, dedicated on Beech Street in June 1893. It accommodated forty patients. The following year, the new Providence Hospital opened in town with beds for one hundred. The old building, St. Anne's, became a home for the aged and infirm.

Holyoke, 1906

In 1890, Springfield had a population of 44,179; Holyoke was close behind with 36, 637; Chicopee, the year it became a city, far behind with only 14,050 in population and still nearly half were foreign born. Hampden County's total population was 135,713.

In June 1895, the trolley line extended from Lincoln and Northampton streets to the "Little Mountain" part of Mt. Tom. In the following year, a cable car funicular was extended up to the top of the mountain. Ella Merkel Di Carlo noted, "The mountaintop belonged to Roswell Fairfield who had bought it for the lumber for his Westfield paper mill." The Mt. Tom Reservation Co. formed, and "For five cents people could ride up from the Main Street Post Office to the park and for another quarter go up and down the mountain."

From a Holyoke newspaper in August 1895:

The popularity of this charming resting place was never more thoroughly shown than on yesterday. Springfieldians are fairly crazy over its beauty, and do not hesitate to accord it superiority over Forest park.

Mountain Park began as a simple pleasure grove and would lead to the birth of theatre on the mountain, and in many decades hence, the Valley Players and one of the nation's most popular summer theaters—created, as an afterthought, by a trolley company.

After Fairfield sold his mountaintop, a summit house was built, and that really was the end of the line because one couldn't go any higher. In June 1898 it was announced, "An automatic telephone has been put in at Mt. Tom and Mountain Park."

President William McKinley at the Mt. Tom Summit House

A year later in June 1899, President William McKinley visited Mt. Holyoke College in South Hadley to attend the graduation of his niece, Grace Howe McKinley. He toured the top of the smaller Mt. Holyoke then traveled across the river to Holyoke. According to Ella Merkel DiCarlo, "He stayed with William Whiting, participated in a parade, and took a ride up to Mt. Tom, exclaiming, 'This is the most beautiful mountain outlook in the whole world.'"

He took a carriage from the train station to Whiting's house. A photo of the occasion on published June 17th shows them traveling in an open carriage, surrounded by crowds lining the road, without any trace of modern security. The image is quaint, but also an uncomfortable portent to President McKinley's assassination the following year in 1901. The *Holyoke Daily Transcript* carried the ominous five-column banner head OUR DEAD PRESIDENT! with his portrait photo edged in black.

***

The President had made his visit just in time, for in October 1900, fire destroyed the summit house, but it was almost immediately replaced with a much grander structure, topped by a golden dome. His visit gave the attraction a boost. If the President of the United States can be a tourist on the mountain for a day, then so could we.

The Holyoke Street Railway opened May 27, 1900 as an electrified railway replacing the horse-drawn streetcars, and eventually extended lines into Oakdale, the Highlands, the town to the south called West Springfield, Willimansett, Chicopee Falls, and South Hadley Center. This was augmented by passenger train service between the towns as well. It was common to take a train from Springfield through connections to Chicopee Falls, Easthampton, or Northampton.

At this time, the area of Mt. Tom that was home to the new park and playhouse was actually part of the town of Northampton. The map was redrawn in 1915, giving the entire length of Mt. Tom to Holyoke.

A 1906 viewpoint of Mount Tom was expressed by Edwin M. Bacon in his book, *The Connecticut River of the Pioneer Valley of the Connecticut – Three Hundred and Fifty Miles from Mountain to Sea*:

Mounts Tom and Holyoke are both accessible by cars and afford from their summits enchanting views. The prospect spread out from Mount Holyoke constitutes the more extensive panorama over the rich alluvial Valley...

Mount Tom is now a public reservation, and it is kept ever fresh in current literature by Gerald Stanley Lee, through his chapbook outdoor magazine "devoted to rest and worship, and to a little look-off on the world."

In this world, summer theatre began to flourish.

The first open-air stage that had pillars and draperies was torn down in 1900 and replaced in 1901 with a new indoor theater future theater-goers would know as the Casino. The entrance was opposite the open-air restaurant.

The Casino seated 1800 under the roof, and 2500 in all including those seated in an uncovered section. It was open on three sides with a roof.

13

Upholstered opera house seats came from the Hartford Opera House, which was being remodeled. A local paper reported on opening week, May 29th:

Bad weather affected the size of the audience, but not the quality of the performance. The 1,800 seats are the most comfortable of any summer park theatre in this vicinity.

For the Casino Stage Company, Willard Dashiell, an actor who would have a long association with the Casino, made an introductory speech at the opening of the theater. One day, the Mountain Park amusement park would include a ballroom where big bands played. On stage nearby, entertainers from circus acts to opera, to Handel's *Messiah* were performed for local audiences who ventured up the mountain.

Pat Casey was the Casino's first manager, followed in 1901 by Robert Kane. A mixture of vaudeville was filtered in with the Mountain Park

Opera Company, which presented melodramas and operettas. By 1904, "flickers" had been added to the fare. In 1905, the players were called the Casino Stock Company, and in 1906, the Casino Opera Company. Frequent name changes seemed to be an effort to draw interest in the venue, still managed by Mr. Kane. In 1908 came the Mountain Park Musical Stock Company, but it was back to the Mountain Park Opera Company the following year.

Downtown new theaters were rising in the brick blocks, and some like the Empire Theatre were showing flickers. The Opera House, founded in the 1870s still carried "legitimate theatre" winter stock, in 1903 presenting *The King of Detectives* and *The Metropolitan Melodrama.*

By 1910, Holyoke's population increased to 57,730, and there would be a housing problem.

MOUNTAIN PARK AND MT. TOM BY NIGHT. HOLYOKE. MASS.

That year was the last log drive locally on the Connecticut River. William Skinner, whose silk manufacturing company was world renowned, died in 1902. That November, his daughters Katherine and Belle Skinner founded the Skinner Coffee House, a settlement house in downtown Holyoke that was in operation until 1942. The city took over operation and ran the Skinner Community House there until 1989. At its inception, it had provided coffee and simple meals for women of the mills to spend their lunch hour in a homey setting.

Holyoke was in a sense a paternalistic society where a few wealthy industrialists controlled much of the activity in town. Was theatre for the masses? Or for the elite? The park was established at the end of a trolley line to get people – mainly the factory workers – to travel farther and spend a larger fare. The mountain was there to be exploited, a built-in natural attraction—not the eighth wonder of the world, surely, but time and again what was being promoted was little more than a cool summer breeze in an idyllic place; exactly the opposite of the brick maze of downtown Holyoke where most of the city's population lived and worked. At the time it was enough of an attraction. Some local companies held their annual company picnics at the new Mountain Park, but is theatre good business, or an appendage of the business community? It enriches the soul, at least as much as the view and a cool summer breeze.

This is our setting. The stage, the mountain, Holyoke, and the valley. The Casino playhouse was organic to this environment; it could not have been established anywhere else.

of live theatre in the valley. In 1844, the Masonic Hall was the venue for the hot play of the day: *The Drunkard's Reform or the Lost Saved*, "In three acts with Beautiful Scenery."

CHAPTER 2

Waiting in the Wings: A Brief History of Theatre in the Pioneer Valley

Massachusetts banned theaters until 1792. In Puritan sensibilities, theatre was akin to sin. The Boston Museum, which actually was a theater and as with many theaters, the owners squelched nineteenth century Puritan squeamishness by calling it a "museum," which suggested culture.

At that time, in the greater Springfield area, *Springfield Republican* editor Samuel Bowles II warned nineteenth century audiences against, "the evil that lurks in every form of pleasure." Samuel Bowles II was not to be confused with Samuel Bowles III, or Samuel Bowles IV; this newspaper with a national reputation had a local notoriety for its successive editors also named Samuel Bowles. The poem, as it was known in the valley:

"There's old Sam Bowles—and young Sam Bowles—
And young Sam Bowles's son—
And young Sam Bowles is old Sam Bowles
When old Sam Bowles is done."

The Springfield newspapers, despite Bowles II's warning, would one day have a large part in promoting theatre in the valley. However, live entertainment began with visiting troupes that tested the waters of acceptability. In October 1821, Blanchard's Olympic Theater played in a tent in what became the Court Square area. It was a traveling circus with acrobats and high-wire artists. It was a crude start to a magnificent legacy

For a long time, the Tilly Haynes Music Hall on Main and Pynchon streets was the only theater in Springfield, and hence the area, but it burned down in 1864. Haynes rebuilt it, and much later in 1881, he sold out to Dwight O. Gilmore, who established Gilmore's Opera House there, until it burned down in 1897. Twentieth century audiences would remember this as the site of the Capitol movie theater that showed Warner Brothers films. Gilmore also established the Court Square Theater.

Court Square Theater, Springfield

Edwin Booth played in Springfield as Iago in Shakespeare's *Othello*. He was the greatest of his generation, and the son of a respected tragedian (unfortunately, he was also the brother of Abraham Lincoln's assassin), but though theatre was becoming more respectable—for who could deny that Shakespeare was more lofty than acrobats—as of 1870 the Blue Laws still prohibited the playing of baseball on Sunday. Mr. Bowles' warning on the evil that lurks in every pleasure left its mark.

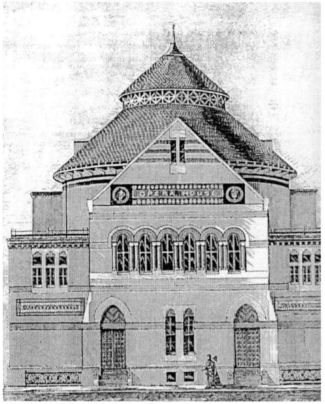

Holyoke Opera House

In Holyoke, the downtown was far behind Springfield in theatre, perhaps not so much because of evil lurking in pleasure; there were fewer impresarios and more industrialists. The Opera House was built in 1877, standing close to the Windsor Hotel and nearby the railroad (which was a necessity for traveling actors, and to transport sets), and a canal. To be sure, in Holyoke, one was never far from a canal. The Hi Henry Minstrels were stranded between Northampton and the Mt. Tom depot in the Blizzard of 1888 on their way to the Opera House. From Ella Merkel DiCarlo's book on the history of Holyoke, *Holyoke-Chicopee, A Perspective*:

The stranded minstrels finally arrived, and were so happy they serenaded everybody at the depot with an impromptu bit of music, and waltzes were danced around the room…the show at the Opera House went on as scheduled though it played to a scant audience, mostly those who couldn't get home and had to stay at hotels in town.

By the 1880s, Holyoke's Opera House was the main venue for theatre and theatre critics. It was noted in the *Holyoke Daily Transcript* that *The Passing Regiment*, described as a comedy-drama, was given at the Opera House Saturday night to a "light audience," and that lead Pauline Markham "…is out of her element."

P.T. Barnum's circus performed at the Water Power Company grounds in 1889. The 1880s was a period of growth in theatre across New England, mainly in big cities with traveling shows and the new craze—vaudeville. One of the premiere newspapers for covering theatre in these pre-*Variety* days was *Byrnes' Dramatic Times*, a weekly newspaper publishing in New York City, where the non-New York theaters were called "Business Out of Town," and were avidly tracked. The doings of Tony Pastor, the Daly Brothers, John Gilbert, Dion Boucicault, Edwin Booth, and Charles Frohman were chronicled in and out of New York.

At the Tilly Haynes' Opera House in Springfield in October 1884, the Union Square Company brought a melodrama called *Storm Beaten* and *Byrnes' Dramatic Times* reported, "gave a very satisfactory entertainment to a large house; the scenery was much admired."

It was noted if performances were well attended or not, and if audiences were welcoming or not, rather like a hobo passing hints to other hoboes for good eats or a job. Touring in these days was still rugged, as this editorial in *Byrnes' Dramatic Times* of November 1884 attests:

There are some managers who have really had the decency to furnish companies, while traveling, with what is an absolute necessity to comfortable travel in these days—sleeping cars. But such managers are still few and far between. The rule is that people are engaged with the understanding, that no matter how much or how little they may travel, they should pay for their own sleeping berths.

Thus, special evils result. In large companies of an opera or burlesque where a number of young women are necessarily employed in small work, at very low prices, many are compelled to sit up nights in the old-fashioned cars, while their more fortunate and better-paid sisters are luxuriating in the comfort of a sleeper. A temptation to go astray immediately ensues…Virtue is thus relegated to the misery of huddling together, while vice answers itself in Pullman palace and boudoir cars.

The sleeping car is really as much of a necessity as a bed in a hotel, but it costs a great deal more money.

In January 1885, Dion Boucicault starred in his play, the Irish melodrama, *The Shaugraun* at Holyoke's Opera House on the 27th. "To a light house," *Byrnes' Dramatic Times* noted. The evening before, the versatile and prolific Mr. Boucicault presented his *Colleen Bawn* at the Court Square Theater in Springfield, "to a very large house."

The Opera House is on the far right.

Though theatre was becoming more popular and, in New England, throwing off the shackles of a lack of respectability, clergymen were now lecturing on the evils of the newest fad—roller skating. They felt it led to the ruin of many innocent girls.

Eva Tanguay, the "I Don't Care Girl" was representative of a new crop of brazen women who performed on stage, though she apparently avoided the evil lure of roller skating. She was one of the very top acts in vaudeville and one of its highest paid performers. Born in Quebec, she grew up in Holyoke where her family came in 1883, following a great French Canadian migration to the city since the 1870s. Her debut took place at Parsons Hall on Dwight Street in 1886 at an amateur night contest. She won a dollar. She was eight years old, and it was the humble beginning of fame and fortune. Decades later, she made one of her last stage performances in Holyoke at the beginning of the Great Depression when she performed at the Casino playhouse on Mt. Tom.

Her act is described in author Trav S.D.'s history of vaudeville, *No Applause—Just Throw Money:*

If anyone embodies the spirit of vaudevillianism, of the triumph of personality, originality, and sensationalism—not only over discipline and craft but even over beauty and talent—that person was Eva Tanguay…Billed as an "eccentric comedienne," her act, at its heart, was that she was nuts. A bad singer and a graceless dancer, with hair like a rat's nest, the homely, overweight Tanguay would put on outrageous outfits, sing provocative, self-involved songs commissioned especially for her and fling herself around on stage in a suggestive manner. She was looked upon as a curiosity, like the "wild man" in a circus sideshow, evincing the same sort of appeal that Janis Joplin and Tina Turner later had in the rock era…But her racier numbers were deemed acceptable because her act was not really reducible to sex. She was just…crazy.

Miss Tanguay reportedly choked a fellow chorus girl to unconsciousness when that woman criticized her performance, and knocked another fellow performer's head into a brick wall. Noticing that scandal brought headlines, which brought more people to the theater to see her, Tanguay started creating controversy, including marriages, to keep her name in the headlines. If that weren't enough, she billed herself professionally as The Girl Who Made Vaudeville Famous. It must have worked. She drew the top salary in the business, at $3,500 per week. Some of her other billings included "Cyclonic Eva

Tanguay," "Mother Eve's Merriest Daughter," "America's Champion Comedienne," "That Girl the Whole World Loves," and "Vaudeville's Greatest Drawing Card." One wonders how many were made up by clever publicity writers, or cleverly made up by Eva.

Eva Tanguay

The Court Square Theater was the jewel in the crown in downtown Springfield when it was established in 1892. All the greats of the late nineteenth and early twentieth century played there: Barrymores, Walter Hampden, George M. Cohan, Mary Pickford, Paul Robeson, Maude Adams, Katherine Cornell, Mrs. (Minnie Maddern) Fiske, Will Rogers, Al Jolson, and Springfield's own Julia Sanderson were only a partial list of the who's who in theatre that played

the city. John Wilkes Booth had appeared in *Hamlet* in Springfield back in 1863, two years before murdering President Abraham Lincoln.

Holyoke was about to make theatre history of its own. Tuesday, May 21, 1895, was the dawn of the new era that would last some seventy years on Mt. Tom—the opening of the Pavilion Theatre. Only a raised platform with a tent cover; the audience sat on the grassy hillside in a natural amphitheater and watched vaudeville and operettas. Early performers included the great Sarah Bernhardt. Light opera and musicals were performed against a painted backdrop. Vaudeville was fifteen, twenty, and thirty cents under Mr. Murray, the manager. The theater was open every evening, with a matinee on Wednesdays and Saturdays.

Sarah Bernhardt

The open air stage is on the far left (above arrow).

The following week on May 28th it was announced:

It is manager Murray's intention to cater to lady patronage this season and disorderly or improper actions on the stage or in front will not be tolerated under any conditions.

Word was spreading, and now that the trolley lines connected the towns in the valley, audiences were coming not just from the workingmen and women in the "Flats", but from more cosmopolitan Springfield. An 1895 Holyoke newspaper reported:

The fine parlor trolley car "Rockrimmon" was at Mountain Park again last night. It was chartered by a party of young Springfield people."

And their chaperone, of course.

It was reported that July 5, 1895 brought a crowd of more than 1,000 to the mountain.

By 1897 vaudeville had gained a foothold; the acts the week of June 27th included the Adelina Ladies' Orchestra, Professor Burke's Trained Dogs, and John Drew, Comedian (grandfather to the famous three acting Barrymore siblings: Lionel, Ethel, and John), all giving afternoon and evening performances. Only the month before, P.T. Barnum's Greatest Show on Earth played in its tent on the Water Power Company grounds, making page one news.

Theatre making page one news: surely the old Puritans, and editor Samuel Bowles (that's Bowles II), must have been turning over in their graves.

Even more astounding and revolutionary, and perhaps to some, disturbing, was a self-made millionaire who rose from humble beginnings and donated several thousand dollars to keep theatre going on Mt. Tom. He was Jacob Barowsky, who arrived in Holyoke from Lithuania as a child with his parents that same year of 1897. He would come to have an enormous impact on theatre on the mountain in the early 1960s. He was not a theatre person, but an inventor and businessman, and as such proved the importance the support of the business community has on theatre. His reasons, even more revolutionary, were altruistic. That would be in the future.

In the 1890s, the theater on Mt. Tom didn't need his help just yet. It was a new world of frivolity, shaking off the dour Victorian restrictions and the tragedies of the nineteen century such as the Civil War and the economic collapse of the Panic of 1893, and looking optimistically toward the coming twentieth century. We knew it would be an age of marvels. The joyous vaudeville menagerie on the mountain included Professor Dunbar's Trained Goats; the Morris' Pony Circus featuring six ponies; a "colored" acting troupe: the Southern Plantation Company; and the Knickerbocker Vaudeville Company, which featured Forrest Tempest, "the Greatest of All Educated Horses." An age of marvels, indeed. Telephones and flying machines were all well and good, but an educated horse—that was something.

Vaudeville was vibrant and joyously egalitarian. Vaudeville historian Trav. S. D. notes in his book, *No Applause—Just Throw Money* that this art form was…

…the first major American institution to offer serious opportunity for advancement no matter a person's race, sex, or religion, and thus had a liberalizing effect on the public—initially demonized and ridiculed, later impersonated, then emulated…and eventually appreciated and loved. By thrusting all groups together, vaudeville became an agent of assimilation.

By 1898, the mountain had become one of the feature attractions in the valley. From a Holyoke newspaper in June:

Mt. Tom is now the beacon of Western Massachusetts and northern Connecticut. A cluster of electric arc-lights has been placed on the roof of the observatory of the Summit House, and the effect is of the light-house order. The light is distinctly seen from Wachusett Mountain, forty-three miles to the east.

From July 1898, a Holyoke newspaper reported:

Denno and Langway, acrobatic wonders, who have just closed a sixteen weeks engagement with the Barnum & Bailey circus at London, do some very clever feats in trick tumbling…

Also in 1898:

John Drew, the popular song and dancing comedian, has been secured as one of the attractions at Mountain Park this week. Drew will be remembered as having appeared several times at the local theatre with road shows.

Perhaps not intentionally insulting Mr. Drew's comedic prowess, the dog act also on the bill drew enthusiastic praise from the Holyoke newspaper:

The troupe of dogs is said to possess more comedy than any other troupe in existence.

In August that year:

The crowd was large last night at Mountain Park to see the performance given by the Southern Plantation company, a collection of colored people who gave a very enjoyable entertainment. The performance opens with an old-time negro act comedy…the olio consists of some very good specialty acts, including a quartet of ladies and gentlemen, who did a very neat song and dance act. The Wilsons also appeared in a refined comedy sketch…. the performance closed with a cake-walk which received enthusiastic applause.

In September 1898 as the summer season was coming to the close:

Enormous crowds witnessed the two performances given yesterday afternoon and evening by the Imperial Star Combination company, which is one of the best vaudeville companies seen in town. The performance opens with Ed Sloan [Sloan Edward?] the black face comedian and banjoist, who had the audience laughing every minute. Sully and Moore appeared in a clever sketch a burlesque on the new woman that is very funny...

John Drew

The stereotype humor prevalent in the day parodied all races, ethnicities and religions on the American social spectrum. At the end of that month, it was reported that::

Barry & Bannon, the Irish comedians, have a very funny act...they kept the audience laughing all the time they were on the stage.

Mr. Berry's (of Berry & Finn—Irish comedians) famous imitation of a Hebrew doing a buck dance which caused the audience no little amount of amusement.

From August 1898:

Fred Wenzel, the well known German comedian...has

been here before with several companies...

Fred Wenzel also performed in stage plays, having appeared in Holyoke the previous year at the Empire Theater in the chestnut *Peck's Bad Boy.*

Other acts included contortionists, "trick violinists," "sentimental singers," and typical vaudeville fare. Mr. William J. Burke was the manager of the theater at this time in 1898 and 1899. It was noted in September that the streetcar fare was twenty-five cents. The summer season of 1900 brought some 10,000 to the park on May 31st. A local paper reported:

This week's show is great. A more disappointed crowd never existed in Holyoke than the several thousand who were forced to abandon the Pavilion last evening.

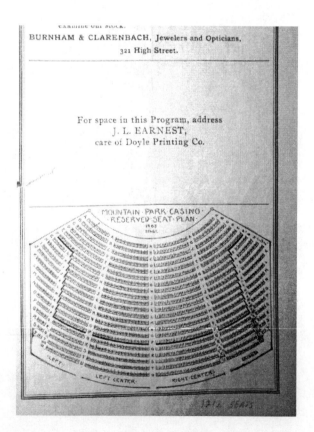

A new theater was constructed in 1901, called The Casino. As vaudeville historian Trav S.D. notes in

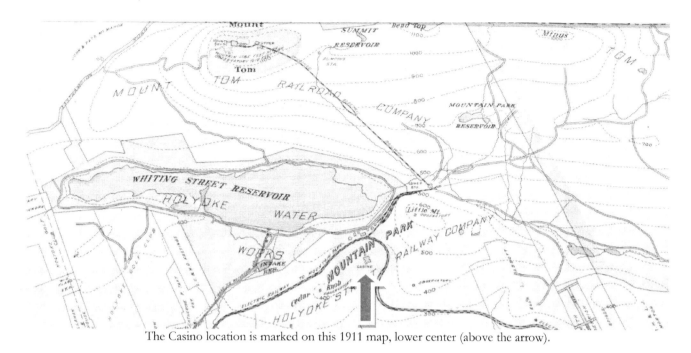

The Casino location is marked on this 1911 map, lower center (above the arrow).

his book *No Applause-Just Throw Money*, "Casino" was a popular name at the turn of the twentieth century that meant "pleasure resort" and "didn't necessarily imply gambling." It was a wooden barn-like structure that accommodated 2,500 seating, and its grand opening dedication was in May that year.

For a 1951 *Holyoke Transcript-Telegram* article, writer Joe L. Markham caught up with Patrick Casey, its first manager. Mr. Casey had also managed an open-air theatre at another recreation park between North Adams and Pittsfield in the Berkshires, and had been lessee and manager at Springfield's Gilmore Opera House and Nelson Theater, both vaudeville houses. During summer months, he would also rent the Court Square Theater and present vaudeville there. Casey, eighty at the time of the 1951 interview, was born in Springfield, but after 1901 left the area and opened a vaudeville booking agency in New York. In 1916 he had established the Vaudeville Managers Association, serving as manager until 1928. Afterwards he went to Hollywood and worked in labor relations for the major movie studios, but retired in 1948 and returned to New England.

***

Vaudeville began the first season at the new Casino, but soon the new Mt. Tom Opera Company took over. Its first production, *Said Pasha*, received good reviews. Many Gilbert and Sullivan operettas were performed in the early 1900s. In 1901, Robert Kane took over as manager of the theater, where vaudeville shared the stage with the Mountain Park Opera Company, which presented melodramas and operettas. At this time, with operettas being more popular, the vaudeville acts would have been used to fill in time between the acts and intermission of the operas and operettas.

The acting company included Charles Fuller, Robert Kane (who directed), Jack Leslie and Florence Ackley. Rather bold both in the variety of genre, mood and tone—the season also included the operettas *The Chimes of Normandy* and the *HMS Pinafore*—and, as in the case of *Cavalleria Rusticana*, did not shy from heavy and difficult material. The last shows of the season were the operas, *Cavalleria Rusticana*, and *The Crimson Scarf.* It was announced in August that during the run of the operetta *Girofle Girofla*.

Beautiful souvenir pictures of Miss Mamie Scott will be

given to all patrons both afternoon and evening.

The offering of a fan photo of its prima donna, Mamie Scott, was both a publicity tool and a clever effort at seeding the community with groupies. At the end of the season, half-tone group photos of the entire Mt. Park Opera Company were given to all patrons. How many Holyoke mantles, piano tops, and scrapbooks they occupied, we can only wonder.

The Barlow Brothers Minstrels opened the 1902 season. The hit of the show was Eddie Leonard.

In that era, Mr. Leonard was considered to be the greatest of all minstrel men, a huge star in his field He frequently headlined at New York's famed Palace, and may be remembered as the author of the song, "Ida, Sweet as Apple Cider."

Improvements were noted to the Casino, with the back being enclosed and the ticket office painted. The local press noted:

Strips of carpet have been laid in the aisles so that the drum-like echo heard when parties were coming down the aisles will be missing.

The Mt. Park Opera Company celebrated its second season with *The Two Thieves*. The company was headed by Emile Barringon and Florence Ackley. Robert Kane returned as manager, and Mr. Kane played the title role that season in *Rip Van Winkle*, where he "scored a big hit". *The Bohemian Girl* played in August with Nannie Dodson the star, portraying the Queen of the Gypsies.

MOUNTAIN PARK OPERA COMPANY
SEASON 1901
❧ ❧ Souvenir One Hundred and Thirtieth Performance ❧ ❧
AUGUST 30th, 1901

William Guild, son of Carlton and Jean Guild who would head up The Valley Players at the Casino in the 1940s and 1950s, recalls exploring the theater as a boy:

It was big, and the stage was Broadway dimensions with all the professional flies, where you would bring scenery in and out from above. I remember a lot of the vaudevillians had left their names scratched on the stairway going down to the men's and women's dressing rooms. The one I remember particularly was Eddie Foy.

***

There were ads in the program for the Murray Hotel—European Plan Exclusively, and Royce's Laundry on High Street, which offered pickup and delivery of laundry by their wagon team. Steiger's department store downtown held a nine-cent sale. The Steiger family-owned department store would have an important role in the future Valley Players on Mt. Tom: not only publishing ads in programs for decades, but leasing the family summer home in Holyoke for The Valley Players to live and rehearse.

Forbes and Wallace, a rival department store in Springfield, also advertised in the programs of this early company. Theatre was becoming posh enough to want to be associated with it. The audience, thumbing through programs while waiting for the show to begin or saving them as souvenirs, would immediately connect with their store ads. Matinees started at 3 p.m., and evening performances were at 8 p.m.

The Chimes of Normandy was back on the roster, as was *Lily of Kilarney, Nell Gwynne,* and *The Black Hussar.* Sunday music concerts were also a feature of this season, which closed September 6th. That opera and operetta were performed jubilantly in a cross between a barn and a large open-air shed is a testament not only to the egalitarianism of summer theatre, but an audience who, perhaps not being able to afford the finer trappings of a night at the opera at the Met, could enjoy a simpler substitute. It was also the scene of the June performance of Lockhart's Famous Performing Elephants. According to the local press:

The great herd of ponderous performing kings of the jungle will be seen to great and particular advantage out of doors. The Casino Theater stage has been rebuilt to insure absolute safety.

Louisa Courtney was the prima donna for the opera company this season. Productions this year included the *Mikado* and *The Pirates of Penzance, Carmen, Faust, Dorothy,* and the season closed with the *Princess of Trebizond* on September 5th. Vaudeville filled in between the acts—perhaps the Casino's having its cake and eating it too.

By 1904, "flickers" had been added to the fare, with a resulting fire. It was reported that some 300 patrons in the Casino fled when the motion picture projector (called a "moving picture machine") threw up flames, possibly from the highly flammable nitrate film of the era. It occurred at about 4 p.m. in the afternoon. The local press reported that though startling to be sure, there was no great danger:

There was a great flash of fire that rose several feet in the air...

No one was hurt, and the paper felt it was a case

of "needless panic."

Operas and operettas were no longer on the bill, as a new company formed called the Mountain Park Stock Company, with tried-and-true middle of the road chestnuts such as *The Telephone Girl, Uncle Tom's Cabin,* and *Triss or Beyond the Rockies* (which was held over two days by popular demand.)

Popular demand was what most theaters, indeed, most providers of any form of entertainment must navigate. Popular demand is influenced partly by what the community needs and what it wants, and often by the whim of fads. Free movies were shown on Sunday afternoon from 3 p.m. to 8 p.m. Downtown in 1903, the Empire Theatre was now showing flickers exclusively. The Opera House staidly carried live theatre, *The King of Detectives* and *The Metropolitan Melodrama.* The Court Square Theater featured Aubrey Boucicault, and seemed to go for the big names.

In 1905, the Mountain Park Players changed their name to the Casino Stock Company, and in 1906, the Casino Opera Company. Frequent name changes seemed an effort to draw interest in the venue, still managed by Mr. Kane. In 1908 came the Mountain Park Musical Stock Company, but it was back to the Mountain Park Opera Company the following year. The dithering over names and genres of entertainment seemed more capricious than a desperate need to attract and keep an audience. They were clearly fascinated at this point by whatever was shown to them. In July 1905 it was reported:

Last night every one of 2,000 seats at the Mt. Park Casino were sold out with 200 people turned away."

A theater manager's dream come true, but the thespians were joined by vaudeville and Collins Moving Pictures. The stock company also used a member of the company to sing or perform specialty acts between the acts and intermissions of the productions that season, which included *The Belle of New York, The Girl from Paris,* a return of *The Telephone Girl,* and *Jack and the Beanstalk.* It was, according to the local press, "the most profitable season the Casino ever had."

Theater on Mt. Tom showed free movies in 1905 as a lure, or to fill-in between vaudeville acts, which were the real attraction. Prices in 1906 were 10 cents, 20 cents, and 25 cents. By 1907, though vaudeville led off the season, the Casino Opera Company brought opera and operetta back to the mountain with a new twelve-week season. Their prima donna was Ada Mead, and W.H. Thompson their tenor; the opening bill, *When Johnny Comes Marching Home.* The company continued the publicity tool of handing out photos of the star, Miss Mead, "richly framed in gold" at every matinee performance of *Tar and Tartar* to reserved seat holders.

DeWolf Hopper, famous for reciting "Casey at the Bat", and husband to his fifth wife, future Hollywood gossip columnist, Hedda Hopper and father to William Hopper (whom you'll remember as the detective Paul Drake on TV's *Perry Mason*), played opposite his longtime partner Jefferson De Angelis in the comic opera *Falke.* The opera season ended August 27th, but was followed with an amateur performance the following week of the ever-popular *The Chimes of Normandy* with local talent from Holyoke and Springfield, under the direction of Emile Barringon and W. Van Volkenburg.

Professor Drake brought his "magic lantern" show "one hundred beautiful views" of The Passion Play of Obergammerau, leading off the 1908 season. The company at the Casino this season were calling themselves the Bijou Opera Company (certainly a change of pace), with Emile Barringon as manager. They opened with the *HMS Pinafore,* but a quick shift was made a week later when the Mt. Park Musical Stock Company was established, superseded the Bijou Opera Company, and presented the comedy "mellerdramer," *The Cowboy and the Lady.* According to the local press:

People were a little upset as they had been accustomed to opera and then had a play thrust at them.

Later generations might wonder at the popularity of opera over a comedy or dramatic play, but such were the tastes of the era. The Mt. Park Opera Company returned under management of Robert

Kane, and opened the next season with *Robin Hood*. Carrick Major, who later performed on Broadway; and Grace Drew, well-known Chicago

prima donna of the era, were the company's leads.

***

A series of postcards published from 1909 through 1913 captures the pre-World War I era of Mt. Tom and the early buildings and pavilions (the dance pavilion graced the park in 1909) in a quiet, pastoral setting, the open-air restaurant and the open-air dance pavilion with its Greek columns, around which ladies in long, sweeping skirts stroll, with gentleman in derbies and straw boaters escorting them. They meet the trolley car, or take in the panoramic view at the Summit House. It seems quiet and idyllic, a world unto itself. That was certainly the intent of the advertising, to pull the city dwellers up to the mountain so conveniently close by, where gracefully tamed nature enhanced the arts.

From 1910 to 1915, more motor cars had access to the mountain, and ads for renting cars for "theatre parties," encouraged the new transportation. The car truly made summer theatre thrive in a way trolleys and trains did not. An ad in the *Holyoke Daily Transcript* advertised the rental of cars at Peltier Brothers Garage on East Street specifically for theatre parties.

In 1911 the Casino Stock Company was the first to exclusively produce stage plays, but folded after

five productions in 1912 and then vaudeville and flickers took over, which had gained in popularity and were cheaper to present. It was not until 1924 that stage plays were again produced at the Casino.

The Casino Stock Company under Willard Dashiell, who had been at the Casino opening in 1901 and delivered a speech to the audience, introduced the company onstage to the audience at the 1911 opening performance. Adora Andrews was the leading lady (who had a long career in stock, but who can be seen in her senior years in her only film performance, in the documentary short produced by the 1939 New York World's Fair: *The Middleton Family at the New York World's Fair*, in which she played the grandmother). Victor Brown was the leading man. Mr. Dashiell played the part of Col. Bonham in their first production, *Arizona*. The local press noted of his leading lady, whom he would later marry:

Mabel Griffith is very pretty, sort of an emotional actress and won many laurels for her acting.

Mabel Griffith remained a favorite of the Casino

audience. A local reviewer had more criticism for the audience than the play:

Slim audience at The Fourth Estate *due to uncertain weather. Two things noticeable lately—late of applause and tardiness of a number of patrons."*

The playhouse sported a new alpine scene backdrop painted by J.W. Murphy of Boston, the scenic artist for the season. E.S. Meniner pulled double duty as the stage manager and carpenter. The special effects were undoubtedly under his supervision as well. In *The Man of the Hour*, thunder, lightning and rain were part of the show on stage, according to the reviewer, which made the play "practically inaudible."

Another name shift created the Casino Musical Comedy Company in 1912, under the management of Lansing Ernest and L.P. Pellissier. They opened with *Coming Thru the Rye* with the largest company up until that time: twenty-eight in the cast. They ended after the fifth production and All Star Vaudeville took over for the rest of the season.

By 1915, more movie ads for theaters downtown filled the newspapers, giving people a reason to stay in the Flats and spend their money there. The Holyoke Theatre showed *Tillie's Punctured Romance* – "Funniest Picture Ever Made" and with it ran, "A Six Reel Keystone with Marie Dressler, Charles Chaplin and Entire Keystone Company." At the Empire Theatre, Mrs. Leslie Carter in *DuBarry*, "A Photo-Dramatization of Her Greatest Success." The Majestic Theatre, "Holyoke's Popular Playhouse" featured still other films, silent movies that were the rage and new curiosity of the era. For the most part, however, the flickers were still looked upon as something for children or the less cultured or less intelligent. Vaudeville, even with dog acts and knockabout comics, was still considered to be on a higher plane.

Competition from motion pictures, however, was a concern for vaudeville and the legitimate houses because it was year-round. The downtown playhouses that featured live theater were winter stock. The Casino on Mt. Tom was summer

stock. Motion picture theaters did not adhere to a particular season; they played constantly – moreover, they could show a feature several times a day without having to pay the cast of the movie for several performances. A stage playhouse had higher expenses in upkeep, in sets, and in payroll of actors and technicians. The movie houses had their cast arrive from the production studio in a film can. In the teens, there were several new theaters in Holyoke exclusively showing motion pictures: The Star Theater showed movies in the first floor of the Crafts Building; the Grand at 407 High Street; the Bijou at 413 High Street; and the Empire at 419 High Street, which was destroyed by fire in 1915. There were also the Wonderland at 301 Main Street and the Palace at 317 Main Street. The Grand Theatre called itself "Holyoke's Leading Photo-Play House," but the Suffolk Theatre actually carried a play in the 'teens when it was not running tango dancing contests. The Empire Theatre carried vaudeville. The only hold out for legitimate theater in the 'teens was Sheedy's Opera House at 461 Dwight Street.

For the next several years, vaudeville was the chief entertainment offered at the Casino playhouse, with occasional plays interspersed as special events, such as the Knights of Columbus Dramatic Club performing in *The Third Degree* in May 1914, directed by John J. Sheehan. These single-performance events were usually in support of a local charity, or as the years of World War I arrived, the Red Cross. Vaudeville had hit its stride as America's most popular entertainment.

In nearby Springfield, the Poli's Palace opened in 1904, as winter stock vaudeville. A new grand venue came to Springfield with the construction in 1913 of the Municipal Group in Court Square, which included a new city hall, a graceful campanile, and the Springfield Auditorium, which would host civic events, as well as concerts and eventually touring shows. Former President William Howard Taft delivered the dedication speech.

Meanwhile, the Court Square Theater on the other side of the common had hit its prime. Maude Adams, probably the most well known and highest paid stage actress of the era, had been originally scheduled to appear at the Holyoke Theatre, but apparently this was cancelled and the Holyoke Theatre offered refunds. She played at the Court Square.

In 1916, the Eastern States Exposition was established in West Springfield, the town just south of Holyoke. Decades hence, the fairgrounds would provide a home to a rival summer theater, the Storrowton Music Fair tent, which would prove a major factor in the demise of the live theatre on the mountain.

Vaudeville gradually proved to be more popular at this time than the operas and operettas at the Casino and continued under the management of Lansing Ernest for several years. After World War I, the only thing hampering the enormous popularity of live stage entertainment (and flickers too), was perhaps the 1918-1919 flu epidemic, in which millions died, and made public assembly a dangerous prospect. By 1921, however, theatre enjoyed another summer season with the danger passed, following the summer vacationers out of town. Up at Mountain Park it was reported in 1921, "tremendous crowds on opening day— hundreds turned away."

1909 postcard

1908 postcard

CHAPTER 3

Enter the Jazz Age and the Great Depression

By 1920, Holyoke's population had reached a high point of 60,203, with one-third of the population foreign born (the population would begin to decrease in the next couple of decades as manufacturing decreased). Chicopee's population, despite its many industries was only 36,214. Most of the land area in that city was still farmland or undeveloped wooded areas. There were several small neighborhood "second-run" movie houses in the city, but no "legitimate" theaters.

In 1920 and 1921 the Holyoke Street Railway Company would suffer less ridership partly because of an industrial decline presaging the Great Depression in Holyoke, and because of the marked increase of the use of automobiles. Holyoke theaters downtown were mainly showing silent movies in this decade: the Strand, the Holyoke Theatre, the Bijou, the Globe, and the Suffolk among them. In 1925, vaudeville on the Keith Circuit also played at the Victory Theatre downtown, which was built in 1920. Newspaper ads did not give street addresses for the theaters – most of which were on High Street or Main Street, and everyone knew that. Downtown, despite the increasing automobile traffic, was still a walker's world. On the mountain, Fred J. Sarr took over management of the Casino for a couple years during World War I, and vaudeville came

under the management of George E. Hammond for two years on the well-known B. F. Keith circuit in 1919 and 1920. *Charley's Aunt* was produced as one of their roster of plays, but vaudeville remained popular from 1912 to about 1924, with only an occasional play produced. In 1924 a re-emergence of stage plays returned with the new Mountain Park Players presented by the Goldstein Brothers of Springfield. Their director was Willard Dashiell, and Mrs. Dashiell—Mabel Griffith—was his leading lady, and this continued through the 1920s. Dashiell would appear on Broadway, including in the original *An American Tragedy* opening in 1926, and had made a handful of silent films. The playhouse under his helm advertised, "Presenting the most popular of New York stage successes." The downtown box office was at the Victory Theatre. However, a smattering mixture of silent movies and Keith Circuit vaudeville continued.

Gift nights and gimmicks to attract customers were offered to the audience down below the mountain. For the first play of one season, *Wedding Bells* by Salisbury Field, the Goldstein Brothers offered to the first couple agreeing to be married on stage during the show, a bridal bouquet, an 18kt gold ring, the marriage license, and a pair of train tickets to Atlantic City for the honeymoon, as well as to pay the fee of the person officiating the ceremony. Other shows that season promised giveaways, usually household items, which could be viewed on display in the window at the Up to Date Waist Company at 327 High Street.

Leading man Irving Mitchell would later appear in a number of Hollywood B-movies and minor television roles. Marjery Williams replaced Mabel Griffith as the new leading woman, as Mabel shifted to character roles. The Goldstein Brothers punched up the publicity for the shows, as they did in this tantalizing piece for *Playthings*.

A new play that has caused all sorts of controversy as to whether some of the questions it raises and the situations it discloses are not a bit too strong even for the modern stage.

Edwardian propriety had been dispensed with, tentatively and cheekily. We're in the Jazz Age now. In July, the musical *Gay Young Bride* featured Tommy Martelle, a noted female impersonator. There were many top acts in the teens and twenties of female impersonators, some quite serious in their imitation, and some rather clownish, but many of these artists came to be well known.

The Goldstein Brothers Amusement Company was back in the 1925 summer season with The New Casino Players, headed by leads Helen Lewis and Jack McGrath. The director was Willard Dashiell. Again, at the start of the season, every actor was introduced onstage to the audience. In their opening show, *In Love with Love*, Mabel Griffith was "deluged with flowers" after the first act. Gift nights were still part of the inducements to get the audience to the theater. Fresh air on the mountain was no longer enough.

In 1926, George M. Cohan's *Mary* was part of the season in August, and late in the month former stock actress Dorothy Beardsley directed *The Naughty Wife*, which marked the first time in Holyoke theatre that a play was directed by a woman. In another generation, The Valley

Players would have most of their twenty seasons' worth of plays directed by one woman, Dorothy Crane.

Other show titles that season reflect the era: *Applesauce, Meet the Wife, The Show Off. The Whole Town's Talking*, with Dorothy Beardsley and King Calder drew a 1,597 house. Between the acts, Miss Marion Severance and Her Orchestra played. A special presentation of a loving cup and flowers was a surprise to Willard Dashiell and his wife, in congratulations for his fifteen years in Holyoke summer theatre.

Early in 1927, a spring flood did damage to much of the city's industry (which would be the first of three devastating Connecticut River Valley floods in the next decade). The Casino, on high ground for sure, escaped the flood and once again provided a summertime refuge for theatre-goers on Mt. Tom. But the opening feature of that season was a portent of the challenge small summer theaters would face in the future—a motion picture.

It was billed as The World's First Exquisite Color Film Featuring Filmdom's Great Star Douglas Fairbanks in *The Black Pirate*. The orchestra from the Victory Theatre downtown provided the musical accompaniment to this silent film.

Then the Casino Players took over with *Laff That Off* with Lillian Merchal and Merrill Matheny in the leads. Some 800 seats sold at 50 cents. On June 27th, fireworks were exploded above the park after the play, which may have been the first time that Mountain Park lit up the night sky, on a play night, a feature that many would remember from their visits in the 1950s.

In 1928, a "winter season" of theatre played in Holyoke downtown, with the drama *Seventh Heaven* presented in April. The company was called the Playhouse Players, and included Mr. Mark Kent, Mr. John Basquil, Mr. Jack Westerman, Miss Virginia Berry, Miss Ruth Abbott. "The Paris Taxi is furnished by Stein's Auto Exchange, 332 Chicopee Street, Willimansett."

Tommy, the next show that ran from April 23rd through 28th featured Dr. William A. Bryant, a former dentist who played in stock around the country, and had the distinction of having appeared in bit roles in two motions pictures in Hollywood: *The Air Mail* with Reginald Denny and Billie Dove, and *Rags* with Mary Pickford. The Playhouse Players presented *So This is London* from May 7th through 12th. According to the local paper:

The Playhouse Players has established themselves as one of the best stock companies to be found anywhere…

The summer playhouse on Mt. Tom at this time was under the auspices of the Court Square Theater, Inc. (another tie with Springfield) proprietors George J. Elmore as business manager and W. O. McWalters as the director. It was noted in the program, "Young children if admitted must be removed at least sign of disturbance. Children in arms not admitted. The management hoped to avoid the above rule which will be rigidly enforced." Shows were performed Tuesday, Wednesday, Friday and Saturday evenings beginning at 8:15, and Saturday matinees at 2:15 p.m. "Popular prices" charged were fifty cents and seventy-five cents for evening performances, and twenty-five cents and thirty-five cents for matinees. "All seats reserved."

They presented light comedies and melodramas. The regular stock company included Mr. Jack Emerson, Miss Mabel Griffith (a favorite on the mountain at the Casino for several summer seasons—no matter what incarnation the playhouse or the company assumed, she remained a constant), Mr. Tommy Kane, Miss Naomi Andrews, and Mr. John Riley. Musical director Leon Girard filled in the intermission with the "Radio March", and selections from *H.M.S. Pinafore*.

The summer season on the mountain in 1928 was again under the auspices of the Goldstein Brothers. Helen Lewis was the leading lady, and new leading man for this season was an Irishman named George Nolan. In the next decade, Nolan would head to Hollywood in sound films and become the leading star George *Brent*. His leading

lady, Miss Lewis (Helen Louise Campbell), would become his first wife. He was perhaps the first of many future famous actors to appear on Mt. Tom.

James A. Bliss directed the company. *Sinner* was the first play, and George Nolan (Brent) was given the job of introducing the company to the audience. He was with the company for two seasons, and often helped out presenting prizes on gift nights.

George Brent

Another special event of the season was when a radio transmission of a Gene Tunney fight was played in the theater after one show. The local press reported:

For the benefit of patrons of the Casino management has arranged to give the Tunney-Heeney fight by radio Thursday night after the show. Every seat for the show will be a ringside seat for the fight without the cost.

This occurred on July 26th, and the bout was broadcast from Yankee Stadium. Gene Tunney beat Tom Heeney by a technical knockout in the eleventh round

EXCLUSIVE OFFICIAL MOTION PICTURES OF
WORLD'S HEAVYWEIGHT CHAMPIONSHIP
GENE TUNNEY BETWEEN TOM HEENEY

Staged Under the Auspices of the World's
Premier Boxing Promoter
TEX RICKARD
SEE!   SEE!
The Close-ups of the Battlers
See the Facial Expressions of Both Boxers
when the Dynamic Punches Crash Thru.
SEE EVERY WALLOP
ACTION IN EVERY ROUND
World's Heavyweight
Champion
HELD AT YANKEE STADIUM JULY 26th New Zealand Champion CHALLENGER

Interestingly, as if illustrating the dichotomy of the 1920s, the first show of the 1928 season was *Sinner*, but the season finished in late August with the old squeaky-clean chestnut, *Peg o' My Heart*.

In 1929, a mixed bags of ups and downs for Mt. Tom: the Mt. Tom Summit House, the third incarnation, burned down and lit up the night sky, visible for miles across the Valley. It was never replaced. On the up side, this was also the year that the beloved carousel and the wooden roller coaster came to the amusement park.

Unfortunately, theatre was on the wane this season, when the Goldstein Brothers yielded, after an opening with Ray Walker's "Song and Dance Review" to a season of Keith Circuit vaudeville, and then in late July, switched to Deluxe Motion Pictures for the rest of the summer. It was reckoned not to be a very successful year for the Casino, financially.

That October, of course, after the Casino and the amusement park were shuttered for the coming autumn, the Stock Market Crash heralded a new era with desperate challenges for many. Theatre, a luxury in the lives of people even in good times, felt the Depression keenly.

In the 1930s, downtown Holyoke had better luck attracting an audience in "winter stock" entertainment, including musical acts at the Valley Arena, which according to local historian and journalist Ella Merkel DiCarlo, "Offered boxing on Mondays, wrestling on Wednesdays and three big shows Sunday featuring big bands, vaudeville

acts and entertainers."

She also noted the racial prejudice that prevented even the most esteemed and famous African American entertainers from staying at a premiere hotel in the city:

Black entertainers who came to Holyoke such as Hubie Blake and Louie Armstrong were denied rooms at the Hotel Nonotuck, [which in the 1940s became a Roger Smith Hotel, and still later known in the 1960s as Holyoke House] *and so often stayed with* [a local African American family] *the Littles.* Black performers also stayed with a Jennings family.

The Mt. Park Players was the new name in 1930, in a string of ever-changing monikers adopted by the theatre company. Musical comedies were the order of the day, the new plan for bringing back the audience, but the attempt failed after a few shows.

Then Willard Dashiell, who had directed several past seasons, took a scouting trip to New York and returned with what he had hoped would be a *dramatic* stock company for Mountain Park. Most of the selections were light comedies. Dashiell directed, and local favorite, his wife, Mabel Griffith was on board for another season as a "character woman." Future Broadway actor Frank Craven (who would become known on Broadway in the original role of The Stage Manager in *Our Town*), starred in *Salt Water*.

Frank Craven

View along Conn. River, Showing Mt. Holyoke Range, Holyoke, Mass.   14

The *WPA Guidebook*, from the vantage point of the Great Depression in the 1930s, looked back on this period in Holyoke:

The American Thread Company and the Skinner Silk Company are about all that remain of what once promised to be a great textile center.

The thirties, and the Great Depression, started the season limping. In 1931 the local area suffered a polio epidemic, schools and theaters closed. A season of RKO Keith's vaudeville played on the mountain. It was recorded that 1,000 seats were sold at 35 cents, 700 seats at 25 cents, and even a few at 50 cents. A bad season, but perhaps fortunate to have on the vaudeville bill that June Holyoke's own Eva Tanguay, the "I Don't Care Girl."

Eva was down and out at this point in her career, having lost millions in the October 1929 stock market crash. She was fifty-one years old, and would retire within the decade, blind and nearly destitute. At the height of her career some twenty years earlier, she was one of the highest-paid performers in vaudeville. Eva's private life, like her freewheeling performing, was similarly uncontrolled, and many of the scandals were orchestrated by Eva purely for publicity. For what she lacked in talent, she more than made up with in daring and a canny insight on what the audience wanted.

But that was behind her in 1931, when her act was old and there were far more sexy wild girls in the silent films whose audience was far larger. Still, in her day, everybody in America knew the name Eva Tanguay. "I Don't Care" was her signature tune, but the songs in her repertoire represent the theme of her act with colorful playfulness: "It's All Been Done Before But Not the Way I Do It," "Go As Far As You Like," "I Want Someone To Go Wild With Me," and what may be considered subtle for her: "That's Why They Call Me Tabasco."

***

At the time of her appearance at the Casino playhouse on Mt. Tom in the last week of June/first week of July 1931, Holyoke, coincidentally, had another Tanguay bringing glory to the city. Young Gerey Tanguay, apparently no relation, had just returned from the Marbles Championship in Ocean City, New Jersey, which had been covered in detail in the newspaper—the city holding its collective breath, apparently, when he was forced to withdraw from competition, battling a bout of tonsillitis. He returned a champion to adulation in Holyoke, bringing with him a gold medal and a bronze loving cup for the Eastern League championships. He also appeared on the vaudeville bill with Eva to give a marbles demonstration. His name is only slightly less prominent than hers in the newspaper ads, but he garnered more attention and articles written about him.

It was not that Eva or her previous fame was forgotten, even if she was eclipsed by a little boy who played marbles better than anybody else. She was billed as "Holyoke's Own Cyclonic Comedienne" and six other "Great R.K.O. Keith

Acts." These included the Bardelangs acrobatic act, Jeanne and Rita dancers, comics Saxton and Farrell, the Wayne Cody Quintette, Alexander and Elmore as master of ceremonies and his stooge sidekick. The Casino was packed the night she played on the vaudeville bill. As befits the star, she was the last act on the bill. She finished her act with her signature song, "I Don't Care." Maybe she didn't.

At the conclusion of the act she was "vigorously applauded." Miss Tanguay told the audience how happy she was to be "home" again. She extended greetings of happiness and health to the audience, and added that she felt their wishes were the same for her.

Like Eva, vaudeville's days were numbered as popular entertainment, and would limp along in the 1930s as radio sped past; the new number one attraction, along with the movies—which now "talked." The legitimate stage never went away, even if it competed with all these forms of entertainment and often lagged behind in box office receipts. The Valley Players management,

Eva Tanguay

looking back on the era from the safer vista of the more prosperous 1950s recalled:

Back in those best-forgotten days of depression, in 1932, when gloom enshrouded the land and money was a disappearing commodity, Broadway producers were almost a vanishing race. The idea of putting on a play seemed suicidal, and theatrical ledgers, it was believed, could be kept, if at all, only with red ink.

Also on the day the review of Eva Tanguay's performance there was another brief article reporting on hundreds of vaudeville players who, only a year ago were earning good salaries, but were now "walking the streets of London penniless and with no work in sight." The Depression had cast its gloom around the world. Also that week, the five-and-ten-cents store J.J. Newberry Company opened on High Street. Here, in the 1960s, Walter Pidgeon, then star at the Mt. Tom Playhouse, would be accosted by adoring fans.

Free "talking pictures" at the Casino made up the

entire 1932 season. A local newspaper article on June 30th reminded the audience that George Brent, formerly known as George Nolan, who had been the star of the 1928 season on the mountain, was now doing well as a movie star in Hollywood. Through the early 1930s there was a mixture at the Casino of talking pictures and Keith circuit vaudeville, until stage plays returned under the Mt. Tom Players and director Howard Hall in 1934. Parking at Mountain Park was reduced to 15 cents, and the best seats in the Casino were reduced to 40 cents. Director Hall announced a guest actor would join the company with each show. Promotion took the form of a direct plea, or admonition, to the community:

Things close to home are never appreciated. Holyoke lags in support of a group that ranks with the best in New England. Unless Holyoke responds to a greater extent, soon the Mt. Tom Players will be forced to pick up their luggage and walk out of the city. The management is losing money every week.

A hopeful plea, to temper the desperation:

The Casino is an open-air one and cooler by far than the stuffy city. The sides are screened so that mosquitoes can be guaranteed to keep away.

Then back to the desperation, and perhaps a note of anger:

Their ability is unquestioned—they are offering Holyoke a chance to enjoy summer theatre with all the rest of New England and yet Holyoke is…being too stupid to realize the fact.

Willard Dashiell, who had tried his luck as an actor in New York and Hollywood for a few months, was back at the Casino in the cast of *Pursuit of Happiness* in early July and remained for the rest of the season in a string of lighthearted comedies in this worst year of the Great Depression.

In 1935 there was an extensive renovation, which according to an unpublished typescript in the Holyoke Public Library History Room and Archives, "changed the barnlike atmosphere into an attractive auditorium replete with a velvet curtain."

George D'Andria, manager of the Chicago Civic Light Opera Company, and himself a former resident of Holyoke, arrived to try his hand at reviving theatre at the Casino with the Mt. Park Casino Musical Comedy Players—surely the longest name to date. The musical director was Fred Hoff, and dances were staged by Solly Fields. Professional visiting companies came, and the first show was *Chins Up*, with a very large cast of thirty, including a ballet unit of fourteen girls from the Metropolitan Opera Company and the Capitol Theatre in New York. All costumes and sets were brought to the mountain from New York.

Despite the hoopla of the opening, the Mt. Park Casino Musical Comedy Players closed after the 4th of July celebration. Mr. D'Andrio cited a "lack of patronage" and the first show had "heavy losses." There were no shows for the remainder of the 1935 season, and the Casino went dark.

But on the horizon, a hope, the same hope that saved millions from starving, also brought income and dignity to thousands of theatre professionals and brought theatre to Depression-era audiences. President Franklin Delano Roosevelt created his Works Progress Administration.

The WPA, one of President Roosevelt's "alphabet soup" of federal agencies that breathed life into Depression-era arts came to bide at the Casino. The WPA produced shows there from 1936 through 1939.

In March 1936, another devastating flood to the Valley brought an already Depression-decimated industrial area to its knees. Not only industry, but homes in the form of block after block of tenements were affected in Holyoke. The entire first floor of the landmark "Battleship" apartment building was under water. An estimated $10 million damage was suffered from flood.

We have a look at Holyoke from yet another WPA source, which provided work to writers producing field guides all over the nation. From the *WPA Guide to Massachusetts*: Holyoke

population in 1938 was 56,139 (already dropping). It's railroad station was on Mosher Street – Boston and Maine Railroad. The nearest small airport was Barnes on Hampton Plains "between Westfield and Holyoke." The city had five hotels.

The manufacturing center, lying along the power canals, has been unusually active throughout the depression. The absence of drab slum quarters usually associated with mill towns is notable.

One factor in creating this prosperous atmosphere is the skilled type of worker employed by the numerous paper mills that manufacture high-grade writing paper, the principal support of the town.

The Essex Hotel

In this respect the city was fortunate that much of its manufacturing was able to sustain during the Depression: across the river, Chicopee lost most of its manufacturing base in that decade. Average labor pay rates during early 1930s were 27 to 35 cents an hour, for the lucky ones. In 1936, the cable car stopped running up the mountain. By 1938 the cars and rails were sold to a junk dealer. Public transit to the park shifted from trolleys to buses.

The Hotel Nonotuck

The Skinner family home of Wistariahurst was now open to the public in limited hours – one must apply for permission at the office of the Skinner silk mills at 208 Appleton Street – presaging its role as a museum several decades hence.

Mt. Tom and Mountain Park are described in the *WPA Guidebook to Massachusetts* in 1938:

…an extensive wooded area through which winds a fine road past heavy growth of laurel. In 1932, ten pounds of the rare mineral babingtonite were found near-by. Some geologists believe Mt. Tom was once volcanic.

The WPA also brought revitalization and substance to artists and technicians in the theatre, and to their Depression-era audiences with the Federal Theatre Project. Theatre critic Burns Mantle noted in his syndicated column in August 1937:

History in the making has a way of sneaking up on us. Frequently it is an established and often fairly startling fact before we really are aware of it. Take, if you interested, the case of the federal theater project. After five months' operation, during which several thousand theater folk were taken off relief and given jobs in their own lines of work, a question arose as to how long the project could continue. Current appropriations were giving out and there was no definite, or at least no official, confirmation of rumors that there would be other appropriations to take their place…to take the jobs away from them would be to put them back on relief.

The program, popular among audiences as well as the theatre artists and business personnel, would continue boldly, but always in a state of uncertainty. It was generally assumed that the program would end sometime, hopefully not until the return of better times. Some dared to hope that the Federal Theater Project would lead to a national theatre.

The Federal Theatre Players of Massachusetts, under the auspices of the Works Progress Administration, re-opened the Casino and provided shows through the summer from Wednesdays through Saturdays. Willard Dashiell, so familiar to Casino audiences, was the director. Admission was 25 cents, and Grace O'Leary, a local actress, "won much acclaim."

It was an interesting season, varied and eclectic. All Star Vaudeville to *Craig's Wife*. For an original play written especially for the WPA it was recorded that:

For the first time in the reviewer's experience the members of the audience remained in their seats until the cast had taken three curtain calls.

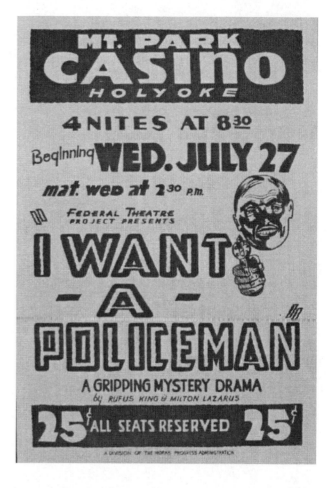

Low prices, an appreciative audience, and a feeling that the theatre was a mutually beneficial, mutually nurturing place at last settled upon the Casino.

Another show, *Sepian Review* presented exclusively by African American members of the Federal Theatre Project, was nothing like the old minstrel shows. The theatre had grown up, and in the 1930s, was delivering a message. The reviewer noted the troupe was popular with the audience, but he felt that they should have eliminated the "political propaganda" in several lines.

The press reported:

The government is now the largest theatre producer in the country with 158 plays showing and rehearsing, 1700 people on the payroll, playing to an audience of 350,000 nightly coast to coast.

In Massachusetts there were twenty-six WPA theatre companies employing eighty performers, presenting shows to more than 40,000 people.

The murder mystery *The Night of January 16th* led off the 1937 season, which provided another mix of comedy and drama. Matinees were held Wednesdays. Willard Dashiell was on board for both acting and directing chores again. The average weekly audience was 1,400.

The 1938 season, again under the WPA, brought Eugene O'Neill's *Ah Wilderness*, starring Wendell Corey, a Springfield native and graduate of Classical (then called Central High School), who would, like George Brent, become famous in Hollywood in the near future.

The democratic nature of WPA shows is exemplified in The Swanee Minstrels featuring sixty people in blackface, a vaudeville offering of *The Black and White Review*, and a restoring of dignity overall with *Return to Death* performed by a company of African American actors. The Federal Theatre Orchestra played between acts, so musicians got to eat that summer as well. We were all over the map and clearly willing to try everything with an élan and bravery missing today.

Wendell Corey

Swanee Minstrels

The Federal Theatre wasn't the only government-sponsored group on the mountain that summer. Another one of President Roosevelt's programs, the Civilian Conservation Corps, maintained a camp on the mountain nearby and performed forestry work. In June 1935 the 1173rd Company was established on Mt. Tom, and created and improved the Mt. Tom State Reservation, a 2,161 acre park with twenty-two miles of hiking trails, Lake Bray, and providing areas for ice skating and cross country skiing in the winter. Chicopee also had its own CCC camp, and would send units to help on the Mt. Tom reservation work. During the weather disasters of the 1936 flood, and the 1938 hurricane, local CCC men and boys were utilized in rescue and cleanup operations. Just a few weeks after the Casino was shuttered for the 1938 season, the worst weather disaster in New England history occurred when the Hurricane of 1938 barreled right up the Connecticut River, leaving much destruction in its wake, and another enormous flood. In 1939, Pioneer Valley name was created to boost tourism and business.

By the late 1930s, the newspapers carried enormous display ads for the movie theaters. In Holyoke that was the Suffolk, the Strand, and Majestic, and Victory, the Globe, the Holyoke Theater, and the Holyoke papers also carried ads for the Willow Theater in the Willimansett section of Chicopee, the residents of which commonly crossed the river to Holyoke for shopping and entertainment.

In the 1930s, Mountain Park still attracted the public with the amusement park and the dance pavilion, where popular big bands such as Duke Ellington, Cab Callaway, Sammy Kaye, Lionel Hampton, and Gene Krupa performed. The theatre was an old and increasingly shabby fixture, but it was no longer looked upon as an added incentive to get people to the park. Louis Pellissier, who had been an assistant to park owner William Loomis, took over Mountain Park in 1929 and purchased new rides and renovated the midway of the amusement park, including children's rides, a funhouse, a ball field, and a weekly Tuesday night fireworks display. He improved the access road for automobiles.

MOUNTAIN PARK

Opens for the Season
Saturday, May 25, 1935

REDUCED RATE ROUND-TRIP TICKETS

from Northampton to Mountain Park can be
purchased from Bus Operaters.

Adults: 35c   Children: 20c

EXTRA BUS - Will leave Academy of Music,
Northampton, for Mountain Park at 8:00 p.m.
and will leave Mountain Park for Northampton at 11:30 p. m. on Tuesday - Wednesday
Thursday - Friday and Saturday Nights.

Northampton Street Railway Co.

According to author Jay Ducharme in his book, *Mountain Park*:

Unlike many parks during the Depression, Mountain Park continued to survive. The Stardust ballroom showcased all of the major big bands, including Glenn Miller, Tommy Dorsey, and Guy Lombardo.

During the Depression the Federal government funded the arts in Holyoke, as it did with many urban areas. According to Ella Merkel DiCarlo, there was an acting group called The Suitcase Theater, led by Norman Thompson, and after rehearsals at the YWCA on Maple Street, the actors would go to Gleason's Townhouse on Suffolk Street for chow mein. Thompson later became a film director working in Japan. One of the actors was Harry Crabtree, who later became a district attorney in the Los Angeles area. George Smith, who acted and sometimes directed, later became an actor in New York. Carlton Vogt, Sr. was another actor. Future columnist for the *Holyoke Transcript-Telegram* and chronicler of Holyoke history Ella Merkel DiCarlo, and Lois Kane Murray, played ingénues.

By 1939, the Federal Theatre Project company at the Casino, which took up their third season on the mountain, was being threatened by conservatives in Washington. By the opening of the season in June, the House of Representatives had voted not to fund it for another year, subject to a final vote by the Senate. Willard Dashiell, who was director of the Western Massachusetts unit of the Federal Theatre Project announced to the press:

We've given up all hope.

Wendell Corey was back for *Tons of Money*, and Walter Hackett's *The Barton Mystery*, as well as *Yes, My Darling Daughter* were also presented before the Casino closed on June 30th as Congress voted not to appropriate any more funds for theatre.

Though theatre was precarious on the mountain, summer theatre elsewhere in New England was enjoying steady, if not spectacular, patronage. Great names in the acting profession toured throughout New England, and many newcomers

to the stage would eventually become famous in Hollywood—where there was no Depression.

New England summer theatre regionally included The Cape Playhouse, which premiered on July 4, 1927, with Basil Rathbone and Violet Kemble Cooper in *The Guardsman*. Bette Davis was an usher in that playhouse. Gertrude Lawrence played at the Cape Playhouse, and would marry its director, in the 1930s. Henry Fonda and Robert Montgomery did their early stage work here. It had begun, according to author Marcia J. Monbleau, who wrote a history on The Cape Playhouse, as a "spare old Yankee meeting house," with hard-backed seats. Katharine Hepburn began her apprenticeship at Ivoryton in Connecticut. Their walls have stories, and the ghosts are grand. Shining stars and just-beginners have walked New England stages. Their voices linger, and it doesn't take much imagination to picture them standing there still.

Other theaters opening in the 1930s were the Ogunquit Playhouse in Ogunquit, Maine, which opened in 1933. Walter Hartwig, its founder, was a leader in what has been called the Little Theatre movement. He also founded theaters in Peterborough, New Hampshire and in Bristol, Connecticut. Ogunquit started in a garage, and among the luminaries appearing there during the Depression were Maude Adams and Ethel Barrymore.

Hartwig wrote in an article for the *New York Times*, published August 4, 1935:

The continued growth and spread of the Summer Theatres that now function through New England, New York, and New Jersey are beginning to assert themselves in other states, may very well indicate what course the American professional theatre will have to take if it is to reestablish itself and command the attention and respect that it enjoyed before the cinema replaced it in the affection of the masses.

Mountain Park parking lot

CHAPTER 4

World War II and The Valley Players

As the Depression wore on, despite a flagging box office, a surge in creativity, eloquence, and in sophistication of themes drove the theatre. According to a *New York Times* article by Ogunquit Playhouse founder Walter Hartwig, published in August 1935:

As the summer theatre has gradually grown into an institution and the standards among the better ones have been placed higher, the public has become discriminating, so that the best actors and best scenic designers are none too good for the summer theatre.

World War II changed the tri-city area of Holyoke, Chicopee, and Springfield, as it had many places in the United States, and pulled communities into a fast-paced and modern world. The most profound change came in the northwest corner of Chicopee, a high plain of tobacco farms and small family farms that was transformed into the huge Northeast Air Base in 1940, named Westover Air Field for Army Air Corps first commander, Oscar Westover, who had been killed in an air crash in 1938. It joined wartime industries providing a plethora of jobs, bringing newcomers to the valley and a huge lift to the economy, which had battered the factory towns and bled money for the entire previous decade.

By 1943, it was a major staging area, where bomber crews were trained, and was the last base they saw before England. Westover Field also made a unique and tragic impact through the wartime crashes in the area, among these a pair of P-47 Thunderbolts from Westover Field that collided over Holyoke in May 1943. One plane crashed into a home on the corner of Linden and Hampden Streets. Occupants of the home were injured. The pilot bailed out and parachuted to safety. The second plane crashed into a brick garage in the alley between Appleton and Essex streets, west of Walnut Street. That pilot, 22 years old and newly stationed at Westover, was killed.

In 1946, another crash of a B-17 Flying Fortress into the rocky southeast slope of Mt. Tom killed twenty-five military personnel. At the time it was rated the worse aerial disaster in New England. Horrified crowds at Mountain Park would have heard the explosion, and witnessed flames leap into the night sky from the burning wreckage. It occurred around 10 p.m. Some civilians, familiar with the area from hiking on the mountain, helped rescuers scramble through the rough terrain to locate the crash site. Unfortunately, there were no survivors from the plane.

There is a monument to the crash on the mountain today.

The play at the Casino that evening would have been *The Hasty Heart*. Paul Rohan recalls the family story:

I believe my mother and aunt had been to a play at Mountain Park the night the plane crashed on Mt. Tom. If I remember the story, they had gone to the play and then came home and then heard all kinds of sirens and wondered what had happened, and later heard that a plane crashed on Mt. Tom. I guess it was nowhere near the playhouse, but there was a sense of familiarity to the location.

Another crash would occur in Chicopee in 1958, a KC 135 plane, killing fifteen people. As many as twelve planes crashed on or around the base in all, mostly occurring during World War II.

Blackouts, gas and tire rationing, no pleasure trips were other new realities and a serious threat to summer theaters not easily accessible by train or public transportation. Those reliant on their audience arriving mainly by car felt the pinch of a diminished audience – yet there were more people able to afford the theatre at this time. Manufacturing switched to a wartime footing. In Holyoke, Skinner mills made silk parachutes during World War II.

The *Holyoke Daily Transcript* listed the names of Holyoke boys in the service. Edward Borucki, local boy feared lost at Pearl Harbor – came home a few months later in February 1942, and later became a Chicopee schoolteacher. Paul Rohan, who grew up in Holyoke, mused of his Depression-era parents:

It was amazing how that generation—well, quite frankly, that generation knew everybody in town.

The 1940s continued with huge and vibrant newspaper display ads for Holyoke's movie theaters: The Suffolk, Victory, Holyoke Theater, Majestic, Bijou, Globe, Strand, and Chicopee's Willow. The ads still carried no addresses; everyone knew where they were. In Springfield, the same with the Capitol, the Paramount, Loew's Poli, and second-run neighborhood houses like the Phillips, the Liberty, the Garden, the Bijou, the Strand, the Jefferson, the Art, the Arcade, the Broadway among them.

At the Court Square Theater in November 1941, the only remaining winter stock "legitimate" theater in town, hosted *Arsenic and Old Lace* with Laura Hope Crews, Erich von Stroheim, Jack Whiting, Effie Shannon, and Forrest Orr. There was also a lecture on current events—the rise of the Nazis in Germany, by journalist and author William L. Shirer at the Springfield Auditorium.

By October 1942 the *Springfield Daily Republican* would be canceling home delivery of newspapers due to gas rationing. They were still readily available downtown, where most of the workers were, but as noted, newspapers were an integral element to local theatre being able to thrive.

The 1940s started with an experiment at the Mt. Tom Casino playhouse, called the Pioneer Valley Drama Festival under co-producers Norman Thompson and David Perkins, and director Lewis Allen. The Casino was now called the Pioneer Playhouse (for the region called the Pioneer Valley). The players were favorite Hollywood butler Arthur Treacher, Diana Barrymore (daughter of John Barrymore), supported by Adrienne Ames, John Craven (who had originated the role of George Gibbs in *Our Town* on Broadway, and was the son of Frank Craven, who had appeared at the Casino in the 1930s), Phyllis Brooks, Tommy Lewis, and Michael Whalen. The *Holyoke Daily Transcript* crowed, "Diana Barrymore Arrives Here For Rehearsal". She traveled with her maid and stayed at the Roger Smith Hotel on Suffolk Street, the city's premiere hotel at the time. She appeared with Arthur Treacher in *The Hottentot*. Treacher, it was noted, "is making Holyoke his headquarters several weeks before his local engagement."

Diana Barrymore

On June 23rd *Up Pops the Devil* with film star Michael Whalen was the first Standing Room

Only event due to his appearance. On June 24th, Arthur Treacher opened with *The Hottentot*, billed as "The Clean Wholesome Laugh Riot." Diana Barrymore played Peggy Fairfax. According to an unpublished manuscript in the archives of the History Room of the Holyoke Public Library, "They closed after six performances with heavy losses."

PIONEER VALLEY DRAMA FESTIVAL
MOUNTAIN PARK CASINO
HOLYOKE MASS. TEL. 2-5140
BOX OFFICE OPEN 9 A. M. TO 9 P. M.
SEATS NOW ON SALE AT BOX OFFICE

WEEK OF JUNE 24, 1940

ARTHUR TREACHER
IN
"THE HOTTENTOT"

It was not for lack of efforts to get the audience up the mountain, with the Holyoke Street Railway abandoning trolleys for a fleet of buses:

We are happy to announce that by special arrangement with the Holyoke Street Railway Company, our patrons purchasing $1.10 seats will be given free transportation to and from City Hall, Holyoke, or if they drive their own car they are entitled to free parking.

Another production in the Pioneer Valley Drama Festival the week of July 8th was *Goodbye Again* (which would later be produced by The Valley Players in 1954). Erik Rhodes (Hollywood comic

character actor, most known for his supporting roles in two Fred Astaire and Ginger Rogers films), Phyllis Brooks and Marcy Westcott were featured, and the cast included Peggy French, John Craven, Gordon Wilson, John McKee, Billy Wood, William Balfour, Lee Parry, and Blanche Hartman. Directed by Lewis Allen, the sets also used furniture on loan from the Roger Smith Hotel and the Hotel Essex at 400 High Street in Holyoke (with a generous full page ad on the back of the program).

John Craven

The following week, the Pioneer Valley Drama Festival would present *On Borrowed Time*, with funds raised to support Broadway's Theatre Wing, under the direction of Antoinette Perry, namesake of the future Tony Awards®.

A show called *Crazy with Heat* with Sheila Barrett and Norman Lloyd (who would soon have a long career in Hollywood, and at this writing, is still attending film festivals at 101 years old), was slated, but was sent to Rhode Island instead. The Pioneer Valley Drama Festival was not a successful experiment. They had suffered a loss of $1,200 per week.

The theatre went dark again before the season was over.

***

At this important moment, the most fortuitous event in the history of live theatre on Mt. Tom occurred when a band of players from a small summer stock company who had lost their digs in New Hampshire came to the valley looking for a new home. The would adopt the name The Valley Players, and lived up to their name as a product of, and an asset to, the Pioneer Valley—most especially to Holyoke as its fame and influence radiated down the mountain to the Flats, to the other towns, and became one of the most well-known and respected summer theaters in New England, where Broadway actors clamored to work, and where future television stars learned their trade.

The war had already started in Europe, and America was on tenterhooks on the sideline. In February 1941, the *Holyoke Transcript-Telegram* announced the plans for newcomers to take over the Casino playhouse and start a new summer theater, that after weeks of investigating other sites in New England, this fledgling group of eight—actors and a director who had operated as the Farragut Players in Rye Beach, New Hampshire, as yet without a new name—had only this week signed a lease with Louis D. Pellissier of the Holyoke Street Railway Company to rent the Casino playhouse in Mountain Park. Nothing was concrete in what kind of theatre group it would be thus far; just the lease. A list of plays was suggested, but not booked. Ned Wayburn, a giant of theatre production, and especially dance instruction, of the late nineteenth and early twentieth centuries (one of his students was Fred Astaire), was considering a partnership with this group to produce a new musical comedy he wanted to bring to Broadway. The leaders of the fledging acting troupe were husband and wife Carlton and Jean Guild.

Mr. and Mrs. Guild have already made several trips to Holyoke and have discussed plans for the summer with various people. Other members of the group expect to visit the city in the near future. They hope to make many *acquaintances here even before they appear on stage at the Casino next summer. The Players are not merely looking forward to next season, they hope to return for many seasons and they want to become, so far as they possibly can, a real part of the community.*

It was likewise announced in *Variety* on February 8th, and on the same day in the *Transcript-Telegram*, of equal import, *the* Ned Wayburn was to meet with Pellissier to possibly establish one in his national string of dance schools in Holyoke, connected with the playhouse. They had dinner at the Roger Smith Hotel, along with the Guilds and Lauren Gilbert and Jackson Perkins, who were other members of the new players. Wayburn was considering utilizing the dance pavilion at Mountain Park, but unfortunately, it did not develop.

Roger Smith Hotel
HOLYOKE, MASS.

The Nonotuck becomes a Roger Smith Hotel.

It was noted from the beginning that the new players were intending not to evoke the star system prevalent in most summer stock theaters, and the public and theatre community debated as to how successfully this model might work. It was a risky experiment, but there was scant summer theatre in the Pioneer Valley, so the Valley Players had found fertile ground.

The Kirby Theatre located at Amherst College would not open this year. The previous summer, Holyoke native Harold J. Kennedy had produced a series of plays there. Mr. Kennedy would return to his hometown in the 1960s to both perform and direct at the Casino. The Valley Players would have been the only summer theater to operate in the Pioneer Valley this summer; except Kennedy did bring another summer theatre to the area this season in an arrangement with the Springfield Trade High School and the Springfield Drama Festival.

Amherst College president Stanley King announced the decision to close Kirby for the 1941 season was due to "the uncertainty of the world situation" and the possibility that some younger members of the faculty normally involved with the Kirby Theatre would likely be in the armed services the coming summer. Some summer theaters in the northeast were closing in similar situations. By May the *New York Times* carried an ad for the new Valley Players along with the schedules of other eastern summer stock companies, and announcements were made in western Massachusetts papers and the *New York Sun*.

Carlton and Jean Guild were at the head of the egalitarian band of players, where there would be no stars. Of all the actors, the Guilds would eventually make Holyoke their permanent, year-round home.

Carlton Guild, business manager of the group, was born in 1908 and was thirty-two when he and his wife came to Holyoke. He was an alumnus of Bowdoin College in Maine. In a 1956 article in *Yankee* magazine, he joked that as a graduate student of Harvard Summer School, he used to spend time with the Farragut Players of Rye, New

Hampshire, where his wife was an actress, and helped to found The Valley Players when the Farragut Players lost their house "to keep a swell gang from breaking up."

Jean Guild, his wife, was a formidable character actress, who read plays, cast actors, solved problems and put out fires.

"If you have a problem and you don't know what to do, ask Jean Guild. The chances are nine out of ten, she'll know the answer," a stage manager remarked to an interviewer in 1962, when the Valley Players were nearing an end.

Jean Guild was a native of West Medway, Massachusetts, daughter of John and Emma Durfee. Jean had toured New England as a young woman for several years giving public readings. She and Carlton had been married since 1933, and had lived in New Hampshire and in Rhode Island where her husband had various teaching positions, and founded the Rye, New Hampshire, group. The Guilds were with the Farragut Players for five years. Jean co-managed The Valley Players and became Director of the Summer School for Apprentices. It was noted in a 1947 play program:

On her rests a major share of the responsibility for choosing the plays to be produced each season. She has the chief responsibility for casting the acting company each spring. And she also sees to it that the twenty-five to thirty members of our organization who come to Holyoke each summer are well housed, well fed, and well provided for in general.

One of the actors, Mr. Lauren Gilbert, was one of the eight Farragut Players who formed The Valley Players, and was another of the co-managers of the group. He had played Shakespeare on Broadway with the Maurice Evans company and was in the Helen Hayes production of *Twelfth Night* the previous year.

Leading lady Jackson Perkins, who was Gilbert's wife, was also one of the original Farragut Players, and had performed in stock in San Diego and Los Angeles. She also performed Shakespeare with Maurice Evans, as had fellow actor John

McQuade. She and Lauren Gilbert had married only about six months before the first Valley Players season in 1941. Other company members played on Broadway in popular current plays, such as Walter Coy, who appeared with Gertrude Lawrence in *Lady in the Dark*. They were a group with an impressive pedigree.

Joseph Foley was from a summer theater in Winthrop, Maine, which he co-managed in 1935. He was "a character man," and would be one of the most beloved and popular members with the audience.

Ann Lincoln, who had played the original sister of Henry Aldrich ("Hen-REE! Henry Aldrich!") on radio, also performed in *What a Life* with Ezra Stone and *See My Lawyer* with Milton Berle. The actors came from a network of varied theatre and radio backgrounds.

Also new to the mountain that year was the radio station WHYN. It was advantageous in this time of earlier technology and no satellites for a radio station to be close to its broadcast tower, and for the tower to be on the highest ground possible. The new radio station made its initial broadcast April 14, 1941.

On May 2nd, Mountain Park opened for the season, and the festivities were carried by WHYN, ensconced further up at the mountain's peak. Mayor Tolpert and Louis Pellissier gave speeches, and a dance at the pavilion and fireworks made up the hoopla of the last U.S. peacetime summer. With the Depression well over, the owners of the Mountain Park amusement park were looking forward to the most prosperous season in years.

World War II was entering its second summer, with the U.S. still on the sidelines. The proceeds for the opening performance at the Casino were donated to the British War Relief.

The public could purchase tickets not only at the door, but reserved seat tickets could be bought at the Park Pharmacy on the corner of Dwight and Maple streets and at the Pleasant Pharmacy on the corner of Pleasant and Hampden streets. Cars were charged 25 cents to park at Mountain Park.

The playhouse had capacity of 1,000 per a 1941 brochure, though this figure would shift a bit over the years with changes and renovations. Some actresses in the new company were feted at the Holyoke YWCA, beginning a long, exceedingly warm relationship with the community. At the event Carmen Matthews read "The White Cliffs of Dover" poem, and a scene from Noel Coward's *Private Lives* was presented by leading man Lauren Gilbert and leading lady (Mrs. Gilbert) Jackson Perkins.

Carmen Matthews, Jean Guild, Gloria Humphries, Doris Poland, and Brightside kids on roller coaster; photo by Raymond D'Addario.

Later that summer, guest actress Carmen Matthews, featured in *Cradle Song*, would visit the Brightside Orphanage in Holyoke. The proceeds of that play would benefit the orphanage. Matthews and Jean Guild were photographed with a bunch of the Brightside kids on the roller coaster at Mountain Park. During the run of the show, the cast was invited to the home of Lt. Col. John R. Drumm, A. C., commanding officer of the 26th Air Base Group at Westover Field for a lawn party, attended by several base officials.

Notables attending *The Cradle Song* included Mrs. William Skinner 2nd, and the wife of Brigadier General John B. Brooks, commanding officer of Westover. It was noted in the local paper that most of the audience wore street attire, rather than evening dress as was more common for theatre audiences of that period.

The local papers, including Holyoke's French language newspaper, *La Justice*, covered the opening. Holyoke's German-language paper, the *New England Rundshau* would also review shows this season. Throughout the next two decades of the Valley Players, which coincided with the heyday of summer theatre, the company enjoyed a great deal of press, both feature stories and reviews, from a variety of newspapers in the valley: dailies and weeklies, and radio.

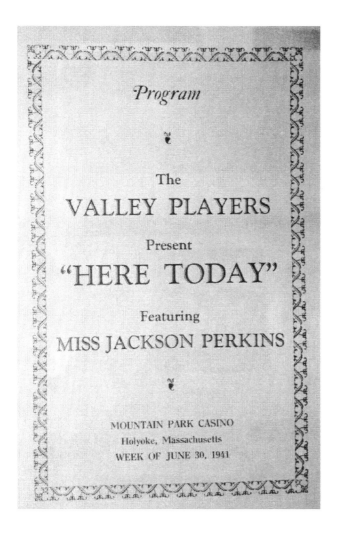

Here Today was the fitting title of the first play produced by The Valley Players, and they would be here at the Casino for the next twenty years, the longest run of any theatre company on Mt. Tom (despite the joking comment they received at the time: "Gone Tomorrow"). Miss Jackson Perkins starred, her husband Lauren Gilbert was in the cast (at first, "Miss" and "Mr." were used in the programs and early press due to the

androgynous first names, but were dropped when the valley got to know the company better), as well as Jean Guild.

Dorothy Crane

The show was directed by Dorothy M. Crane, the second woman ever to direct in Holyoke, but Ms. Crane would be the main director for this company for the next two decades, which would likely make her the person who directed more shows than anyone in the history of theatre in the Pioneer Valley. She was one of the founders of the group, who had been a manager and director of the Farragut Players at Rye Beach, New Hampshire. After the summer seasons ended, she returned to Newport News, Virginia, where she taught drama in the public schools and directed. She had met grad students Lauren Gilbert and Jackson Perkins at the University of Michigan, and they all were reunited at the Farragut Players, from which The Valley Players evolved.

A 1949 article noted:

Miss Crane, a quiet-spoken woman with a low, pleasing voice, has no trouble with temperamental actors and actresses in the Mountain Park Company, "because we don't have a person who isn't as interested as I am in getting out a good show." If there is a case of pyrotechnic temperament, the player is not invited to join the company the following year. Such cases have been rare, Miss Crane reports.

Opening night was met with a downpour of rain, and attendance that week reached only 1,681, but fortunately, there were better days ahead. Springfield radio station WMAS broadcasted from the Hotel Charles in Springfield, where host Milton Hale reviewed the play on his late afternoon program:

Last night's audience at Mountain Park Casino enjoyed every line and situation, and gave the company a well-deserved number of curtain calls at the conclusion of the play…A good deal of credit should go to Dorothy Crane, the director of the group, for she has taken a simple plot play and turned it into a comedy that hits on all high.

Prices were 39 cents for unreserved matinee seats, for reserved seats: 55 cents, 77 cents, and 99 cents for evening performances. Evening performances began at 8:20 p.m., 8:00 p.m. on Tuesdays. The Saturday matinee began at 2:20 p.m.

Jean Guild

The front page of the *Holyoke Daily Transcript and Telegram* of Wednesday, July 16, 1941, carried news of Nazis battling the Russians, and a cheesecake shot of Mary Elliott, Valley Players ingénue, sunbathing on the banks of the Connecticut River by the rented cottage of fellow actress Ann Lee in South Hadley, where some of the players were billeted that first summer.

Night Must Fall starred Mr. Lauren Gilbert and Jean Guild playing the elderly murder victim. It was remarked in the notes of a 1947 program looking back upon this production that many of the nearly 2,000 people who attended the show "still remember and talk about it, recalling with especial vividness the climactic sudden parting of the curtains at the back of the stage."

In *Cradle Song*, Carmen Matthews appeared as a guest featured player. Like many of the guest performers, or "jobbers," she became acquainted with Jackson Perkins and Lauren Gilbert when they were all appearing with Maurice Evans in his Shakespearean productions on Broadway. The founding members of The Valley Players were well connected in the theatre world, and they cast a wide net for visiting actors, frequently drafting old friends.

George Washington Slept here was presented in August. *Springfield Daily News* reviewer W. Harley Rudkin loved it.

Every time I mention Jackson Perkins the word "versatile" comes out of the typewriter almost of its own volition. One day I will dig up a new adjective for this, er—versatile lady, but it won't do her justice.

The technical crew, headed by Chief Electrician Talbot Peterson, or "Pete", was also versatile. For the Alaskan setting of *Petticoat Fever*, he needed to recreate the Northern Lights. Pete managed to find a motor-driven color wheel and according to the *Springfield Union*, "practiced for hours to achieve the illusion of the aurora borealis."

The Vinegar Tree was the final show of the season. According to the Northampton's *Daily Hampshire Gazette*:

High Street 1940s postcard

There was a good-sized audience present at last night's performance and it responded to the players' work as if reluctant to see the season end...there is mention made now of continuing the theater next summer. Assuming that the same level of achievement will be repeated, the group will be more than welcome.

Likewise, the *Springfield Union* celebrated the first season, and urged the company to return.

For the first two weeks at the Casino, finances were not too rosy. Then the Players put on The Cradle Song *and gave part of the proceeds to Brightside...that week was the turning point and since then success was never in doubt.*

Comment cards turned in by the audience all urged the players to return.

The *Springfield Daily News* later on that month of September ran a frustrated editorial on the prospects for Springfield theatre, as the Court Square Theater faltered between plays, vaudeville, and movies. The headline, "Is Legitimate Theater

Wanted Here?"

After a winter and summer of stage productions in this city, the question of whether or not Springfield would support a legitimate theater remains unanswered. Northampton, and Holyoke will; Hartford and New Haven will—but Springfield? No one knows.

Despite being the home of the lauded Court Square Theater, it did not have a repertory company but instead hosted touring shows, usually not for more than one or two performances. The Springfield Drama Festival, Harold J. Kennedy's experiment in summer theatre at the Trade High School "was not an outstanding success." It was the regretted opinion of this editorial that the community was interested in light comedies and musicals, but not dramas. Even though the Trade High School plays starred well-known names like Francis Lederer, as well as Kitty Carlisle and Tallulah Bankhead, they were not well attended.

Ladies and gentlemen, if Tallulah Bankhead can't pack

them in solid—who can?

Miss Tallulah would eventually make her way up the mountain in the 1960s with her own brand of divinely funny chaos as we will see in a later chapter.

Springfield had always been a theatre town, though in the past generation, it had sprouted movie theaters rather than playhouses. There was a certain ignominy in a community not being receptive to live theatre.

The following March 1942, when Lauren Gilbert and Jackson Perkins visited Holyoke and stayed at the Roger Smith to confer about what plays to produce in the upcoming second summer season—just their having supper in town made the papers, so eagerly had The Valley Players been taken to Holyoke hearts.

By that time, the United States was at war.

***

In the spring of 1942, W. Harley Rudkin of the *Springfield Daily News* jubilantly reported that The Valley Players were coming back.

In one short season The Valley Players became a tradition, both in personnel and in good theater. They made a lot of friends last year. Starting from scratch they gave a season of summer stock that did not have to apologize to anyone.

The public is quick to realize when it has a good thing, and word soon spread that there was something going on at the Mountain Park Casino that no one who liked good entertainment should miss. As the season wore on, that patronage grew. If it does the same this year—and there is every reason to believe it will, the company will have to start breaking out the SRO signs early in the summer.

An honorary new member of the company was Carlton and Jean Guild's son, William, who was interviewed for this book:

My mother was actually carrying me during the first season in 1941. I was born in February '42, so I was almost born in a trunk, as it were. I grew up with the theatre. I was fascinated by it. The actors were great. It was like

the best time of my life is when the summer came. I just loved it.

Even before the season began there was speculation as to how long the nation's summer theaters would be able to operate, in view of gas and automobile restrictions, restrictions on building and clothing material—and the loss of men to the service—and how that would hamper the ability for the show to go on. The driving restrictions were particularly difficult to overcome, as most summer theaters were in rural areas, accessible mainly, sometime only, by automobile. In the case of The Valley Players, the trolley line that had created the park was long since disbanded, and Mountain Park was accessible only by bus and car. Nobody walked up the mountain, or at least only the very hardy did. A venue like the Springfield Trade School, located downtown, would have been much more accessible, and should have been more successful, especially with the big names that appeared there.

W. Harley Rudkin of the *Springfield Daily News* beat the drum for local summer theater:

I would be unhappy to see this revival of the summer theater wilt and die just as it is getting nicely started once again. Western Massachusetts has two very fine theatrical enterprises of this nature: The Berkshire Playhouse at Stockbridge and the extremely capable Valley Players group which is coming to the Mountain Park Casino again this summer. I believe that the public will not willingly let them give up, at least without making a fight of it.

A good summer theater is a great advantage to any community, and, regardless of restrictions, I believe the public will support it…There will probably be more "theater parties" this year than ever before. Neighbors will form contracts whereby they will use one car one week, another the next…desire for good theater will furnish the motive and ingenuity will find the way.

The 1942 season on the mountain led off with the aptly named play, *Theatre*, to a great audience reception, featuring "Miss" Jackson Perkins. Familiar to Holyoke theatergoers was Willard Dashiell who had managed the summer stock company and appeared as an actor at the Casino in the 1920s, in a guest role for the first show.

Another old friend was Ernest Woodward, who as the program noted:

...is no stranger to Holyoke, having begun his professional career here nearly a generation ago at the Opera House in the company then operated by Ralph Murphy. He has already discovered many old landmarks and has renewed some old acquaintances. He had also recently signed a movie contract.

The program filled us in on the winter activities of the company—for instance, who was on tour, like Gaylord Mason. Ada McFarland appeared with Maurice Evans and Judith Anderson in *MacBeth*. Lauren Gilbert returned from a winter of radio work and also recorded several books for the American Foundation for the Blind. Ann Lee had been on radio in *Big Town* with Edward G. Robinson and *Woodsbury Playhouse* with Charles Boyer; and in the *Screen Guild's* "The Awful Truth" with Carole Lombard, Robert Montgomery, and Ralph Bellamy; the *Lux Radio Theater* with Barbara Stanwyck and William Powell; *Fibber McGee and Molly* and others. In the early 1950s she would run her own summer stock company in Santa Fe, New Mexico, and a winter season theater in Phoenix, Arizona. Norah Adamson played on local radio, including a role as the Gingerbread Lady in the children's show, *Bread Box Review,* on WHYN.

It was noted that for the first show, furs were supplied by the Hudson Fur Company, furnishings by Kane's Furniture Company, and the afghan was loaned by Mrs. Owen Marra of McAuslan and Wakelin local department store. Summer theatre is a community endeavor one way or another. Reciprocating, in July members of The Valley Players appeared at locally well-known Steiger's family owned department store in Holyoke to sell war bonds.

W. Harley Rudkin of the *Springfield Daily News* welcomed The Valley Players back for their second season, with a nod for the murder mystery *Love from a Stranger.*

My weekly salaam to Jackson Perkins, an actress of fine talent and keen understanding...Top bit of the evening

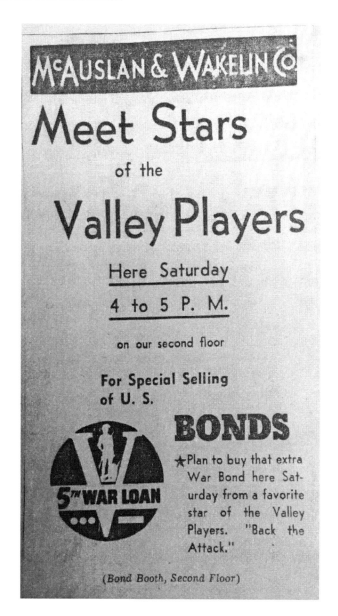

was her puttering with the cushions on the couch just after it has dawned on her that she has been living with murder. This automatic reaction while fighting for emotional control was exactly the right touch.

Followed by a couple of comedies, the 1942 season was well attended and The Valley Players were building momentum. In the farce, *Out of the Frying Pan,* W. Harley Rudkin mused:

They're doing everything but swinging from the chandeliers at the Mountain Park Casino this week...the Valley Players simply pull out all the stops and let 'er roll.

For *George Washington Slept Here* in August 1941, both young Harold Dumais and Brian Quinn, who had minor roles, were from Springfield, students at the Norah Adamson School, and Brian had played parts on local radio at WSPR in the children's show *Aunt Patty's Gang*. The Valley Players began to use locals sporadically embedded in their Equity casts.

The Valley Players presented *The Milky Way* in August, a comedy featuring John O'Connor. Other members of the company appearing were Jackson Perkins, Lauren Gilbert, Joseph F. Foley, Kent Adams, Mary Elliott, and John McQuade. McQuade had performed with Maurice Evans in *Hamlet* and *Richard III*. It was his first Valley Players appearance.

John O'Connor had toured the previous year with theatre greats Alfred Lunt and Lynn Fontanne. Kent Adams, The Valley Players' so-called "Male Juvenile" had performed with Orson Welles' Mercury Theatre in New York City. Phyllis Leon and Adele Lipkin were the youngest members of the apprentices that first season, both from Norfolk, Virginia.

Dorothy M. Crane was back as director for the season. In a *Holyoke Transcript-Telegram* article from 1961 that reviewed her career and noted her then 189 plays with The Valley Players:

Dolly Crane knows exactly how many steps it will take the girl who has a walk-on part to get on and off the stage. Dolly Crane had to plan rehearsals like this. While the Valley Players are performing one play in the evening, next week's play is being rehearsed in the afternoon. There isn't time for trial and error, for doing something just to see how it works.

Dolly gives the stage and Mountain Park Casino its share of credit for helping rehearsals run smoothly. It's as large or larger than stages in New York theaters.

Rehearsals can be plotted from what theater people call the "New York floor plan." Entrances, exits, locations of doors, windows, and furniture and stage groupings have already been developed and refined by the company which originally produced the play.

A ten-page program included small ads from Hudson Furriers on Suffolk Street in Holyoke, and the Main Street General Store, the Log Cabin restaurant at the entrance to the Mt. Tom State Reservation on Easthampton Road, and Bee's Beauty Shoppe on Suffolk, Hampden Ale from the brewery in Willimansett, the Colonial Pharmacy on Dwight Street, and the Park Pharmacy. The Roger Smith Hotel – featuring dancing nightly on the "Yankee Doodle Roof" to dance bands, served dinner from $1, and there was no cover charge. Ads for Steiger's department store urged us to choose our next winter's furs now, and an ad for the amusement park invited us to walk up the hill to sample the Midway.

Another "actress" was Miss Bucket, a cat whose "only experience was in the streets of Holyoke." The Guilds would return to their winter digs in Rhode Island at the close of the season, and most of the rest of the cast and crew scattered for "winter stock" work. It was reported of young company member Mary Elliott:

Mary Elliott is the only one of the Valley Players who may carry on this winter in Holyoke, for Miss Elliot is under contract with RKO to be groomed as a promising young starlet for the movie screen. As the VP ingénue, she has contributed many fine performances this summer...

For the ten-week season, actors Lauren Gilbert, Jackson Perkins, Joseph Foley, and Jean Guild were paid $400 for the season, or $40 per week. They represented the main cast, and visiting or occasional actors were paid less. Ann Lincoln worked for one week in one show and was paid $25. Director Dorothy Crane was paid $400 for the season, the same as the principal actors. The Valley Players paid a $13 license fee to the City of Holyoke, and some $1,253.99 in royalties to the play publishers.

As regards the individual productions, *Night Must Fall* cost $990.74 to produce, and the highest production costs of the season were from *The Male Animal* at $1,214.92. Advertising done locally appeared in the *Holyoke Transcript*, the *Springfield Union*, the *Springfield Republican*, the *Springfield Daily News*, the French language Holyoke paper *La Justice*, the German language *Rundschau*, and the *Holyoke Saturday Democrat*. Ads were also placed in newspapers in the northern valley town of Greenfield, Massachusetts, and south as far as New York City. In the following decade The Valley Players would cast a wider net for advertising, but it was early days, and the war would limit civilian pleasure travel. They appropriated $42 for radio spots to their neighbor

on the mountain summit, WHYN.

By 1942, tickets were also offered in Northampton at Dickinson's Drug Store, and reservations could be made through Holyoke, Northampton, and Springfield phone numbers (four-digit phone numbers of the day). Tickets could be reserved at the Park Pharmacy on Dwight Street and Martin's Pharmacy on Hampden Street in the Highlands section of Holyoke. Buses ran from the City Hall to Mountain Park every fifteen minutes and from the Lyman Street railroad depot as well.

An ad for the Kathleen Smith Music Shop on Maple Street, opposite the Strand movie theater in the program for the third show of the season, *Yes, My Darling Daughter*, urged the community to...

Buy bonds for security, then consider a PIANO for a more cheerful home during gas-less days ahead.

Gas rationing and tire rationing during WWII, and pleasure driving not being allowed would seriously affect summer theatre – which is routinely not in the cities, and therefore there is little to no public transit and the venues are not easily accessible. Materials for building sets, and fabric would be restricted, and advertising took a hit when by October 1942 the home delivery of newspapers would be canceled due to gas rationing. If attracting an audience and maintaining their loyalty was difficult for professional theatre before the war, the realities of wartime added new hurdles.

But the show went on. The Guilds noted in the playbill production notes for the start of the 1942 season:

Yes, it's mighty good to be back. We've been looking forward to this season ever since the end of last summer. You know, we didn't realize at the time how many real friends we have made here during our first season.

Alfred Paschall, who appeared occasionally in minor roles, was usually "our very efficient and likeable stage manager." Technical staff would occasionally take minor roles on stage through the next two decades.

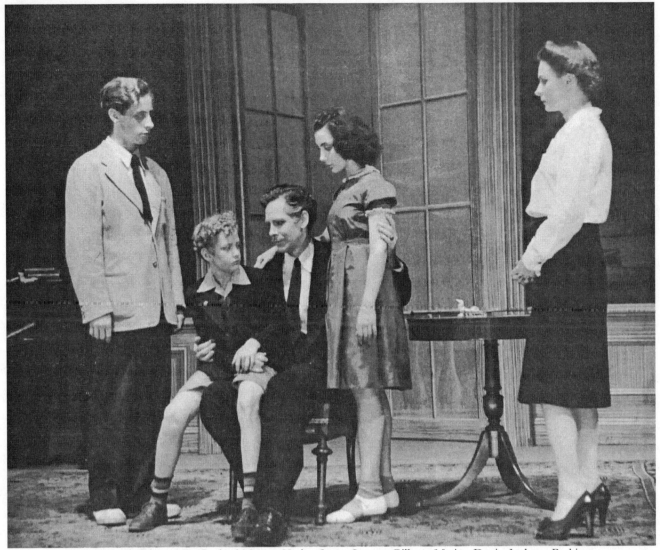

Watch on the Rhine 1942, Gaylord Mason, Harlan Stone, Lauren Gilbert, Marion Davis, Jackson Perkins

Watch on the Rhine was the sixth show of the season on August 3, 1942. This seminal show had been the hit of Broadway in 1941, and most of the Broadway cast made up the national tour 1942. That tour was currently on break for the filming of the movie in Hollywood. On this, and in many productions, The Valley Players were choosing not just chestnuts, but current shows that were recent hits in New York and, in the case of the subject matter of *Watch*, very much in the news. Lauren Gilbert starred as Kurt Mueller, the underground fighter against the Nazis. Gilbert's real-life wife Jackson Perkins played his American-born wife, Sara. Jean Guild was the formidable Fanny, the family matriarch. Maurice Wells played the duplicitous villain of the piece, Teck de Brancovis. Gaylord Mason played oldest

son Joshua, and two younger children in the cast were played by Harlan Stone as Bodo, who already had New York stage experience at eleven years old, and Springfield girl Marion Davis, who was thirteen years old and a drama pupil of Valley Player Norah Adamson. She had also appeared in local radio in *Aunt Patty's Gang* and the *Bread Box Review*. (Ann Blyth played the role as a child on Broadway. That fall she would resume the national tour of the show, which brought her to Los Angeles and the offer of a screen test that launched her film career.)

Springfield Daily News theatre critic W. Harley Rudkin, noted of little Harlan Stone:

...he hadn't seen the part until Thursday of rehearsal

week…and that meant a terrific amount of work…I told him I liked his performance; he bowed slightly, thanked me and made pleasant conversation although it was apparent that he was almost asleep on his feet…Despite the rigors of rehearsals, Harlan found time to have fun. They came to look for him one afternoon, and finally discovered him in a tree armed with a long, ancient flintlock from the prop department…Below and patiently playing whatever game he was involved in was…a friendly little Scottie belonging to Lauren Gilbert and Jackson Perkins.

Mr. Rudkin, who had reviewed the national touring company production at The Bushnell in Hartford the year before with the original cast (and lamented that Springfield was not able to attract more national touring companies to the Court Square Theater), continued his adoration of Jackson Perkins in the role of Sara Mueller:

I found Jackson Perkins more believable than Mady Christians, who originated the character. Quick, loyal, tempestuous—she is the strength a man needs when his own begins to fail…I know it to be an absolute fact, yet I still have difficulty in understanding that this production has been in rehearsal only a week. It is a masterly piece of work by gifted and enthusiastic craftsmen.

The *Holyoke Daily Transcript* lauded with play with a touching and thoughtful analysis that speaks volumes for what The Valley Players was becoming, and the place it was to fill in the Pioneer Valley for two decades to come:

The Valley Players had a very definite plan, when they came here last year, that they would give this bewildered Valley relaxing plays. They would make people laugh with good farce or they would now and then throw in a thrill. They thought we needed that. And of course we do. But this week they have come to town with something of real value to us as a play. Also it reveals the friendly Players of the Valley group in roles that demand other standards. They are proving themselves. Of courses, Jean Guild is unfailing…No one can longer date Jackson Perkins as a pert, brilliant performer of brittle roles

only…Watch on the Rhine gives her a new personality…her voice is choicely handled and her whole play-up to Lauren Gilbert, who rises to a new top as Kurt Muller [sic], is fine for its restraint and sense of genuine power. The patrons of the Valley Players are having a rich week with Watch on the Rhine, every role handled with full measure of the great theme.

The program for the week of August 10, 1942, contained an insert, titled *Joint Appeal of the American Theatre Wing War Service, Inc. and The Actors' Fund of America.* As part of the Summer Theatre Managers Association, the Valley Players carried the message that those donating to the theatre organization "…will be combining patriotism with the greatest of all homely virtues—charity." The American Theatre Wing supported the Stage Door Canteen, which entertained and fed service personnel during the war, with an average nightly attendance during the war of 3,000. The Actors' Fund took care of the sick and aged members of the theatre community. During the week of August 10, 1942, summer theatre patrons all over the U.S. were asked to contribute. Antoinette Perry was chairman of the board of the American Theatre Wing, and her name, of course, would later be bestowed upon the annual Broadway prize, the Tony Award®. Also sitting on the board at this time were acting greats Helen Hayes, Gertrude Lawrence, and Josephine Hull. Katharine Cornell sat on the board of the Actors' Fund of America. The Valley Players would devote one show each season for the next two decades to raise proceeds for The Actors Fund.

So far the new gas rationing law in the U.S. was not hurting theatre in western Massachusetts. According to Springfield drama critic W. Harley Rudkin:

War or no war; rationing, Western Massachusetts theater lovers will still patronize something they like—even if they have to get there afoot or on bicycle. If you don't think so,

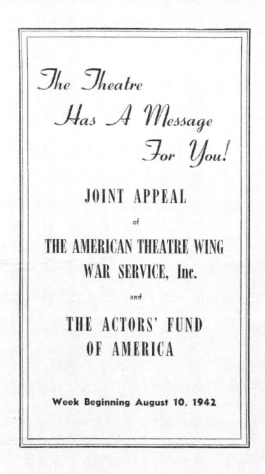

ask Carlton Guild, business manager of the Valley Players, now breaking all attendance records at the Mountain Park Casino…It is proof positive that people want value for their money and that they will patronize those projects that provide it.

The theatre's most famous newspaper, *Variety*, also reported in August 1942:

In spite of gas and tire curtailments, The Valley Players, now halfway through their second summer at the Mountain Park Casino, Holyoke, are breaking all records for that theatre.

The only legitimate company operating this summer in Western Massachusetts, the Valley Players are selling the 1,000-seat house out well in advance…Automobile traffic to the park still heavy, but buses are also getting big play Army men from nearby Westover Field are regular patrons of Casino productions.

But male juvenile player Gaylord Mason wouldn't finish the season; he was about to be drafted. The war would have an effect on professional theatre just as it would on professional sports. However, unlike professional sports, some actors who were not eligible for military service, either because of age or health issues nevertheless volunteered to perform for troops in the U.S. and abroad in war zones. The theatre lost more personnel, both men and women, to the war than did professional sports.

There was also the matter of blackouts which made a dark night on a heavily wooded mountain a greater adventure than in a downtown theater which could keep interior auditorium lights on, but ensure that outside lights were not visible. Rudkin reported on the unusual and unexpectedly fun experience at the Casino:

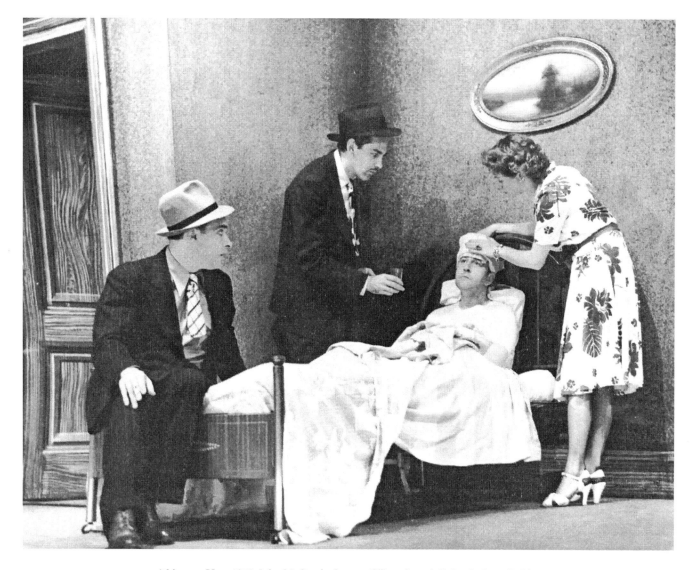

3 Men on a Horse 1942, John McQuade, Lauren Gilbert, Joseph Foley, Jackson Perkins

So engrossed was the audience in the tomfoolery of Three Men on a Horse *that Dorothy Crane's announcement from the stage that a blackout was in effect brought a gasp of surprise from a capacity house. The only disturbance came from one harried gentleman who went climbing about the place in the dark looking for a telephone. He was an air raid warden, whose conscience bothered him because he couldn't figure out how to get to his post.*

But if things were calm and peaceful out front, it was quite the reverse backstage. Although the Valley Players *were prepared for the blackout any night it might come, it is one thing to grope around with a flashlight in theory and quite another to put it into practice…The blackout couldn't have come at a worse time in the season as far as handling sets*

is concerned…there are three sets…and even under normal conditions the cast was continually taking the wrong turning and winding up somewhere far removed from where they should have been…with the stage practically dimmed out, it was something of a feat.

At the announcement, the backstage and beam lights were doused and the stage lights dimmed to a minimum…Action was still visible, and the audience didn't even notice it until the director told them…Then matches began to flare in the audience as patrons tried to read their programs…But a quick admonition put an end to that…Patrons sang during changes and generally had a wonderful time…Most common statement heard when the intermission finally came was, "I'd rather be here than at home."

Three Men on a Horse, a rollicking racetrack comedy featured everybody's favorite character man, Joseph Foley. Willard Dashiell, who had managed and appeared on stage at the Casino in the 1920s, had a small role as a barkeep.

Nothing But the Truth, which played the week of August 24, 1942, featured guest "jobber" Ralph Edwards, who was then a hit on radio with his game show *Truth or Consequences* that ran Saturday nights for the past three years. The television version awaited him in the future, as well as his other long-running and popular show *This is Your Life*. Jackson Perkins had invited him to Holyoke after she had been a guest on his *Truth or Consequences* program. The comic play's title, *Nothing But the Truth*, was also playful jest on his radio show title. His character in the well-known plot must speak only the truth for twenty-four hours to win an expensive bet. The Valley Players demonstrated that putting on the latest New York hits was only one tactic to draw in an audience.

Another was to play the publicity game. Being a national radio figure, news of his Valley Players appearance was covered by The *New York Herald Tribune* and other papers across the country.

The last show of the season was Noel Coward's sophisticated comedy *Private Lives*. A review called it "a most successful season...If early indications from the counting room are reliable, the attendance will reach 40,000 against last season's 26,000."

Jackson Perkins played Amanda, Lauren Gilbert "in his most inviting role" played the erstwhile husband, and also featured were Ann Lee and Joseph Foley. Jean Guild had a brief role as a French maid. Louise (Louie) Mudgett, publicity director, and who would become as well-known a fixture at the plays on and off stage, addressed the audience between acts and invited them to meet and greet the players at the end of the show. A great number did. According to the *Springfield*

Daily News article, "The snugging of the wooden shutters at the Casino Saturday night will close down the popular summer company and playhouse and bring the first legitimate harbinger of fall."

Ralph Edwards

Lauren Gilbert topped the actors for appearances and salary for the 1942 season at $2,086.35. Jackson Perkins (his wife) earned $400 that season with far less performances. Both season director Dorothy Crane and Jean Guild earned $1,821.20.

The producers bade farewell in the "souvenir" program that featured photos of the 1942 season:

We are not going to say goodbye, for we are already thinking about and planning for next summer. We wish we could say, 'We'll surely be back in 1943,' or even 'Some of us will certainly be back, and the Valley Players

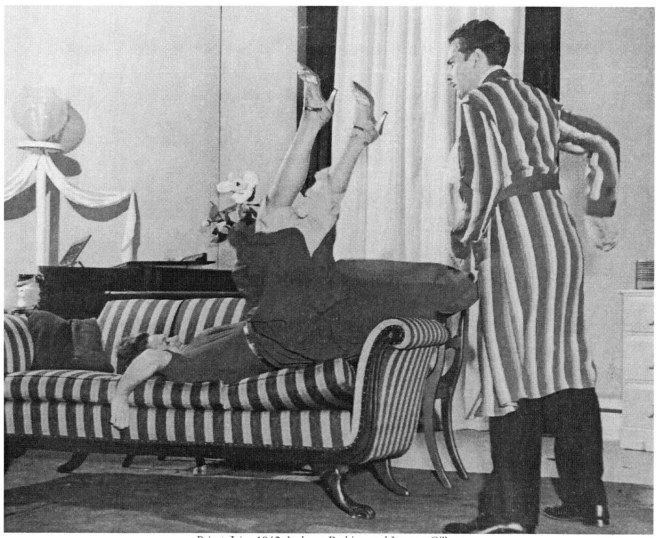

Private Lives 1942, Jackson Perkins and Lauren Gilbert

will continue their productions next summer.' World conditions naturally forbid any such statement. But the theater has a way of living, even of flourishing, in war time. If any summer theaters, however few, open their doors next June, we believe that the Mountain Park Casino will be numbered among them. We shall not cease working to that end.

It was a heartfelt and even noble statement, but there would be no 1943 season for The Valley Players. The wartime restriction of pleasure driving, the rationing of gasoline, forced the entire Mountain Park amusement park to close in 1943, and The Valley Players were only tenants of the Casino; they did not own the property.

William Guild also notes:

In '43 because of the war and the draft they couldn't get young leading men.

Famed choreographer, dancing teacher and showman Ned Wayburn, who in the previous year had considered opening another in his chain of dance studios in the dance pavilion at Mountain Park, died as The Valley Player's second season came to an end. He had decided to hold off and let The Valley Players have a chance to get established before he made a move to join them in business. One wonders what he would have made of a dance school on the mountain, with his "Midas touch."

Just as there were welcoming editorials in the local press at the beginning of the season, there were farewell editorials at the end.

This particular group of players has given us cheer and something that we could call "esprit". They have lived themselves into our own life now. They have made many people see more clearly the painstaking sacrifice that the actor's life has to be. Mr. and Mrs. Guild, and their co-workers have felt that nothing they could do could possibly be too good for Holyoke…May we meet again next year.

Joseph Foley left The Valley Players at the end of the 1942 season to enlist in the service. He was one of the original founders and managers of the acting company. Bertram Tanswell had joined The Valley Players in 1942 and would direct many shows as well as act. He performed in many plays and radio programs both in England, where he was born, and in the U.S., where he became a citizen.

Bertram Tanswell

In 1943 the "New" Holyoke Theatre downtown, "The Playhouse Beautiful" as its programs stated, kept theatre going downtown at this period during the traditional theatre "winter stock" months. In March *Twin Beds* and *Mrs. Crane Steps Out*, and *Laugh That Off* were among the plays produced by the stock company that included Hall Shelton, Grace Carney, Frank Lyon, Philip Arthur (future Valley Players member), Louis

Kirtland, Ruth Amos, Harry E. Lowell, Guy Palmerton (who would come to manage other New England summer theaters), and Eleanor Harrington. Mr. Lyon and Mr. Palmerton were also the Production Director and General Manager, respectively. Many were local (Eleanor Harrington's bio calls her "a Springfield girl,") and had performed in summer stock around New England. In April, the plays included *George and Margaret* and *The Family Upstairs*. *No, No, Nannette*, and *10 Nights in a Bar-Room*, in what was advertised as a "musical swing version" would round out the season.

The company was managed by Holyoke native Harold J. Kennedy, who would later find his way up the mountain for summer theatre in the mid 1960s when the Mt. Tom Playhouse and touring packaged shows with known stars would replace the resident repertoire company from 1964 to 1965.

Early in 1943 it was expected that Mountain Park and The Valley Players would be open for business that summer, requiring and receiving permission to open from the Office of Defense Transportation, a new wartime regulatory committee, solely for the amusement of the service personnel at the nearby Westover Field in Chicopee, as well the war workers in the heavily industrialized Holyoke-Chicopee-Springfield area.

Other summer theaters, however, had already closed due to wartime restrictions: The Harrison Hall Players in Fitchburg, the Cape Playhouse in Dennis, the Peterborough Players in New Hampshire, the Monomoy Theater in Chatham among them. *The Billboard* remarked:

The hue and cry was centered around the fact that most summer theaters are in isolated areas, accessible by auto only, and what with the conservation of gas and rubber, many veteran cowbarn producers just let the weeds grow high around their properties for the summer.

In April 1943, Willard Dashiell, the actor who had made the introductory speech to the audience on the stage of the new Casino in 1901, who had acted and managed acting companies at the Casino in the 1920s and 1930s, and lately had a few small guest roles with The Valley Players, died, leaving his widow and former co-star Mabel Griffith. Dashiell had also been a playwright, and directed for the old Poli Stock Company in Springfield. Though he began as a lawyer, he drifted into theatre, known for his "splendid" baritone and singing professionally in opera companies, reputedly being the first American to sing Wagner's *Parsifal*. He performed on Broadway. He also appeared in silent movies with Tallulah Bankhead and Mabel Normand. Stock theatre, however, was his true love, and where he played, toured, and directed for the remainder of his life. He first came to Holyoke at the Empire Theater downtown in *Great John Gantry*. He and Mabel Griffith played at the Mt. Tom Casino when they eloped to Hartford, Connecticut, and were married by a justice of the peace.

The playhouse on Mt. Tom was only a stop on their tour, but they loved Holyoke, and remained here the rest of their lives, taking a house in the Smiths Ferry section of the city. He is buried in the Smiths Ferry cemetery.

***

A few weeks after D-Day, The Valley Players opened for 1944.

The Casino was spruced up when some 300 new seats were installed, with a flat floor and soft drink bar on one side of the lobby, aisles recarpeted, and the theater painted. The local papers filled pages with bios of newcomers to the company. Prior to the opening, the company went down to local department store (and longtime playbill advertiser) McAuslan & Wakelin Company to sell war bonds. The Oracle column of the *Holyoke Transcript-Telegram* rejoiced:

Holyoke greets the Valley Players. They give us the sign that we are past the peak of our war limitations. The program for the season is rich with promise…it is something to have the Mountain Park play season open.

Claudia led off the 1944 season. It had been a hit on Broadway in 1941 and was the vehicle that brought star Dorothy McGuire to Hollywood. Elaine Ellis took her role for The Valley Players.

Beatrice Newport was in the cast, who had performed at the famed Pasadena Playhouse, and whom most of the audience would remember from her work on the long-running *Ma Perkins* radio soap opera. The Guilds addressed the audience about the lost year in the program:

We are very glad to be back. It was a great disappointment to us not to be able to return in 1943. Our plans for last summer were practically complete when the pleasure-driving ban made the operation of the theatre impossible.

Another kind of ban affected the traditional Mountain Park evening celebrations—there were to be no fireworks held during the war.

After final curtain on opening night, a live radio broadcast on WHYN with interviewer Ward Gardner, who spoke with the director and cast, was conducted on stage before the audience to re-introduce the valley to The Valley Players. It had been the largest "first night" audience since the company had come to Holyoke in 1941. Jean Guild received applause just for making her first entrance in a minor role as the cook.

Westover Field brought enlisted men and women every Thursday night to the Casino playhouse in convoys. The base newspaper, *The Westover Flyer*, carried reviews of all the plays.

Blind Alley, the fourth show of the season featured John O'Connor, just back from a year in the Army Air Corps. Gary Striker, also in the cast, was a fourth grader from Springfield's Frederick Harris School. Other shows included young people from the Trinity Players of Springfield, and a Holyoke girl on vacation from Emerson College where she was studying drama and speech.

The continuing ban on driving and gas restrictions posed difficulties for one Hartford critic in his effort to cover The Valley Players. *Hay Fever* brought the reviewer from *The Hartford Times*, in part because:

This summer stock company is the only one…available on anything approaching a convenient public transportation schedule for Hartford…One can catch the 11 p.m. bus, which connects with an 11:45 train to Hartford from Springfield. It takes 15 minutes to get from Mountain Park to downtown Holyoke. The 10:30 bus from the park leaves time to see almost the entire play and allows for connections.

Almost the entire play? How many patrons also had to miss the ending? The reviewer comforts us that on Saturday nights, it's possible to stay for the whole show, because there is an 11:30 bus, which allows one to make the train leaving Holyoke at midnight. Clearly a Connecticut resident, he pokes gentle fun at the Massachusetts Sunday Blue Laws—which required a list of censored words to be removed from the script— and posted for public review in the lobby. The irony may have been lost on the Blue Law administrators, but not on the reviewer or, one presumes, the audience.

Jean Guild won raves for her featured performance in *Hay Fever* ("She was a very good actress," says her son William Guild), and Helen Harrelson, who would join the company, appeared for the first time. Alfred Paschall had a minor role. He had been The Valley Players stage manager, but left with Ralph Edwards after his show of the previous year to join Mr. Edwards' radio *Truth or Consequences* staff as stage manager. He came back this summer for an extended visit. Claudine Shannon, one of the current stage managers, had a small role in this play. Another stage manager was Ken E. Andrew, who also took small parts throughout the season, as did publicity director Louise (Louie) Mudgett.

For *Charley's Aunt*, the *Daily Hampshire Gazette* reviewed noted of the curtain call:

…the players take their bows in fixed position suggestive of the old Daguerreotypes, with the exception of [star Bertram] *Tanswell, who does a final bit Charley's Aunt clowning as the curtain finally rings down.*

In *Broadway*, a 1920s style review (which would be produced again at the Mt. Tom Playhouse in the sixties with Merv Griffin), Jean Guild wowed them in a blonde wig and bird-of-paradise costumes, "was delightfully slap happy in a song and dance number, with Alfred Paschall as her inebriate husband." The cast were hopeful young hoofers, and John O'Connor a gangster. Carlton Guild, business manager, even joined in with a minor role as a barkeep.

The producers noted in the last program of the season:

We hope that you have enjoyed the weekly radio interviews with members of our company and the brief pre-views of our plays which have been broadcast over WHYN each Monday during the season.

The radio show's sponsor was McAuslan and Wakelin Co., a department store on the corner of Dwight and Maple streets, "(meter parking)". The box office was at the Kathleen Smith Music Shop at 269 Maple Street.

The *Springfield Union* ran a feature on how The

Hay Fever 1944, Helen Harrelson, Steven Elliott, Al Paschall

Valley Players were coping with wartime shortages, making what materials they had stretch as far as they could go, and noted new competition when some New York producers had opted to keep their plays running all summer, taking advantage of the massive closings of summer theaters unable to operate under wartime shortages and restrictions on gas and materials.

The *Springfield Union* noted that the playhouse on Mt. Tom was helped to no small degree by Holyoke stores, which lent furniture and props, and their crew remaking old secondhand furniture with ingenuity, though the theatre was not exactly run on a shoestring. Chief Electrician Talbot "Pete" Peterson noted that in terms of cables, switchboard, and technical wizardry, they had, "as much backstage equipment as any Broadway show, and were better equipped than any of the 26 stock companies" that were then running during wartime.

The season ended with Gaylord Mason, Robert Emhardt and John O'Connor heading off to Broadway for winter work with Helen Hayes.

In January 1945, the Shubert production of *The Merry Widow* played the Court Square Theater – and garnered only a small article in comparison with the giant movie display ads on the entertainment page; it was dwarfed by them. The operetta performance was sponsored by The Playgoers of Springfield. The Victory Theater in downtown Holyoke, which showed movies, touted itself as "Holyoke's only air conditioned theater." The movie theaters, with war workers downtown, were doing a land office business in this era.

Back on the mountain in Holyoke, husband and wife team ("Mr.") Lauren Gilbert and ("Miss") Jackson Perkins were absent for the 1944 season due to Gilbert's military service and Mrs. Gilbert's following him to his posts in Washington, D.C., and California, where he was involved with motion picture assignments for the Navy. They had three children, including the set of twins that were born only the past spring. It was noted in the program for the play *Over 21*, that:

…only a few weeks after her eldest child, Claiborne, was born, her husband, Lauren Gilbert, changed his civilian clothes for a Navy uniform.

They spent the war living in cramped wartime housing projects. Old friend Edward A. Wright of the Farragut Players was on hand to fill in this season. But the just before the 1945 season commenced, it was announced that the Gilberts would be joining The Valley Players company again, and that they had taken a house on Wellesley Road for the summer. Jackson would appear in most of the shows this season, while her husband would appear only in the season opener: he costarred with her in *Blithe Spirit*, and then had to return to the Navy after his fourteen-day leave.

Carlton and Jean Guild were back from their winter digs in Newport, Rhode Island, where he was head of the English Department in the public school system.

Papa is All was the second play of the 1945 season. It was recalled in the producer's notes in a 1947 program:

Jean Guild still has nightmares about her experience of coming on stage for the third act on opening night and discovering that the all-important wall telephone which her first lines were supposed to be about and which had to be used in a few minutes simply was not there! There was much improvising on stage to stall for time much scurrying about back stage with no solution in sight but to drop the main curtain and begin the act all over again—a disgrace which thus far (yes we're rapping vigorously on wood) we have never yet incurred. Gaylord Mason did some of his best quick thinking brought the telephone on stage installed it and no sooner done than it rang, and the play proceeded.

Another episode of bad luck occurred that week when Jackson Perkins "who gave a brilliant performance as Mama on opening night, was taken seriously ill." Director of the show Dorothy Crane stepped into the role on the next night with only a few hours' notice "and played it without a single prompt, and, still more to her everlasting credit, gave a truly fine performance, continuing in the part for the rest of the week." It brought in the second-highest profit rate of the season at $604.31. It was topped by *Murder Without Crime* at $741.41.

Once again, the military from Westover Field were guests of The Valley Players every Thursday night. Convoys left the base at 7:15 p.m., and they received special rates on other nights. Terry Little joined the cast, having been introduced to the company through "his friend and former fellow actor, Corp. Jon Collins of Westover Field."

The program was twelve pages, and included ads from Steiger's, now promoting itself as an "Official War Bond Agency"; Child's Fine Footwear on High Street; Leo J. Simard, Jeweler on Suffolk Street; E. O'Connor & Company, which had been established in 1888, sold "Quality Clothes" on High Street. Ads appeared for shoes and shoe repair by Napoleon Bail on High Street next to the *Holyoke Transcript* building, the Kane Furniture Company on Dwight Street, and Anita—for "sophisticated apparel" and "choice millinery" on Maple Street. The City of Holyoke Gas and Electric Department sponsored an ad, as did Bee's Beauty Shoppe on Suffolk Street, the Highland Laundry Company on Pleasant Street, and McAuslan & Wakelin Company department store at High, Dwight, and Maple streets.

For *Kiss and Tell*, local companies supplied props for the play: the local Coca-Cola bottling company in Springfield, the Pioneer Valley Ginger Ale Company, and Hampden Mild Ale supplied by the Hampden Brewing Company. The Philip Morris company also provided cigarettes. The program for this play also marks possibly the first mention of the noted (or notorious) fireworks in Mountain Park:

Our Tuesday evening performances for the remainder of the season will begin very promptly, and intermissions may be shortened, in order that the play may be over before 10:30 when the fireworks will be displayed.

Regular reviews by weekly papers, which often maintained a columnist or critic on staff, seem remarkable in comparison to the lack of coverage of professional theatre by them in our current era. The *Belchertown Sentinel* ran a column "Old Steeple Soliloquies" in which the reviewer remembered the old-time stock shows of his youth at the Casino on Mt. Tom, and approved of the newer fare by The Valley Players:

The present summer stock is more than a mere financial enterprise. It is almost a school of the theater, where young people do a lot of studying and get a great deal of experience for not much more than good board and room. More than likely, every member of the company is in, or through college, and definitely interested in theater for its artistic rather than for its commercial possibilities. The youngsters are chaperoned to a degree unknown by most of the adolescents in the audience…One commendable difference between modern and ancient stock companies is that there is no longer likely to be one "leading man," one "leading lady," and one "villain," all of whom must have star parts each and every show. The lead this week is probably the maid, or the chauffeur next week. 'The play is the thing' with groups like the Valley Players…week-by-week, patrons become real fans and have their favorites, who get applause whenever they first appear each week….When the movies came into full flower, some of us feared for the future of the "legitimate," which we loved for all its corniness. We didn't need to worry. Too many people were born with a love for the theatre and a willingness to work like galley slaves for their hobby to surrender entirely to the Hollywood blitzkrieg…with "A" tickets up in gallonage, you could do much, much worse than renew your acquaintance with the footlights at the old Casino at Mountain Park.

Mr. Guild, business manager and the only non-actor among them, was also brought back for the next play, *Arsenic and Old Lace*, as Lt. Rooney. The program notes teased that he would have to join Equity soon.

During the run of *Arsenic and Old Lace*, the reporter Olive Pearson Rice of the *Springfield Republican* spent the day with The Valley Players, and gives us a view on what it was like for a summer stock company during wartime. She describes a big, rambling summer home of the Steiger family in the Highlands of Holyoke where most of the company lived. The rest rented rooms in nearby homes. Albert Steiger had emigrated to the U.S. from Germany as a boy. He began as a peddler, founded his first store in Port Chester, New York, and eventually relocated to western Massachusetts, starting his family chain in Holyoke in 1896, with future stores in Springfield and in Connecticut.

You come on it suddenly around a bend in the road and pass its gardens and terraces on your way to park beside the garages.

It was quiet early in the morning when she arrived, with most of the actors still asleep, not having gotten to bed until "the bell in the steeple strikes 3 or 4 in the morning."

Mrs. Lee Carson, "A pretty little white haired woman" was hired to do the food shopping and prepare the meals. She collected the ration books of the actors and tussled with shortages on a grand scale. Breakfast was a "free for all," lunch was buffet style, and for supper this night there would be meatloaf with tomato and mushroom sauce, baked potatoes, vegetables, sliced peaches, and cake. Sunday dinner, of course, was chicken. Nearby farms provided the eggs, and twenty-two quarts of milk were delivered at a time. Sugar was carefully doled out and restricted.

Three young apprentice actors paid their way by cleaning. In the afternoon, the large living room served as their rehearsal space. "Miss Hayes," Gaylord Mason's dog, a Sealyham terrier named for Helen Hayes, lived with them. "Miss Hayes" had the canine lead in *Kiss and Tell* in New York, and reprised her role with The Valley Players.

She has been a riot: in fact she practically brings the house down whenever she appears on the stage.

Gaylord Mason's ration books came in the mail this particular morning, forwarded by his family, who had already lifted all but one shoe stamp in it.

Ronald Telfer, in "snazzy pajamas and blue silk bathrobe" meandered around the kitchen with his own mail in one hand and a can of fruit juice in the other. The arrival of the mail brought "a wild scramble."

Martha Jones, "a cute glamour girl ankles in wearing a raspberry chambray sport dress and her head done up in a kerchief. She is married to Robert Emhardt, whom she met and married when both were acting with the Lunts in *The Pirate*." Emhardt is described as having a "Churchillian voice."

Helen Harrelson is a curly-haired ingénue busily ironing on the back porch in a spare moment.

Randall Brooks, set designer, showed up for lunch before heading back to the Casino. Wartime restrictions made paint scarce, "among other items and each set has to be freshly painted for

each week's performance."

Back at the house a New York car is parked by the driveway. It belongs to Jackson Perkins. She lives down the road a bit with her three children, the twins are only a few months old. Her actor husband, Lauren Gilbert, is in the navy.

She grabbed a sandwich and told reporter Olive Pearson Rice that she learns her lines in the morning when she is most rested.

Watching her during rehearsal it is easy to see that she has the art of relaxation down to a science. One minute she is storming in a tense scene; that over, she completely relaxes in a comfortable chair. She manages to look regal even in a checked gingham dress with her head wrapped up in a scarf.

Rehearsal is a serious business. Miss Dorothy Crane, the able director, sits ensconced in a cretonne-covered wing chair by the fireplace and not a flick of the eyebrow or an inflection of tone escapes her notice. She builds up scenes, prompts, does the sound effects, and generally whips the play into shape to her liking.

The Steiger estate.

Merrell Hopkins, stage manager, sat in the other chair, and when not involved with The Valley Players this summer, she was a theater department instructor at Smith College in Northampton.

After that evening's performance, the blue-green

curtain was lowered after the final curtain call, and the players, in a caravan of cars and the company station wagon headed back to the Steiger place "for another raid on the overworked refrigerator" and a few more hours' work as they read their next play. They rehearsed one play in the morning, performed a second play in the evening, and read the next coming play in the wee hours.

The Valley Players gave six evening performances. After they "break" set from one show on Sunday afternoon, they start rehearsal for the current play on a new set in the evening.

In between times you'll like as not find some of them giving out programs or taking in tickets.

A young ingénue joining the company for *Kiss and Tell*, playing the part of Corliss Archer, was Betsy Drake, who had performed on Broadway and was slated to head to Hollywood for a screen test; she had recently signed a movie contract with producer Hal Wallis to make two films per year, released through Paramount. She would also marry Hollywood star Cary Grant.

Carlton Guild was back on the boards playing Mr. Willard, a house painter, while his wife, Jean Guild, played the maid. "There are no small parts…" as the saying goes. They sold photos of scenes from some of the plays for fifty cents each.

Snafu, the comedy whose title meaning was delicately explained in the program, included Lucille St. Peter in the cast, another local young actress, a graduate of Classical High School in Springfield, and who had appeared in local radio on WMAS and WSPR.

On August 18th, the newspapers ran ads for Mountain Park and for The Valley Players, presenting *Snafu* with Jackson Perkins and Terry Little, and *The Torch Bearers* next week with Hugh Franklin and Helen Harrelson, "A completely mad comedy featuring Jean Guild," and also at that time celebrating the resumption of pleasure driving and birth of the "golden age" of summer theatre. Interestingly, unlike the movie theaters, the Casino listed phone number, prices and times. The movies did not need to lure the audience inside.

V-J Day occurred that week, bringing an end to World War II. Mountain Park had received instructions to close because of a lack of police protection during the wonderful, but chaotic spontaneous celebrations around town (and around the valley), and The Valley Players were requested to cancel that evening's performance, but not before early arrivers had already come to the playhouse. It was recalled in a 1947 program, "It was one grand mix-up. We never did get the Tuesday night tickets all straightened out; but the occasion, we all agreed, was well worth the resulting confusion. We also canceled the Wednesday performances and ran special matinees Thursday and Saturday."

The end of the war also brought an *immediate* end to gas rationing on August 15th. "Gas Rationing Ends Today" – trumpeted *Holyoke Transcript-Telegram* on page one of the August 15, 1945, issue. It was as jubilant a headline as the news of peace.

Fireworks at Mountain Park, which had been resumed as well, sometimes presented a challenge for the theater staff and patrons, aswell as for the Holyoke Street Railway Company, which ran the public buses to the park from downtown. Trying to work the third act to avoid the noise of the rockets' red glare and bombs bursting in air sometimes made shows run past the last scheduled pick up by the bus, but it was recorded that the Street Railway was ever cooperative.

The war and the season ended with, ironically, the pre-war cautionary tale of Nazis and their indoctrination of German youth in *Tomorrow the World*, which ran the week of August 27 through September 1, 1945. Hugh Franklin was the featured player, with Martha Jones and young Paul Porter Jr. Jean Guild had to take over for Jackson Perkins, who fell ill.

Paul was thirteen years old at the time he appeared as the problem child in *Tomorrow the World*, and his bio in the program had a number of regional stage credits. He had appeared in *My Sister Eileen* in New York, and had some sixty movies and around 250 radio appearances to his credit. Paul played the boy influenced by Nazis in the same role on Broadway, where his father, Paul Sr., was stage manager. Phyllis DeBus, ten years old, appeared in touring companies, and appeared in *Lady in the Dark* on tour and on Broadway. Other young people in the cast, Allen Knox, Robert Sabin, Richard Williams were all from Springfield. Increasingly, when the child role was not a starring role requiring experience, local amateur child actors were allowed to join the cast of pros.

The program notes that the end of the season would send company members Gaylord Mason, Robert Emhardt, Helen Harrelson, and Terry Little back to New York like birds flying south at the end of the summer. Director Dorothy Crane was to return to Newport News, Virginia, for the winter. Hugh Franklin was off to join Ethel Barrymore's touring show, *The Joyous Season.*

Evidence of the suddenness of the Japanese surrender, and the ignorance of the atomic bomb that precipitated it, showed in an ad ran in the last program of the year, sponsored by the town newspaper, the *Holyoke Transcript-Telegram*:

To Beat Japan *will take all the fight American fighting men have.*
Stay with them.
　1) Keep that war job.

　2) Keep Buying Bonds.
　3) Keep doing all your country asks.
　　It's a tough road to Tokyo.

The Roger Smith Hotel, promising dining and dancing and "man-size drinks of star quality," featured Allen Chambers and His Society Music in the cocktail lounge on Tuesday through Friday, and in the new Patent Leather Room on Saturday.

After this last show of the season – and the end of the war – The Valley Players were to fold their tent, so to speak, for the winter. The program noted:

By this coming Sunday night, the big house at Wyckoff Park will seem pretty much deserted. Martha Jones will he joining her husband, Mr. Emhardt in New York…Probably the last to go will be Merrell Hopkins, our stage manager, who has to wait until next week to return furniture and properties to their rightful owners.

Louis D. Pellissier, president of the Holyoke Street Railway company, who started as a conductor on a trolley line in 1892 (earning 14 cents an hour and boarding at the Bon Ton hotel) and later came to run the company, celebrated his fiftieth year in business in a newspaper tribute, with an especial note of pride for The Valley Players, which he "confesses is one of his greatest accomplishments, the bringing to Holyoke of such an outstanding company."

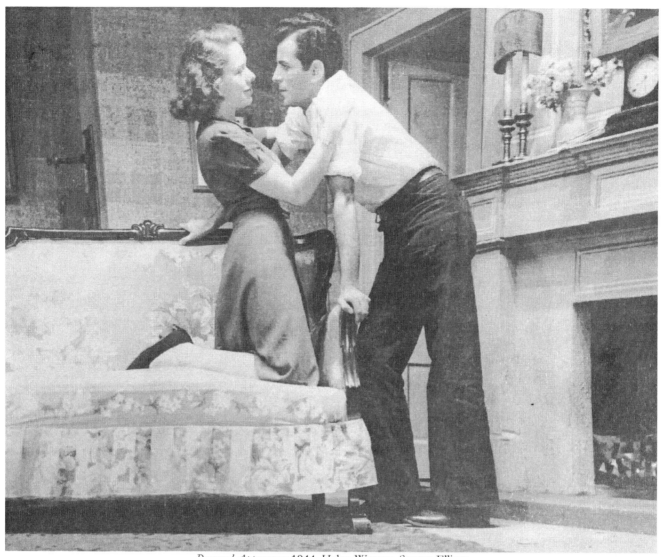

Personal Appearance 1944, Helen Wagner, Steven Elliott

as dish-washing, window cleaning and unpacking of food stuffs.

When the T.T. reporter visited the Steiger estate yesterday afternoon, she found the popular Carlton Guild and his wife Jean, and leading man Gaylord Mason basking in the sun on the expansive lawn enjoying a few hours of relaxation before 'hitting the grind' of memorizing lines.

CHAPTER 5

A Post-war World and a New Audience

Mountain Park opened for the first post-war season on April 27, 1946. "It's Mt. Park Time!" proclaimed the ads.

The local newspaper announced all the regulars who were gone during the war and were back from service, especially favorites Joseph Foley, and Lauren Gilbert and his wife Jackson Perkins, and that George Alan Smith, graduate of Holyoke High School was just back from the Navy where he served in the Pacific. Smith was also a playwright, and director. W. Harley Rudkin, theatre critic of the *Springfield Daily News* rejoiced:

Springfield theatergoers will not have to travel far for their summer stage fare. The nearest spot is the Mountain Park Casino, in Holyoke, where the Valley Players will return Monday. Starting from scratch, and with a theater that had languished in other hands, this lively organization has built itself a staunch following through the best possible gleaner of good will in the world—first-class productions.

The local paper eagerly followed them as they took up residence again in their usual digs: the summer home of Albert Steiger, the founder of the local department store chain, Steiger's:

…some of the Valley Players are already 'moving in' for the summer months, midst the bustle of such practical tasks

The first peacetime season after World War II brought *Ten Little Indians* and *Angel Street* as mysteries, *The Corn is Green* as a noted drama of the day, and comedies such as *The Man Who Came to Dinner*. These were popular plays, which have become the "chestnuts" of regional and community theatre today.

Evening admission prices were $1.20 and 85 cents for reserved seats, 60 cents for unreserved seats. Matinee seats were all unreserved, at 60 cents for adults and 25 cents for those under eighteen years old. The box office was still located at the Kathleen Smith Music Shop on Maple Street. Phone reservations could be made at the Holyoke telephone exchange number of 8175, but those calling from outside of Holyoke could dial the operator and ask for Enterprise 6042. Tickets could also be purchased at the Hotel Bridgway on Broadway in Springfield.

It was noted in the program that buses leave City Hall in Holyoke for Mountain Park at quarter past and quarter of the hour, and return on the hour and half-hour. Buses also ran to the Park from Northampton and Easthampton. The program for the first show of the season reflected the excitement of the annual get-together and acknowledged that The Valley Players were becoming an expected part of the summer.

Many of our company are now back with us again for what has become a kind of annual summer reunion—indeed, so many of our group return from year to year that the Valley Players are more of a family than a business organization, and Holyoke long ago became for us not merely a pleasant place in which to live and work for the summer, but a home.

As we look back over the years to our initial season in 1941, we are aware of how many changes have taken place in the world at large and in our much smaller world of summer theater.

The program had grown to sixteen pages. The theater was redecorated and two additional rows of seats were put in and other improvements were made in the dressing rooms and office. They had weathered their early years and the war, and were in for a new "duration," – the postwar world. The first show of the season, *Hope for the Best*, had a title that certainly exemplified the relief and the uncertainty that lay ahead, both for the nation and the little wooden playhouse on the mountain.

There was a new sense of freedom after the war – personal freedom to move about without travel restrictions. It was noted in the program for *Angel Street*:

This summer it is possible once more to travel and find relaxation in new surroundings…We hope that if you are near another summer theater you will visit as many of their productions as possible.

One cast member, Hugh Franklin, had spent the winter season touring with Ethel Barrymore in *The Joyous Season*. At the beginning of the 1946 summer season, he returned to the Valley Players, and brought his new wife with him, novelist Madeleine L'Engle, who at that time had published *The Small Rain* and *Ilsa*. She would become famous to generations of young readers for her *A Wrinkle in Time*. The couple had married in Chicago in January. She became a member of the acting company for this season. Her debut role was Emily Brent in *Ten Little*

Indians, in which her husband, Mr. Franklin played the part of Dr. Armstrong. They became the parents of a little daughter the following summer. Miss L'Engle did have local roots as well—she was a graduate of Smith College in Northampton.

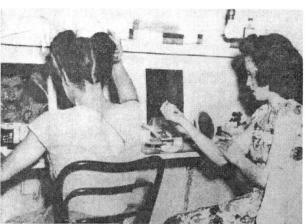

Ellen Andrews and Helen Harrelson 1946, in the dressing room, *Holyoke Transcript-Telegram* photo.

The war left a generation of veterans who would become the focus of post-war life: in politics, in culture, and in economics—in all areas of American society. It is no wonder that the program bios of these actors listed their military experience. The Valley Players who, in a world before television, presented the same actors week after week in the summer to an audience who came to know them, welcomed their warrior cast back "home."

Joseph Foley returned from the Pacific and more than three years' service in the Army Air Corps. Holyoke native George Alan Smith, stage manager, was back from the Navy. Guest actor Raymond Greenleaf, it was noted, had served in the Army in World War I, and in the Navy in World War II.

During the war, future regular Howard Ledig, had his acting career curtailed for five years. He rose from the rank of Private to Major and served with the 13th Armored Division of General Patton's Third Army. Eric Elliot, future guest actor in *The Barretts of Wimpole Street* in 1947, served in India in the Intelligence Department of the Royal Air Force. Miriam Stovall, future Valley Players actress, played in U.S.O. productions during the war in Italy, France, Belgium, and Iceland. Bertram Tanswell returned from nearly a year's service with the ETO, entertaining American groups.

John Bryant had joined the Army in 1941, first with the Signal Corps, and then was reassigned to Capt. Maurice Evans in charge of live entertainment in the Pacific. J. Harris Melia, who worked principally in publicity, but who would also take minor stage roles in future, was a veteran of the Battle of the Bulge.

Donald F. Hermes, began designing sets for the company in 1946, had served in the army from 1942 through 1946. A 1953 program mentioned that future player Hal Holbrook was a "veteran of the Second World War," and that Norman Twain, who appeared in *Three's a Family* in the summer season of 1956 had served with the 101st Airborne Division.

Beatrice Newport, it was noted in the program for *The Late George Apply* in July, had toured with *Blithe Spirit* for the USO in the Pacific for several months. Ruth Elliot performed for the USO during the war in New England.

Doris Belack, as noted in the program for *Little Accident* in August, made transcriptions for the Office of War Information (OWI) during the war. In the same program it was noted that Mel Roberts made Naval training films.

Many in the audience were also returning from war service and adjusting to civilian life. The veterans in the audience would have the most profound impact on live theatre in the country. They had been a generation that grew up during the Great Depression, and if they had not the opportunity or could afford to see a stage show then, they were nonetheless familiar with the Broadway greats because at this time, Broadway was the driving force of popular music. Show tunes were the top hits of the day on radio. During the war, service personnel saw stage shows brought to their camps and they developed a taste for theatre that would not have been otherwise available to them. Now with jobs, a booming economy, and expendable income, they were primed for a great time.

Ellen Andrews was a newcomer to the Valley Players, having performed on radio for the previous five years on the *Campbell Playhouse*, and in the radio soap opera *Right to Happiness* in the part of Connie Wakefield. She had also performed on Broadway in *Too Hot for Maneuvers* with Richard Arlen, and had just closed *Apple of His Eye* on Broadway with Walter Huston.

William Guild recalls growing up:

We always had an actor living with us as well in the summer, for several years it was Ellen Andrews, who was a brilliant actress.

Louise "Louie" Mudgett was back as a stage manager and sometime actress in bit parts. It was reckoned in the program that Louie was perhaps the most familiar to the audience as the person "who greets our patrons so graciously as they enter."

Interestingly, the program for *Hope for the Best* thanks the co-producer of the New York presentation of the show "for the use of the original atlas globes." The Kane Furniture Company on Dwight Street offered Simmons mattresses and Philco radios.

That summer, program ads included Steiger's, which offered summer play suits, bathing suits, pedal pushers, bareback dresses, and short sets. The night club "The New Casino in the Sky – Atop the Roger Smith Hotel" urged, "The play's the thing—but before the curtain goes up, dine and dance…" or top off the evening "with a delicious bite and a tall glass—more dancing and lots of fun after the show." Music was offered by The Continentals, and the cocktail lounge was touted as air-conditioned—a new post-war feature coming to many businesses before it ever reached homes.

W. Harley, theatre critic for the *Springfield Daily News* dropped in on a midnight reading of the play *The Hasty Heart*.

Shop IN **SOLID COMFORT**

at Air-Conditioned

The cast had just finished an evening performance of Hope for the Best, *and most of them were then rehearsing* Angel Street. *So being bears for work, they started right in on another play. This was at 11 p.m. All they had for the next day was a rehearsal for* Angel Street *and a performance of* Hope for the Best. *Time on their hands, practically.*

"Cracking a script" is always fun to watch, and judging from the way the cast went at it, fun to do as well. Dolly Crane, who had been in bed with pneumonia, met us at the door with the cheerful announcement, "I'm allowed to sit up today."

Miss Hayes (Gaylord Mason's dog, not the actress)…took the center of the stage almost at once. Her part was extremely simple. She chomped on a bone.

There was a slight pause while Miss Hayes was politely told to go hustle her lunch someplace else, and then Dolly looked around, saw that everyone had "sides" [scripts], and then the balloon went up…Those people never go to bed. I don't know when they sleep. George Smith, the stage manager, was quietly studying a script of The Hasty Heart *and wondering where he could get a Victorian highboy for* Angel Street. *Stage managers lead very complicated lives. Theirs is a never-ending search for*

something they are never sure they can get.

…as I shambled sleepily for the door, I got caught in the rush for the kitchen where a ravenous bunch of actors were preparing to combine a late supper with breakfast in order not to spoil their lunch. I don't see how they do it.

Unfortunately, one actor, John C. Taylor Jr., who was slated to join the cast of *The Hasty Heart*, suffered an eye injury, forcing him out of his first chance at professional theatre. Taylor, twenty-five years old, had won the community theatre Springfield Playhouse award for best male lead for his title role in *Emperor Jones*. His day job was at Springfield Auto Gear and Parts Company, where a piece of metal flew into his right eye, requiring several stitches, and doctors at Wesson Memorial Hospital worked to save his sight. William Brown, of Cambridge, who had played the role only the week before for the Cambridge Players, was rushed in to take over the part of Blossom in the war play.

The producers noted in the program for *Little Accident*, the week of August 19-24:

Choosing the plays for one of our ten-week seasons is a long-range undertaking, beginning the previous summer and extending usually until early June. It would be easy to dream up an ideal list of ten shows, but practical matters forbid mere wishful thinking. For the present season, well over fifty plays were read or re-read, each by at least two people; and various other plays well known to us were thought about.

Many problems had to be considered, such as the best use of the members of the company and of the jobbers (actors engaged for a short term), so that no actor would be given too heavy or too light a schedule, and so that at least some jobbers could be engaged for more than a single week.

Headshots of all the company were published in that last program of the season, in the formal and

Ten Little Indians 1946, Howard Ledig, Madeleine L'Engle, Raymond Greenleaf, Edward A. Wright, Joseph Foley, Ellen Andrews, Gaylord Mason, Jean Guild, Hugh Franklin and Bertram Tanswell

rather glamorous style of portrait photography of the day.

It was the beginning of the height of summer theatre, at least in New England, where several groups or more flourished from the late 1940s through the late 1950s. In the era before television, people went out more, with little to keep them home, and socialization, particularly after the austerity of the war years, was welcomed.

Hollywood adolescent Roddy McDowall appeared that season with the North Shore Players in Beverly, Massachusetts in *Young Woodley*. Bert Lahr was at New England Mutual Hall in Boston. Grant Mitchell and Taylor Holmes were at the Cape Playhouse in Dennis. Elaine Stritch was at the Provincetown Town Hall. Frank McHugh was at Lakewood in Maine.

Ten Little Indians played on the mountain with Madeleine L'Engle drawing praise for her role as a prim spinster with the holier than thou attitude in a show where pretty much the whole cast gets murdered. Raymond Greenleaf, visiting Hollywood character man, was said to be splendid

in the pivotal role as the judge. Mr. Greenleaf next took the lead in *The Late George Apley*. The reviewer for the *Holyoke Transcript-Telegram* crowed:

If the Valley Players were a baseball team, their score this season could not be a more enviable one. It seems to be just one hit after another.

The *Springfield Union* visited the Steiger estate up in the Highlands that summer, noting that the winding driveway was a bit rocky and posed a threat to thin tires. Some fifteen members of the cast resided here, and twenty-eight or more sat down to dinner. Reporter Francis Merrigan visited with Carlton Guild, who confessed that the previous day had been tough, with both his wife Jean Guild and Gaylord Mason coming down with laryngitis, and publicity man J. Harris Melia was ill, while Madeleine L'Engle had dental issues requiring three extractions. Her husband thought she'd be okay for the next show, but Mr. Guild ruminated, dropping himself into a wicker chair on the porch and lighting a cigarette, "You never know how they'll be after the anesthetic."

He sounded like a man with experience in these

The Corn is Green 1946, John Randall, Robert L Baker, James Anderson, Edward C. Purrington Jr., Gaylord Mason and Jean Guild

matters. As the day wore on, Melia was found to be suffering from acute appendicitis, and he was subsequently relieved of his appendix at Holyoke Hospital. While they waited to see if Gaylord Mason's voice returned, Mr. Guild reminded the interviewer ruefully that there were no understudies in summer theatre. "We get along with ingenuity, the grace of God and who knows what else."

Guild took the reporter through the house, where some of the actors were rehearsing in the living room, and others were trying on costumes in the dining room for the upcoming *The Corn is Green.* The Steiger summer "cottage" was…

…a wonderful spot for lying around, sipping tall cool ones on the porch which overlooks the valley, and just taking life easy…but the Valley Players don't have time for that.

'There's lot's to do,' Guild said, 'Indeed there is…one play

is still being presented when they're working on another, and that doesn't allow for much leisure.'

William Guild remembers with amusement:

What used to drive my mother crazy was she had a very good memory for lines; she had to, to do one-week stock. But when I was three or four, because they'd take me to rehearsal and I'd sit in the back and I was very quiet. And she'd be giving me a bath and I'd start with the first line in Act One and just go through everybody's lines. And she told me later, "It was the most frustrating thing that you knew my lines before I did."

What a Life, yet another take on the tales of Henry Aldrich and his clan with young Jay Sawyer in the lead, earned the biggest profit that season with $1,345.49, and the lowest profit came from *The Man Who Came to Dinner.* However, profit is not always an indication of popularity, and often has more to do with the expense of a particular show.

But Not Goodbye 1946 John O'Connor and Joseph Foley

The Man Who Came to Dinner boasted a very large cast. Including penguins, one presumes. Expenses ran $2,930.74 for this show. Perhaps the penguins, even as stuffed toys, were Equity actors.

But 1946 was a splendid and profitable season for The Valley Players. Despite a proliferation of summer theaters this first peacetime summer, not all were doing financially well. An undated newspaper article in the Valley Players scrapbook for 1946-1947 notes a lack of air conditioning in most of them was part of the problem for lower turnout and that the Provincetown Playhouse had shut down mid-season because of that. The writer muses that The Valley Players having no star system was part of what kept it fresh and vibrant.

Olive Pearson Rice of the *Springfield Sunday*

Republican visited the *What a Life* production from a backstage perspective:

Actors and crew were in positions in the wings. They all waited tensely for that second when the rising curtain would galvanize them into action at the signal given by George Alan Smith of Holyoke, stage manager. The hush was nerve racking [sic]...

...Then up came the arm of Mr. Smith, and up went the curtain as Milo Miles and Harry Desnoyers pulled on the great ropes. On went the footlights and off went the house lights as Talbot Peterson expertly manipulated his two switchboards. The show was on...

The play called for a lot of teen agers and they continued to enjoy themselves in the wings, but with an eye out for Joseph Foley who, as the irascible high school principal constantly stomped off the stage in high dudgeon and went on a way into the wings before he snapped out of character…

…in the back of the theater where Michael Jess, stage carpenter, is sawing "corner blocks" and "key stones," of which he uses about three dozen in each set…Mr. Jess is a native of Holyoke…[remembering the greats in his career] *There was Ethel Barrymore, he reminisces, as his eyes shine with pleasure at the remembrance. She had just come of age and was playing in her first show,* Captain Jinks of the Horse Marines. *Other well-known names roll off as he recalls those gay and glorious days: William Collier, John Drew, DeWolf Hopper and six-foot Jerome Sykes whom he liked a lot; "a nice gentleman," he avers, with whom he worked in* Pinafore. *Minnie Maddern Fiske is remembered next, and Kyrley Bellew, E.H. Sothern and Julia Marlowe and Robert Mantell. All these visited Holyoke when Mike was a lad…*

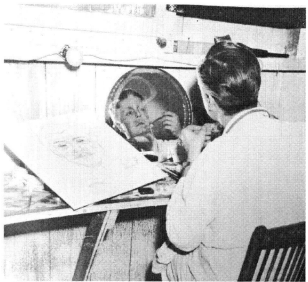

The Man Who Came to Dinner 1946, Alfred Paschall making up as Sheridan Whiteside.

He toured with the greats, but returned to Holyoke in 1914 and worked at the Suffolk Theater in stock, where Donald Meek, and later George Brent (as George Nolan) appeared. He had worked with The Valley Players since they began.

It comes straight from the heart when he says they are the nicest people he ever worked for; and that, in fact, is the consensus of the crew.

Louise Mace of the *Springfield Union* had high hopes for the future of summer theatre at the end of that 1946 season:

Curtains in summer theaters went down with a happy, hope-filled thud last night, resounding contrast to the slow, inert descent in 1941. In that year of war certainty for the country straw hat producers knew the odds were against 1942 reopenings. They have no ominous prescience in 1946, despite the between-the-darkness-and-daylight condition of the world. This first postwar rural season settled for years to come the public's attitude toward living theater. The people want it; all that can be given them, and this feeling is neither pretence nor a rush to enjoy a benison long denied. There is every reason to believe that stage drama has taken new and vital hold of popular imagination. Concede much of this renaissance to the influence of returned veterans whose appetite for entertainment was both awakened and stimulated by the valiant USO troupes.

This last remark about veterans being influenced by USO troupes is important. The service introduced a generation of men to education opportunities for obtaining high school diplomas and college degrees, which before would not have possible for them—as well as to theatre.

Springfield is in luck to have the Valley players so close at wheelhand. The group is theater worthy, composed of professionals whose winter months are spent with Broadway or touring companies. All, with minor exceptions, are seasoned actors despite the fact that none is yet a Times Square star, although this may come true in time.

***

The *Holyoke Transcript-Telegram* once again paid tribute to their hometown acting company at the beginning of the 1947 season:

Before the war the summer theater was gaining sway in other parts of the country, but naturally war activities, shortages, and gas rationing restricted most group's programs. The Valley Players were a happy exception to this decline. All during the war, battling uphill all the way they carried on across Casino boards. They were urged to continue because they represented a valuable contribution to the taxed summer entertainment facilities for the large Westover Field military contingent. They attracted nationwide attention in their efforts. They gather together a crackerjack company, and they carried on despite the war.

Now in the past two years we have seen a very impressive rise of the summer theater…Some places attract big stars who want to spend a week or two on a sort of busman's holiday out in some old barn really enjoying parts they've always wanted to play. The Players don't rely on this method but theirs is just as good…The automobile makes the diverse theaters of the summer circuit readily accessible to all and sundry and the word is coming to us that a great part of the Pioneer Valley has taken to supporting this playhouse. Their name now rings true as the Valley Players…

In 1947 the phone number had changed to 2-3273, but was Enterprise 6042 for Springfield, Northampton, and Chicopee. In Holyoke that year, the home of Judge Hildreth became the Yankee Pedlar restaurant, according to DiCarlo, "known as a top eatery up and down the Valley."

Toto's on Route 5

One of the ads in the program this year was for Toto's, a unique eatery on Route 5, just two miles from Mountain Park. Offering dining and dancing, the place was noted for its novel construction, shaped like a zeppelin. However, a fire destroyed its unusual design, and the reconstructed version continued to serve customers without the zeppelin, and advertised faithfully in The Valley Players programs until the late 1950s.

Bertram Tanswell played the title role in *Uncle Harry* the week of June 30 through July 5, 1947. Anne Follmann and Ed Fuller were newcomers to The Valley Players with this production. Like most other performers with the Valley Players, they had experience in regional theatre, on Broadway, and on radio.

At this period, Donald F. Hermes was the set designer, and George Alan Smith was the stage manager, and in *Uncle Harry*, both of these "techies" appeared on stage. It was not unusual for the Players to draft usually non-acting staff into small stage parts when needed. Edward C. Purrington Jr., who served as second stage manager, was also used for small roles. He was a Holyoke native, a 1947 graduate of Holyoke High School.

Jean Guild, founder, producer, and character actress, also collected tickets at the front. In 1947 the Guilds moved permanently to Holyoke, in a large house on the corner of Lincoln and Northampton streets, and Carlton Guild was appointed to head the English department at Westfield High School, his "day job" from September through June. The Guilds now made their home in Holyoke year-round, and Jean's father lived with them, though she confessed that, despite attending one show per week, her father was really more of a baseball fan than a theatre fan.

The Barretts of Wimpole Street required a very large cast, and all hands on deck (or on stage) were needed, including techies Mr. Hermes and Mr. Smith. Beatrice Newport played the lead role of Elizabeth Barrett Browning, and it was recorded in the program's production notes that she had "made a hurried trip from Hawaii to Holyoke to be with us again." She had performed in regional theatre and on Broadway, and had been visiting family in Honolulu and played a performance there of *Joan of Lorraine*. She had been a member of the Valley Players for the entire 1944 season.

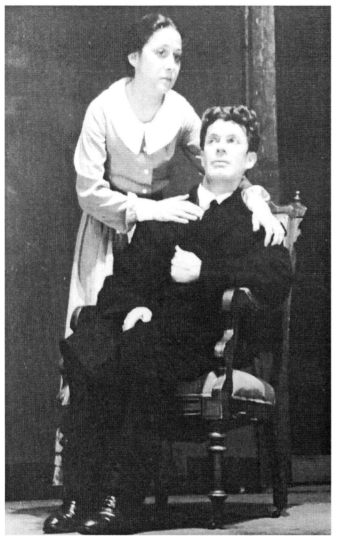

Anne Follmann and Bertram Tanswell, *Uncle Harry 1947*

The Barretts of Wimpole Street 1947, Howard Ledig,
Beatrice Newport

It was noted in the previous program that the coming performance on Tuesday of *The Barretts of Wimpole Street* would begin at 8:15 instead of 8:30 p.m., "in order to avoid conflict with the regular Tuesday evening fireworks." A playhouse inside an amusement park may have had its whimsical challenges, but there were drawbacks.

William Guild laughingly recalls another moment:

When we did Our Town, *Louise Mace, who was a drama critic for the* Springfield Union, *started her review by saying, "We've got to support the Valley Players—they can no longer afford scenery."*

That was a classic to us. My dad called Louise and

explained to her that that was the way it was, and she just hadn't listened when the Stage Manager says, "We're not going to have any scenery."

Evidently Louise Mace did not remain confused for long, for her review of July 22, 1947 expressed her admiration for the effect:

They gave a beautifully moving performance and not one character moved an iota from this rarified orbit.

Thornton Wilder's *Our Town* had its summer night sounds embellished by Willard Cary, veteran newspaperman, actor, and famous mimic of bird and animal sounds, on board, fresh from doing the job on Broadway, as well as earning two walk-on parts in the roles of Farmer Carter, and Professor Willard.

The Barretts of Wimpole Street 1947, Eric Elliott, Ruth Elliott, John Randall, Ed Ford, Helen Harrelson, Robert Jeffers, Don Hermes, Clifford Lamont, Beatrice Newport, and Gaylord Mason

Ed Fuller and Jean Guild played Doc and Mrs. Gibbs. A thoughtful remark from the reviewer at the *Holyoke Transcript-Telegram*:

During the war lots of Americans had time to sit in far-off places and think about the life they wanted to live. Up at the Casino, the Valley Players are presenting an engrossing and rewarding reading of Thornton Wilder's noteworthy drama, Our Town, *and Mr. Wilder gives you two hours to think about life and the way you are living it.*

Cast of *Our Town*

Our Town 1947, Jean Guild and Beatrice Newport

For *Our Town*, the large cast included many locals in walk-ons as townspeople or the church choir. John O'Connor played the Stage Manager who narrates the proceedings in Grover's Corner. The program noted, "He once remarked that, as a New Hampshire man himself, every line of *Our Town* was sacred to him." Both Jean Guild and Joseph Foley played the same roles they did when they performed the play with the Farragut Players.

Willard Cary was also in the Broadway cast of this play and the national tour. For help in gathering the townspeople, Miss Grace D. Healy, director of drama for Holyoke High School, and Mrs. E. G. Moriarty of the *Holyoke Transcript-Telegram* were thanked. We see that a great many of the plays featured large casts, which is not something professional theaters, especially smaller regional

theaters, tend to do these days; as the larger the cast, the more salaries have to be paid and the more expensive it is to produce a show. Old-time large-cast shows are now mostly left to college, high school, and community theaters—where the cast is not paid, and the larger the cast, the more relatives are likely to pay to see them.

For Lillian Hellman's *The Little Foxes*, two actors were engaged to play the servant roles: Enid Raphael, who had played with Basil Rathbone in *Heat Wave*, and also had performed for eight years in Europe in films and nightclubs, and musical comedy. She also ran her own theatre company that played in the South and on the West Coast. Charles Benjamin had appeared on Broadway, and had played in the film version of *The Emperor Jones*. The Guilds were meticulous about casting the plays, and it is evident that even the minor roles were carefully considered and usually filled (unless they were walk-ons) with actors of considerable experience and auspicious background. But not always. A maid's role in

Return Engagement that summer was played by Mary Landry, who was the real-life housekeeper of former stage manager and now guest actor Alfred Paschall.

***

The Little Foxes 1947, Gaylord Mason, Joseph Foley, Alfred Paschall and Ann Lee

A request was made in another program that summer:

If you have in your attic unwanted furniture, dishes, silverware, draperies, or other things that you would be willing to give us for stage furnishings, please leave word at the box office.

That fall, male juvenile lead Gaylord Mason was off to Hollywood for a screen test at M-G-M. Marjory Miller of Longmeadow, who had appeared as a young ingénue in the 1945 season, was off to Broadway in *A Young Man's Fancy*, with a new stage name—Mardia Miller.

It was noted that the average production

attendance was nearly 5,000 this summer, exceeding that of many New England summer theaters.

***

In February 1948 heavy snow and strong winds made the roof collapse on the right wing of the stage. It might have been a harbinger of the season to come, a season of challenges, including plays and casts that had to be shifted around due to contractual troubles. Alfred Paschall, due to appear on stage in a break from his *Truth or Consequences* stage managing gig, was required by his doctor to take the summer off due to nervous exhaustion. *Voice of the Turtle* on which there was

Voice of the Turtle 1948 Helen Harrelson and John Bryant

a royalty release issue, rang up the curtain on the first play of the season. The *Catholic Mirror*, denouncing summer theatres for producing plays with sex as a theme singled out The Valley Players and called for a boycott of this play.

It was noted in a *Boston Post Magazine* article by theatre critic dean Elliot Norton, that of all the nation's summer theatres open for business this season, nearly half of them were in New England, some sixty-nine theaters, with seventy-four others among all the other states combined.

Anne Follmann received great notices in *Kind Lady*. The *Holyoke Saturday Democrat* called her,

…without a doubt one of the best actresses that ever graced the footlights at the Casino. Not affected, a voice that is soothing, and a grace in acting that is just natural…Looked like old times when Jean Guild, Joe Foley and Ruth Elliott all came together for their first entrance. And did the house come down!

A thunderstorm did not cancel the show, but the local reviewer from the *Holyoke Saturday Democrat* confessed:

It's not good for the nerves! Great credit must be given to the Valley Players the way they stood up in the first and second acts. Most of them must have had sore throats the next day. It's quite a job to try to drown out thunder and rain…Carlton Guild was very busy putting down the side windows during the storm…You will have to go far to see a better actress to perform than Jean Guild. She is great in any kind of play and if the part is not interesting she makes it look good and interesting…

That was in Ruth Gordon's comedy, *Years Ago*. In the following week, the torrid *Rain*, the weather fit the theme perfectly:

Favored with hot, humid weather, the Monday night opening found the atmosphere of Rain *extending from the superb stage set with its hibiscus and bougainvillea-draped terrace…*

In a future program for *Chicken Every Sunday*:

Wednesday matinee will be cancelled if official local…weather report promises an afternoon temperature of 100 or more.

The Guilds noted in a program that theatre was changing in the post-war world:

Many of the plays written in the 1920s or early 1930s have lost their original appeal. They "date" in subject matter, in characterization, in dialogue, in the kind of humor or sentiment used, or in other ways. So when Little Accident, *which Burns Mantle selected as one of the ten best plays of 1928-29, was mentioned for our schedule this summer, our first reason to it was a dubious one…but when we read it, we found it still as good a comedy as we had thought it to be some seventeen years ago.*

Three new members joined the company as

Dear Ruth 1947, Gaylord Mason, Bertram Tanswell, Ruth Elliot, Helen Harrelson, Jean Guild, Joseph Foley, and Howard Ledig

"jobbers" for *Little Accident*: Gloria Peterson of Springfield, who had studied acting in Boston and New York and performed on local radio for WMAS; and Doris Belack, who had begun her career studying acting at New York's American Academy and doing regional theatre, and during the war made record transcriptions of radio performances for the Office of War Information. Telling for the decade ahead, she had also appeared on television, which was in its infancy. Mel Roberts also appeared on television and had played in *My Sister Eileen* in New York, and toured with other plays, but during the war he made training films for the Navy. In the last program, for a play aptly named *But Not Goodbye*, The Valley Players generously gave a plug to a one-day- only performance of *Life with Father* coming up

on Wednesday, September 25th at the War Memorial Auditorium in downtown Holyoke by a touring company. Winter stock had become less prolific than summer stock in Holyoke by this time, but there were still facilities for its presentation and one presumes and hopes, still an audience for it.

In 1948, Holyoke population was 56,426, with twenty-five schools and twenty-five churches. Chicopee was gaining in population, largely due to the Air Force base and the carving out of new suburban neighborhoods in its vast area of former farms and undeveloped wooded areas, now 45,000 with twenty-two churches. During the coming decade, Chicopee's population would surpass Holyoke's.

WHYN, the radio station on the mountain, applied for a television license in 1948. In 1953, the new television station broadcast for the first time and began as Channel 55. The studio was on the foundation of the former Mt. Tom Summit House. According to an article in a local historical monthly, *Chickuppy and Friends Magazine*, "Getting up and down the mountain was a major project. Without an adequate road to the summit, studio guests had to endure a bumpy, treacherous ride up the mountain and down again in the back of a four-wheel drive pick-up truck."

Some 400 new seats were installed in the Casino replacing older seats in the center section. Barbara O'Leary Halpin of Holyoke, interviewed by the *Holyoke Transcript-Telegram* in the 1980s in a retrospective article on Mountain Park, recalled her days as a teen taking the bus to the Casino playhouse to see the shows. She later became an usher. As an adult she became a teacher, and had worked part-time as an executive secretary for the Valley Players for fifteen years from 1947 to 1962 when the group disbanded.

"It was a wonderful place and the shows were just terrific. They had great productions." She had no desire to become an actress herself, but was drafted to play bit parts in several productions. "Occasionally, I would fill in to play the part of a maid. That's the only role I ever played. It was wonderful acting alongside all these professionals. I remember playing the maid in *Witness for the Prosecution*."

She encountered young actors such as Hal Holbrook, Simon Oakland (then billed as Si) and Hugh Franklin before they had gone on to greater success. "I also met Helen Hayes at the Casino. She came to see an ingénue who was at the Casino one summer. It was a very exciting time in my life."

The Casino was reported by the *Holyoke Transcript-Telegram* to have drawn audiences of around 1,000 people per night. Summer 1948 introduced the first twelve-play season, and began, uncharacteristically, with a three-person play, *The Voice of the Turtle*. Special notices in the programs addressed the competing fireworks at Mountain Park, with obvious deference to the Monday, July 5th fireworks for Independence Day.

You Can Take it With You was the profitability champ in the 1948 season, grossing $5,287.40 total receipts and an attendance that week of 6,459. The lowest grossing show was *Kind Lady*, with a total of $3,208.37 receipts, and an attendance of 3,547. That was the second show of the season (the first or second shows of the summer season generally did not do as well as ones later in the summer).

The *Voice of the Turtle* was the first look back to the war years, and the program notes make an interesting reference to how quickly one era can melt into another.

Dealing as it does with the last war, The Voice of the Turtle *has already become a "period piece" and a "costume play". It must seem almost impossible to the women in our audience—and to the men, too, for that matter—that what we thought high style just three and a half short years ago can have suddenly become outmoded. The period for which this play was written was one in which world-shaking events were taking place. The most important thing that could happen to any soldier at that time was the chance for a week end of fun. It was a period of "let's live for today", the "New Look" was still unborn in the mind of Christian Dior—and this week's audience will have a chance to judge whether or not they'd prefer to have it still unborn.*

Kind Lady 1948 Louie Mudgett and Beatrice Newport

January Thaw 1947, Phyllis DeBus, Jay Sawyer, Joseph Foley, and Anne Follmann

Kind Lady was a murder mystery that included Louie Mudgett, the company's community publicity representative, in one of her occasional small roles. The program notes reminded the audience she had "the widest personal acquaintance with our audience, whom she has greeted in the lobby of the theater during all our seven seasons."

Anne Pitoniak, future television and Broadway actress and Tony® nominee, featured in three shows in 1948, was a local actress from Westfield, and graduate of Westfield High School and the University of Connecticut, who had been a former member of the Cleveland Playhouse before she came to The Valley Players. By the time she had played in *Father of the Bride* in Holyoke in 1953, she was married, had a son, was living in Westport, Connecticut, and had performed on a number of television shows. The program for *You Can't Take it With You*, in which she played the flamboyant Russian Countess Olga, notes that Miss Pitoniak was a Westfield native, whose involvement with the company came through The Valley Players' scenic designer Edward Sheffield. He met her while she was touring with the USO in the Far East Command.

He was in charge of production at the Ernie Pyle Theater in Tokyo.

Since Westfield is only fourteen miles distant, this was a rather round-about way of making our acquaintance, but that's how it happened.

Jacqueline Paige was a former Radio City Music Hall Rockette and had also played with the Lunts for years and with Helen Hayes for six years. She and John O'Connor were another of several married couples in the group. O'Connor, who was also a playwright, had performed in summer stock after graduating from college in 1931, and married Miss Paige after his army service.

The *Holyoke Saturday Democrat* lauded Jacqueline Paige in *Rain*:

Miss Jacqueline Paige is demonstrating, and without an alibi, that she is a great actress. Her work as Sadie Thompson, in the play, is of the highest order and she compares very favorably with Jeanne Eagles.

Wednesday and Saturday evenings were most popular nights, Mondays received the lowest audiences. Up until now, in the past seven years, the highest attended show was *The Barretts of Wimpole Street*. Ticket prices were increasing in straw hat theater, noting the top price for Stockbridge was $2.94.

The *Ghost Train* impressed the *Springfield Union* in its overall presentation:

The local company could have been satisfied just to rollick through this old-fashioned melodrama. Instead they have given painstaking care to reproduce set, costumes, makeup, and acting styles as they were in the '20s...The Clear Vale, ME station is a masterpiece of stage setting, for which we must thank Donald Hermes. Nothing has been overlooked. You feel gritty just seeing it. And those who work behind the scenes win more laurels this week by providing superlative costumes and makeup, just as they must have been when this play was first produced. The knee-length chiffon dresses, the Herbert Hoover collars, the Arrow-collar ad makeup, all are priceless.

To go with it, the cast revives the stilted gesture and all the other stage business that enthralled us 20 years ago. They

must have had fun doing it; it's delightful to watch...Bertram Tanswell stars as the overwhelmingly silly Englishman whose whim lands the group in its sad predicament, and with all the stops out as he dances through a slapstick role. Jean Guild makes the most of another plum, a New England spinster overtaken by brandy. The crotchety old station master is a part right down John O'Connor's alley. Then there are the "straight" parts, beautifully dead-panned by John Bryant and Ruth Elliott as the honeymooners, and Ed Fuller and Jacqueline Paige as the quarreling couple...

For the program of *Guest in the House* in August 1948, the Guilds noted:

There was a time, not so long ago, when we were still hesitant about introducing plays that fall into the category of "drama" or "serious theater." Some companies we know of come to financial grief when they attempt such offerings. Perhaps our audiences are above-average intelligence and culture. We like to think so, although we do believe in fundamental human nature and the similarity of people in different communities.

They noted that *The Barretts of Wimpole Street* and *The Little Foxes* had done very well.

Tons of Money 1948, Mary Jackson and Bertram Tanswell

Mary Jackson was a guest player, or jobber in *Tons of Money*. She may be best recalled today for her recurring role in the television series *The Waltons* as Miss Emily, one of the dotty elderly Baldwin sisters. She was thirty years old at the time she played in Holyoke, a veteran of stock and touring companies, and then living in New York. She was a guest at the home of Mr. & Mr. Phillip Hopkins on Fairfield Avenue for the run of the show. The Hopkins, taking their job as hosts seriously, took her on a sightseeing tour of Holyoke, the Skinner Mills, Westover Field, Hastings Heights, and "wound up with a spaghetti dinner at a local restaurant." She had been invited by Bertram Tanswell, whom she had met years previously, to appear in the show as his wife.

Tons of Money 1948, Joseph Foley and Jacqueline Paige

Accent on Youth was the final show of the 1948 season. Portrait photos of all the company were included in the program. Average attendance beat that of the 1946 and 1947 seasons. With the end of summer, publicity representative and actress-when-you-need-her Louie Mudgett would head back to Boston for her fall-through-spring job managing dramatics for the Metropolitan Boston and Cambridge YMCAs. She had been with the company since it started in 1941.

As always, we shall hope to do at least one play, as we say, "For ourselves," because we think it is a fine play, because we feel that producing it will be a rewarding experience for us, and because—well, you know, because we just want to do it.

That play was *All My Sons* in this season, and in the previous year it had been *Our Town*.

Both proved far more popular than we anticipated, and

that pleased us, too.

That Christmas, Bertram Tanswell gave a reading of Charles Dickens' *A Christmas Carol* at the Second Baptist Church in Holyoke, as The Valley Players' contribution to raise funds for the First Congregational Church building fund.

***

The 1949 season brought a few new faces, including Tom Carpenter, who it was noted was a war vet, as was Stephen Reese, who had served in the Navy in the Philippines from 1943 through 1946, and Jean Bellows, a young actress who was the daughter of artist George Bellows. She replaced Jacqueline Paige. The first play was *George Washington Slept Here*, which the company had also produced first in 1941. In 1949, Jean Guild, Joseph Foley, John O'Connor, and Louie Mudgett all reprised their original roles from the 1941 version.

George Washington Slept Here 1949, Joseph Foley, Dickie Simmons, Robert Emhardt

A couple of children in the cast, Betty Lou Keim and Dickie Simmons were old theater veterans who attended the Children's Professional School in New York City. A few minor roles went to some locals in the cast: Virginia Lee of Holyoke, Nancy Carpenter of Longmeadow, and Richard

Erikson of West Springfield. Some workers in the box office, like Alice Mary O'Donnell, Jean Purrington and J. Harris Melia also took minor roles on stage from time to time. The Guilds' young son, William, made his stage debut in a walk-on role in *My Sister Eileen*.

Richard Maxson began as one of the artists exhibiting work in the lobby during the shows (the Casino hosted a new art exhibit by a local artist each week during their two decades' tenure), progressed to join set designer Donald F. Hermes on The Valley Players' sets, and then found himself drafted for walk-on parts.

Laughter is probably still echoing around the Mt. Tom Range after last night's opening of Apple of His Eye *at Mountain Park Casino. John O'Connor and Anne Pitoniak are featured in the riotous comedy around the December-May romance of a prosperous Indiana farmer and a hired girl.*

The Heiress featured Miriam Stovall as the psychologically bullied daughter and Hugh Franklin as her autocratic father. The *Springfield Union* reported:

Miss Stovall is remarkably effective as the girl, impressing her portrayal with delicacy of speech and a haunting quality that lights the complexities of her inner turmoil and eventually fires them into the steel of character very like that of the father who both loved and disdained her. By the end of the week her performance should be only slightly superlative.

It is good to have Mr. Franklin back. He is an actor of polished grain and his portrait of the father is fineness itself and perfectly contained yet highly flexible and fluent. The two actors work together with choice understanding.

Unfortunately Peter Harris makes a shambles of the role of the suitor. He is not right for the part, lacking vigor, suavity and romantic persuasiveness. He seems to have little idea of the role's meaning.

In the program notes from *An Inspector Calls*:

...you might well be confused by the last pages of the script and might leave the theater thinking that Mr. Priestley

[the author] and the Valley Players (at least this week) were just plain crazy...the plan soon moves from a routine police questioning of smugly complacent people to matters which not only can but do concern all of us in whatever year of our Lord we may be living. Of the characters in the play, Sheila [played by Miriam Stovall] *first and best realizes the nature of the situation: that here there can be no equivocation, no pretense, no escape. So must it be, at some time, with all of us.*

Why, then, the ending? Should the curtain comedown when the Inspector says, "Good night"? Or should the play go on through its following satire of human relationships— that instinct we all seem to have not facing our shortcomings—but end on the tone of Sheila's last speech, omitting the final telephone call? Admittedly, it's the final telephone call that may bewilder some people.

We'll leave the answers of such questions to you, to argue pro and con if you will. As for us, it's the kind of play we enjoy doing, because it is both what we think is "good theater" and also something that we can "get our teeth into." It's a better play even than we thought before sides were passed out to the actors and they gave a first reading which hit us like an electric shock. We hope you'll enjoy it, too.

Westfield native Anne Pitoniak was back for another season. It was noted in the program that during the "last war" (a phrase which in 1949 had an ominous sound, as if anticipating more to come), Miss Pitoniak was a member of the Veteran's Hospital Radio Guild, which visited vet's hospitals and helped the patients to write, produce, and direct their own radio shows.

The program notes were also generous and appreciative toward the actors. Of Ruth Elliot, who was featured (the word "starred" is characteristically avoided in the family of Valley Players):

Although this is her first featured part, she has often stopped the show or come near to it. Witness what she did in Dream Girl *as Miss Delehanty in just four words ("Hi," "Yeah," and "Why not?" plus, of course, a "getup" and a "slow take")...An agent who happened to see the play told her she should have tried out for "Billie Dawn" in* Born Yesterday.

POPULAR PLAYS *by* POPULAR PLAYERS

Miriam Stovall

TWELVE WEEKS
OF PERFECT
ENTERTAINMENT
JUNE 20 TO
SEPTEMBER 10

John O'Connor

Jean Guild

FOR THE BEST
SEATS CALL OR
WRITE FOR A
RESERVATION
WELL IN ADVANCE

Joseph Foley

The Week — The Play

The Week	The Play
June 20—25	JENNY KISSED ME
June 27—July 2	G. WASHINGTON SLEPT HERE
July 4—9	AN INSPECTOR CALLS
July 11—16	PARLOR STORY
July 18—23	DREAM GIRL
July 25—30	APPLE OF HIS EYE
Aug. 1—6	THE HEIRESS
Aug. 8—13	BOY MEETS GIRL
Aug. 15—20	THE BAT
Aug. 22—27	MY SISTER EILEEN
Aug. 29—Sept. 3	FRESH FIELDS
Sept. 5—10	THE LATE CHRISTOPHER BEAN

Dorothy M. Crane, *Director*; Donald F. Hermes, *Scenic Designer*

The Featured Players

Joseph Foley, Miriam Stovall, Tyler Carpenter
Jean Guild, Joseph Foley, John O'Connor
John O'Connor
Edward Fuller, Anne Pitoniak
Miriam Stovall
John O'Connor, Anne Pitoniak
Miriam Stovall, Barnard Hughes
Peter Harris, Barnard Hughes, Ruth Elliott
Jean Guild, John O'Connor
Jean Bellows, Ruth Elliott
Jean Guild, Miriam Stovall, Edward Fuller
John O'Connor

William Dodds and Edward C. Purrington, *Stage Managers*

Edward Fuller

RESERVATIONS ARE
HELD FOR YOU
UNTIL 8:10 (ON
TUESDAY, AND
JULY 4 AND SEPT. 10
UNTIL 7:40)

Jean Bellows

Barnard Hughes

RESERVATIONS ARE
HELD INDEFINITELY
IF YOU AGREE TO
PAY FOR TICKETS
NOT CALLED FOR

Ruth Elliott

We may note the remark also indicates that agents and other theater professionals were regularly a part of The Valley Players audience, scouting talent. Talbot Peterson, known as "Pete," the company electrician had been with the group since it began in 1941, and he also got plaudits in the programs. A Springfield native, he then lived in Northampton and had worked as well as the Plaza Theatre and the Calvin in Northampton since the 1920s.

Many of you out front may never have seen him or know anything about him, but to us, he is next to indispensable.

The Guilds commented on the evolving tastes in theater as the mid-century approached:

Speaking of "old timers" among plays…we are perpetually interested in resurrecting one or another of them. Some of them "date" badly as we read them nowadays; others don't seem to. But they are rather risky business. We aren't sure how some of the really older ones would go, meaning especially by that the real old melodramas like East Lynne. *And, if you would like to see one by way of variety, and for auld lang syne, would you prefer to has us do it "straight" and as nearly as possible in the original manner, or "tongue-in-cheek"? Seems as though we are always asking for your opinions, but we never get enough of them.*

The end of the season brought the usual reminder to reserve seats for next year by writing to the gloriously simple address: "The Valley Players, Holyoke, Mass."

The Guilds ruminated:

At the end of this year, our eighth season, we find ourselves looking very happily in two different directions. Although the general uneasiness in the business world has prepared us for smaller attendance this summer, our audiences have been as large as those of 1948, which had been our banner year…the ups and downs in attendance last summer has given place to more regular and steady attendance…Ever since our first summer of 1941 we have been convinced that nowhere could there be a more ideal place for a summer theater than here in Pioneer Valley, nor could one hope to find elsewhere a more friendly, helpful, and responsive community of people than those who live in this region.

According to author Jay Ducharme in his book Mountain Park:

By the 1950s, he [Louis Pellissier] *decided it was time for the Holyoke Street Railway to get out of the amusement park business. That decision led to the park's renaissance.*

An article that winter as usual kept the audience abreast of the activities of their hometown theatre group. Many were touring, while Ed Fuller and Anne Pitoniak were doing radio work in New York. Some of The Valley Players, like Hugh Franklin and Joseph Foley, were finding winter season jobs on TV. That December, Jean Guild gave a reading of *The Littlest Angel* at the Women's League of the Second Baptist Church.

All This Week
Matinee Tomorrow
THE
Valley Players
AT THE
MT. PARK CASINO
are presenting

Ruth Elliott

Edward Fuller

"LOVE RIDES THE RAILS"

A REAL, OLD-FASHIONED MELODRAMA
WITH SINGING, DANCING, AND SPECIALTY NUMBERS

EVES. 8.30 (Tues. 8) 85c-$1.50
Mon. Nights Only 60c-$1.50
Wed. Mat., 2.30 60c—
Under 16, 25c

TEL. HOLYOKE 2-3272

From N'ham., E'ham., Amherst
Ask for Enterprise 6042

Tyler Carpenter

Bertram Tanswell

Apple of His Eye 1949, Betty Lou Keim, and John O'Connor

Fresh Fields 1949, Madeleine L'Engle, Miriam Stovall, and Edward Fuller

Guest in the House 1948, Anne Pitoniak, Edward Fuller, Helen Harrelson, and Jean Guild

Return Engagement 1947 Miriam Stovall, Ruth Elliott, Mary Landry, Beatrice Newport, Alfred Paschall, and Joseph Foley

Pursuit of Happiness 1948, Jean Guild, John O'Connor, Edward Fuller, Joseph Foley, Bertram Tanswell,
Helen Harrelson, and John Bryant

The Ghost Train 1948 Bertram Tanswell and Jean Guild

CHAPTER 6

The glory days of summer theatre.

The Pioneer Valley was changing. After the war it became even more diverse in population, and was enjoying a business expansion. At Westover Air Force Base in Chicopee, tensions mounted as C54 and C57 transport planes brought supplies, fuel, and relief (and candy) to an isolated Berlin during the Berlin Airlift. The Strategic Air Command took over operation of the base in 1955, and hosted long-range stratosphere bombers, B52 bombers, and nuclear weapons as the Cold War was fought behind the heavily guarded gates. Beyond, in the suburbs that surrounded the base, children learned to "duck and cover" and every window on every home rattled when a bomber came in or took off, casting its long black shadow over their roofs.

The now-famous annual Holyoke St. Patrick's Day parade was first held March 16, 1952 (a parade was held only sporadically in years before this). The trolley line to the amusement park had long since been removed, and even buses were not the main conveyance to the mountain these days. The auto ruled the road, and took people out of the cities. Springfield had 66,849 cars registered in 1954, double the 1945 number. Movie theaters, like their patrons, were moving to suburbs.

Mountain Park was sold by the Holyoke Street Railway Company. John Collins of Wellesley, Massachusetts, who also ran Lincoln Park amusement park in Dartmouth, Massachusetts, purchased Mountain Park. It was reported that Mountain Park had lost some $20,974 since 1949. Mountain Park, under new ownership, with giant clown heads and brightly painted midway attractions in vibrant pastels created an otherworldly scene, theatrical on its own, just a short distance from The Casino. The park was still the place to be for families on Sundays. Large employers such as Steiger's and Monsanto in Springfield held their company picnics here. Carnival barkers and the clatter of the ratcheting cars on the wooden roller coaster broke the nightly summer chorus of crickets, and fireworks thundered on the mountain and lit up the black, starry sky, visible from all over the valley.

Radio station WHYN celebrated its tenth anniversary in 1951. In 1954, the studio moved to a new building on Liberty Street in Springfield across from the former Springfield Airport. The following year, Channel 55 became Channel 40, and in 1959, joined the ABC affiliation. By the time it had relocated from the mountain to a new studio, one of its on-air personalities would have a unique perspective on the development of The Valley Players. Barbara Bernard worked at the station from 1955 until 1975, when she retired from broadcast television. Her roots with WHYN went back to 1944 when, as a student at Mt. Holyoke College in South Hadley, she worked for the fledgling radio station when it was located in that town. She continued in radio when she and her husband moved to Pittsfield for a time, and then when they returned to the Pioneer Valley, she resumed work with WHYN radio, interviewing local people for a program called *It Happened in Your Own Backyard.*

WHYN, and Barbara Bernard, made the leap into television with a talk showed called *Today's Woman* in 1955, which was later renamed *The Barbara Bernard Show.* Several circumstances would link her to The Valley Players: being an avid theatre-goer and attending many of their plays, interviewing actors and actresses from the company (and other theatre groups) as guests on her television program, by the serendipitous coincidence of living on the same street as the Guild-Valley Players headquarters and having them for neighbors (where they borrowed clothes, furniture, and props from her on occasion), and by actually appearing in a walk-on in one play for the 1959 season. Mrs. Bernard, in an interview for this book recalls:

The Valley Players was in existence when we moved here. So I actually got to go to Valley Players plays before I started interviewing. That was the amazing part. I had great knowledge of The Valley Players, and it was fun then to really become able to help them. They were great. My husband and I began to go to The Valley Players the day we moved to Holyoke.

Hal Holbrook and his wife Ruby became friends.

She was pregnant. She borrowed some of my maternity clothes to wear. They all lived here in Holyoke, some of them lived in Liz Corcoran's mother's home. There were several houses where people would rent their rooms out to these actors and actresses.

The Valley Players grew, thrived, were challenged, and ultimately, reached their zenith in the decade of the 1950s. Their rise echoed the heyday of summer theatre in this country. The Guilds continued their prudent management of the theater, and a look at the accounts records meticulously kept by Carlton Guild, donated by Mr. Guild to the Holyoke Public Library, give a poignant picture of the nuts and bolts of running a home-grown theater—or we should say, the nickel-and-dime aspect. Some of the season financial accounts are typed, the hard and uneven impressions of the manual typewriter on onionskin typing paper, or fuzzy carbons, or kept in sharp, firm hand in gray-blue fountain pen in on a lined analysis pad.

Each season from 1950 to 1959 ran twelve weeks, except 1953, which ran thirteen weeks. The advertising budget ran to $1,663 in 1950, more than the costume budget, as it was through most seasons. We may muse that borrowing clothes

from Barbara Bernard helped keep the cost down.

Insurance fees in 1950 amounted to $571, and came in at $738 by the end of the decade. FICA and Unemployment amounted to $336 in 1950, and more than quadrupled by 1959 at $1,446. The Guilds rented the Casino theater from Mountain Park for $3,000 for the 1950 season. The rent jumped to $6,396 in 1956, but was reduced to $4,800 by 1959.

Total payroll for actors—regulars and guess actors, or "jobbers" was $10,612 in 1950. By 1959, the actors' salaries came in at a total of $11,743, the technical staff at $10,425, and others including Carlton Guild, came in at $6,625, rates which were fairly steady throughout the decade.

Train fares for the actors, and expenses to run the station wagon to pick them up from the train

POPULAR PLAYS *by* POPULAR PLAYERS

Jean Guild

FOR THE BEST
SEATS CALL OR
WRITE FOR A
RESERVATION
WELL IN ADVANCE

John O'Connor

Jacqueline Paige

FOR THE BEST
SEATS AT THE
LOWEST PRICE
COME ON
MONDAY EVENING

Gaylord Mason

The Week	*The Play*	*The Featured Players*
June 18—23	— GOOD HOUSEKEEPING	Jean Guild, John O'Connor
June 25—30	— THE MAN	Gaylord Mason, Pamela Simpson
July 2—7	— BORN YESTERDAY	Nancy Wells, Si Oakland
July 9—14	— THE FIREBRAND	Phil Arthur, Archie Smith, Jacqueline Paige
July 16—21	— GOODBYE, MY FANCY	Jackson Perkins
July 23—28	— THEIR HEARTS WERE PURE	Phil Arthur, Hal Holbrook, Nancy Wells
July 30—Aug. 4	— TWO BLIND MICE	Gaylord Mason, Jean Guild, Louie Mudgett
Aug. 6—11	— THE JOYOUS SEASON	Jean Guild
Aug. 13—18	— SEE HOW THEY RUN	Gaylord Mason, Ruby Holbrook
Aug. 20—25	— COME BACK, LITTLE SHEBA	Jacqueline Paige, John O'Connor
Aug. 27—Sept. 1	— CANDLELIGHT	Gaylord Mason, Archie Smith
Sept. 3—8	— THE FATAL WEAKNESS	Jean Guild, Jacqueline Paige

Dorothy M. Crane, *Director*; Hal Shafer, *Scenic Designer*   William Dodds and Edward C. Purrington, *Stage Managers*

Archie Smith

RESERVATIONS ARE
HELD FOR YOU
UNTIL 8:10
TUESDAYS
UNTIL 7:40

Nancy Wells

Hal Holbrook

RESERVATIONS ARE
HELD INDEFINITELY
IF YOU AGREE TO
PAY FOR TICKETS
NOT CALLED FOR

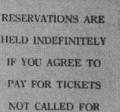

Ruby Holbrook

depot were part of the expenses in these years. Most actors up until this time arrived in Holyoke by train, but that would quickly change with the shift to jet travel, when they'd have to find their way from Bradley Airport in Windsor Locks, Connecticut, or Boston's Logan Airport.

Gross ticket sales, however, did not keep pace with costs, despite the popularity enjoyed by The Valley Players and summer theatre in general during this decade. In 1950, gross ticket sales amounted to $4,545, the highest of the decade. By 1959, sales decreased to $3,996. Average costs, conversely, were $4,109 in 1950, and $4,322 by 1959 (reaching a peak in the 1957 season at $4,907.

The profit for the 1950 season was $5,400. The lowest profit level was in 1958 at $113. The following year, 1959, brought the only loss year of the decade, leaving The Valley Players in hole by $3,380. (The highest profit of the decade came in the 1956 season at $8,250.) The highest grossing show of the 1950 season was *The Philadelphia Story* at $5,435.68, attendance 6,742, and the lowest grossing show was *The Damask Cheek* at $3,876.38 receipts. The lowest attended show was *The Traitor*.

Carlton Guild bought ads in newspapers in Springfield and Holyoke, and as far away as Amherst, Greenfield, Hartford, and New York City, and spots on local radio stations WACE in Chicopee, WARE in Ware, and WHYN.

Life With Mother 1950, Ralph Longley, Marian Hatfield, Miriam Stovall, Louise Wallis and Jean Guild

In the valley at that time, Springfield's Court Square Theater was now showing movies, older features such as *The Victor Herbert Story* and *The Scarlett Empress*, and Laurel and Hardy features. The grand old theater's days were numbered.

The newest innovation in entertainment, drive-in theaters, were springing up in the valley, including The Airline in Chicopee, the Riverdale in West Springfield, and the Sundown between Holyoke and Westfield at Hampton Ponds on Route 202.

The indoor theaters used air conditioning, not surprisingly, as their main selling point in the summer.

It was business as usual for The Valley Players, with the downtown box office again located at Kathleen Smith's music store at 267-269 Maple Street. A new control board was put in place backstage, and "6,000 feet of new rope strung across approximately 135 recently installed pulleys." Prices ran from 60 cents for a matinee performance, 25 cents for children under sixteen, and 85 cents through $1.50 for evening performance seats.

One is struck by the accessibility of the audience to the Players. The Guilds offered, in the first program of the 1950 opening show:

If you are interested in the mechanics of back-stage production, you are welcome to take a look around after some performance (except on Saturday, when we have to strike the current show and set up the next one). On a Saturday evening, you might like to remain "out front" for awhile and watch the crew at work.

There were nods in the program to Milo Miles, head of the props department since 1941, and Henry Desnoyers, who since 1942 had been head of the local stagehand's union.

Jackson Perkins, one of the founders, was back with the company for the first time in five years. The annual first meeting and buffet supper was held at the Guild residence on Lincoln Street, and actually covered by the local papers. "Our Valley Players" read another headline:

Valley Players are more generously supported than they were at the start...They have earned that. They give so splendidly. You don't see careless, off-side play in a Valley

Players production. They respect their art. They have learned to enjoy their following quite as the playgoers have learned to appreciate the artistry and honest teamwork of the Players...Perhaps we in Holyoke do not know what fame this group of players had brought to Holyoke in the world of drama.

The movies are splendid. Television is bringing good plays to the fireside. But there is nothing quite like the spoken drama, where men and women of talent express the dreams and ideals and sins and weaknesses of the race—hold the mirror up to the people. Holyoke can well boast of the vicarious culture of her neighbor colleges. But the Valley Players are her own.

People come from all the towns and villages up and down and across the valley to drink in what the Valley Players mean...Moreover there is something very beautiful about the setting for the Valley Players. You are away from the traffic and dusts and crowds up there in Mountain Park and yet you are just a few minutes away from the whirl of things. It is very beautiful there under the trees. There are no distractions. You don't get the barny feeling or the old, arty items that some of the summer circuits affect...So here's "hands all round" to our Valley Players in this beautiful Junetide.

Archie Smith joined the cast of *Peg O' My Heart*, but was headed back up to his regular gig at the summer theater in Kennebunkport, Maine. The Guilds urged the audience, "If you're motoring up that way this summer, drop by and see him and say hello to him for us."

Of the aforementioned *Peg O' My Heart*, a refreshing analysis by *Springfield Union* reviewer Louise Mace:

Without depriving it of durable essence or affronting it with an air of condescension they play it straight and with a likeable deference for what it was. What it seems to modern audiences is a pleasant and likeable page from a theater era when plays were about people unaffected with neuroses and perfectly willing to be illustrations of both the good and not so good of which human nature is composed.

The post-WWII era, through the Korean War and dawning Cold War, brought introspection to the types of plays chosen, as well as the remarks in the programs. Like using local amateurs and

Peg O My Heart 1950, Betty Oakes and Ralph Longley

relying on local interest to maintain and sustain the theater, The Valley Players was not apart from the world down below the mountain, but very much a part of it.

The Traitor, playing in early July, spurred a contemplative note in the program by the Guilds that reflected the tensions of the era:

When we scheduled The Traitor *early last Spring, Russia was known to be in possession of the atom bomb, the H-bomb had already dwarfed it in the public imagination, and the cold war was still reasonably cool. The Fuchs trial had been held and Senator McCarthy and others were in hot pursuit of "fellow travelers." But developments in Korea had not been anticipated, and a continuance of the unstable peace was being confidently assured by those in high places.*

The Traitor 1950, Edward C. Purrington Jr., Edward Fuller, Albert Rosetti, Miriam Stovall, and Joseph Foley

Not that recent developments would have caused us to drop The Traitor *from our 1950 schedule, for we believe it to be a very well constructed play, provocative of thought as well as of excitement. Moreover, we have never regarded the American people as ostriches, but rather as looking unpleasant matters squarely in the eye and being confident in the face of possible disaster.*

Heady stuff, right there above the ad from Steiger's, and Daniel F. Waters Co., Holyoke's oldest bookstore for 50 years at 284 High Street.

...You will find in this week's play some characters who sympathize with communism for a time until reality breaks in upon them. You will find raised questions of academic and of scientific freedom, of world vs. national security, and of other matters. That is, you will find them if you care to

look for them.

Phil Arthur appeared in the play, a veteran with over ninety plays, forty TV appearances, and 100 radio roles. His pedigree was joined with the tongue-in-cheek note that "making their first appearances of the season this week are Carlton Guild, business manager, and J. Harris Melia, in charge of box office." Such egalitarianism, or necessity, made for good fellowship.

For *The Royal Family,* the celebrated comedy of the 1920s lambasting the Barrymores, the program noted:

Plays of the 1920s have not, in general, stood up very well under the test of time, but The Royal Family is one of the

The Royal Family 1950, Jean Guild, Edward Fuller, Phil Arthur, Jackson Perkins, Miriam Stovall, and Nina Probette

notable exceptions, burlesquing without coarseness or bad taste, sentimentality without bathos or mawkishness, revealing a vital and vibrant humanity in the midst of chaotic confusion.'

Jackson Perkins was back this season, having added to her professional bio in the program with TV gigs such as the prestigious *Studio One*, along with touring on stage, while guest actress Nina Probette's career began in 1908, and had included Broadway, vaudeville, and her own stock company in Cleveland.

For *The Winslow Boy* that season, as was the custom for casting child's roles, a professional child actor was recruited; in this case, young Barry Truex had played the same role in stock with Basil Rathbone. However, it was a local girl from Longmeadow who played Dinah in *The*

Philadelphia Story.

The producers ruminated that summer:

Why more people don't read plays we don't know, but we do know that they are missing a lot of easily acquired enjoyment. In an age of digests and condensations and "shorts," the overlooking of the printed drama at first seems an anomaly.

Many wondered at the prospect of television resulting in a loss of audience, however an interview with players Helen Harrelson and Hugh Franklin was more optimistic, with the actors of the opinion that though movies and minor league baseball had suffered from competiton from television keeping audiences at home,.live theatre would remain strong.

Philadelphia Story 1950, Tyler Carpenter, Helen Harrelson, Hugh Franklin, and Edward Fuller

Paul Rohan grew up in Holyoke, where his father was a teacher and eventually vice principal of Holyoke High School. While his father was away in the war, his mother and aunt, who lived with them, along with a friend, were avid playgoers and regularly attended shows at the Casino. After his father returned from the service and Paul was born after the war, the family continued to see most of the shows from The Valley Players era on through to the Mt. Tom Playhouse years in the mid-sixties.

So that was just of part of life. Now, when there was a play that was appropriate for a child, my aunt would tell my parents and I won't say it was a weekly event for me, but during the summer I'd probably see two or three plays.

Sometimes we'd go on an evening and I'd spent X amount of dollars on rides at MountainPark, or throwing beanie bags at one of those concessions. They'd give me a dollar amount that I could spend, and then it'd be, you know, walk down the hill to the playhouse.

It was also in the news that August that The Valley Players' old barracks, the Steiger estate, former summer home of the Steiger family in the Wyckoff Park area of Holyoke owned for several years by Edwin D. Ballard, was sold to Clarence A. Bemis for the purpose of reselling the home, the apartment-garage, and to develop the remaining 10 acres of the estate.

Helen Harrelson was a hit in *The Philadelphia Story.* Her husband, character man and perennial

Love Rides the Rails 1950, Edward Fuller, Ruth Elliot, Ralph Longley, Albert Rosetti, Carlton Guild, Joseph Foley, John Marion, Walter Swift, J. Harris Melia

favorite, Joseph Foley, played her ex-husband in the play, and when his line required him to call her a "battle-axe,"…

…Joe couldn't repress a little smile when he said that and the audience was quick to pick it up.

Joseph Foley and Helen Harrelson had been married in June 1947, and fellow Valley Player Lauren Gilbert gave the bride away. There were several married couples in the company making The Valley Players a family affair, including Martha Jones and Robert Emhardt, Jackson Perkins and Lauren Gilbert, future members Ray Gandolf and Blanche Cholet, and of course, the Guilds. Marian Hatfield and William Dodds, who both worked in the publicity and business departments and had occasional minor roles on stage (just about anybody could be drafted to perform on stage), were married. During World War II, Marion had toured Europe with the USO in *Dear Ruth*, and had played in other stock

companies.

A rollicking departure occurred with *Loves Rides the Rails, or Will the Mail Train Run Tonight*, an old-time "mellerdramer" (actually written in 1940 and premiering in Stockbridge, Massachusetts) featuring the entire company, and pianist John Marion, well-known locally for his playing at the Valley Arena, and the Holyoke and Victory theaters. The Guild's son William had a minor role, and the actors were announced in the program as Miss and Mr. (or Master in William Guild's case), likewise to get into the spirit of the event:

All Members of the Audience who are Ladies and Gentleman Will Please Remove their Hats.

Some members of the company also doubled in special "olio" acts. Not certain how the audience would react to this type of frivolity, a note was put in the program to introduce them to the world of nineteenth century theatre protocol:

You – the audience – are much more a part of the production than usual. Not only are you invited, you are expected to cheer and applaud, to hiss and boo, to stomp and whistle to laugh, to weep (if you must) as the opportunity presents itself and as the spirit moves you…

It was a huge hit, so much so that many in the audience came back more than once and requested more of this kind of show. A reviewer noted:

It is difficult to determine at times who is enjoying the whole thing more, the audience or the actors. Given leave to hiss, boo, stamp feet and whistle, the audience needed no persuasion, and entered into the spirit of the play with no little restraint…an ensemble number of "By the sea" with "bathers" in old fashioned bathing suits is a marvel to behold…on any laugh meter, the production goes over the top.

Old-fashioned bathing suits were courtesy of the Jansen Knitting Mills in Boston.

It achieved the first capacity matinee. To accompany this show, in a splendid valentine to the history of theatre, the Casino lobby, which doubled as an art gallery presenting the work of local artists during each production, featured a photographic exhibit during the run of this old-time "mellerdramer" of illustrious actors and actress of the 1880s

Proving that actors had achieved respectability in the twentieth century that they may have sometimes lacked in the nineteenth, members of The Valley Players were invited to St. Andrew's German Reformed Church toward the end of that season for their annual garden party. An editorial in the *Holyoke Transcript-Telegram* expressed appreciation for their taking part in community activities:

…the Valley Players were coming over to eat frankfurts and cold meats and baked beans and sauerkraut and the most wonderful kuchen, just as we were. We liked that. We are devotees of the Valley Players and do fully appreciate the great gift this group makes for us in our summer season. We realize all of them as fine men and

women devoted to one of the highest cultural arts in the world. We claim them as Holyoke's own…we could feel very near to Louie Mudgett…Pretty Ruth Elliot is as pretty off the stage as on. Ralph Longley brought his charming wife…This is the best season attendance-wise the Valley Players have had. They get closer to the Holyoke public from season to season and that's the way Holyoke gets closer and closer to the Valley Players. They are our folks. We are their folks. And that's all good.

The 1950 season reached record attendance, and the future looked bright. The notes in the final program of the season looked forward to the next season, which would be the tenth anniversary of The Valley Players – and their 100th performance.

***

The champ in both box office receipts and attendance for 1951 was the comedy *Born Yesterday*, at $5,087.58 and 6,182 attendance. The lowest was *The Fatal Weakness*, the last show of the season, at $3,607.66 total receipts, and an attendance of 4,091.

The programs always took special care to note when a minor role was played by a local person. The opening show of the season included a student, Ann Dowling, from the Northampton School for Girls. A new regular member of the company was Mac Gress, from Hadley, and a graduate of Hopkins Academy and of Northampton Commercial College. As was noted of other veterans, he had served overseas during World War II with the 3rd Division, had been wounded in action, and during a long convalescence, began to consider the stage as a career.

New to the company was nineteen-year-old Nancy Wells, whose father's family had originally come from Holyoke and where he, James Wells, began his own theatrical career some forty years previously. He trod the boards at the Holyoke Theater in the old Shea Stock company, and also at the very Casino with the Emile Barringon-Bijou Light Opera Company. His daughter Nancy began her theatre career with The Valley Players, and took the lead in *Born Yesterday* this season.

The Firebrand 1951, Jacqueline Paige, Archie Smith, James Courtney, Phil Arthur, Carlton Guild, and Gaylord Mason

Jackson Perkins would be back for only one show this season, as she was touring as Mrs. Darling in *Peter Pan*, with Hollywood stars Jean Arthur and Boris Karloff.

Two other newcomers to the company would eventually enjoy greater fame. Si (billed as Simon in his later career) Oakland, who came to The Valley Players for the lead role of Harry Brock in *Born Yesterday*, a part he played in stock previously. He had Broadway experience, as well as television. Many will recall his 1970s turn as the boss of (and bane of his existence) Darren McGavin in the hit cult show *The Night Stalker* as well as character parts in films, including the detective in the hit musical *West Side Story* (1961).

The other was Hal Holbrook, who joined the company in 1951 along with his wife Ruby. He had desperately wanted The Valley Players job so he could qualify for his Equity card. Holbrook, who would in future years enjoy a long career on stage, films, and television, would perhaps enjoy more fame than any of The Valley Players alumni. But he owed them a great debt – not only did he get his Equity union card, he actually premiered his full-length, one-man play *Mark Twain Tonight!* with The Valley Players at the Casino on Mt. Tom. That would come at the end of the decade.

For now, he was a newly married man traveling the country with his young actress wife, trying to get established in a career full of challenges and disappointments. The 1950s brought new hope. Their plan, according to Mr. Holbrook's memoir *Harold*: "…we would drive up to Holyoke,

Massachusetts, and pay a visit to Bertram Tanswell, who was with the Valley Players summer stock company. We'd let them take a look at us. Just in case."

Holbrook, who had lived in eastern Massachusetts part-time as a boy, visited The Valley Players with his wife Ruby to see if they could find a place in the group. From his memoir:

Off to Holyoke. We were nervous about this trip because we did not want to seem too pushy or to embarrass Bertram….We drove along the handsome Connecticut River past Springfield, where I had boarded the train with Grandpa for those overnight rides to Cleveland, snug in the upper berth. My past was beginning to connect to my future. I was in New England again.

We arrived in Holyoke just in time to see the play that night, You Can't Take it With You…. *in the hands of a company of professionals who could project their characters into the cavernous space of the Mountain Park Casino it was hugely enjoyable. Jean and Carlton Guild ran this theater, and after the show everyone came together at the Guild's home to drink beer and run lines for the next week's play. We were made welcome, but it was like dropping in on a family preparing for a wedding or the imminent birth of a baby. It wouldn't do to hang around, so we left on Monday for the drive back to Granville.*

The Holbrooks did not have Equity cards yet. Bertram Tanswell, a New York actor had a…

…steady summer job with the Valley Players in Holyoke…We had a dream, a wonderful dream, baby, to inspire Bert to inspire Carlton and Jean Guild of the Valley Players to let us in and give us Equity Cards. By such devious means are careers launched, but the odds are maniacal. We did not beg Bertram to help us, we just knew our dedication would mean something to him.

They were overjoyed when the Valley Players hired them.

Holyoke came through! We were hired for the summer. We would each be in six to eight of the twelve plays and get our Actors' Equity card. We were going to step across the big threshold…It was a big leap of faith for them. We had to prove ourselves. We stepped into the arena as youngsters, surrounded by a company of men and women from twenty to seventy years old and playing their own ages, not a band of college actors playing ages way beyond their own. Standing on the rehearsal stage with John O'Connor and Jacqueline Paige at Holyoke was a different experience…Yet they were kind. In the dearest tradition of the theater, they were going to give us our chance. We were family now.

Holbrook lends his impressions of the Holyoke summer theater that gave them their big chance:

The audience in Holyoke's Mountain Park Casino loved their actors, but you had to win their respect first, and the reviewers from the four newspapers covering the plays would be judging our worth to the company on this first shot out of the box. The play was The Firebrand.

The Firebrand was a lavish play set in 1535 Florence. The program noted of the Holbrooks:

Two young people with greater ability enthusiasm, and energy would be hard to find

The program also noted with amusement the restraints of propriety on certain shows:

In questionable situations, we prefer the light touch, not taking the matter seriously not stressing it or making an issue of it. Back in '44 when we gave Sunday performances and were subject to the blue laws of the Commonwealth, we were often amused by having to post where all could read the words of the text which state censorship forbade us to utter on the Sabbath.

Two Springfield dailies wrote theatre reviews, one Springfield weekly, two Holyoke dailies, and a Northampton daily. Coverage was far more extensive of theatre at this period, including interviews and feature stories on a few different local radio stations, soon to be joined by two local television stations. Local programming was far more common in this era, and local theatre benefited by the attention. Even the weeklies, as previously noted, carried professional play reviews.

Hal Holbrook gives us a glimpse into the rehearsal schedule at Holyoke:

While The Firebrand *was playing eight performances,*

POPULAR PLAYS *by* POPULAR PLAYERS

FOR THE BEST
SEATS CALL OR
WRITE FOR A
RESERVATION
WELL IN ADVANCE

Jean Guild

John O'Connor

FOR THE BEST
SEATS AT THE
LOWEST PRICE
COME ON
MONDAY EVENING

Jacqueline Paige

Gaylord Mason

The Week	The Play	The Featured Players
June 18—23	GOOD HOUSEKEEPING	Jean Guild, John O'Connor
June 25—30	THE MAN	Gaylord Mason, Pamela Simpson
July 2—7	BORN YESTERDAY	Nancy Wells, Si Oakland
July 9—14	THE FIREBRAND	Phil Arthur, Archie Smith, Jacqueline Paige
July 16—21	GOODBYE, MY FANCY	Jackson Perkins
July 23—28	THEIR HEARTS WERE PURE	Phil Arthur, Hal Holbrook, Nancy Wells
July 30—Aug. 4	TWO BLIND MICE	Gaylord Mason. Jean Guild, Louie Mudgett
Aug. 6—11	THE JOYOUS SEASON	Jean Guild
Aug. 13—18	SEE HOW THEY RUN	Gaylord Mason, Ruby Holbrook
Aug. 20—25	COME BACK, LITTLE SHEBA	Jacqueline Paige, John O'Connor
Aug. 27—Sept 1	CANDLELIGHT	Gaylord Mason, Archie Smith
Sept. 3—8	THE FATAL WEAKNESS	Jean Guild, Jacqueline Paige

Dorothy M. Crane, *Director*; Hal Shafer, *Scenic Designer*   William Dodds and Edward C. Purrington, *Stage Managers*

RESERVATIONS ARE
HELD FOR YOU
UNTIL 8:10
TUESDAYS
UNTIL 7:40

Archie Smith

Nancy Wells

RESERVATIONS ARE
HELD INDEFINITELY
IF YOU AGREE TO
PAY FOR TICKETS
NOT CALLED FOR

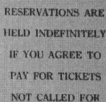

Hal Holbrook

Ruby Holbrook

Monday through Saturday, we were also rehearsing Goodbye My Fancy *to open the following Monday. While* Fancy *played its eight performance schedule we'd rehearse the next play, and so on down the twelve-week summer season. We rehearsed five hours a day, but only two hours on matinee days, Wednesdays and Saturdays, and we learned the lines at night after the evening's performance. Jean and Carlton's rambling old home became our clubhouse, where there was close companionship and plenty of beer on ice. We cued each other over and over until we had nailed those pages of lines into our brains. Sleep was the only thing that was rationed.*

In an on-camera interview for the locally produced television documentary, *Mountain Park Memories,* Mr. Holbrook recalled,

You had to learn all new lines. A new play...I can't even believe today what we did. You'd stay up till 2 o'clock working real hard on your lines. You'd go back, you're trying to get six, seven hours sleep. Get up, rehearse all day, do the show again at night, then learn the lines in the middle of the night for the next. And you do that every night, every day, week after week. And it took spirit.

Mr. Holbrook's chapter in his memoir, *Harold,* on The Valley Players is filled with delightful reminiscences of specific plays. He would receive his first featured role for The Valley Players in *Candlelight* in late August.

It was The Valley Players 10th season and the *Holyoke Transcript-Telegram* lauded the "fine sincerity" of the group.

Mr. and Mrs. Guild are citizens of Holyoke. They and their splendid corps, and that includes everybody from the pretty girl who hands you your program and takes you to

PRESENTING

THE HERO	THE HEROINE	THE VILLAIN

Phil Arthur	Nancy Wells	Hal Holbrook

In The Valley Players' Production of
'BECAUSE THEIR HEARTS WERE PURE'
ANOTHER RIOTOUS, OLD-TIME MELODRAMA
ALL THIS WEEK AT THE MT. PARK CASINO
Eves. 8:30 (Tues. 8:00), $1.50—85c; Mon. Night Only $1.50—60c
Wed. Mat. 2:30, 60c—Under 16, 25c—Tel. 8243

your seat, to stars of every production—show the something of hospitality that makes the Valley Players a high asset to our summer life. Here's to the Valley Players at age ten. May they live long with us and prosper.

Another editorial in the *Holyoke Saturday Democrat*, "Our Valley Players" – note the *Our* – remarks on the high quality of the shows and performances, but something else, distinctly a sense of pride and ownership:

The company took a chance, a gambling chance to try and revive the Casino. Holyoke, as you know is pretty hard to please when it comes to stage shows, and it required faith and confidence to leave an established playing residence to come to Holyoke... and how glad we are that they did!... Their faith in Holyoke had paid big dividends and Holyokers in returned opened their hearts to the company and backed them enough to warrant their stay in Holyoke.

Another show was a rousing reprise of the old-time "mellerdramer" genre that had been so well received and successful in the previous season. This time it was a show with a local flavor— *Because Their Hearts Were Pure* was presented with a local slant, set in the Pioneer Valley. The actors and actresses were, according to the manner of the nineteenth century, introduced as Mr. and Miss, and Master William Guild again took a minor role. His mother Jean played yet another widow woman, Mr. Hal Holbrook played the villain, Sebastian Hardacre, manager of the Westfield Bank. Bertram Tanswell played a "Connecticut River Rat". Set in Holyoke, Northampton (Jacqueline Paige, as chairman of the Northampton School Board "stole the show – She's a riot!"), at "Shanghai Mamie's" in Springfield, and a forlorn orphanage in Chicopee. Some of the cast also performed specialty acts, and John Marion was back at the piano.

The program noted that *Love Rides the Rails* of the previous season had been the most popular of all the shows. Naturally, as any company would, The Valley Players went back to the well.

Many came to see it a second time during the week, and many more urged us to revive it another year, or at least to present a play similar to it.

According to the *Daily Hampshire Gazette*, the audience became so involved in the spirited show, at which they were encouraged to cheer the hero and boo the villain:

One dignified elderly lady was last night heard yelling to the villain [played by Hal Holbrook] in a soprano voice: "Drop dead, you snake in the grass."

As the summer continued, it was usual for guest actors scheduled to perform to ask to be released from their commitment for more, as the program put it, "remunerative engagements," but The Valley Players always managed to find substitutes in a large network of friends and colleagues. This season Archie Smith was off to a better gig on TV, and they got Glen C. Gordon instead, late of the movies where he appeared opposite Arthur Kennedy in the film *Bright Victory*.

The Valley Players began welcoming more and more amateur players regularly to fill minor roles, beyond the occasional need for a local drama club student. Among the locals taking a minor role this season was Tom Lennon, who appeared in *Come Back Little Sheba* in August. He was from Springfield and had performed in community theatre locally for some fifteen years, including the Civic Theatre and Repertory Players. He also directed for Longmeadow, the Trinity, and the Chicopee Players. The Valley Players, despite

Come Back Little Sheba 1951, Carlton Guild, John O'Connor, William Dodds, Jacqueline Paige, Jean Guild

their Equity cards, was a truly egalitarian setting and community-based. Jerry Melo also came from community theatre, the Call Board Theater of Springfield. On the back of the program for the last show of the 1957 season – prime ad space – there was an ad for Springfield's Call Board Theater commencing its seventh season of an impressive roster of six plays at the Museum of Fine Arts.

Real-life husband and wife John O'Connor and Jacqueline Paige were featured together in *Come Back, Little Sheba,* and actor Bertram Tanswell stepped into the director's shoes for this show. According to an article in the *Transcript-Telegram,* which followed the couple through a rehearsal process, the O'Connors stated they preferred The Valley Players above all summer stock groups

with which they'd worked:

"It's pleasant here. The response of the community is encouraging, and it gives the actors without top billing a chance at solid roles. It gives us a chance to grow dramatically."

Another feature article covered in depth the set, the furnishings and props for the show and where they were obtained, or scavenged. The Feinstein Leather Company on High Street loaned a period suitcase, Steiger's donated a red slipcover for the couch, plumbing fixtures, and an old icebox – including a nightly block of ice, all needed for the show. Lilacs, however, they had to import from Rhode Island, as the season had passed locally.

One has to marvel at the amount of press The

Valley Players received. There was even a listing of the ushers posted in the paper. The program, always growing, featured ads this season for the Hofbrau Café at 674-676 South East Street in Holyoke, Pete's Restaurant "across from the Victory Theater," the Holyoke Bowl-O-Drome at 158 Elm Street: "air conditioned."

As the season wound down, the program noted where The Valley Players were bound in the fall and winter months:

One of the few actors in existence who know what they will be doing in future months, Mr. Holbrook and his wife will take their "Theatre of Great Personalities" on tour throughout the country for the fourth successive winter, at the conclusion of which we hope to find them heading back to Holyoke for another, and this time full, season of summer stock.

The Guilds said farewell for another year, not with the anxious hope of continuing the playhouse for another season, as was the tone of past programs, but with the comfortable knowledge there would certainly be another season as part of the normal passing parade of life.

The squirrels and chipmunks are chattering away, telling us to pack up and be off so that they may reserve their rightful tenure during the colder months ahead. The field mice are beginning their incursions, and in the quiet of an early morning an old groundhog wanders up and down the aisles as if trying to choose the best seat in the house from which to view the winter scenes…

…goodbye now. May your pathways be pleasant and prosperous until another summer reunites us.

The Oracle column of the *Holyoke Transcript-*

Telegram again bade farewell to The Valley Players…

Not all the summer Play Houses can look forward to the next season as we in this community can look forward to our Valley Players. We didn't create our Valley Players. They created us as a following….

But this included an ominous, unintended perhaps, prediction when quoting a *Falmouth Enterprise* interview with Arthur Sircom, who was leaving the Cape Playhouse after eleven years:

"The situation in Dennis as in all summer theaters is getting more difficult every season, more difficult to do the kind of things one reaches for. Package shows are here to stay, for a long spell anyway, and it is going to be very difficult or the producer in the future to be anything more than a booker." We Holyokers do not think the Guilds and the splendid group they have built together find our Valley so limited. And yet they say the Cape theaters made more money than ever during the summer past.

The lengths to which Holyokers, or at least the local press, regarded The Valley Players as family can be sensed in many ways, including the lead editorial in March 22, 1952, announcing the distressing news that publicity representative and chief greeter of the public at the playhouse door, Louise "Louie" Mudgett required recent hospitalization due to illness and would be missing the upcoming season. The writer regarded her contributions as paramount to the success of the company:

…the company made good, but the "angel" that protected them; made the patrons like the cast and the company was the lovable Louie Mudgett at the door…ladies like Louie are few and far between…We know that contact with the patrons, plus the splendid air of the mountain will do more to bring her back to health than anything else…Yes, Louie, "Home" is the Casino Theater in Holyoke; a place you have helped make famous; a summer theater which will always honor the name of Louie Mudgett…

Both Holyoke papers called for prayers, and cards to be sent to Miss Mudgett at the Boston hospital to which she had been confined for the past two months.

Smith residence Lincoln Street, Hal Holbrook, possibly Ruth Elliot, and Simon Oakland, with unidentified boy.

A group photo of the cast for the first show made the front page of the *Holyoke Transcript-Telegram* on June 10th. They posed outside by a tree on the property of the Lincoln B. Smith residence on Northampton Street, where they rehearsed in a brick barn. "We are not an arty community," admitted the editorial of the *Transcript-Telegram* on June 13th, but:

…We are a theater-loving people…The Valley Players are strictly of a high order. They are prosperous enough now to provide beautiful settings for their plays. The educational and cultural values of what the Valley Players mean to Holyoke can be yard-sticked. It seeps into our life. It adds to what Holyoke means in the world of culture. Such additions do something for all of us. Here's to the 1952 edition of the Valley Players. May it out-do and out-sell all the seasons behind them as part of Holyoke's life.

***

The 1952 season brought a return of the

Holbrooks, whose first child, their daughter, Victoria, was born just two months before the season in Holyoke commenced in June. From his memoir, *Harold*, Holbrook recalls:

On Sunday, the day off, while the whole cast cavorted around a swimming pool made available by a sainted supporter of the theater, Victoria visited us in her mother's arms and was the center of oohs and ahs and gentle touches from our tenderhearted comrades.

The pool was at the home of Lincoln Smith on Northampton Street, across the street from the Guild home. The cast rehearsed in Smith's barn for years. Holbrook discusses the working relationship as well of these tenderhearted theatre comrades while rehearsing *Gramercy Ghost*, the third show of the season, in which he and his wife Ruby were paired for the first time in featured roles:

Mac Gress spreading cheer and concern; John O'Connor and his wife, Jackie Paige, polite and kind, a wealth of understanding etched in the creases life had worn into their

Hal Holbrook, Ruby Holbrook, baby Victoria Holbrook, possibly Guild residence on Lincoln Street

Lincoln Street picnic, Hal Holbrook, Ruby Holbrook across, facing camera, Valley Players company.

Faces; Ed Fuller, new this week and watching carefully; and Jean Guild and our director, Dorothy Crane, a little edgy about moving things along. And then Bert Tanswell, our friend playing the charming ghost of the title, the actor doing his job, working for laughs, and carefully observing us. There was something ironically sweet about the sly efforts of his ghost to bring our characters in this play

together—Ruby and me. It was like an unplanned vote of confidence the play had asked him to deliver.

Now maturing into its second decade, The Valley Players seemed to hit its stride in the 1950s, which some regard as the zenith of summer theatre. Television would not yet be the competition it

Lincoln Smith residence on Northampton Street: Simon Oakland and Bertram Tanswell

Lincoln Street picnic, Jacqueline Paige, Dorothy Crane, unknown, John O'Connor, unknown

The Luck of Caesar 1952, Jean Guild, Stanley Greene, and Nancy Wells

would become in future years, and prices were affordable in an era where the middle class was rising to unprecedented economic power and fulfillment of the good life. Ads in the ever-growing program this season included W.T. Grant's on High and Dwight Streets. As always, Toto's on Route 5 had a prominent ad which featured a headshot of the featured actor or actress of the week. Toto's started a program of offering 10 percent off on meals and on theater tickets when purchased at the same time.

Jean Burns, and her daughter, Maureen, of Springfield, both had roles in *Season in the Sun* in July; the program mentioned their experience in local community theatre including Springfield's the Call Board Theater. One might note that

community theatre has also a place in the life's blood of a community, and without a professional full or part-time theater in town, is the only substitute for professional theatre that many communities enjoy. It is a vibrant replacement.

The 1952 season displayed a few departures, showing The Valley Players was not settling into a rut, but remaining relevant and dynamic. *The Luck of Caesar* was an original play written by George Alan Smith, a former stage manager for The Valley Players, and a native of Holyoke (Holyoke High School class of 1932). The play was set in a New England factory town.

Stanley Greene, who appeared in the play, was a visiting guest actor and one of the founders of the

A Streetcar Named Desire 1952, Si Oakland, Nancy Wells, Hal Holbrook, John O'Connor, Miriam Stovall, and Edward Fuller

American Negro Theatre. Even these many years later, the actors' bios in the programs were still listing their wartime service to the country. Mr. Greene entertained the troops. Playwright Mr. Smith served in the Navy as a Chief Pharmacist's Mate.

Si Oakland played the Stanley Kowalski role in *A Streetcar Named Desire*, with Miriam Stovall as Blanche, and Nancy Wells as Stella, a great leap from the light comedies that opened the season. By doing the latest plays, especially ones which had struck a chord, or struck like lightning, in American popular culture, The Valley Players were rather daring in inviting comparisons. Their *Streetcar* was well received, both by critics and the audience, which is always assumed to prefer lighter fare:

Judging from audience reaction and the prolonged applause as the curtain fell, the Valley Players were more than successful in the demanding challenge they accepted.

It was the season Ted Tiller, destined to become a favorite, joined The Valley Players. His first appearance was in August for the comedy *Room Service*. It was recounted in a future program that Ted Tiller:

…had audiences rocking back and forth so much with laughter that seats broke right, left, and center. In spite of this damage, we invited him back in 1953 for seven parts.

Ted Tiller, as part of his acting career, also put on marionette shows, and wrote scripts for radio and television, including *Omnibus*, and the children's series *Mr. I Magination*. He was a playwright, and

122

The High Ground 1952, Eleanor Farnese, Jean Guild, Ruby Holbrook, John O'Connor,
Jackson Perkins, and Lee Firestone

directed and acted on Broadway (including in *No, No, Nanette*, *The Great White Hope*, and *Witness for the Prosecution*), in regional theatre, and on television during a forty-year career. He performed with The Valley Players in Holyoke for the next eleven years.

Local television personality and columnist Barbara Bernard says of Tiller:

He just was a superb actor. He could do anything. He could do an accent, and he was in practically every show, every summer. Sometimes he had the lead, and sometimes he would have a minor part, but he always did so well.

William Guild concurs:

Ted Tiller was particularly a favorite of the audiences. He was a very deft comedian.

Of Tiller's role in *When We Are Married*, the newspaper noted:

Ted Tiller makes an enormously funny hen-pecked husband who breaks his bonds and puts his wife in her place…while Jean Guild makes an excellent domineering wife…

Jean Guild, a driving and guiding force of The Valley Players since its inception, divided her time between the enormous tasks of management and casting, and appearing in supporting roles through the season, but always in each season there would be at least one play that had a featured or starring role for her. For 1952 it was as Sr. Mary Bonaventure, the nun who aids a convicted killer and investigates a mystery in the suspense drama *The High Ground*, or *Bonaventure* by Charlotte Hastings. Claudette Colbert played her role in the movie version *Thunder on the Hill* (1951) with Ann Blyth playing the role of the condemned prisoner, played by Jackson Perkins for The Valley Players.

Country Girl starred John O'Connor and Jacqueline Paige:

The *Country Girl* 1953, Jacqueline Paige, John O'Connor, Simon Oakland, Mac Gress, and Edward Fuller

Unlike last week's production, The Country Girl *is theater, not a show. The players under Miss Crane's firm direction are close to make it so.*

The farce *Happiest Days of Your Life* featured Ted Tiller as headmaster of an English boys' school, with Jean Guild as the headmistress of a girls' school.

The *Springfield Sunday Republican* offered:

Every summer company should have the chance to relax at this point from the rigors of steady stock production, and so, perhaps, should audiences. The Players are seizing the opportunity by galloping about with abandon, engaging in hearty horseplay and slapstick which, if this memory serves, is unprecedented. Director Dorothy Crane has given the cast the go signal and last night there was no stopping it.

That play also featured Douglass Cummings, twelve years old, in town from New York, where he was a working actor, and had appeared on TV in *Mr. Peepers* and *Captain Video.* Jean Burns, Jean Jones, and Don Thomas of Springfield were also in the cast, as well as Sally Donovan from Longmeadow.

Holbrook's wife Ruby was absent from the roster this year, and as one program explained that was due to their fifteen-month old daughter Victoria:

…whom Mrs. Holbrook is already having to drag off stage by force. Leave her unguarded for a moment at rehearsal, and you'll find her right in amongst the actors.

Hal Holbrook and Ted Tiller were both praised in another farce, *See My Lawyer.*

Room Service 1952, Ted Tiller, Mitchell Erickson, J Harris Melia, and Hal Holbrook

Ted Tiller is priceless as the somewhat more than eccentric Robert Carlin…His entrances bring joy to the audience every time. The biggest acting load is carried by Hal Holbrook as the lawyer Archer Lee…Mr. Holbrook does it very well, sustaining a frantic pace without a lapse.

The Valley Players managers noted of Holbrook in a program at the end of the 1953 season:

Admirable actor as he was from the outset in 1951, his work has broadened and deepened and humanized as season after season unfolded. One of the greatest rewards of summer-theater management is to see a fine actor mature in ever-greater and greater achievements. All that we can provide is the opportunity: the credit for making the most of it belongs to the actor. Mr. Holbrook, we believe, will go far in the world of theater.

The local press had equally warm thoughts that summer towards the acting company:

The Valley Players have made this community a richer place in which to live during the summer season. They've made for us a happy feeling that they belong to us… The Valley Players themselves, as persons, make a happy factor in our community life. A group with high standards as individuals, people you wish you might know better and still be able to invest them with the glamour that they lay upon us. We could wish we might show ourselves as hosts eager to do them honor, we thank Carlton and Jean Guild for choosing to settle into our Holyoke life and for wanting to stay with us.

An article reminded Holyokers of a long-ago leading lady on the Casino stage—Mabel Griffith, who had married actor and producer Willard

See My Lawyer 1953 Virginia Low, Ted Tiller

Dashiell. Now widowed, she lived in retirement in an Oak Street apartment. She recalled for the interviewer that she and her husband came to love Holyoke so much, they built a house in the Smith's Ferry section, which they called "Journey's End," and to which they always returned after touring. She was originally from Chicago, and had played in stock all over the country, in the hits of the day, such as *East Lynne*, and *Stella Dallas*. She had retired from acting during the Depression, and helped out at the local Red Cross and Visiting Nurse Association and the Boys' Club, and took at job as a timekeeper at one of the city's paper mills, National Blank Book. She was a great fan of The Valley Players.

The final show of the season was certainly a departure for The Valley Players—it was a "packaged" touring show produced by Fred F. Finklehoff and James J. Elliott and directed by Elliott, showcasing an entire cast of visiting performers, with not one of The Valley Players company participating, save set designer Hal Shafer. Intended to be a Broadway tryout, it

received mixed reviews by critics and the audience, who were perhaps missing The Valley Players, and the mournful "farewell" editorials blanketed the local newspapers.

***

In 1953, with Mountain Park under new ownership by John Collins, with the amusement park run by his brother Dennis and son Jay, there was a question as to just how the arrangement with Mountain Park as the landlord of the Casino theater would change. The Guilds claimed they knew nothing more than what they read in the papers, were not initially contacted directly, but then received verbal agreement that the show would go on.

Actress Anne Follmann would return this season after an absence of five years. In the early 1940s, the Players had rehearsed in the open air ballroom of the park, later at the Steiger home in Wyckoff Park where most of them lived together during the summer. When the Steiger house was sold, they rehearsed in the old merry-go-round house in the amusement park, but this offered little privacy. The Smith barn on Northampton Street was working out for another season this year. The Smith home offered storage space, kitchen and restroom, and a swimming pool in back. Some of the actors, including Anne Follmann, boarded at the Smith home. Expenses for 1953 included use of the swimming pool at 176 Linden Street for $75 per season, and hosting a party for $210.

This summer Carlton Guild was lauded in the press for arranging for Blue Cross and Blue Shield health coverage for his players, even though Equity did not require that.

The program featured ads for Jack August seafood restaurant on Bridge Street in Northampton, Filene's in Northampton and South Hadley, Grants at High and Dwight Streets in Holyoke, Hotel Northampton and Wiggins Tavern, which advertised air-conditioned dining rooms, lounge, and guest rooms. The Apremont Bowling Lanes also promoted air conditioning, "Meet Your Friends and Bowl in Comfort."

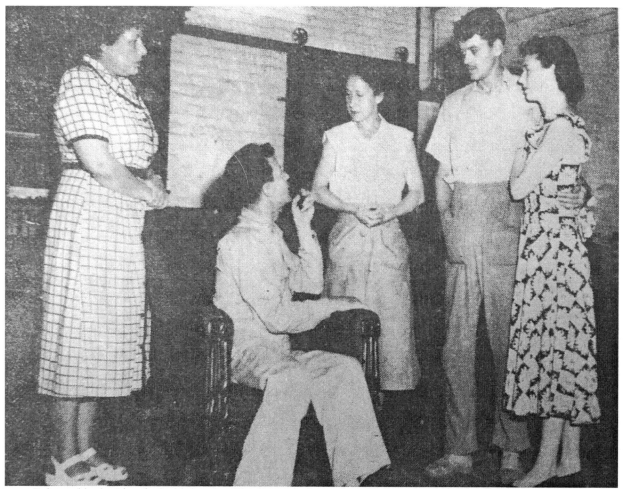

Rehearsal in the Lincoln Smith barn on Northampton Street, Jean Guild and Hal Holbrook are among the cast.

Steiger's and the Yankee Pedlar remained staunch supporters, as well as Dreikorn's bread, the *Holyoke Transcript-Telegram*, Toto's, the Kathleen Smith Music Shop, the Holyoke Water Power Company, Mel's "Home of Real Italian Food" specializing in chicken and spaghetti. Catalina swimsuits were on sale at Saltman's at 252 Maple Street, opposite the Roger Smith Hotel.

There was, as usual, a note about the 8 p.m. curtain on Tuesday, as opposed to 8:30 on other nights, because of the fireworks. Some people, inevitably got mixed up and arrived late.

Parking got to be a problem with more cars (visiting the amusement park, not only the theater) and limited space, though under the new ownership, the 25 cents fee was dropped and parking was now free.

Actor Bertram Tanswell doubled on community publicity with Louie Mudgett. The program noted that, "People are always stopping us on the street to say they saw Lauren Gilbert or Joseph Foley on television just the other night." Mr. Gilbert sometimes appeared on TV with his wife, Jackson Perkins, who lately had a gig on Broadway as the mother in *Peter Pan*. James Van Wart, the stage manager, also acted on stage from time to time. Anyone who stood still was likely to get cast in a play.

Westfield native Anne Pitoniak appeared in *Father of the Bride. Bell, Book, and Candle*, was a popular show, with Miriam Stovall and Hal Holbrook in the lead roles. The final show of the season was the comedy, *Gigi*, with Holbrook again in the lead as Gaston. It had been a financially successful season with *Father of the Bride* earning top box office receipts. During the first month of August when a hot spell visited the valley, it was recorded

Affairs of State 1953, Hal Holbrook, Jacqueline Paige, and Helen Harrelson

that over 300 cancellations were received, with a loss of about $1,000. *Bell, Book, and Candle* went on, however, despite a registered 110 degrees on the stage. And another editorial congratulating them on another season, and pleading with them to return.

Westover Air Force Base in Chicopee continued to swell the population of that town and bring newcomers to the area. In 1953 and 1954, the part of the base called Stony Brook was a secret area for the storing of nuclear weapons. Strategic Air Command took over Westover in 1955. Mt. Holyoke had a nuclear bomb-proof command post for the Strategic Air Command, locally called The Notch, which began in 1956, about 400 feet below the summit of Mt. Holyoke. This sector played a prominent role in the Cuban Missile Crisis as a secret photographic lab there developed the reconnaissance photography of

Cuba.

In May 31, 1955, *Holyoke Transcript-Telegram* published a feature on the polio vaccine being offered at clinics set up in local schools. Polio was even now, as it had been for the 1918-1919 Influenza Panidemic, a reason for keeping people away from theaters, especially in summer.

In 1956, the Skinner silk mill, one of the oldest manufacturers in the city and a signature company in Holyoke, discontinued the manufacture of silk fabric. In 1959, Wistariahurst, William Skinner's family mansion, opened as a museum. Youngest daughter Katherine Skinner Hubbard had been the last full-time resident. She and her children donated it to the city.

In May 1956 construction locally on the Massachusetts Turnpike began, and would cut

JFK, Mrs. Kennedy holding baby Caroline ride on a float in the St. Pat's Parade, Holyoke, 1958.
Photo by Ann Lynch Beebe, author's collection

through the south part of Holyoke bordering West Springfield and become a major east-to-west artery in Massachusetts. It was completed a year later.

The Holyoke St. Patrick's Day Parade of 1958 featured special guests Senator John F. Kennedy and Mrs. Jacqueline Kennedy, who rode on a float and waved to crowds lining the street. JFK was the first winner of the parade committee's new National Award, which after his death would be called the John F. Kennedy Award. The first parade ball was held at the Roger Smith Hotel.

At Mountain Park these summers were the heyday of "Dodgems" and the Ferris wheel and cotton candy. From author Jay Ducharme's book on *Mountain Park*:

From the top of the wheel, the riders had a breathtaking vista of the Pioneer Valley. At night, the bright lights circling the wheel were visible from miles away ... After

sunset, the park was a sparkling wonderland with strings of bright white lights crisscrossing the midway and colorful signs everywhere. The Ferris wheel anchored the center of the midway with its giant circle of bulbs.

Jacob Barowsky, the young boy who arrived as an immigrant to Holyoke in 1897, had since founded the local General Cleaners and had invented the household cleaner Lestoil, which in 1959 earned some $25 million in sales. He would play a major role at the end of the decade to save The Valley Players, at least temporarily.

Expenses for the 1954 season included operating the Dodge truck and the 1934 Ford Panel truck, the City of Holyoke property tax, $90 to the police, and "fogging Casino." In the program for *Gently Does It*, which ran the week of June 28 through July 3, 1954, the management noted:

Production costs are still very high (about $4,000.00 a week) considering possible box-office returns; and one or

Magnificent Yankee 1954, Mac Gress, Harry Crane, Arthur Trudeau, James Daggitt, William Brooks, Robert Furey, Manuel Duque, Jerry Melo, Vern Jones, Walter Case, John O'Connor, and Ann Driscoll

two fluffs, misses, or whatever you want to call them, might put us out of business. We have to be good, for your money—and for less money than you would pay, as we have paid on occasion, to see something like half a show at an uncomfortable angle with 50% visibility of the stage in a metropolitan theater.

At best (and we're convinced that here in the Pioneer Valley is the best), summer-theater operation is not a lucrative business. Its greatest rewards are not monetary. They are personal. One is the satisfaction that comes from doing a good job and having it appreciated and enjoyed by others. Another is the many friends one makes...

The Holbrooks were not on hand for the 1954 season. One newcomer was Stephen Pluta, who had served with Armed Forces Radio Service in Korea – young men were Korean vets now. Michael Enserro was new to the company this year, and one program note recalled his arrival with fellow actor Howard Ledig, when the Guilds, and actor Edward Fuller along for the ride, piled into the company car to drive down to Holyoke's station to meet the train. They ran lines in the car ride on the way home.

Jacqueline Paige was a hit in *Gently Does It*, a mystery comedy. From the *Holyoke Transcript-Telegram*:

Miss Paige plays the juicy part of a British barmaid...with a Gracie Fields flair. In fact, she drains every drop out of playwright Janet Green's lines, and adds an extra nip to the part for good measure.

Si Oakland played his part as the murderer, "with intensity and force...slowly but surely, the full house Monday night realized that Oakland...was...a psychopathic killer." Si Oakland played lead Johnny Case in Philip Barry's sparkling *Holiday*, with Ellen Andrews as Linda and Nancy Wells as her stuffier sister Julia. Young Mac Gress was the tipsily depressed younger brother Ned. John O'Connor was the smug patriarch.

Howard Ledig returned to The Valley Players with *My Three Angels*, a comedy about escaped convicts infiltrating family life. John O'Connor emerged from the minor supporting roles to take the lead in *The Magnificent Yankee*. It had been repeated in the press time and again that one of

The Girl From Wyoming, 1954, Ruth Elliot and cast.

the chief charms of The Valley Players was their mixing up their cast, using them on all roles, not having "stars," but having a well-rounded repertory of players who could take a character part one week, and the lead the next. The audience apparently loved both the familiarity of seeing their same favorite actors week after week, but also the novelty of seeing them always in something different.

John O'Connor's turn as Justice Oliver Wendell Holmes, who had died the previous year at ninety-four years old, was his seventy-sixth role for the company. In the audience for the Wednesday evening performance was actress Helen Hayes.

The "first lady of the American theatre" was reportedly moved to tears. Miss Hayes had just finished a four-week stint at the Cape Playhouse in Dennis, and was on her way back to her home in Nyack, New York, when she stopped off at Mt. Tom especially to visit John O'Connor and his wife, Jacqueline Paige, who were friends who had

appeared on stage with her in New York. Her teenage son, future film and television actor James MacArthur (and slated to return to the Cape to play one of the sons in *Life with Father* that summer), was with her. According to the *Transcript-Telegram:*

She told members…that she was impressed with the entire establishment at the Casino and thought the play was a fine production. She said that O'Connor's portrayal of Oliver Wendell Holmes Jr., was excellent and sensitive.

Virginia Low, who had played in *Holiday,* and was a friend of Helen Hayes, accompanied her back to New York.

The Girl From Wyoming was another comedy-musical old-time "mellerdramer," a wild west parody that, as usual, went over well with the audience. Comic character man Ted Tiller took the villain's role this time, and the Guild's son, William, had a minor part. The old English music hall song, "Don't Go in the Lion's Cage," a fond mother's words of warning to her daughter set the

Chicken Every Sunday 1954 John O'Connor, Curtis Bayer, Janice Burns, Jacqueline Paige

silly, raucous tone. Specialty numbers in the olio acts also included "Are You From Dixie?", and "True Blue Lou." Elsie Cappel, who operated a dance school on High Street, supervised the choreography.

The specialty numbers were marvelous. The Players have shown that they are all very versatile in the many roles they have played in the past; but this week I believe they have awakened hidden talents in many.

In *Goodbye Again* from July 1954, stage manager Robert Colson played the part of the bellboy. Nine-year-old Robin Jones of West Springfield, and his mother, Jean Jones, both had roles in the 1954 season. Enid Schwartzwald was between her sophomore and junior years at Holyoke High School. She played the maid. Paul Rohan, who had attended Holyoke High School recalls:

I know it was always considered to be kind of a plum when somebody who was good, like in the high school drama club, would get asked to be in some of the plays at

Mountain Park.

A later program noted that two critics liked the play, but others did not and "persuaded a lot of people not to see it."

Let's remember that a reviewer is a contentious person doing a difficult task with really remarkable accuracy...He or she may be overpraised or underpraised as on a few occurrences. But you are our final and ultimate WORD.

People wanted to know why The Valley Players didn't do winter shows, "We simply can't," was the usual answer from the Guilds, who noted that just planning and preparing for a summer season was a year-round job. In their off time, they also attended local community theatre shows.

In the 1954 season, several actors from the Valley Players taped brief announcements for local radio, to be broadcast on WHYN, the Springfield station, WACE, the Chicopee station, and WREB, the Holyoke station to run at different times of the day. Publicity in this area may have been hard sought, but it was evidently generously granted. The *Springfield Sunday Republican* ran a "rotogravure" supplement section filled with photos of The Valley Players rehearsing, the backstage techies at work. Another newspaper, the *Brockton Enterprise* visited the Casino and wrote a mini travelogue for the Town Crier column on the trip to Holyoke:

The highways are well-moteled. Around midnight their "No Vacancies" signs glare at you in the dark. Some brag they have television, hot-water showers, controlled heat...It has an excellent hotel, the Roger Smith, where they give you your second cup of breakfast coffee free.

One of Holyoke's most delightful eating places is the Log Cabin. Not an inspiring name, but an interesting restaurant and perched up on a hill...if you do call and make a table reservation, when you get there and are seated, you find a little card on your table. It has your name and the time you reserved the table for on the front. You open it and inside find a bright new dime with a thank-you note from the management for making the reservation. The dime is to repay you for your phone call.

Chicken Every Sunday 1954 Ted Tiller, Jean Burns, Judith Love, Jacqueline Paige

Pretty slick…

Another thing the Log Cabin does is to put a card on each table. The card says, "Grace Before Meals." Inside you find the Catholic, Jewish, and Protestant forms of grace…

The writer also praises the Yankee Pedlar restaurant in town, and remarks on the long traffic jam of cars due to a drive-in movie theater on the way home. Just where, he doesn't mention, but it probably didn't matter. In the 1950s and 1960s, they seemed to be everywhere. But they posed no threat to business for The Valley Players. Their demise was more likely due to a new source of live theatre in the valley—but not quite yet.

The main challenge this season, as for all seasons, was the weather. They decided to capitulate to the thermometer this year. A note in the program of

The Magnificent Yankee for the week of August 2-7, 1954:

The Wednesday matinee will be canceled after next week if the official temperature at noon is, or definitely promises to become 100 or more! Our experience has been that we get the really unbearable heat, when we get it, during latter August or early September. We still remember too fervidly the matinee of Bell, Book and Candle *last summer. Probably we're getting older. Anyway, we don't want to go through that again.*

Another fact of theatre life to consider:

Theaters should be built like accordions, to expand and contract according to the size of the audience. But since they aren't, we often have to disappoint people on Saturday evening for whom there would have been seats earlier in the week. We've already sold out on several Saturdays…

Reviewing the comedy *Chicken Every Sunday*, the *Daily Hampshire Gazette* of Northampton noted:

Ted Tiller and Jean Guild, as usual, were two of the funniest people on stage…he is one of the most versatile performers in the company…Miss Guild…was hilarious. She played to the hilt the boozy singer, even intoning quite operatically the last few measures of, appropriately enough, "Drink to Me Only With Thine Eyes." She can do more by merely lifting an eyebrow that most can do by taking a pratfall.

Local television personality and newspaper columnist Barbara Bernard remembers of Jean Guild, "She talked like this, you know, (indicates the big-yawn of mid-Atlantic stage speech), oh, she was so dramatic, and she was delightful."

Don Grigware recalls his childhood impression of her, "A splendid actress, who was best as matriarchs and authoritative women. She had a haughty, rather imperial look about her, like a schoolmarm, so I never approached her except once for an autograph."

Peggy Bowe, who would take lessons in speech and drama from Jean Guild, regarded her as the most influential person in her life:

She didn't really look anything like her, but, like Eleanor Roosevelt, she was an imposing figure. Jean Guild was an Imposing Figure. She was a mature, full figured woman—not fat—but substantial, more rubenesque and she walked with amazing carriage. Always very erect, like she was making an entrance. There was nothing phony or flamboyant about her—she was not heavily made up, but she had a presence about her that made you notice her and pay attention. As the years of our association continued, we became close, but not in a demonstrative way. Maybe a hug at the holidays or the end of the school year but you could tell she really cared about her students. In keeping with the times, she was always MRS. GUILD, even my parents called her Mrs. Guild—but they were of that generation.

The Bishop Misbehaves featured Jean Guild, Howard Ledig, Virginia Lee, John Oliver, Jacqueline Paige, Robert Colson, Jerry Melo, and Mac Gress. A review in the *Daily Hampshire Gazette* August 16, 1955:

The Valley Players, it must be set forth, are a very talented group, usually adding to the material they select. Many times they have taken a mediocre play and through a spirited and expert performance have provided an evening of scintillating theatre. The same effect is made with The Bishop Misbehaves.

The *Holyoke Transcript-Telegram* review both praised and found fault with Jean Guild's performance in this play:

Miss Guild has the uncanny ability to make each and every performance a tour de force of her dynamic personality. For most of her roles, this is a definite asset. For one as…subdued and skimpily drawn as last night's, it is not. She did not succeed in creating the character of the sister…the rest of the performances were quite good.

For *Chicken Every Sunday*, the company "family" expanded again as Jean Burns, of Springfield, brought her little daughter, Janice, into the company. Also in that show was Lucille Gibbs, a Springfield teacher, and Curtis Bayer, a Springfield boy.

It was also the summer they said goodbye to a former company member, Anne Follmann, "whose courageous and spirited battle against cancer ended in her death on August ninth…" According to her obituary in *The Billboard*, her illness had forced her to give up a Hollywood contract. She was forty-one, survived by her husband, her mother, and a sister. Her battle with cancer lasted over four years, through which time she continued to appear on the Casino stage and elsewhere. She had originally been signed to play in *The Magnificent Yankee* this season, but due to treatments, needed to bow out before the season began. Her obit was edged in black in The Valley Players' scrapbook.

Louis D. Pellissier, founder of the Holyoke Street Railway, which was responsible for the existence of both Mountain Park and the Casino playhouse, died at eighty-five years old, still working for his bus company. He had been in business over sixty-three years, beginning as a trolley worker, picked by William S. Loomis to join the ranks of management.

21—Holyoke (Mass.) Transcript-Telegram. Thurs. Sept. 2, 1954

Deaths

Anne Follmann, Valley Player, Of Cancer At 41

Anne Follmann

Anne Follmann, 41, well known to Mt. Park Casino audiences, died Aug. 9 in a New York hospital after a long and one-half year battle with cancer.

Mrs. Follmann became ill in 1949 but after treatment continued periodically with her work. She was scheduled to play the part of Fanny Dixwell Holmes in the Valley Players production of "The Magnificent Yankee" last month. Mrs. Follmann read the script last winter and according to Carleton H. Guild, business manager for the Valley Players, liked it very much. However she became seriously ill in March and notified the Players she would be unable to take the part.

She made one appearance here last season when she took the part of Mother Hildebrand in "The Velvet Glove" in July of '53. Those who saw the 1947 and '48 productions at Mt. Park will remember her performances as Letter in "Uncle Harry," Marge Kags in "January Thaw," Elsa Meredith in "Made in Heaven," Mary Herries in "King Lady" and Mrs. Davidson in "Rain."

Mrs. Follmann made radio and television appearances and appeared in New York off-Broadway productions. She was associated with the Hedgerow Theater during the past five years.

When Mrs. Simons was in Holyoke she stayed with Mr. and Mrs. Lincoln B. Smith, who formerly owned a home at 1625 Northampton St. A resident of New York city, she is survived by her husband, Joseph Follmann.

Anne Follman Grand Actress

We had the good fortune a few years back meeting Anne Follman at the Casino before a performance.

She was a grand actress tested by the many featured parts given to her by the Valley Players Director, Miss Dorothy Crane.

She was a highly cultured woman, very delicate in appearance and so very nice to meet.

She fought a losing fight to cancer . . . this week's program at the Casino brought the sad news of her death August 9th. She will be remembered for her very fine performances at the Casino, and the patrons who attended last year's plays at the Casino will recall applauding Anne Follman . . . that was to be her last play at the Casino.

It seems as though a member of the family has left us . . . J. B.

A theatrical landmark over in Springfield was seeing its last days. The Court Square Theater, renowned in the area since the nineteenth century, was not only closed, but facing the wrecking ball. Almost immediately, eyes turned to The Valley Players as the last best hope for live theatre.

***

The 1955 season featured a string of recent hits from Broadway.

New to the company for *The Southwest Corner* in June was Constance Simons from Chicopee, who had first been taken by her parents to the Casino to see The Valley Players when she was a sophomore at Chicopee High School. She decided then she wanted to be an actress when she grew up. She saw many more plays after that, and as a senior, joined the local community theatre group, the Chicopee Community Players. Apprenticing in stock, she was awarded the Mary MacArthur Scholarship to the American Theatre Wing, set up by Helen Hayes in memory of her daughter Mary, an aspiring actress who died from polio. Constance appeared in minor roles on TV. She would stay with her parents during her performances for The Valley Players, and bring her career dream full circle on the Casino stage.

Jerry Melo was known to valley audiences as a community theatre player with the Springfield Civic Theater and the Chicopee Community Players, the Somers Playhouse, and was one of the founders of the Call Board Theater of Springfield, who graduated to a place in the company in a few shows the previous two years, but in 1955 would appear in ten shows. The Valley Players had occasionally filled slots for walk-ons with amateurs, or even non-actors, but as the fifties progressed they displayed a remarkable generosity to newcomers from the world of community theatre. Jean and Carlton Guild frequently attended local community theatre and were familiar with the amateur actors and actresses.

Two new ingénues, Kathy Nolan and Nancy Devlin, real-life sisters, would be featured this summer, both with experience in stock. Louie Mudgett was back greeting the audience at the door. Joseph Foley, one of the founders of The Valley Players, their beloved character man returned from television roles to try his hand at something he'd wanted to do for a long time: a dramatic part. He was slated to star as the unbalanced Captain Queeg in *The Caine Mutiny Court-Martial*.

The welcoming editorials in the local press outlined the season to come, with a settled-in tone as the company was nearing middle age in its fourteenth season. Or maybe only the audience was entering middle age.

Dial M for Murder continued their streak of obtaining the rights of the latest plays to perform, with Ellen Andrews in the lead as the wife whose

Sabrina Fair 1955, Joan Cappel, Walter Swift, Enid Schwartzwald, Virginia Low, Harry Crane, and Frank Wolff

husband wants to have her murdered. According to the *Springfield Daily News*:

Even the Fourth of July fireworks display between the second and last acts couldn't break the tension...

Though regular members of the audience no doubt accepted the Mountain Park fireworks display during the program as a simple fact of life at the theater, one wonders what first-timers and visitors to the valley thought of the thunderous spectacle.

This show was directed by Jacqueline Paige, rather than the resident director Dorothy M. Crane, and won over the critics.

The next show, *Sabrina Fair*, would feature Virginia Low, who had traveled occasionally with Helen Hayes, as she did when Miss Hayes visited the Casino in the previous year. Low had befriended the actress while still a child, having tossed flowers at the curtain call of the famous actress. They had since appeared together in a couple of plays and TV shows, having toured with *Mrs. McThing* for five months in 1953, and in What *Every Woman Knows* in 1954, and on TV in the *Schlitz Playhouse of Stars*, and on the *Motorola TV Hour*. Low would appear with The Valley Players for the whole season of 1955.

Sabrina Fair (which would be presented on Mt. Tom again in the next decade with Kathryn Crosby in a touring production) won plaudits for lead Virginia Low. The macaw used for one brief scene was supplied courtesy of the Forest Park Museum in Springfield. It was actually a cockatoo that the character Sabrina was supposed to have brought back from Paris, but the cockatoo that had been arranged to play the role unfortunately died before the show went up so, as happens in the theater, the understudy went on and became a star.

Or not.

They insured the macaw for $50. *Sabrina Fair* was the highest grossing show of 1955 at $5,812.51, with a top attendance of 5,736. The lowest ranking play that season was *The Bishop Misbehaves* with receipts of $2,593.35 and attendance of 2,669.

The season continued a streak of late hits, and the next play on the roster, *The Caine Mutiny Court-Martial*, reached a pinnacle of dramatic excellence—and a tragic end.

Joseph Foley, one of the founders of The Valley Players, was a longtime favorite as a comic character actor. He really wanted to try dramatic roles, however, but was afraid audiences wouldn't take him seriously. Along with his stage comedic roles, he had his regular gig on television as the high school principal in *Mr. Peepers*. His first attempt of a dramatic role at the Casino was in *The Traitor*. In July 1955, his greatest role was starring as Captain Queeg in *The Caine Mutiny Court-Martial*.

The press was buzzing with the news that the valley's favorite comedic character actor was taking the lead role in a powerful drama. Because of his familiarity among the regular Casino audience, the show drew a capacity audience every night. He earned resounding praise. From the *Transcript-Telegram*:

This very much loved player, for so many years with the Valley folks, does something more than one of the best roles he has ever given his admirers…He has done a great line of "character" parts in his years at the Casino. This time he has a master role and he is indeed the master.

The *Springfield Union* called the play "one of the

most significant dramas of our time," and found Foley's work equal to others who played the role on Broadway and the screen.

Northampton's *Daily Hampshire Gazette* thought both Foley, and Howard Ledig, who played Lt. Barney Greenwald, were outstanding.

The *Transcript* reviewer used the ominous word "taxing" to describe the effort of portraying Queeg, a taut, emotional role, a character who mentally unravels by the play's end.

Joseph Foley outdoes himself in the taxing role of Queeg…who starts out on sure ground and then struggles hopelessly in the quicksand of his own fears and failures.

Local theatergoers should make a point not to miss this Mountain Park Casino offering, for it will be remembered long beyond the current season.

Foley and the cast received several curtain calls, and a standing ovation opening night.

These reviews came out on Wednesday, July 19th, after Tuesday's opening night. Taxing, to be sure, and long remembered, certainly—Joseph Foley died of a heart attack the morning of Friday, July 21st.

He had been diagnosed with a heart condition three years previously, and had complained of the heat during the Thursday evening performance. He rose early Friday morning at the home of Mrs. Faith Jenks on Lincoln Street, who rented rooms to the actors in the summer. Foley was dressing to go to a dental appointment when he was stricken. Michael Enserro, who played Capt. Randolph Southard in *The Caine Mutiny Court-Martial*, was another boarder. Mr. Enserro heard Foley fall, and ran to his room, discovering his body on the floor only seconds later.

Enserro called Dr. Samuel Potsubay, but before the doctor arrived, Foley was dead. He was forty-five years old.

William Guild was a paperboy delivering the *Holyoke Transcript-Telegram*. He recalls:

I still remember delivering it the morning after Joe Foley died, and he was on the front page, his photo. And he had been told by his doctor he had serious heart problems, and he was told to not act again, that he would get too emotionally involved with the characters.

Joseph Fitzgerald Foley had been a founder, and a regular member of The Valley Players company from 1941 to 1953, except for four years during which he served in World War II. From 1953 to 1955 he was a guest player, taking on more work in television. He had played some seventy roles for the company, and had also appeared on Broadway. Previously he had been married to Helen Harrelson, who had also acted with The Valley Players, but they were divorced at the time of Foley's death, and Foley had not remarried. An uncle from Michigan had been visiting him in Holyoke during the production.

With the kind of accolades usually reserved for sports heroes, the local press mourned an actor who was not a native of Holyoke, or even New England, but had become an adopted son. The *Transcript-Telegram* ran its lead editorial the following week:

It was something of an omen that, for his last appearance on his home stage, the audiences rose to its feet in acknowledgement. Indeed there are those who say that the last night went over the edge in its power.

It was a grand final offering in the art of Joseph Foley loved so much, and served so well…We who so enjoyed the art he gave to us will long remember that Joe Foley left us in a high hour and for us who have been bowing before him this week there is a "sense of the triumphing night—with her train of stars and her great gift of sleep."

It is a sweet rest we invoke for our Valley Player who has made his last curtain.

The remaining Friday and Saturday evening performances were cancelled. Paul Rohan remembers being a child of about nine years old in 1955 when, being babysat by his grandmother while his parents and aunt worked, his grandmother had received a phone call:

They had canceled the play, which was like an unheard of

thing, because the lead actor died.

As the *Springfield Union* reported:

The stage where Joseph Foley spoke his last lines as an actor will be dark.

The Caine Mutiny Court Martial 1955, Joseph Foley

***

It was noted in a program from August that former company member Alfred Paschall also died, and so the company had to say goodbye to three of its family: Mr. Paschall, Anne Follmann, and Joseph Foley.

A few comedies followed in the wake of the magnificent, and tragic, *Caine-Mutiny Court-Martial*. The show went on.

Weather proved a formidable impediment when flooding from Hurricane Diane washed out the entrance to Mountain Park and the performances on August 18th and 19th had to be cancelled. (This occurred as well the following year, canceling one performance of *Laburnum Grove*.)

The Remarkable Mr. Pennypacker 1955, featuring John O'Connor and Jacqueline Paige.

The Remarkable Mr. Pennypacker, a family comedy, featured many local youngsters in the cast from Springfield, West Springfield, Longmeadow, Chicopee, and Easthampton.

At the end of the 1955 season, an ad on the back of the program reminded the audience that the amateur group of players, the Call Board Theater of Springfield, would begin its fifth season in October.

The Valley Players management noted in 1955:

Although our actual productions are a seasonal adventure limited to twelve weeks, a vast amount of our time during the other forty weeks of the year is devoted to the planning and preparation which they entail. When we are asked, as we have been, why we do not operate a year-round theater somewhere, we reply that this summer theater is pretty much a year-round occupation. During the months when it is not open for you to enjoy, there is scarcely a day when we are not giving at least some thought to it.

***

The year 1956 brought the fifteenth season for The Valley Players. Such numbers bring anniversary celebrations, but to large extent, it was business as usual. The lead play *The Tender Trap* opened on a chilly evening, proving at least that not all summer nights were sultry on the mountain.

More welcoming editorials for The Valley Player in the local press as the summer season began:

Of course Holyoke is a better place in which to live summers than it would be were it not for our friends, the Valley Players. Let's make the most of them.

In a portent of things to come, Louise Mace of the *Springfield Union* reported on the New York flutter of interest around former Valley Player Hal Holbrook, who apparently was working up a one-man show based on the life of nineteenth century American author Mark Twain that he was performing in a Greenwich Village nightclub. It wasn't a play as yet, really more of a skit, but it had promise.

Ruby Holbrook came back for one performance in 1956 in the comedy *A Roomful of Roses.* Husband Hal made a "secret" visit to the Casino to see his wife perform. Along with their daughter Victoria, they also had a son, David, not quite a year old. Mrs. Holbrook was lauded in the press as charming and sensitive in her role as the mother of teenage Nancy Devlin.

Dorothy Crane directed *The Seven Year Itch* that July. The *Holyoke Transcript-Telegram* review:

From chuckles to uproarious laughter evidenced at the Valley Players production…during the opening night performance Monday, the play was a popular one with the audience.

The play featured Constance Simons, the Chicopee girl, graduate of Chicopee High School, who had been brought to the playhouse as a child in 1945 and decided she'd wanted to be an actress when she grew up. Also in the cast, Kevin Burns, young son of Jean Burns in the cast, and Debra

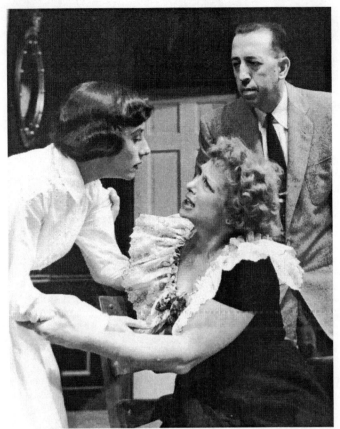

The Bad Seed 1956, Ellen Andrews, Jacqueline Paige, and Carlton Guild

Koff, "Miss Holyoke," and a member of the Mt. Holyoke College drama club.

The mysterious and romantic late Broadway hit *Anastasia* drew raves with Ellen Andrews in the lead, and Jean Guild as the grand dowager empress.

Strange Bedfellows included Carlton Guild's administrative assistant, Barbara O'Leary in the cast (who, in the off-season was also a fourth-grade teacher in Springfield), as well as a couple of local high school students, a junior high student who was usually an usher, a sixth grade teacher at local Highland School, and a Mt. Holyoke College professor.

The top play from a business perspective in the 1956 season was *The Solid Gold Cadillac*, grossing $7,289.44 with an attendance of 6,104. It drew mixed reviews, featured Jean Guild in the starring role, and several local amateur thespians, including Molly Hosman of Chicopee, who had

also appeared in *The Tender Trap* earlier in the season. Milton Hayward of East Longmeadow; and Patricia Maier of West Springfield, a college senior, debuted with The Valley Players.

Ted Tiller suffered persistent nosebleeds during the week of the production, and John O'Connor took over the Friday night performance on less than a day's notice, and less than an hour's rehearsal on stage.

The program for *The Solid Gold Cadillac* had an ad on the back page for its next show, Maxwell Anderson's *The Bad Seed*, with the disclaimer:

Not a play for the overly impressionable or emotionally inclined, its stark and incisive realism and relentless horror make it an unforgettable experience in theater. With this note of caution, we invite you to see an ideally selected cast in a superb production of the most successful work by one of America's most famous craftsmen.

The Bad Seed 1956, Howard Ledig and Claudia Crawford

Though The Valley Players had demonstrated an uncommon willingness to fill roles with amateurs

The Male Animal 1956, Howard Ledig, Evelyn Davis, and Jerry Melo

from time to time, there were some roles, especially for children playing leads in the show, that needed professional actors in the role. Claudia Crawford played the wicked child in *The Bad Seed*. Already a veteran, she had performed on stage since the age of four off-Broadway, appeared on many television shows such as *Kraft Television Theatre*, *Robert Montgomery Presents*, and comedy/variety shows hosted by Garry Moore, and Milton Berle in those days when live TV was like vaudeville training, only with an audience of millions. She also had performed on Broadway. She was nine at the time of this production, and was a student at the Professional Children's School in New York.

Claudia had tackled her role, according to the

Springfield Daily News, "with unnerving effectiveness." Though comedies were admitted crowd pleasers, the press invariably took an awed and respectful stance toward the dramas, as if, even after all these years, they were still amazed to find an acting company of such powerful versatility right here in the valley—those same people who could crack us up on stage one week, could move us to tears, or shock us the next.

Evelyn Davis appeared with the group for the first time in *The Male Animal* in August 1956. She had appeared on Broadway with Orson Welles and Helen Hayes and Melvyn Douglas, as well as a number of television shows, and the motion picture *The Shrike* with June Allyson.

Don Grigware remembers Virginia Low in *The Rainmaker*:

She was remarkable, and that was the first time I ever saw that play. I can still see and hear Starbuck telling Lizzie "to believe that she's pretty". What power in Nash's beautiful words!

The program notes for the next play, *The Rainmaker*, make an interesting observation on possible audience attitudes in the New England factory town below the theater, as it makes a veiled plea for the audience to keep an open mind:

Attend to it, enjoy it as a diverting story, if that is all you find, but perception will pierce the surface layers to profounder messages and other rewards.

It is, to repeat, in considerable measure fantasy, and thereof we have observed that the practical folk of this region have less appreciation than for other wares. It is not that they never lift up their eyes to the hills around them, not that they never find occasions to meditate on life's hidden meanings in the pleasant peacefulness of their valley. Rather, perhaps, it is that the ruggedness of the early New England life afforded little tolerance for free flights of fancy. Pragmatism, essential to survival, became the inheritance of later generations, including our own.

Special mention was made of director Dorothy M. Crane. This was the 168th production of The Valley Players, and she had directed, to this time, 152 of them. Robert Colson, who was sometimes drafted into minor roles, was actually the group's stage manager, "holding book" in theatre lingo, since 1952. It was said of him:

In the course of his daily work, which usually begins before 9:00 a.m. and often ends well after midnight, he locates and transports most of the furnishings and properties used on stage. He also acts in from four to six plays a season, and his performances are gems of characterizations, such as Dr. Bird, the opinionated psychiatrist in The Caine Mutiny Court-Martial *or the doctor in* Three's a Family.

The program for *King of Hearts* included the names of the many volunteer ushers for the season. It was also mentioned that those wanting to have their names on the mailing list for the next season may drop a postcard to, simply, "The Valley Players, Holyoke, Mass." Was the postal service so much more efficient with such scant information, or were The Valley Players so obviously well-known?

Ted Tiller had been with the group since 1952. At this time he was also writing for the Arlene Francis *Home* television program. He also served The Valley Players this season as "our New York casting representative."

Making his debut with The Valley Players in *King of Hearts* was Schuyler Larsen of Jackson Heights, New York, nine years old, and a veteran of television roles, the Hyannis Melody Tent, and a production of *The King and I* at New York City Center. David Black, from Springfield, was eleven years old. It had been a season of quite a number of children's parts.

Ralph Levy of Northampton had his MA in Theatre and was a member of the Northampton Circle Players.

Program ads at this time included a number of local businesses: Cray's Soda Company on Northampton Street in Holyoke, Service Typewriter Exchange, Inc. on High Street, the Highland Variety Store, "The Only Store of its Kind in the Highlands" and Carey's Flowers of South Hadley.

The Valley Players were operating in the black, but costs were rising. Salaries, as for any business, comprised the largest expenditure, about 45 to 50 percent of the operating costs. Equity had determined that non-musical theater performers' salaries should be set at $55 a week minimum to $75, depending on the size of the theaters. The Valley Players paid $65 base rate minimum. They had raised ticket prices this season from a maximum of $1.75 to $2, and a minimum of 60 cents to $1, which were still lower than most professional theaters.

In a portent of the future, Carlton Guild remarked to the *Holyoke Transcript-Telegram* at season's end that he did not feel big name guest stars would "operate well here because audience in the area is not of the resort area 'high spending' kind," a view which future Casino/Mt. Tom Playhouse manager Hugh Fordin would come to adopt after two years of trying to attract an audience with big names. Guild, however, felt the profitable 1956 season was also due to "the fact that people are beginning to leave their television sets." That would prove to be more wishful thinking than accurate.

The same article also mused that tent theaters, which had become a growing fad in summer theatre, were able to do well financially because they could attract a larger audience. A tent theater would come to the valley in the following summer, and would have a profound impact on The Valley Players.

***

The 1957 top show was *Witness for the Prosecution* with $7,098.33 receipts, and an attendance of 5,833. Carlton Guild placed ads in the *Westover Flier* (the newspaper of Westover Air Force Base in Chicopee) in the *Catholic Observer*, the *Chicopee Herald*, the *Springfield Jewish Weekly*, and on radio stations WACE and Holyoke's WREB. Brad Davis interviewed The Valley Players on his radio program *Show Time* at Chicopee's WACE Monday through Friday at 9:30 a.m.

The season led off with a very special show, a rare one-man show created entirely by a Valley Players alumnus: Hal Holbrook. The show: his now-famous *Mark Twain Tonight!*

He had come a long way in only a handful of years since he was a struggling actor, newly married, and traveling the country in search of work in regional theatre. He had finally found a place at The Valley Players in Holyoke for two seasons, but worried he was not being challenged and that there were no breakout roles for him in this seasoned and tight group.

Holbrook, in a letter to his wife Ruby March 3, 1952 –

"…The letter from Carlton Guild has speared my dreams

in flight. I see the logic of your counsel that we return to Holyoke this summer instead of taking the more challenging job in Minnesota, but in all three respects— salary, roles, length of time I'm wanted—I feel set down. My talent, whatever it is, just doesn't fit the type required at Holyoke. Hackwork is what they want from me, K.P. detail I did last summer, acting without heart and soul, and without desire which is so terribly important to me…."

In 1954 Hal Holbrook went to New York and had a regular job on the radio soap opera, *The Brighter Day*. He did regional theatre, and appeared in clubs in New York with skits on some new material he had worked up himself – on the nineteenth century humorist Mark Twain. It would be his making as an actor. He performed his Mark Twain persona on *The Ed Sullivan Show* and *The Tonight Show* with Steve Allen on television, and by the end of the decade, would debut a full-length one-man show on Twain—at The Valley Players as a special guest performer in 1957.

Mr. Holbrook notes from his autobiography, *Harold*:

On June 6, just before heading to Holyoke, I got another appearance on NBC's Tonight Show *with Jack Lescoulie as host. Would that help me fill the big open-sided Mountain Park Casino in Holyoke? I wondered.*

Mark Twain Tonight!, presented at Holyoke in its first full-length version, was a career-making event for Hal Holbrook. It opened The Valley Players' sixteenth season. The reviews were fabulous.

From Louise Mace of the *Springfield Union*:

"…a unique and rewarding program…in all life, so it seemed, there was Samuel Langhorne Clemens himself, complete with immaculate, comfortably wrinkled white suit, brisk red tie, drooping white mustache, ample white headpiece, and the inevitable cigar…a re-creation of a man and a mind in a deeply kneaded personification."

From the *Daily Hampshire Gazette*:

His portrayal is both a science and an art. He has paid scrupulous attention to detail, from the shuffling walk to the twinkle in his eye. Hal Holbrook never draws a breath on stage—it is Mark Twain even when he tells a story requiring the dialect and mannerisms of three or four additional characters. A remarkable piece of showmanship, Mark Twain, Tonight *at the Casino through Saturday merits your attendance.*

The *Holyoke Transcript-Telegram* called it "a fascinating artistic masterpiece…the young Mr. Holbrook, remembered as the company's handsome leading man a few year ago, is dropped from mind the instant Mark Twain enters the stage…"

Hal Holbrook as Mark Twain at the Casino 1957

Barbara Bernard, who attended the opening night performance, remembers:

I thought: this is going to fall flat on its ear, or it's going to be something so different. Well, it was—and it was magnificent. He came out in that rumpled white suit. Oh, he was terrific.

William Guild recalls:

It took him two hours to put on that makeup. You know, back then you had to use putty and all kinds of stuff that they can do so easily now. But I mean he was late twenties or maybe thirty. But I used to drive him up to the theater three hours before the performance for the week that he was doing it, and we would sit in the dressing room while he did makeup, and talk. I have very fond memories of that. He was kind of like an uncle in a way.

In less than two years, Holbrook's one-man show would be a smash on Broadway.

Unfortunately, possibly as lead show of the season (typically a slow spot in the season rotation), possibly because of its experimental nature, *Mark Twain Tonight!* was the lowest earner of the season, coming in at $3,002.45 receipts, and an attendance of only 2,510. The highest numbers of the season went to *Witness for the Prosecution* at $7,098.33 receipts, and an attendance of 5,833. Among the expenses of the season was "Actors' Train Fare and Drayage" of $582.78, up from $447.42 the year before.

William Guild, who had just graduated from the John J. Lynch Jr. High School when he performed at the Casino in *The Loud Red Patrick*, admits:

I was never an actor. No affinity for it. I was a good director. But I did everything in the theater. When I was like nine I started taking tickets in the evening. At the age of ten I started cleaning that enormous theater. Then I went from taking tickets to cleaning the theater, to working in the building of sets, and then became the assistant stage manager, and then became the full stage manager—and this is while I was starting college in 1960 and '61 and '62. I was majoring in directing at Boston University. And I went on to get both a bachelor's and a master's degree from BU in directing. And that's where I met my wife (actress Hannah Brandon), *was at Boston University.*

Also in the cast were Constance Simons and Lee Graham, both winners of the Helen Hayes' Mary MacArthur Scholarship to the American Theatre Wing, which the actress sponsored and named in honor of her late daughter. Holyoke native Nancy Dreikorn also appeared this season. She was of the family that owned the Dreikorn's Bread bakery and advertised faithfully in The Valley Players program, the ad conspicuous for its orange illustration of the Dreikorn's wrapper on its bread.

Patrons were reminded in the program not to smoke in the theater, and if smoking outside, to make sure that matches and smoking materials were completely extinguished, and never to discard them in the grass. The dry spells on the heavily wooded mountain during the long hot summer could be disastrous for careless smoking. Fire inside the theater here was perhaps not even as great a threat as fire outside of it.

This season, after the Thursday night performance of *Speaking of Murder*, the audience was invited backstage and on stage, to marvel at the behind-the-scenes magic of theatre. Showing one's sleight of hand was never part of the purchase price of a ticket, but The Valley Players were nothing if not open and welcoming to the community. It didn't seem to harm the mystique, and in the future more such opportunities were planned.

Their rehearsal space now, having vacated the now sold Lincoln B. Smith residence, was described as a quaint old barn adjoining Barthello's Rest Home on Northampton Street.

One member of the audience in *The Reluctant Debutante* was Leo Carillo, long a Hollywood favorite character actor and currently star of TV's *Cisco Kid*, playing sidekick Pancho. He came with Pat Casey, who had been first manager of the Casino back around the turn of the century. Carillo was in the area to make a personal appearance at Agawam's Riverside Park amusement park. Casey and Carillo were acquainted from early theatrical days when Casey was a booking agent in New York and had signed Carillo. They met up for supper at the Jack August restaurant in Northampton and decided to take in the show at the Casino. Carillo also entertained the kids at Springfield's Shriner's Hospital for Crippled Children before leaving the area.

The Reluctant Debutante 1957, Lee Graham, modeling fur for Langley furrier fashion shot, Neil Doherty photo.

Dorothy Crane stepped out from the director's chair and took a small walk-on in *The Desk Set*, which according to the *Springfield Union*, brought down the house. Also, Jacqueline Paige as lead Bunny Watson and Jean Guild as Peg:

…are grandly funny in a Christmas Eve bout with the bottle, and in the course of a romp Molly Hosman does a standout bit of characterization.

Strong supporter of The Valley Players, Mrs. William Dwight, Minnie, of the *Transcript-Telegram* died late July 1957. As Carlton Guild offered in a letter to the *Transcript*, "Monday nights at the Casino won't be the same now, but we shall remember her stopping to talk with us at the door…her written letters and editorials…"

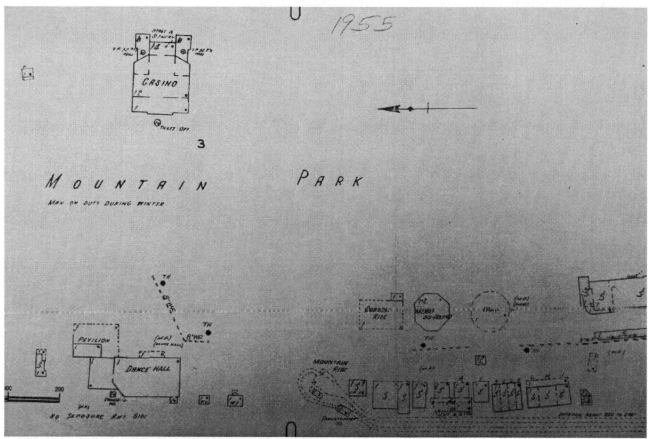

Mountain Park specifications, 1955

There were some eighteen summer theaters in Massachusetts running in 1957, and the *Transcript-Telegram* crowed:

There is always one place where Holyoke gets on the front page so that our town looks like the Capitol of Massachusetts. That is the annual New York Herald-Tribune's *story of the Straw Hat Circuit in New England.*

The attendance was lower this season, a drop of nearly 5 percent from 1956. Carlton Guild noted that most summer theaters were experiencing a decline in business, but more so for theaters, like the Casino, not situated in resort areas. The main problem, as Guild expressed it, was to keep ahead of continually rising prices, noting that when they began in 1941, it took about $1,300 per week to meet expenses, which had risen to $5,000 cost per week in 1957. Though expenses had quadrupled, their ticket prices had barely doubled in that time. Still, they ended up in the black.

The Republican lamented that only the lighter comedies brought the public out in large number, a common complaint of critics and theaters. But what does the public think?

Dennis Collins, former manager of Mountain Park, died at the end of that season. He had operated it with his brother John.

The 1958 season began with a chilly June, a "bone-chilling" June on the mountain as some papers reported, due to the capricious New England spring, but Jean Burns and Henry Barnard, featured in the thriller *Night Must Fall* received great notices. A few weeks later, Agatha Christie's *The Mousetrap* continued the audience appreciation for English murder mysteries.

The 1958 season top show was *The Matchmaker*, Thornton Wilder's much-produced favorite, which in another decade, of course, would be given the musical treatment as *Hello, Dolly!* Ruby Holbrook returned for this show and was well received as Mrs. Molloy. The *Springfield Union* thought the production was brilliant, and the

The Matchmaker, 1958, featuring John O'Connor as Horace Vandergelder, Ellen Andrews as Dolly Levi
and Ruby Holbrook as Mrs. Molloy. William Guild played August.

performances superb, with regular favorites John O'Connor as Horace Vandergelder and Ellen Andrews as Dolly Levi.

Endearing family comedies like *The Happiest Millionaire* always did well. *Separate Tables* was one of those plays more geared to please the acting company. Intense and challenging dramas *The Diary of Anne Frank* and *Cat on a Hot Tin Roof* were jewels in the 1959 season, but it was perhaps no surprise that *Teahouse of the August Moon* took the high spot of the season with receipts of $6,029.06, and an attendance of 4,759.

The proscenium was painted in the spring. The management had good news for the playgoers as regards their autos:

The owners of Mt. Park have agreed to let you park on the grass near the theater when the main parking lot is full and the ground is not too wet to drive on.

Advertising included all the usual local papers and would extend to the Beth El Brotherhood, Hadassah Program in Northampton, the Holyoke Police Relief, the Jewish Community Center High Holidays issue, *Kuryer Codzienny,* the Providence Hospital Guild, the *Westfield High Herald.* There was an ad in the program for WACE in Chicopee, "Western Mass.' Most Powerful Radio Signal" and a half-page for Steiger's announcing the marvel of the age: "We're Completely Air Conditioned." Another ad touted lawn furniture from McAuslan and Wakelin.

Miranda, the mermaid comedy, included Wini Haslam in the cast who as a child was on WJZ radio, and did *Wini 'n the Weather* on WHYN-TV, also from the Call Board Theater. Among fellow Call Board Theater member Jean Burns' acting jobs was playing Sylvia in *The Women* for the Doctors' and Dentists' Wives Association of Chicopee.

Twin sisters Joy and Joyce Renjillian were students at John J. Lynch Jr. High School in Holyoke. Other shows in the season included Richard Pervonga, a teacher of drama and English at West Springfield High School. Was using a non-Equity cast more and more a way to save money?

Businesses helping with props were acknowledged: Steiger's, Holyoke Hospital, the Holyoke Public Library, Holyoke Taxidermist. A.G. Spalding sporting goods in Chicopee was specifically thanked in the program for *The Happiest Millionaire*. The Kathleen Smith Music Shop still sold tickets downtown in the shop at 267-269 Maple Street next to the Strand Theater. To reserve tickets, phone Jefferson 8-8243.

Ads through the season included Kay's Drive-In Restaurant on Rt. 5 for steaks, chops, and seafood, Doane & Williams on Chicopee Street in the Willimansett section of Chicopee, and as always, Toto's, and the Hotel Northampton. Except for the Hotel Northampton, none of those businesses, as with most of the advertising that has been noted, exist any longer.

They closed the decade faltering financially, but evidently still hopeful for a receptive audience and yet another season.

From Barbara Bernard:

It was very interesting about The Valley Players, there was always a show live—at the same time during the day there would be a show in rehearsal that would go on next week, and at the same time there would be a reading of a show that would be the third week. So the people in The Valley Players really worked, and it has always been my feeling that to try to do a new show every week, which they did, was just too much. It was not financially successful, and it

was really difficult on the actors.

***

Early in 1959, The Valley Players scrapbook began to be filled with terrific notices of Hal Holbrook's success in *Mark Twain, Tonight!* on Broadway. A letter from Holbrook thanks the Guilds for their congratulatory telegram. His letter, which was also quoted in the *Holyoke Transcript-Telegram*, remarks:

I am especially glad about one angle of this success—it surely is a wonderful vindication of the faith you had in the show—a faith which has been very helpful to me.

In April 1959, a small newspaper clipping in The Valley Players' scrapbook revealed that a tent theater was to be established on the grounds at the Eastern States Exposition that summer, to be called Storrowton Music Fair. Storrowton, locals to the Pioneer Valley will know, is the name of the recreated nineteenth century village on the grounds of the exposition, a permanent living museum. Around this quiet oasis are the exposition buildings, including an impressive row of replicas of each of the New England statehouses. In September, the annual state fair, celebrating all six New England states is held, one of the largest in the country. Year-round events are held on the fairgrounds. This year, at the far western edge of the property, between the state houses and the dike along the Westfield River, was the spot for a huge circus-like tent to house the theatre-in-the-round of Storrowton Music Fair.

Their founder and manager was circus promoter Walwrath "Wally" J. Beach. A full slate of musicals in the big tent for its inaugural year would lead off with the lavish *The King and I* on June 15th and bring a new show each week running Monday through Saturday. The tent would seat 1,972 people, larger than the Casino by several hundred, and would accommodate a twelve-piece orchestra of local musicians under a different guest conductor for each show, as was the manner of traveling "packaged" shows.

Louise Mace, theatre critic for the *Springfield*

Janus 1959 Ellen Andrews and Ray Gandolf

Republican juggled both the traditional yearly editorial welcome back to The Valley Players, and marveled with great interest in the shiny newcomer:

Over a period of years a resident company, which is basically unchanged in management and varies in acting talent just enough to salt the old with the new, becomes like an old and trusted friend. The Valley Players are in this fortunate and well earned position. The Music Fair at Storrowton is a newcomer from which lively and merry doings are expected.

Each is a branch from the mother tree of Theater, and for centuries each branch has flourished and dispensed its refreshing fruits.

What its dress, however it is presented, wherever it wends its way across footlights, from the conventional proscenium or down the aisles, it will be theater.

That April, *Springfield Union* also reported on the upcoming season planned by Jean and Carlton Guild in the "Valley Players' headquarters at 176 Lincoln Street, the Guild home. They discussed casting and plays with Ted Tiller and Ellen Andrews, "the company's New York representatives who had come to Holyoke for the first intensive conference of the year." Good news for longtime fans: Hugh Franklin would rejoin the company after a nine-year absence for a role as Mr. Frank in *The Diary of Anne Frank* in August. He was the husband of novelist, and former Valley Player, author Madeleine L'Engle. Bertram Tanswell, after a five-year absence was also coming "home."

Advertising was placed in the *Agawam Independent*, the *Agawam News*, the *Berkshire Eagle*, the *Easthampton Inquirer*, the *Westfield News Advertiser*, and the *West Springfield Record*, and newspapers as far up the Connecticut River Valley as Vermont.

Janus was to be the eighteenth season opener, a Broadway comedy, with Ellen Andrews, Jean Guild, Ted Tiller, and also Bertram Tanswell in the cast.

"We have to plan a 12-week season very carefully in advance," Mrs. Guild explained, "in order to provide variety for our audiences, to use our resident and our guest actors to best advantage, and to distribute our technical staff's most demanding production loads. As a result, the release of a play we hadn't really counted on—or the loss of a play we felt sure of—can cause a lot of other changes. It's not just a simple matter of taking out one play and putting in another. Right now we're very excited and pleased over the prospects for our 18ᵗʰ season, in the course of which we shall present our 200ᵗʰ production at the Mt. Park Casino."

Also in this newspaper edition, another article on the recent success of Valley Players alumnus Hal Holbrook, who was then appearing at the Forty-first Street Theater in New York, where *Mark Twain Tonight!* had opened Monday night. He was called "leading man with the Valley Players" in 1951, 1952, and 1953, "and who tried out his one-man show, *Mark Twain Tonight!* there the week of June 10, 1957." His play was now making "a resounding hit" in New York.

Every one of the metropolitan reviewers wrote of Mr. Holbrook's portrayal in glowing terms. Tuesday morning there was a long queue at the box office and a somewhat dazed but extremely happy Mr. Holbrook finds it difficult to believe this had happened to him.

Knowing that eventually he would chance his impersonation of Mark Twain on Broadway, Mr. Holbrook chose the Valley Players' Casino as the scene of his "big stage" tryout of the program. Previously, he had presented the Mark Twain characterization in miniature, as it were, at a small New York night club, and it attracted uptown attention. Also, Mr. Holbrook has toured most of the country in appearances before clubs and civic organizations.

Walter Kerr, drama critic of the Herald Tribune *concludes his notice, "Mr. Holbrook has, of course, good material to work with. What with his own sly and patient inventiveness, and the bland, bare-faced howlers his author has bequeathed him,* Mark Twain Tonight! *is rich, robust, and mightily entertaining."*

Critic Arthur Gelb of the *New York Times*, called it:

...an extraordinary show...The result can only be described as brilliant...Everything about the evening is perfect—the intimate theater, Mr. Holbrook's faultless characterization and the uproariously funny selections from Twain that he has chosen.

Don Grigware notes:

Hal Holbrook was a class act and his wife at the time was lovely Ruby. He did Mark Twain there, and years later I saw him in it on Broadway and went backstage to tell him that I had been an admirer for many years. He was very quiet, just smiled and thanked me.

Hal Holbrook played Mark Twain many times over many decades (and at the time of this writing, continues to bring his marvelous performance to audiences across the nation). In 1982, he played in Springfield at the Symphony Hall, and was interviewed by the *Springfield Union*:

The first performance (of Mark Twain) I ever gave that was a full-length performance in its present format of two hours in a theater [rather than a school or cabaret] *was at the Valley Players...*

He recalled of his time as a member of the company:

I used to have a lot of fun on the stage...As the season wore on we'd get a little tired and it was easy to find things amusing. We'd kind of break up a little on the stage. Something would strike us as so funny we'd have a hard time holding a straight face.

New to the company in the 1959 season was Ray Gandolf, who would come to be known in later decades as a television news writer, a sportscaster and anchor, and in the late 1980s as the co-host, along with Linda Ellerbee of NBC's pop culture documentary series *Our World*. Gandolf's wife, Blanche Cholet, a veteran of television and regional theatre, also performed in some shows at the Casino that season. Ruby Holbrook was back for a play that summer.

Half-page ads for Lestoil appeared in the program this season, a reflection of the support of local businessman Jacob Barowsky. The product was said to clean lawn furniture, cars, all painted surfaces, and golf balls.

An anonymous contributor to this book:

As a teenager during the Valley Players' last few years I was one of the crew that directed theater-goers to spaces in the Casino's parking lot. Actually, there wasn't much of a lot—flashlights in hand, we pointed drivers to spots among the trees surrounding the place. When the show was a hit we stuck around to help folks exit the park; otherwise, they were on their own. The hits were mostly musicals: The Boy Friend *and* Little Mary Sunshine *among them. Besides the two bucks we were paid per night (three on weekends) we were sometimes given popcorn and we could watch the show for free on any night we worked. As a result, even today I can do a credible job on most of the songs from those two shows.*

Side by side reviews began the 1959 theater season for Storrowton Music Fair and the Valley players in the *Springfield Daily News*. Reviewer Carroll Robbins noted the chilly weather was a challenge at the Casino on the mountain, but the "coat-clad" audience enjoyed the opener, the comedy *Janus*. Special praise was given to Jean Guild and newcomer Ray Gandolf, and resident funny man Ted Tiller.

W. Harley Rudkin reviewed the musical *The King and I* at Storrowton with a plaudit that seems, in hindsight, so much like an opening salvo:

A new and refreshing era of theater came to this area last evening with the gala opening of the Storrowton Music Fair's presentation of The King and I. *This was the night that a great many Western Massachusetts theatergoers had been waiting for and they flocked to the music tent…*

For those who may not be familiar with the physical techniques of theater in the round, some of the effects may be surprising.

You never can be quite sure where you are going to see an actor, or from what direction a voice will come.

It might be right next to you, or somewhere in the audience on the other side of the tent.

But the overall impression is what is important, and the capacity audience at Storrowton last evening obviously was enjoying itself…

This is good theater in a most desirable setting. It is something we need.

Louise Mace of the *Springfield Union*:

A new theater era broke over Springfield Monday night with the opening of the spacious and colorful Music Fair at Storrowton. Wally Beach, who watched the marquee lights go out for the last time at Court Square two years ago, has seen his great purpose realized: to restore living theater to Greater Springfield. He has done so in the grand manner.

That theatre had never left "the greater Springfield" area must have been a source of chagrin to Carlton and Jean Guild, who cut this article out of the paper and pasted in their Valley Player's scrapbook of the year 1959. That they welcomed another theater with camaraderie is certain, but the attention paid the new enterprise must have left them stunned. Their world was about to change due to a tangerine-and-green-striped tent.

So chilly was opening night for both theaters that the *Springfield Union* called it "parka and mitten weather." Another particular problem both summer theaters occasionally shared was unique to the Pioneer Valley—the deafening roar of the military aircraft from Chicopee's Westover Air Force Base. They were, in that era of the Cold War, an almost daily occurrence, and unsettling for those who grew up in the valley—but could be quite frightening for visitors not accustomed to life in the flight path.

But Wally Beach weathered both the weather and the bombers, with congratulatory telegrams from many, including Springfield's own long-ago stage star Julia Sanderson, and for good luck, a talisman from the old Court Square Theater: a wooden "belaying pin" used to fasten curtains high above the stage, a gift from a Gilmore descendent of the original Court Square owner.

The *Springfield Sunday Republican* devoted an entire "pull out section" to the opening of Storrowton Music Fair, with pages and pages of huge display ads from area businesses wishing luck to the new venture. To be sure, theatre was in Wally Beach's family, and in his blood, and his energetic promotion was something which the Guilds of The Valley Players could only look upon with awe. They had received many years of faithful support from the local press, with a gratifying amount of coverage not only from the dailies in the area, but from several weeklies as well in an era where just about every publication had a theatre critic on its staff, where covering local theatre was just as much a factor in circulation as hard news or high school sports.

But Beach's commandeering of the attention of the local press was masterful. The Valley Players may have gotten its share of editorials and feature stories, but the *advertising* that local business placed in the papers in honor of Storrowton's opening had to make the Guild's mouths water. With painstaking perseverance, The Valley Players had slowly increased the pages of their programs and garnered more local advertising to support the programs, but if Jacob Barowsky had not stepped in this season with a generous donation, The Valley Players might not have withstood all the attention Storrowton was getting.

The King and I had a cast of forty, and the techies backstage numbered sixty. One hundred people on the payroll just to put up this single show. Not all the shows produced at Storrowton would be this grand, but it was a spectacular opener.

A Storrowton play later that month, *Say Darling*, was the last review published by *Springfield Union* theatre critic Louise Mace, who typed the journalist's old-time code "-30-" at the end of her column for the last time. Storrowton presented her with a bouquet of American Beauty roses

before the show started. She had begun her career in 1917, a new graduate of Emerson College in Boston, when she was hired by publisher Sherman Bowles, a descendent of that famed Bowles family of Springfield newspaper publishers, for the *Springfield Republican*. When she began her career, Springfield was a lively theatre town, with many vaudeville houses, and Broadway touring shows coming through town. She had interviewed Walter Hampden when he played *Hamlet* at Court Square in 1921, and she was quoted in her farewell in the paper, "I saw the Court Square Theater rise to its pinnacle in the world of theater… I saw it die."

She closed her roll-top desk at the newspaper office for the last time, remarking, "I am convinced the living theater is indestructible. I wish it were."

Must there always be a fall, an inevitable third act of going out of business for theaters, especially in smaller communities?

By July, the typical summer heat had returned to warm things up in the valley, and *Dracula* played at the Casino on the mountain in another creative change of pace. *Teahouse of the August Moon* was the big show of the season, for which a beat-up Army Jeep was found and moved on stage, and well as the loan of a local goat.

The *Holyoke Transcript-Telegram* devoted a few-pages spread to the Valley Players with many photos to celebrate the 200th show. In late July, Ruby Holbrook was featured in Agatha Christie's *Spider's Web*, and her husband Hal showed up to cheer her on opening night, surprising his wife, and delighting the audience at the visit of a favorite son who'd made good. Holbrook's visit to the theater drew more headlines than did the play.

That August, the *Springfield Republican* also turned its attention back to The Valley Players with a rotogravure photo section on the 200th production.

There were a string of comedies, and Jean Guild stole the show in *Anniversary Waltz* as the interfering mother-in-law. Ellen Andrews and Ray Gandolf were the couple; Miss Andrews was by now a favorite, and Gandolf was becoming a reliable and appealing leading man.

The Diary of Anne Frank was produced this season, having made a huge hit on Broadway four years earlier. Performances were lauded as outstanding, with special note of Hugh Franklin's being lured out of retirement to play the role of Mr. Frank, and Katherine Henryk, who played Anne, knew something very personal about the material. She had been born in Poland. Her parents were theatre professionals, and they became refugees at the outbreak of World War II, fleeing to Portugal, then to the United States. Her father worked on radio for *The Voice of America* and Radio Free Europe. It was noted of Katherine in the program:

It is a story that comes closer to her life than to most.

Jean Guild was listed in the programs as General Manager, Carlton Guild was Business Manager, Dorothy M. Crane was Production Manager, with Louie Mudgett still on community publicity.

At the end of the season, it was reckoned that The Valley Players might not open in 1960. They had averaged some 3,000 per week attendance, down from 3,700 weekly attendance in the previous year. *Teahouse of the August Moon* was the best-attended show. Carlton Guild was quoted in the *Springfield Union*:

"People just aren't as interested in drama as they were years ago."

The Valley Players finished up the season with *Cat on a Hot Tin Roof*, with Katherine Henryk playing Maggie the Cat, another of the remarkable transformations from one week to the next in a company that did not have a star system; everyone displayed versatility in tackling a wide range of roles, from leads to minor roles. Ray Gandolf was Brick. Jean Guild and Walter Boughton were Big Mama and Big Daddy. It received excellent reviews and much praise. The reviews were quickly followed by wondering if The Valley Players would return the next year.

Cat on a Hot Tin Roof broke even; *The Diary of Anne Frank*, which received glowing reviews, suffered a loss of somewhere between $200 to $300.

Over at the Storrowton Music Fair, their highest weekly attendance was for *Oklahoma!*, a sellout at 14,000 people that week. They were to end their first season in the black, rare for new theaters in the United States.

A *Transcript-Telegram* article of September 3rd was probably the first to openly suggest that Storrowton was taking the audience away. William Guild concurred that this was his parents' assertion as well. They may not yet have imagined it would mean the end of The Valley Players:

What killed it was the Storrowton Music Tent over in West Springfield, Mass. We started to lose money on it the minute they opened.

Night Must Fall 1958, Jean Guild and Henry Barnard

Anastasia 1956 Howard Ledig and Ellen Andrews

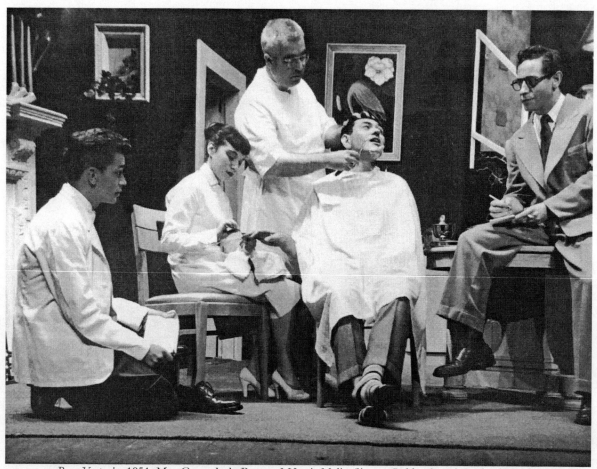

Born Yesterday 1951, Mac Gress, Judy Barger, J Harris Melia, Simon Oakland, and Gaylord Mason

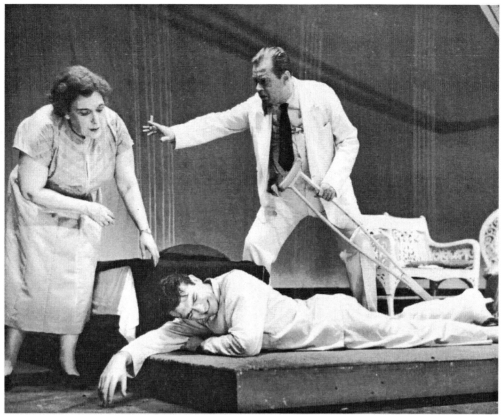

Cat on a Hot Tin Roof 1959, Jean Guild, Ray Gandolf, and Walter L. Boughton

Father of the Bride 1953 Mac Gress, Edward Fuller, Francis Donovan Jr, Anne Pitoniak, and Claire Kirby

Grammercy Ghost 1952 Bertram Tanswell, Ruby Holbrook, Edward Fuller, and Hal Holbrook

Late Love 1954, Jean Guild, Sylvia Meredith, and Ellen Andrews

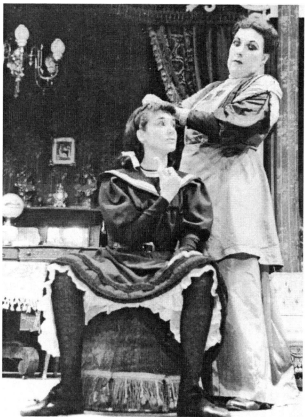

Gigi 1953, Claire Kirby, and Jean Guild

Dear Delinquent 1959, Katherine Henryk, Blanche Cholet,
and Ray Gandolf

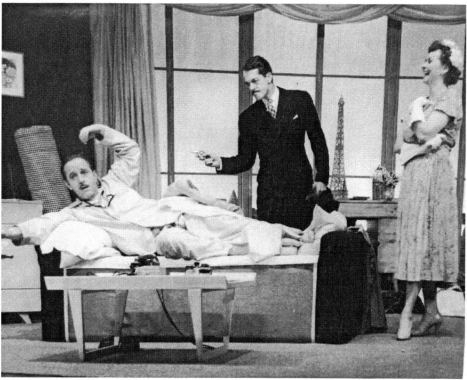

Nina 1953, Joseph Foley, John O'Connor, and Jackson Perkins

Will Any Gentleman 1959, Katherine Henryk, Bertram Tanswell, and Molly Hosman

Witness for the Prosecution 1957, John Gaffney, Don Thomas, Ronald Irving, Ellen Andrews, and John O'Connor. Neil Doherty photo.

Teahouse of the August Moon 1959

The tickets were very inexpensive. Of course, they were up at Mountain Park and there was a certain time every night that Mountain Park used to blow off fireworks. I think it was around 9:30, as soon as it got dark. So they always had to stop the plays at that time. They were so thrilled when they could time their intermissions at that time.

George Murphy, who worked as an apprentice at the Mt. Tom Playhouse in the 1964 and 1965 seasons, could vouch for this practice continuing in the 1960s:

That's true. They really did that. When I was up there, it wasn't as constant as that, but I remember once or twice, not that many times, where that would happen. And people would start migrating over there. I think they might announce it in the park, and they would have a short display. And as soon as they broke, you know, for intermission, they'd have sparkling, all this stuff, and sometimes it would run a little long. Or sometimes — two times it happened, if it ran a little long, then the theater, you know, we'd wait. The actors would probably get upset, I don't know.

Paul Rohan, who was taken to the theater many times as a child by his parents:

You could just go up there and watch the fireworks. You know, the intent was if you were in the area, you'd hit the midway and spend some money. But the fireworks were free and they always had, like, a fire truck standing by. The final firework was usually an American flag.

Barbara Bernard also recalls the refreshment stand that sold birch beer soda.

Oh, it was so refreshing, and everybody raved about it. And sure enough, if you were lucky, you were having your cold birch beer and the fireworks would go off. And when they were done, you'd go back to your seat for the second act.

William Guild remembers:

Oh, yes, Tuesday night. Tuesday night we started at 8:00 instead of 8:30. Everybody did 8:30 back in those days. In fact, Noel Coward wrote a one-act called Tonight at 8:30, but yeah, we would stop the show. We would time it with the fireworks, and then the audience would traipse up

CHAPTER 7

"What's Happened to the Theatre?"
Danny Kaye – "White Christmas"

How does theatre fit into a community, become part of the flavor and character of a community? It needs a community for support. Does the community need the theatre?

A Holyoke newspaper, undated, rejoiced that the Valley Players "have almost signed a lease for their Casino home for next year and with options for yet two more years." The post-War era welcomed live theatre as a right, privilege, and reward for all that had been endured for a generation, as noted a long and laudatory editorial, "Summer theaters are now the order of New England's holiday season." It notes that The Valley Players' audience came from all over the Connecticut Valley.

It would be a grave lessening of our joy in summer living if the Valley Players could not be summoned back…we, as a play going community, are grateful for the prosperity of our friends the Valley Players who can now maintain a director of stage settings like Hal Shafer…the nightly applause for his décor when the curtain goes up must be music.

Barbara Bernard recalls:

Auntie Mame 1960 - featuring Sue Ann Gilfillan in the title role, with Jean Guild as Mother Burnside

the hill to watch the fireworks. And traipse back down, and on we'd go. And I remember that vividly, being a kid, you know, it was exciting to me.

Nobody knew then in the warm summer night, the stars sailing above Mt. Tom, that there would be only a handful of seasons left, and that The Valley Players were to be soon at the end of their timeline.

Carlton Guild spread the advertising dollar as far as he could to all local papers, weeklies and dailies, and they read as a roll call of community newspapers that, for the post part, no longer exist. Train fare and drayage expenses had lowered to $437.40. Train service wasn't what it was anymore since the privately owned railroads were scuttling their passenger service in favor of more lucrative freight contracts.

The top grossing show of the 1960 season was *Auntie Mame*, at $6,388.44, with an attendance of 4,088. Lowest receipts came in for the drama *The Desperate Hours* at $2,929.11 and a low attendance of 2,266. The season represented a careful mix of the old chestnuts like *Life with Father* and *Arsenic and Old Lace*, and newer plays, but those were still very well known such as *Picnic*, and *Sunrise at Campobello*.

In 1961 The Valley Players donated to the Holyoke Police Ball, while the late Broadway hit *A Majority of One* was slated for the season, as well as *Inherit the Wind*, and *Ah Wilderness*, and a charming bit of nostalgia—parody this time—*The Boy Friend*.

In the late 1950s, drive-in movies had reached a zenith, and though hampered by a limited season in New England, the valley saw a surprising number of them being carved out of the woods and farms at this time: the Parkway Drive-In on Parker Street in East Springfield, the Round Hill Drive-In in Springfield, the Hadley Drive-In on Route 9 in Hadley, and the East Windsor Drive-In just over the line in Connecticut, Chicopee's Air-Line, the Riverdale in West Springfield, and the Sundown.

Television, of course, had begun to hit its stride and was a most formidable competition for the attention of their traditional audience of World War II vets, now in middle age, that might have preferred to stay home.

***

The 1960 season was noted, by the end of that summer, to be:

The most arduous of production seasons that we have ever presented.

But a great deal of work had been done before the season started. An apprentice program was expanded in which young people between the ages of sixteen and twenty-two would be accepted to learn theatre craft, taking lessons, building sets, working backstage, even taking minor roles. It was a program for which students from New England, New York, and as far away as California applied and paid tuition to attend. They would quality for Equity membership.

These apprentices took classes three mornings a week, and worked many hours in the theater, including appearing in plays. They received instruction in dance, makeup, stage technique, and other aspects of theatre. Half of the fifteen slots were taken by students local to the greater Springfield area.

A roster of new and decidedly young faces joined the regular company as actors: James Secrest, and Nuella Dierking, who had stock and TV experience. James Bernard, who had appeared at Lakewood, was a Holyoke native. The *Holyoke Transcript-Telegram* photographed the company outside the Casino. It was a young cast, a vibrant

new beginning, though veterans Ted Tiller, Jean Burns, and Walter Boughton were back, and in front, kneeling on the ground was the ever-frail-appearing but resilient Dorothy Crane, back for her nineteenth year of directing.

James Secrest later became a good friend of William Guild and his wife Hannah:

Mart Crowley wrote a play about a party Jimmy gave called Boys in the Band. *[NOTE: which opened off-Broadway in 1968, made into a film in 1970.] And Jimmy was supposed to play the lead in it off-Broadway, went on to be a Broadway show and then when on to be a movie, but he and Mart had a falling out, and so Mart took him out of the play and put in Kenny Nelson, who did it very well. He was playing Jimmy. I watched the movie again about ten years ago and it's very interesting because Mart Crowley had given him a lot of Jimmy's characteristics and he picked up them and did a very good, not an imitation, but he played it like Jimmy would have played it.*

William Guild also, as an adult, renewed ties with actress Helen Harrelson long after The Valley Players ended:

I stayed in touch with Helen for many years. When I was living, Hannah and I, in Manhattan, she was working some play in New York and so we had her take my car, because I didn't want to keep switching sides of the street every day. And she took the car out to where they lived, which is, I don't know, Westchester County, I think, and drove it in for a couple years. She was a sweetheart.

The Valley Players received a Holyoke Chamber of Commerce salute, and public support from Mayor Samuel Resnic, who urged Holyokers to attend the shows.

They led off strongly with *Auntie Mame*, with Sue Ann Gilfillan in the title role. She had played the same role in Williamstown the previous summer. In a departure from previous seasons, the names of feature players were placed above the title on the program. It was the largest opening night audience in years, and a photo of the audience in their seats was taken from the stage and published in the *Transcript-Telegram*. Men in suits and ties,

The Desperate Hours 1960, spectacular set by Robert T. Williams

women in summer frocks, pearls, hats, sweaters draped over their shoulders. No one would dream of attending even a movie dressed casually, let alone live theater.

The Guilds' son William joined the crew as a stage manager this season. A new actor in minor roles this season was John Ulmer, who would later direct at StageWest in West Springfield. William Guild would work under him as a stage manager there, eventually taking over directing chores himself.

Picnic was critically successful, called "brilliant." *No Time For Sergeants* continued the string of familiar late hits, undoubtedly chosen to strike a chord with the audience, and the sure-fire audience pleaser, the chestnut *Life with Father*, with Walter Boughton in the title role. Jean Burns, who had taken many minor roles as a guest actor, had now joined the company as a regular. "She was a good actress," William Guild recalls, "Very nice person." Like Burns, who had been acquired from local community theatre and had performed in several shows for The Valley Players from 1952

to 1957, and became a regular member of the resident Equity company in 1958, there were more and more cast members gleaned from the ranks of amateurs; perhaps, along with the use of student apprentices, this was an indication of management trying to reduce costs by avoiding higher salaries.

William Guild notes:

Equity allowed a certain percentage of the cast to be non-professional. I think they opened that up a little bit more back at that time.

Sunrise at Campobello and *Mister Roberts* rounded out a roster of popular plays with which the audience would certainly be familiar. An audience, it was evidently reckoned, would turn out, if not always for comedies and lighter fare, then at least for plays which were already familiar to them.

It was another family affair for *Arsenic and Old Lace* when Jean Guild played a lead role as one of the sweet, but homicidal, sisters; husband Carlton played one of their victims, and son William was

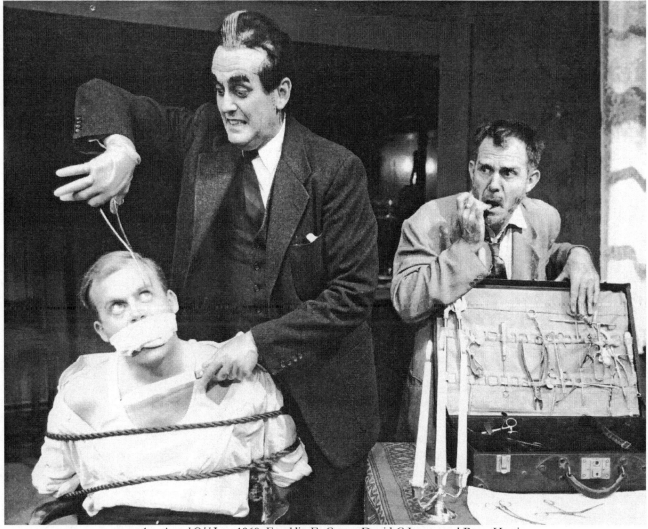

Arsenic and Old Lace 1960, Franklin E. Cover, David C Jones, and Peter Harris

undoubtedly in the wings "on book." Jean Burns shared the lead with Jean Guild as the two dotty Brewster sisters.

The program notes for this show recalled when The Valley Players had originally presented this comedy in 1945. Both Jean and Carlton Guild were in the cast that time as well. The management reminisced of those days when Jean:

...was also primarily responsible for housing and feeding almost the entire company in the big Steiger place in Wyckoff Park.

The Desperate Hours had Jack Gianino and James Secrest as armed intruders to the suburban home of Walter Boughton and Jean Burns. The set for this production, designed by Robert T. Williams,

was exceptional: a two-level set of the house looking so much like a child's dollhouse, with all the rooms exposed so the audience could see the action in every room as it was happening at once to the members of the family held hostage by gunmen. Alternating with the main set were two smaller sets that were moved on and off some *twelve* times. The audience gasped when the curtain went up and revealed a two-story house.

It was noted in one rave review that a couple of bats got loose in the Casino, attracted by the stage spotlights, and a toad just off stage appeared to be watching the show from a slit under one of the doors on set. Wildlife on the mountain was usually more discreet, but the park was cheek by jowl with the wilderness, so it wasn't unheard of for the neighbors to drop in.

Arsenic and Old Lace 1960, Walter Boughton, Peter Harris, David C. Jones, Jean Guild, and Jean Burns

Tea and Sympathy rounded off the season with mixed reviews. There were no rumors that it would be the last season this time, though the farewell articles did express the hope that they would return, no longer taking it for granted that they would. "Certainly they deserve more support than we have noticed on opening nights," wrote the reviewer from the *Springfield Daily News*.

Peter Duryea, son of the famous Hollywood actor Dan Duryea, was an apprentice this season, an Amherst College student and acting hopeful, who had a small role in *Tea and Sympathy*, and would be best known in the next decade for many television guest roles.

The end of the season brought predictions for the next summer, including the possibility of a musical to celebrate their twentieth anniversary. The end of the summer also meant a new epoch

in the lives of the Jean and Carlton Guild, as their son William began his freshman year at Boston University in the school's Theatre Division. He had recently graduated from Holyoke High School. He had spent the summer as one of the two stage managers for The Valley Players.

Perhaps not so coincidentally, his mother Jean Guild began conducting classes in voice, diction, and acting for students from eight years old to eighteen at the Elsie Cappel School of Dancing on High Street, as a way to help pay for her son's tuition.

William Guild offers a reflection on his years growing up "above the shop," as the saying goes:

It was an enchanting time for me. It wasn't really the real world. I didn't fit in with the kids in high school. We didn't have bullies or anything like that back then, this

Life with Father 1960, Walter L. Boughton as Father, and Shirley Bryan as Vinnie, with Marsha Pettit, and James Secrest as Clarence Jr.

was the fifties. But I just didn't have many friends in high school. I had a few, but I was much more interested in the theatre and films, and we did have touring companies in Springfield from time to time during those years, the late fifties.

Of his parents:

Distant would be the way I'd describe them. They never argued. I never heard an argument. I never heard a raised voice during all my childhood and teenage years, ever. And so I had a very odd upbringing because I didn't have any siblings and they were only children, so I was the only child of only children. They just didn't communicate well. I don't know what "well" would have been at that time in my life, but I just never saw a display of affection or a

display of anger. And if I ever raised my voice, which was rare, my mother would say, "We don't do that in our house." And that's how I was raised, so it was very frustrating for [his wife] Hannah, when she would want to argue about something that I would get quieter and quieter.

I believe they both loved me. I certainly loved them. I loved working with my dad when we were taking tickets together one year. I loved cueing my mom, taking her through her lines.

Don Grigware lends another child's perspective on the world of the Casino. His father, Don Sr., had an office job, but worked at Mountain Park on weekends and some weeknights in the

166

Mister Roberts 1960

summer, usually running concessions in the park and also at the Casino.

He chatted with the actors, got autographs for me and would always say what a nice person this or that one was, but he was a white-collar by day, blue-collar by night guy who had little interest in entertainment except to watch The Red Skelton Show *on TV; he absolutely loved him—so did I! Now my mother, she was another story altogether—Irish from a family of ten kids, a singer and would have been a great actress, had she been given the opportunity.*

My dad would take me with him to the Playhouse summers and I would roam around trying not to get into trouble. I would peek into the parking lot and watch the actors arrive about an hour before curtain and then when the performance began, I would sneak into the theatre, crouch down behind the seats of the last row and watch the play. Carlton Guild, who ran the theatre at the time of the Valley Players, did not want me in the theatre and was very strict about me not being in there, so I had to sneak in and out when the house lights were out. I think I was so infatuated by watching the actors strut around onstage and speak with perfect diction, I knew that if I had my

druthers, I would become an actor...I wish I had been less shy and had auditioned.

In the program notes during the 1954 season, the Guilds offered a discussion on the philosophy of summer theatre:

Why, then, it is reasonable to ask, does anyone get involved in the producing of plays? As far as New York City is concerned, we don't know. But for ourselves, it's different. Production costs are still very high (about $4,000.00 a week) considering possible box-office returns; and one or two fluffs, misses, or whatever you want to call them, might put us out of business. We have to be good, for your money—and for less money than you would pay, as we have paid on occasion, to see something like half a show at an uncomfortable angle with 50% visibility of stage in a metropolitan theater.

***

In 1961 Holyoke began to lose its enormous industrial base as factories were sold, moved South, or just went out of business. A large Puerto Rican migration to the valley and to Holyoke in search of employment was unfortunately met with fewer opportunities because of the dwindling manufacturing. In 1961, the Skinner company sold out to Indian Head

Mills, which in turn, closed a year later. It had been Holyoke's oldest family-owned business. All over the alley factory closings in the 1960s, including Indian Motocycle, Westinghouse, and the Armory in Springfield, changed the tenor of life.

Sunrise at Campobello 1960, Franklin E Cover and Mary Holland

In 1961, Interstate 91, which in future would also, like the Mass. Pike, become a major artery in the area, finally crept up from Connecticut as far north as the Springfield–Connecticut line. The section from Hartford to Springfield opened. In 1963 the proposed section to build from Springfield to Holyoke received approval. By the end of the decade, I-91 would cut a swath through Holyoke, and through Mt. Tom. Between the Pike and 91, Holyoke was X marks the spot. Did I-91 increase access to the tri-city area, or only make it easier to pass it by?

Conversely, the Boston and Albany Railroad, which had brought people directly in to

downtowns for generations, closed thirty-four passenger stations across Massachusetts.

Polio, despite the Salk vaccine, was still an issue in 1960 as Springfield schools delayed opening to October 2nd due to an outbreak of infantile paralysis.

The drive-in theaters were still thriving, but we were starting to lose the neighborhood second-run movie houses: the Bijou and the Globe in Holyoke, and Chicopee's Willow. The Majestic in West Springfield would, decades hence, experience a rebirth, but not as a movie theater—as a "legitimate" playhouse.

The Gazebo 1960, David C. Jones, Ted Tiller, and Jean Burns

***

Between the Valley Players and Storrowton, summer theatre had reached a wonderful and exciting climax in the Pioneer Valley. Barbara Bernard, between writing play reviews and hosting her television show, was very busy:

My husband loved the fact that he got to meet all these famous stars. The plan was on Monday night I would go to the Storrowton. It opened on a Monday, and then on Tuesday on my show I would interview the stars. If it ran for two weeks, or if they had a kind of a slow run of tickets, Wally Beach would call to see if maybe I could interview somebody else. So quite often, I would interview maybe two people, the star and then somebody else from the show. That Tuesday night, my husband and I would go to the opening night at the Valley Players, and then on Wednesday, I would interview people from that, but usually the star. Sometimes, because it was a repertory theater, I would have the same person on maybe two or three times during the summer because they may have a lead in this week's play, and next week they would have a minor part.

In 1961, Mountain Park owner John Collins died at the age of fifty-six. His son continued at the helm of the park, and expanded it. Big bands at the pavilion gave way to rock and roll—The Animals, Herman's Hermits, The Beach Boys and

others. It became a favorite spot for high school proms, and sock hops with Phil Dee, the disc jockey from WHYN-radio.

The Guilds sent out a letter in May 1961 announcing complete redecoration of the Casino, with new paint, new lobby and restrooms, new carpeting, seat covers.

None of this could we have done ourselves. The financial resources which we lacked have been provided as a public service to you, to the community, and to our entire area. Without this support, our theater could not have continued. With it, and with your support as theatergoers, it will enter upon a new life.

Admission was kept at a maximum price of $2.50, "far lower than that of other professional companies." The fee for being a Patron was $27.50 for the entire season of eleven weeks: first choice of seats, with the ability to change tickets for other nights.

They also installed a new amplification system "designed to bring equal audibility to all parts of the auditorium."

Although the Valley Players have long prided themselves on their ability to make their voices carry easily to the 27th row, there has always been a slight "dead" spot about two-thirds of the way back…

The actors never saw the set until a few hours before opening curtain. They continued to rehearse in a barn on Northampton Street near Lincoln Street.

The 1961 season saw the use of better paper for its programs, the cover with a splash of orange in it, a more decorative departure. Bigger ads, more of them, included regulars Dreikorn's bread, Steiger's, Holyoke Water Power Company, as well as for the Schine Inn in Chicopee, just off the turnpike – a sprawling motel with seven restaurants, cocktail lounge, four bowling lanes, 200 "luxurious rooms," and a pool. Construction had been completed September 1959, the newest in the chain of Schine Enterprises hotels. Some stars appearing at the Casino a few years' hence would stay here, and at the Howard Johnson's on

Northampton Street, no longer staying at downtown hotels.

There was also an ad for the new Mt. Tom Ski Area, now sharing the mountain above the park, which had opened in December 1960. The full back ad on one program was taken by Steiger's, which announced not only the continuing miracle of air conditioning, but the availability of shopping by "charge-a-plate."

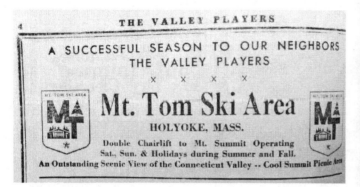

The Valley Players' 1961 scrapbook also contains a clipping about Jacob L. Barowsky of Lestoil Products, which had been sold to Standard International Corp., who donated $24,000 to Valley Players, $15,000 of which was used to improve the sixty-two-year old theater. The rest of the money went for advertising, mostly in newspapers and a bit of direct mail, but $4,500 was earmarked for a thirteen-week TV spot drive.

In an interview for this book, Barbara Bernard recalls the Barowskys, as "very lovely people (who were also neighbors). They had a grandson who was interested in theatre. So they decided to subsidize the Valley Players."

The programs carried a new roster of "angels," with Mr. and Mrs. Jacob Barowsky, and Mrs. Seymour Barowsky topping the list. Others included William Dwight, Otto Dreikorn, Thomas Epstein, Robert Steiger, Mr. & Mrs. William H. Hubbard (of the Skinner family), and Marcus Printing, Hadley Falls Trust Company, Holyoke National Bank, Orr Cadillac, Hano, Co., Inc. manufacturer of business forms (this was still Paper City), Holyoke Savings Bank, Mechanics

Savings Bank, People's Savings Bank, an ad for Dorothy Dodd women's clothing store downtown, and for Yale Gentin on Riverdale Street in West Springfield. The program grew to twenty-four pages. Toto's restaurant, which had closed, was missing in the ranks.

Jacob and Adeline Barowsky,
and Holyoke Mayor Samuel Resnic

Carlton Guild's program notes were less folksy now, less like introspective essays and more like business reports. Missing was longtime community publicity representative and sometime actress Louise "Louie" Mudgett. David C. Jones was welcomed back. He had spent a season touring in regional theatre, including a gig at the new Storrowton Music Fair in West Springfield.

New to the company was actor James Coco, winner of the off-Broadway Obie Award of the previous season. Critic Robert Levey of the *Holyoke Transcript-Telegram* did not feel *Inherit the Wind* was up to par:

...did not meet the challenge of the play, despite the admirable efforts of the two principals James Coco and Walter Boughton, the play moved awkwardly, revealing the

The Boy Friend 1961, Sure Le Page, Ellen Leef, Denis Donahue, David Black, Barbara Gingras, Patricia Hohol, Linda Jorczak, Peter Beck, Eloyce Buijnicki, Diane Mroz, Valentine Doyle, James Secrest, Susan Lance, Ian Brown, Ronni Bloom, Louise Hesse, James Pompeii, Susan Cansino, Peter Harris, Louise Magee, Barbara Bernard, Robin Barnes.

haste of preparation. It was an enjoyable evening of theater, but it was also an example of a fine script receiving a less than fine presentation…the sets were mediocre and manipulation of the large cast by Dorothy Crane was at times unwieldy…the performances of Boughton and Coco are, in themselves, worth seeing.

Walter Boughton was also busy as the director of plays at the Kirby Memorial Theater at AmherstCollege in Amherst, Massachusetts. It was his third summer with The Valley Players. He also had experience playing summer theatre in "packaged shows" (which would be the kind of theatre done by the Mt. Tom Playhouse in 1964, and by the Storrowton Music Fair) where visiting stars and principal players travel from theater to theater (and where he had played in *Cat on a Hot Tin Roof* opposite Hollywood star Veronica Lake), but he declared he preferred performing within a resident stock company, such as The Valley Players. Boughton inevitably played "heavy" roles.

Polly Campbell and David C. Jones were company favorites, whose comic roles in the mystery *Rebecca*, based on the celebrated novel by Daphne du Maurier, playing Beatrice and Roger Lacey, seemed almost to outshine the featured

actors. The *Holyoke Transcript Telegram* noted that the minute they made their entrance for the costume ball scene, they received audience applause. The *Agawam News* remarked, "Those two don't even have to try!"

Sai Springwell, who played the ingénue role of the young second Mrs. de Winter, was praised by The *West Springfield Record*:

Audiences at the Mountain Park Casino this week are being pleasurably treated to an annual experience—that of seeing a bright, fresh, new star rising on the horizon; an unmistakable emergence of a definitive stage personality from an unexpected source. Summer theaters usually make use of well known stars as attractions to go with their stock companies but it is not too often that they produce stars from the ranks of their companies.

Just where in the drama we first realized we were witnessing a star in the making, escapes us now, but take our word for it, this girl is a child of destiny. She's just theater, through and through.

Reviewer Florence Moreno of the *Agawam News* advised her readers to: "Don't walk—run! To the Casino this week to see *The Boy Friend*. You'll have the most delightful evening!"

The Boy Friend 1961, James Pompeii front, rear: Susanne Cansino, Barbara Bernard, Peter Beck, Judith Love, David C. Jones.

The Boy Friend was the musical send-up of 1920s frivolity, with featured a large cast, some of whom had been in the off-Broadway production of this play. Local television personality Barbara Bernard, of WHYN's (Channel 40) *The Barbara Bernard Show*, played a small, but flashy, walk-on role as "Miss Riviera of 1926."

Another newcomer for the season was SusanneCansino, who as noted in one program was born in Carnegie Hall where her parents ran a dance studio. She was from the famous dancing Cansino family, cousin to Hollywood film star Rita Hayworth. The *Springfield Union* noted of Susanne that she "is a block buster in her own way. Their 'Won't You Charleston with Me' number brought down the house."

The *Holyoke Transcript-Telegram* reported:

Had the cast taken a deep, deep breath following last night's final curtain and started the show once more, a gleeful first night audience would have happily sat through The Boy Friend *again and would have remained as excited, delighted, and awed by the graceful, tasteful production.*

Bob Levey, reviewer for the *Transcript* likewise applauded Susanne Cansino:

Susanne Cansino was lively and witty as Maisie, and was terribly funny with her posturing in parody of the flapper.

She was paired with James Pompeii, a young man with an unusually radiant stage personality and enormous musical comedy talent, especially as a dancer.

Northampton's *Daily Hampshire Gazette* marveled that The Valley Players, for whom musicals were rare, would turn so effortlessly to a musical:

Perhaps the most surprising about this production is the apparent ease with which the resident company turns to musical comedy…

The word is getting around that the Valley Players have a big hit on their hands so if you want an evening that will be remembered for a long time, order your tickets now to this gay musical show. When the final curtain comes down, you will wish it could begin all over again.

Reviewer W. M. Manta of the *Chicopee Herald* remarked:

It would appear as though, finally, this reborn organization is shaking free of its growing pains and realizing that its patrons have come to join in the fun of play-going rather than sit awe-struck viewing a play ill-chosen and ill-performed. In this type of production, the presence of amateurs, apprentices, and neo-professionals is permissible…but not without the understanding that this is acceptable rather than procedure on the part of any group dedicating themselves to good living theatre.

He also urged, less severely:

Don't give up your only opportunity to see the sedate Barbara Bernard trip the boards…

Longtime Valley Players friend and supporter Barbara Bernard recalls being prompted to get into the act in her small role:

The reason for that was they felt that having somebody who was well-known, it would draw audiences. And, of course, they took my picture and I'm in this bathing suit. This was done in rehearsal, so that appeared in the newspapers, and they sold out every night…now, I cannot honestly say people bought tickets to see me in a bathing suit.

But a lot of people who had never gone to the Valley Players, they did go, and it was a great show. I think I had five lines, and I hope I didn't screw them up. But it was a bit of a grind because I was on every night, and I was doing a television show during the day, and then

getting into this bathing suit. And then a big stripe across my 'bazoom'…Miss Riviera. But it was fun. They asked me to do it and I would say yes to anything that Valley Players asked me to do. They were such a lovely, lovely group of people.

It was the highest grossing show of the season at a soaring $9,394.11, with a grand attendance of 5,246.

Elsie Cappel, local dance instructor, did the choreography for *The Boy Friend*. Jean Guild ran an ad in the last program for her speech, drama, and acting classes as the Rita Mitchell Guenther Studio, formerly the Elsie Cappel dance school at 280 High Street.

Jean Guild and Ted Tiller, normally character actors, both took the leads in the wistful and poignant comedy/drama *A Majority of One* playing an elderly Brooklyn Jewish woman and an elderly

Under the Yum Yum Tree 1961, Susanne Cansino and Vincent B Carroll

Japanese diplomat, respectively. They received excellent notices in what some reviewers felt were their best performances.

It didn't all run smooth. *The Sound of Murder* got off to a rocky start:

The production was plagued with a variety of opening night mishaps that even extended to the traditional stage accident of a misfired pistol, and the possibility of the play's success was inhibited by both the mishaps and the not too absorbing plot of the mystery. By the last week in the season, *Under the Yum Yum Tree* received enthusiastic reviews, and one reviewer, W. M. Manta of the *Chicopee Herald* felt the overall season gave much to rejoice:

If the Valley Players are going to try as hard to improve themselves next season as that have raised their standards this season, then we would say bravo!!!..and when does the sale of the 1961-1962 season start?

Now that the summer theatre series is coming to an end all the followers of out of town entertainment should lend ear, heart and pocketbook to the efforts of your own city in the direction of improving by doing things in the performing arts. Patronize your concert and theatre groups and you will be helping Chicopee grow in a direction that your children's children will enjoy.

Manta's remarks also underscore the reality that

The Valley Players was not perceived to be only a Holyoke attraction, but belonging to the Pioneer Valley.

John J. Collins Sr., one of the operators of Mountain Park, as well as president and treasurer of Lincoln Park in New Bedford, Massachusetts, died in the summer of 1961. The Collins family had acquired Mountain Park in 1953. The park was actually under the direction of his son, John J. Collins Jr., at the time, who was a resident of Holyoke.

As usual, the end of the season brought feature articles on where the cast and crew were bound for until next summer. Many, like James Coco, were off to New York theatre, others to TV and radio. College professors, like Walter Boughton, were back to Amherst College and other schools. The sister trio of Barbara, Mary, and Louise O'Leary, general secretary for The Valley Players and box office staff, went back to their teaching jobs in the Springfield and Holyoke public schools. The Guild's son, William, who had served as stage manager, was back to Boston University where he was majoring in theatre directing.

William Guild recalls of those years:

The interesting thing I think also why the public liked us

so much was that the actors were there pretty much for a season, or at least eight to ten plays if not the full twelve, and they all stayed in people's homes. They rented rooms in people's homes in the Highland area, which is where we lived on Lincoln Street. So those people really got to know them and really liked them. So that was part of it. They'd drag friends off to see shows that they were playing leads in when there was somebody in their home. Simon Oakland rented a room from this tiny elderly lady who'd rented her room to several other people over the years, Mrs. Humphries. I've never forgotten her. I mean, she was maybe five feet, probably four-foot-ten, and Si was like six-foot-three. And when I brought him to her house and introduced them, she said, "Now, you're a good boy, aren't you?" And I've never forgotten that, because he was a sweetheart. But he was there to do Streetcar Named Desire, among other things.

***

The Pleasure of His Company 1961, Patricia O' Morran
and Ted Tiller

The 1962 season was to be The Valley Players' last year. Nobody predicted that at the beginning of the season; it came as a shock at the end. The season opened on a tenuous, but still hopeful note with a grateful nod to local businessman Jacob Barowsky in the program:

When we came to an apparent parting of the ways a year and a half ago, Jacob L. Barowsky came to the rescue for the benefit of all of us and of this entire area. The owners of Mountain Park assisted us most generously. Many others contributed in various ways, not the least of which was by purchasing patron subscriptions. Thus we got our financial feet back onto firm sand.

But could they sustain it for another year? The *Holyoke Transcript-Telegram* offered a note of warning:

The response at the box office has been disappointing. Nearly all of us go to see a Valley Players production once in a while. We would not like to think there was no play at Mountain Park for us to attend when the mood strikes. For some families it is the only live professional theater their children can see.

But the Valley Players can't exist on such casual support. Its costs are high, its prices low. Furthermore, the season is short and plagued with the uncertainties of summer weather. The company must have the security of heavier ticket-buying than has been the case this year.

The Valley Players are an asset to the city. What they need in the way of support is modest, but they have to have it. We should think some of our industrial and commercial institutions might be interested enough in keeping the Players here to purchase blocks of tickets, to be distributed to their employees or clients in any way they fancy…If Holyoke wants them to stay, it must respond promptly with a vote of confidence at the box office.

They started off with a small, but popular comedy, *Critic's Choice*. The program was back to black and white and the original cover design. Would this be a bare bones season?

Next up was *Blood, Sweat, and Stanley Poole*, featuring the returning James Coco in his only appearance with The Valley Players this season. The show was a hit, with an audience…

Invitation to a March 1961, Richard Kronold, Polly Campbell, and James Secrest

George Murphy, a teenager who would work at the Mt. Tom Playhouse in two years' time as an apprentice, was in the audience:

And at that time, language was—nobody swore, but they did on stage, and I remember this one scene—you know, how things come back in your past and you can picture it? Whether it's five years ago or forty years ago? I picture a scene of a guy sitting in a chair and this other big guy standing down, and the whole stage was bathed in nothing but blue light. And I just thought that was fantastic. There was something about it.

The next day I go down to High Street in Holyoke and I'm going to a record store, and here's the actor that was standing over the actor in the chair, screaming and yelling and cursing at him. He's leaning in a doorway! And I walked by and I said, "Man, that was one terrific show last night."

[Gravelly voiced, gangster-like] "T'anks, kid." It was like something out of a gangster movie. "T'anks, kid."

…that seemed willing to applaud indefinitely when the final lights went up…The honors go principally to James Coco, a gifted comedian of the sort who can make even silence uproarious.

Rebecca 1961, Sai Springwell and Jean Guild

Strong plays such as *Death of a Salesman*, and *The Miracle Worker* were jewels of the season. Linda Gale, who had done the part in a national tour, played Helen to Sue Ann Gilfillan as Annie Sullivan. A powerful and moving production, the *Transcript-Telegram's* Oracle column begged people to go see it. It drew letters to the editor in praise.

The Pursuit of Happiness, a Revolutionary War romantic comedy about the old New England custom of "bundling" required the expected period props, and it was perhaps for this show that a musket was required.

When Peggy Bowe was a young girl living with her parents in Holyoke, she remembers her father getting a phone call from the Guilds. Her father, Bob had once owned the Pioneer Valley Gun Shop in Holyoke and was friends with Neil Doherty, a professional photographer who both worked for the *Transcript* and had taken most of The Valley Players production photos. When the Players were in need of a gun for a production, Doherty recommended his friend and a connection was made. Bob Bowe began helping out The Valley Players when…

I was made to get all dressed up, and we got to go to the play. My dad's compensation was three free tickets…then the phone calls came every few weeks for the rest of the time they owned the theater; Dad provided the guns. Dad did not want a credit in the program for safety reasons.

Possibly for *The Pursuit of Happiness*, Mr. Bowe was asked to produce a Revolutionary War era musket, which he did not have, but also being a modeler, he did have a couple of plastic models of muskets, which he offered, and warned the company just to hold the fake gun, not to place it down on anything, or the audience would hear the sound of a piece of plastic and not a heavy metal gun. Theatre, after all, is about illusion.

The show was also a throwback to a previous season, having been produced here in 1948. Only Jean Guild was left of the original cast. She received a tribute in the program:

Here is a monumental record, combining magnificent performances, an actress with the almost superhuman

responsibilities of general management of the company. That the Valley Players had a beginning, that they have continued for so many seasons, that they developed such high standards of production, such professional integrity and such closely knit friendships, are part of the measure of her achievement. The road has been long. It has never been easy, especially for one whose task has ever been to make the rough places smooth for others. Now in her 181st performance at the end of her 21st season as a member of our acting company, the labors and disappointments and griefs of these many years are quieted and enriched by memories of accomplishments which few are able…to attain.

The Guilds were guest speakers in January 1962 and at the Holyoke Business and Professional Women's Club, where they spoke on aspects of managing a theatre and theatre arts. In May, the *Holyoke Transcript-Telegram* called for support of The Valley Players on its editorial page, with the pointed headline "They Can't Live on Kind Words":

Everyone is glad to see that the Valley Players are all ready for another season at the Mountain Park Casino…The Players have already received encouraging support in the form of advance season ticket reservations, but they make no bones about the fact that they need more. The local company was rescued from financial shoals last season by Jacob L. Barowsky…But to stay in good shape the Players need the steady support of regular customers…if Holyoke people want the Players to carry on with the solid entertainment they have provided for 20 seasons, they mustn't leave it to somebody else to support them.

A theatre company can't run on a one-season-at-a-time basis. Plans for plays and personnel go around the year and depend upon continuing financial security. The Players need the assurance of steady patronage from Holyoke.

Dark of the Moon was said by the *West Springfield Record* to be a "very super-duper production…too, we would like to add a bravos on the choral work of the players, for it was outstanding, especially during the revival meeting at the Buck Creek Church."

With *Roman Candle*, director Dorothy Crane

celebrated her 200th production for The Valley Players, and the local paper recounted her career as one of the managers and director for the Farragut Players for seven years before her long stint with The Valley Players. Her memorable feat of taking on the lead acting role in *Papa is All* in 1945 with only a few hours' notice was re-told.

More particularly, her detailed and rigorous schedule was noted and given appreciation for its uniqueness and success. Ms. Crane plotted each show during the winter well before the season, not only the actor's blocking, but the lighting, sound, and other elements for each scene. She was Director of Speech Arts and Extra Curricular Activities in the Newport News, Virginia, public schools at that time, and also directed community theatre there. In between acts of the show, the full company and backstage crew gathered on set, brought Crane out on stage, and presented her with a huge bouquet of American Beauty roses.

John Gordon, new theatre critic for the *Springfield Union*, broke the rumor that the end was near for The Valley Players when Carlton Guild released an ambiguous statement in August.

In his weekly prepared release on the coming attraction at the Casino, he [Carlton Guild] referred to the "final production of the 21 years" summer plays. Thursday night Guild said the ambiguity of the statement was intentional, adding "we are not sure what is to happen" before another season rolls around.

Guild admitted that Jacob L. Barowsky of Holyoke, founder of a detergent manufacturing concern, has been the financial backer of the Valley Players since last year. He underwrote the complete renovation of the Casino and modernization of the interior to make it less a shed and more a proscenium theater.

"Mr. Barowsky has other interests and what his attitude is toward continuing his aid to the Valley Players is not known," Guild said.

William Guild offers another aspect to their business relationship with Mr. Barowsky:

He wanted to keep the theater going, and he could afford to do it at a loss, but he was a very difficult man and there were certain plays that he didn't want us to do, and he was very dictatorial. Having run it by themselves for twenty years, they just couldn't work with him.

Little Mary Sunshine featured a young cast, the long anticipated musical that spoofed the musical comedies of the 1920, in which seven members of the cast had been in the off-Broadway production. It was a lightweight, enjoyable spoof.

But The Valley Players would go out with dignity.

In August 1962, the Valley Players performed their last show: Tennessee Williams' *The Glass Menagerie*. Broadway and television actress Grace Carney starred as Amanda. Ray Girardin played Tom, with Marilyn Cunningham as the sensitive daughter, Laura. Clark Warren was the Gentleman Caller. Ted Tiller directed.

It was their lowest attendance.

The Valley Players Present GRACE CARNEY RAY GIRARDIN in THE GLASS MENAGERIE with MARILYN CUNNINGHAM CLARK WARREN

MOUNTAIN PARK CASINO
Holyoke, Massachusetts
WEEK OF AUGUST 27 - SEPTEMBER 1, 1962
229th Production

The Miracle Worker in late July was the top show of the year in attendance at 4,080, and the lowest was the final show, Tennessee Williams' *The Glass Menagerie* at a pathetic 1,629.

The Valley Players paid ten payments of $400 each for rental of the Casino from the Mt. Tom Amusement Co., Inc. They bought ice from the Holyoke Ice and Fuel, bought lumber from the Street Lumber Corp, and paper supplies from City Paper. The payroll for the 1962 season was $28,252.33, actors and crew. They were contributors in material ways to the City of Holyoke.

One young man, Jim Othuse, then of Williamsburg, who went on to a career in designing sets and lighting for the theatre, began as an apprentice at the Valley Players that last season.

I remember loving every day that summer of 1962, when I

was eighteen. I understand that was the final year of the Valley Players after a long and illustrious run and I am so glad I got to experience a technical apprenticeship with the company. I commuted all the way from Williamsburg, Mass. every day. I still have the three letters from Carlton Guild, dated February, March and May of 1962, explaining the details of the program, the schedule and the commitment he and Jean Guild were expecting of me...I am still designing sets and lighting for theatre and loving it. I cherish those days at the Casino that led to my career.

The headline in the *Springfield Sunday Republican* was like a death-watch: "Theater-Lovers Pulling for Survival of Casino." It was rumored, but not definite—at least not officially announced—that The Valley Players were pulling the plug on twenty-one years of their theatre company on the mountain.

End of operations of the Valley Players and closing of the now modernized Casino would be a loss to the area. Western Massachusetts has a cultural heritage to carry on and the loss of any of the art forms or forums would reflect an artistic regression...The Valley Players long have been considered among the leading units furnishing summer theater entertainment and are worthy of presentation. That the stock company may be in financial difficulties is no reflection on management or productions staged. Many theaters of the like are in trouble throughout the country.

The writer of the article, John M. Gordon, recounted the mounting production costs plaguing summer theaters, and competition from other sources of entertainment. He makes an interesting comment:

But if any summer theater is to be considered an area of responsibility it must be loosed from the shackles of provincialism imposed by some who cry loudest for a wider base of support—a thought some boosters of the Valley Players might do well to consider.

He mentions the Holyoke Chamber of Commerce had been undertaking a campaign to continue the Valley Players' tenure, and acknowledged Jacob Barowsky's enormous contribution.

Jacob L. Barowsky, Holyoke industrialist who has done so much for the Mountain Park theater in the past two years is to be commended for his personal and financial efforts

and the regret expressed that his considerable contributions were not matched in interest, at least, by others who enjoy legitimate stage fare.

The program carried a note in an ad box on the last page:

With deepest appreciation to Mr. and Mrs. Jacob L. Barowsky of Mountainview Drive. Had they not come to the rescue of the theater when deficits of the 1959 and 1960 seasons made further operation impossible for those who had managed the company for 19 years, the Valley Players' 217th production would have been their last.

Many people lamented the prospect of our demise in 1960. Mr. and Mrs. Barowsky did something about it. They gave us two more years in which to bring another 22 productions to the still too few thousands who came for the enjoyment and beauty and wonder and greater understanding and appreciation of human existence which the theater, at its finest, offers to mankind.

It sounded like goodbye. There were no see you next year notes. However the decision had been made, and young William Guild knew it was the end at the last performance.

It broke my heart when we closed. The last lines that Tom says are "Blow out your candles, Laura…("for nowadays the world is lit by lightning") …"

The last night of the production I just sobbed. I was outside watching through these—we had these big, big, huge open-air windows to let a cross breeze through. And I didn't want to go in the theater to see that. It was just so heartbreaking for me because it was the end.

Interestingly, the review of *The Glass Menagerie* ironically reflects perhaps the sensibilities of a future generation for whom theatre is not the first choice of entertainment:

The Players production is too real, too down to earth and

has bypassed the delicate air of recollection in which all things are soft. They have lost the haunting beauty of memory.

Theatre critics, newspaper editors, and letters to the editor in newspapers up and down the valley, from Springfield to Greenfield, mourned the passing of an era. In years to come, many of these publications were to, one by one, to go out of business. Like Laura blowing out her candles, for nowadays the world is lit by lightning.

At the time *The Glass Menagerie* was playing at the Casino on Mt. Tom, Victor Borge appeared in his comedy show at Storrowton Music Fair of West Springfield in its third season.

The Williamstown Theatre, a summer theater begun in the 1950s in the far northwest corner of Massachusetts at Williams College, was also running its final show of the season. It was the late hit musical *Once Upon a Mattress*, and it would be the shape of things to come for theatre on Mt. Tom – and a new director to infuse a new leadership – Nikos Psacharopoulos.

CHAPTER 8

Another Opening, Another Show

In October 1962, Westover Air Force Base went to its highest alert level ever during the Cuban Missile Crisis. The Cold War spiked a fever.

Senator Edward M. Kennedy and his wife Joan Kennedy marched in the 1963 Holyoke St. Patrick's Day Parade. The following year, they returned, despite their mourning of the senator's brother, President John F. Kennedy, who had been assassinated five months previously. A prize-winning float depicted President Kennedy's grave at Arlington National Cemetery, guarded by servicemen.

Peggy Bowe began taking speech and drama lessons from Jean Guild that fall of 1962 after the last season of The Valley Players. Her parents had seen the ad in "the good old *Holyoke Transcript.*"

An only child, Peggy recalls she was quite timid as a girl and the lessons gave her confidence. Jean Guild was her teacher for some six years until Peggy graduated from Holyoke Catholic High School in 1968. She notes:

Junior and senior years, or maybe just senior year, she gave up renting the studio at Elsie Cappel's and started just having us in her living room, which was great fun, because

then we got to play with her cats. Sometimes she would make cookies. She was just a neat lady.

Peggy had attended shows from time to time with her parents as a child, as her father had supplied the guns that were needed as props for certain shows. She was in the audience for *Write Me a Murder,* when Jean Guild played Dr. Elizabeth Woolley.

She came in and had to give somebody a shot, and I was thrilled because we were at that play and that was my *Mrs. Guild.*

My mother was a great one for the tradition that you always had to give any adult that you were involved with, like a teacher, a Christmas present. One year my mother had learned how to make what she called dusters. It was a wire coat hanger that you bent and you would take rug yarn and cut it into, say, five-inch pieces, and then you folded it in half and then pulled the strings through the loop around the wire. And it made this fuzzy thing, but it was a great duster. It was especially good to use for your blinds. I mean, it was goofy, but people loved them—so I made one, wrapped it up, and gave it to Mrs. Guild. She went home and opened it up at Christmas, and she called me up and she said, "Peggy, is this a duster?"

"Yes, ma'am."

"Oh, I just think it's terrific." And then whenever I went back, the next week, she said, "I'm absolutely in love with that thing! That's the best thing anybody's ever given me!" For the next several years, every Christmas, I made Mrs. Guild another duster—even when I was in college—it was a great excuse to stop and see her for a visit.

Even after I went for the Army, she would run into my mother at Stop & Shop and say, "I miss Peggy, there's no question about that, but boy, I miss those dusters." I think my Mom made a couple and dropped them off.

She was kind of a larger-than-life figure, but yet she was the most down to earth, warm person.

Peggy entered speaking competitions, won medals, eventually attended Emerson College and had a career in the Army from which she retired as a lieutenant colonel. Public speaking was a skill she'd started learning from Jean Guild, whose influence in her life was "hugely important." On one occasion, it served her when she delivered the eulogy for Holyoke's Maurice Donahue (President of the Massachusetts Senate 1964-1971), who was Peggy's uncle. The Maurice A. Donahue Elementary School is named for him, as is the UMass Donahue Institute, and the Donahue Building at Holyoke Community College. Peggy received many compliments for her eulogy, and some years later, then Senator John Kerry remembered her speech when they met on another occasion, and he remarked. "That was one of the nicest eulogies I've ever heard."

The fact that he remembered blew me away. But that goes back to the confidence that Jean Guild instilled in me as a young school girl.

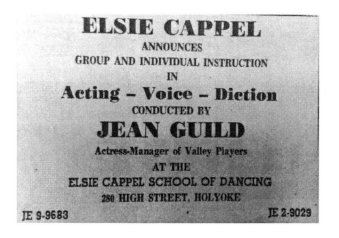

Peggy Bowe still tears ups when she speaks of the impact Jean Guild had on her life.

She gave me incredible self-confidence that I never had. I mean, I was a scared little only child that was afraid of my own shadow. Well suddenly, I met this dynamic woman who believed in me and treated me with respect and dignity, and encouraged me.

Sometimes she and the other students asked of Mrs. Guild why she wasn't still in theatre.

Always, it went back to the financial. You know, "It's a wonderful business, but the world is changing," and the television and the proliferance of movies, that live theatre just really couldn't compete. They weren't making money for the Players to survive.

But if the Guilds were done with managing a theatre company at the Casino, the old playhouse was not empty yet. Nick Psacharopoulos from Williamstown was in the wings, ready to have a go at it.

By December, the city became involved to try to continue theatre on the mountain, with no apparent hope of reviving The Valley Players, and the attempt was to utilize the playhouse with whatever attractions could be found. The *Holyoke Transcript-Telegram* headline:

Area-Wide Effort is Planned for Summer Theatre at Mt. Park.

Local theater-goers learned today that the Holyoke Chamber of Commerce is sparking an area-wide effort to sustain a summer theater at the Mountain Park Casino. The Valley Players have terminated their operation here, after 22 years.

Possibilities for a new summer theater organization to be known as the Pioneer Valley Players will be presided…at the meeting room of the Holyoke Savings Bank.

Nikos Psacharopoulos, executive director of the summer theater at Williamstown and instructor in directing at Yale Drama School will speak about what he believes can be done at the Casino. He has visited Holyoke several times during the past few weeks and is enthusiastic about organizing a summer theater here along the lines of the Williamstown theater.

Psacharopoulos, a native of Greece, had directed stage shows at Williamstown, as well as for television. A founder of the Williamstown Theater Festival, perhaps his most important credential was that, as it had been reported, "It has just been announced that the Williamstown Theater made a small profit in 1962 for the second consecutive year."

A small profit. Williamstown, however, was a non-profit theater with the self-described mission of having "no package shows and a minimum of the light, frothy fare customarily associated with the straw hat circuit." This might well describe The Valley Players.

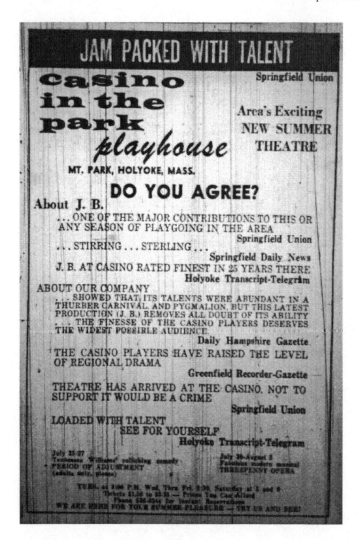

JAM PACKED WITH TALENT

Springfield Union

casino in the park playhouse

MT. PARK, HOLYOKE, MASS.

Area's Exciting
NEW SUMMER
THEATRE

DO YOU AGREE?

About J. B.
...ONE OF THE MAJOR CONTRIBUTIONS TO THIS OR
ANY SEASON OF PLAYGOING IN THE AREA
Springfield Union

...STIRRING...STERLING...
Springfield Daily News

J. B. AT CASINO RATED FINEST IN 25 YEARS THERE
Holyoke Transcript-Telegram

ABOUT OUR COMPANY
...SHOWED THAT ITS TALENTS WERE ABUNDANT IN A
THURBER CARNIVAL AND PYGMALION, BUT THIS LATEST
PRODUCTION (J. B.) REMOVES ALL DOUBT OF ITS ABILITY
...THE FINESSE OF THE CASINO PLAYERS DESERVES
THE WIDEST POSSIBLE AUDIENCE
Daily Hampshire Gazette

THE CASINO PLAYERS HAVE RAISED THE LEVEL
OF REGIONAL DRAMA
Greenfield Recorder-Gazette

THEATRE HAS ARRIVED AT THE CASINO. NOT TO
SUPPORT IT WOULD BE A CRIME
Springfield Union

LOADED WITH TALENT
SEE FOR YOURSELF
Holyoke Transcript-Telegram

The Casino became "Casino-in-the-Park" as if to reiterate the special location of this Mountain Park theater.

While not directly connected as yet with the new theater here the Guilds are enthusiastic and have confidence in the new production team. They feel that the new blood has something to offer and something which Holyoke theater goers will enjoy.

With Psacharopoulos was Robert Mathews as executive producer. Richard H. Anderson joined as costume designer, also from Yale Drama School. He had experience with costuming and makeup for many companies. David Nancarrow was production manager. The Executive Committee board included such Holyoke business professionals as Richard C. Whitney, William H. Smith II, Frank W. Schreier, Mrs. George Beraud, and Donald Dwight. The play programs were now several glossy pages, with headshot photos of all the cast and production heads.

Six guest directors were slated for the season, including F. Curtiss Canfield of Yale Drama School, who had been involved in theatre at Amherst College from 1927 to 1954. The new Casino-in-the-Park had a nine-play lineup that carried a respectable mix of recent Broadway hits and theatre classics, among them *Threepenny Opera*, *Pygmalion*, and *Romeo and Juliet*. Shows were Tuesday through Saturday evening, with two shows on Saturday at 5 p.m. and 9 p.m. It was run, similar to The Valley Players, as a stock company. Season ticket prices were touted for $16, $23, and $28.

The season began with *A Thurber Carnival* that the *Holyoke Transcript-Telegram* thought "bright and amusing. The cast was very good. And it was different—a novelty."

On July 15th, Archibald MacLeish's Pulitzer Prize-winning play, *J.B.*, was presented with George Ebeling in the title role. In the previous week he had played Colonel Pickering in Shaw's *Pygmalion*. Ebeling had performed on television, including soap operas.

Pygmalion, according to the *Transcript-Telegram*, "ran into some production troubles because it had a poor director. Still audiences who saw it late in the run found the famous Shaw comedy in good shape and liked it."

J.B., however, "was stupendous. It was a superior artistic achievement that could stand comparison with the very best." The *Springfield Union* called it "...one of the major contributions to this or any season of playgoing in the area."

The *Daily Hampshire Gazette* remarked that the company, "...showed its talents were abundant in *A Thurber Carnival* and *Pygmalion*, but this latest production [*J.B*] removes all doubt of its ability...the finesse of the Casino players deserves the widest possible audience."

However, the opening night audience had only 150 to 200 people.

Meanwhile, the Cole Porter musical *Can-Can*, starring Patrice Munsel and Robert Alda at the Storrowton drew a standing-room-only audience—in a tent that held nearly 2,000 people.

A Period of Adjustment, the only full-length comedy by Tennessee Williams was next (clearly the new management were boldly driving towards modern plays), but drew mixed reviews; according to a *Holyoke Transcript-Telegram* article the production had the misfortune of running during a heat wave, but also "met the disapproval of some, ourselves included, though who thought it was a poor play. A good many people who was it thought it was very funny. The acting was good."

The following play, *Threepenny Opera* did better:

…put the Casino in the Park back in the company of the angels. It is top quality. It is tremendously entertaining. Audiences love it. Some of the critics in the area who raved about J.B. *thought this was even better.*

Weigh this up and the tally is clear. The Casino in the Park is good, in fact better than we dared dream.

Cast regular Anthony Zerbe (who was a well-known for his television appearances on *Naked City, Route 66*, and the daytime soap opera *Edge of Night*) played a street singer. Stephen Elliott was Mack the Knife. Elliott had played some fifteen years earlier at the Casino with The Valley Players. The show was held for a second week.

Anthony Zerbe

casino in the park *playhouse*

JULY 30 - AUG. 3

THREE PENNY OPERA

Peggy Bowe recalls:

I can remember as a pre-teen, teen they would often have actors from soap operas. The actors would get "sick" on the soap opera. And my mother was a big soap opera watcher so I was familiar with many of them. So I would see this guy or that guy that was a heartthrob on the soap.

Ads appeared in the program for the Schine Inn, and the Highpoint Motor Inn in Chicopee (hotels, like the movie theaters, had moved to the suburbs), and Jack August seafood restaurant in Northampton. Holyoke businesses included Jubinville Package Store on Main Street, and Child's shoes on High Street in Holyoke and a Bridge Street, Springfield location. Other advertisers for the season included the Yankee Pedlar restaurant, the *Holyoke Transcript-Telegram*, and the local Friendly's restaurant chain, promoting local restaurants on 233 South Street and 435 Appleton Street in Holyoke, and 63 King Street in Northampton, and 1554 Riverdale Road in West Springfield, as well as longtime advertiser, Dreikorn's bakery, locally known for their sandwich bread and rolls.

A Far Country starred future film and television star Anthony Zerbe as Sigmund Freud and Janet Sarno as his patient. Among the supporting cast playing a maid was Barbara Heisler, who would later become familiar to area listeners for her talk show on Holyoke's radio station, WREB in the 1970s and 1980s.

On August 21st the show was *Fashion! Or Live in New York*, with Louise Shaffer as the show stealer in this comedy. A note in the program from Robert Mathews:

We follow in the footsteps of a dedicated and capable theatre enterprise. For some twenty years, the Valley Players have made summer theatre going a habit—even a tradition in the Pioneer Valley. We now begin an attempt to uphold through our own ideals, aims and means that tradition for which personally and professionally we have great respect.

The finale of its only season was *Romeo and Juliet* with future film and television actor Nicholas Pryor and Margaret Cowles.

"Casino Players in Romeo and Juliet Provide Thoroughly Rewarding Evening…Janet Sarno as Lady Capulet "deserves special plaudits" according to reviewer Donald R. Dwight; Walter Rhodes as Mercutio also drew praise.

The reviewer, whose family owned the *Transcript-Telegram,* complained, however, about the tradition of fireworks:

One circumstance beyond the control of the players—the Tuesday night fireworks at Mt. Park that erupted during the second act—did nothing to sustain the play's mood. It strikes this reviewer, if both the Casino and the Mt. Park management are in accord that they could benefit each other mutually, that some more satisfactory arrangements could be evolved for the fireworks.

Halfway through the season, critic Anabel B. Murphy gave her assessment of Casino-in-the-Park, and lent some interesting thoughts not only on the course of this new theatre company, but of the very question whether theatre was to survive on the mountain. There was a duality to Casino-in-the-Park: this hybrid name typifies the conscious attempt to link to the well known and beloved Valley Players that occupied the Casino Theater for a generation, and yet attempts to entice the audience with something different, something new, reminding the public of the newness of the organization. This was a new theater that needed to be investigated and tried on for size.

Ms. Murphy's article attempts to remind the public of Holyoke's great theatre heritage on the mountain, and entice a younger audience to the Casino ("In the Park.") But it also plays a kind of devil's advocate role which kept the producers on guard and questioned whether, indeed, the new theatre group—or any theatre group—was up to the challenges of pulling a loyal audience up the mountain in the summertime.

Holyoke was changing. The enormous factory base of employers was dwindling as companies went out of business or moved South, and the nineteenth-century cavernous brick mills were growing silent. The working families who once escaped to the cooler heights of Mt. Tom in the summer months had moved to the suburbs, and bought air conditioners. Soon a new group of immigrants from Puerto Rico would take their newcomer's place in the brick workers' housing and apartment blocks, but would run up against a greater challenge to find work at a time when so many larger employers were leaving.

Much of the audience these days came not from the Flats, but from the suburbs and arrived by auto. With competing sources for entertainment, particularly in the suburbs, the downtowns of Holyoke and Springfield were losing the audience that had made them exciting and profitable centers for a century.

Critic Anabel Murphy recounted that the Casino-in-the-Park was established by the Pioneer Valley Theatre Foundation, a group of citizens led at first by the Holyoke Chamber of Commerce, "who wanted to keep a summer theater alive in Holyoke, as an economic, cultural and social asset to the community."

It is, first, a notable and noble act for a community to hold a summer theater up with such respect and to work to keep it alive, but as Ms. Murphy reminds this idealistic group of supporters, in a tone that sounds as much like chastisement as a voice of reason:

For these complimentary aims to be realized, the project has to break even financially. In this undertaking money is not an end, but a necessary means….where do we stand, past the half-way mark? Is the Casino in the Park any good? And is there an audience in this area for it?

Though the theatre group headed by Nikos Psacharopoulos and Robert Mathews may feel that only the second question was really a question from the start, the civic group headed by Richard C. Whiting and William Smith II has had both questions to answer.

…Our judgment is that if you saw any five plays now on Broadway, or on Broadway last winter, you would not have spent your money as well as you would have if you had bought tickets for the five shows that have been put on at Mountain Park so far this summer.

If you had gone to five other summer theatres in any one week this summer, you wouldn't have done nearly as well…The Casino in the Park Playhouse is good, in fact better than we dared dream, it has grappled with all the woes of any brand new undertaking, all the unexpected trials inflicted by balky equipment, sick actors, slender financing, New England weather…and it has come up with two genuine triumphs, two good shows, and one that was a matter of opinion.

In all five, the standard of acting and of production has been way above summer theater average. We have been particularly impressed with the technical excellence of these productions.

The second question, about whether there was an audience for this summer theater, no matter how excellent the quality of its productions, was the more uncomfortable notion. Most theaters and, indeed, most businesses must face the possibility that its products may be a hard sell, or that there is no market at all.

Is there a local audience for good theatre that is enlightening as well as entertaining? Are there enough people who enjoy this kind of entertainment and enough people who want a summer theatre in Holyoke to put a first season across? Not yet.

She notes the audience is spread over a wide geographic area, as far away as Greenfield to the north. The theater sought support from theatre-lovers, and also from citizens who, if not theatre-lovers, would support a local undertaking and align themselves with a source of community pride. Her frank assessment: "Good will that is not expressed in ticket sales does not do much good."

Nobody knows how many people there are who would be sorry to see the theater go under, but who have not yet attended any shows. If this is a sizeable group, it could make the difference…It will be especially disappointing to those people—and there are between two and three thousand of them—who have found the Casino in the Park to be a source of delight and need only a few hundred recruits to their happy company to be able to keep it here. The weeks ahead will tell.

Sue Ann Gilfillan

The reviewer of *Romeo and Juliet* for the *Springfield Union*, "R.E.B.", noted that the audience sizes through the season were small, and wondered what could be done to stimulate the box office, but had no answers.

We feel sure the Pioneer Valley Foundation will try again. They have learned a lot and can profit from experience. We would hate to see all theater sacrificed because of lack of a paying audience for so called better shows.

The Casino-in-the-Park did not survive its first season.

That year of 1963 was also, as it happens, the fifth anniversary of the Storrowton Music Fair. In early June, several pages of the *Springfield Sunday Republican* carried article after article, features, interviews, sidebars, on the upcoming season, pages of ads from local businesses congratulating the producer Wally Beach and the Storrowton Music Fair managers. Clearly, they were an advertising juggernaut.

In comparison, the Mountain Park amusement park carried a few isolated ads on the kids show featuring Huckleberry Hound and Yogi Bear, and *The Howdy Doody Show*. *Carnival* was opening at the Storrowton. The same ad carried the next two weeks plays: Lee Grant and Mamie Van Doren in *Silk Stockings*, followed by star of television's *Your Hit Parade* Dorothy Collins in *The Unsinkable Molly Brown*.

Huckleberry Hound?

Also celebrating its fifth summer season were the Ivy Players based at Springfield College. Like Casino-in-the-Park, they were also leading off their season with *A Thurber Carnival*. The Casino couldn't have been happy about the coincidence.

Also carrying an ad that June day in 1963 was the Majestic Theater in West Springfield, which was a small neighborhood movie house showing second-run films, sometimes movies that were a generation old – John Wayne's *Flying Leathernecks*. No one could have predicted that in another forty years Storrowton would be gone, the Casino playhouse on Mt. Tom would be gone, and the

Backstage at the Casino

little Majestic would become a thriving equity winter stock theater, one of the few venues left in the Pioneer Valley for a regular season of live theatre.

But another attempt was made the following year of 1964, not with a repertory stock company this time, but with a series of visiting packaged shows. It would throw off both the names and the association with the Valley Players and the Casino Theater. The Mt. Tom Playhouse would give theatre on the mountain one final exciting encore, not unlike a sparkler with a white-hot blaze just before it dies. Or like the Tuesday night fireworks over the midway of Mountain Park.

I had a second cousin who lived in Holyoke, with his wife and children. Actually, I stayed at their house while I was raising the money for the theater. Their last name was Levin-Epstein, and they lived in Holyoke. But that was my first time in that part of western Massachusetts. I had grown up in the Berkshires, but on the New York side, so it was closer to Pittsfield and Kent, but never that part of it. I grew up in Brooklyn. I went to Syracuse University School of Drama, to my parents' insisting. I wanted to go to Notre Dame and become a football player. Well, they said you've got to go to a theatre school, because I had done a show in high school that I wrote and directed and all that stuff. So they said, "No, you've got to go to a school that at least has a drama department."

The shows at the newly re-named Mt. Tom Playhouse were packaged shows, many of them beginning their regional or national tours at the theater. According to Hugh Fordin:

The director would be there and also the advance director would come for about three days and then would leave because he'd have to go to the next theater. But I would say out of the ten shows, five of them were mine. So, yeah, and the advance director would come, talk to the technical director, talk to the set designer, make sure that everybody was going to be in a comfortable housing accommodation, and that's how it happened.

CHAPTER 9

The Final Curtain

The Pioneer Valley was changing. First it had the growing, and then it had the pains. The infrastructure was under continuous construction: the area's first "super highway," Interstate Route 91, snaked its way up north from Connecticut, and the Massachusetts Turnpike crisscrossed east to west from Boston to Stockbridge. Train service was dying in the 1960s before Amtrak was instituted in 1971. Actors drove to Holyoke, and stars flew into Bradley Field in Windsor Locks, Connecticut, the nearest large commercial airport; or to Logan Airport in Boston and then traveled two or more hours by limousine to the western part of the state. A few were still put up in one of the last of the area's grand hotels: the Hotel Northampton in nearby Northampton, but fewer were staying at the Roger Smith and other local downtown landmarks, and instead were lodging at chain motels in the suburbs. The supporting players, as always, were usually on their own.

Hugh Fordin, described by the *Holyoke Transcript-Telegram* in 1964 as a "young, personable and energetic man," entered the story at this point, a theatre producer who would turn the Casino into the Mt. Tom Playhouse for its last two seasons. He also had Holyoke connections, though he grew up in Brooklyn, New York. From an interview with Mr. Fordin for this book:

Opening night was Monday, and usually the only rehearsal was just Sunday night. Says Fordin, "Most of the time, it was Sunday night, so Monday was easy, you know, opening night. Of course, they were used to the show."

Ten shows played for the season, with eight performances Monday through Saturday, and matinees on Wednesday and Saturday. It took some juggling to make it all go like clockwork.

Even juggling the shows, and then a few cancellations at the last minute, not of just my engagement, but the whole show, and then trying to find another show in its place. Wasn't easy.

Carlton Guild was on staff as the business manager for the first show, with Len Bedsow as stage manager, and Richard R. Chamberlain, Jr., as the technical director. Jean was also on board as the assistant box office treasurer. The Guilds

being present for the first season at least suggested a continuity with the glory days of The Valley Players. However, well before the season was over, Carlton's involvement ended, and he devoted himself solely to teaching at the Westfield High School. "He was a very good writer, and apparently a very good teacher," William Guild says of his father. Jean Guild's name lingers a few plays longer on the program as assistant to the box office treasurer, and then her association with the Mt. Tom Playhouse also ended. It occurred quietly and without fanfare.

William Guild notes that his mother adjusted to not being at the helm:

She had always been in the box office when she wasn't acting. It was like one of those things you'd never see now, where people did all kinds of different jobs.

Hugh Fordin notes:

The operation was not up to par when I took it over. I mean, it wasn't equipped for big shows. It was basically, you know, a little theater that had a large auditorium.

But I tried to renovate as much as I could to make it like a really star operation, very much on the order of what the Ogunquit Playhouse was like.

Hugh Fordin recalls the investors purchased a "bungalow colony" on Route 5, just about a mile and a half past the entrance to Mountain Park that consisted of about twelve bungalows and a motel for some of the visiting actors. The audience, since the days of The Valley Players, was not local only to Holyoke anymore. Fordin discover his audience was really no longer centered around the mountain or the factory city.

It turned out in retrospect that most of the people that came to the theater were not from Holyoke at all, but were from Longmeadow and West Springfield and Springfield, because Holyoke, by and large, was a depressed area.

In June, representatives of the Greater Holyoke and Springfield industry and business concerns were invited to become special emissaries in spreading the word about the new playhouse. They were given a champagne party, a tour of the refurbished theater, along with, as the *Holyoke Transcript-Telegram* reported, "special order pads, season brochures and posters." A photo showed Hugh Fordin with a group of ladies and one gentleman from local companies such as American Pad & Paper, Gilbert & Barker, Van Norman Machinery, Wesson Maternity Hospital, Hunting Company, the *Wall Street Journal* and others, and the International Ladies Garment Workers Union. It was a hopeful and realistic

acknowledgment that to be successful, the company needed to be community oriented, as had been The Valley Players for so many years. That had been one of their chief successes.

However, the official moniker of the enterprise was *Hugh Fordin's Mt. Tom Playhouse.* One wonders if this personal mark of ownership led to a loss of community "ownership." It was always "our" Valley Players. Now it was Mr. Fordin's playhouse.

Theater Returning to Mountain Park ran the headline in June, and came the announcement that the new concern would feature stars of Broadway, motion pictures and television, "and it is going to be under a young, dynamic leadership." Hugh Fordin, it noted, "has been bustling in New York and byways lining up the elite of the theater for the Holyoke shows and success has been his."

Mayor Daniel F. Dibble presented a proclamation to Mr. Fordin on the opening of the playhouse, and declared his intention to invite the visiting stars each week to city hall to present them with a souvenir from the city.

There were two refreshment stands, one in the playhouse for soft drinks, ice cream and candy. One in the blue and white striped tent adjacent to the playhouse that sold beer, wine, champagne, as well as soft drinks. Restrooms were in a smaller building next to the theater.

Evening shows started at 8:30 Monday through Friday, and Saturday's evening show started at 9 p.m. Matinees were Wednesdays and Saturdays. Prices for matinees were $3 for the front orchestra and side divans, and $2 for the rear orchestra. Prices for the evening performances Monday through Thursday were $3.75 for the front orchestra, and $3.25 for the rear orchestra and side divans. On Friday and Saturday evening, the prices were $3.95 for the front orchestra and $3.50 for the rear orchestra and side divans. Also $2.50 and $1.75 for Monday through Thursday side divans; $3 and $2.25 for Friday and Saturday evening side divans; and $2.60 and $1 for matinee side divans.

A few large display ads hit the *Holyoke Transcript-Telegram* with photos of the disembodied heads of greater and lesser Hollywood and television stars who were to be the roster of celebrity players to the mountain: Eve Arden, Alexis Smith and Craig Stevens, Van Johnson, George Hamilton, Arlene Francis and others. The 1964 season put the headliners above the shows:

Cesar Romero in *Strictly Dishonorable*.
Genevieve in *For Love or Money*.
Arlene Francis in *Kind Sir*.
Tallulah Bankhead in *Glad Tidings*.
Van Johnson in *A Thousand Clowns*.
Peggy Cass in *Bachelor's Wife*.
Merv Griffin in *Broadway*.
Lloyd Bridges in *Anniversary Waltz*.
Kathryn Crosby ("Mrs. Bing") in *Sabrina Fair*.
Fernando Lamas and Esther Williams in *Once More with Feeling*.
Martha Raye in *The Solid Gold Cadillac*.
Members of Broadway touring company of *Stop the World, I Want to Get Off*.

If the performers were to be among the elite of the entertainment world, would the audience also be required to be elite to afford to attend? Was the workingman audience of days gone by still going to be a fixture at the newly named "Mt. Tom Playhouse"?

The technical support staff numbered between fifteen and twenty, aside from the young apprentices, which all lived locally. Fordin advertised for apprentices in the local paper:

Every summer theatre needs apprentices…they are so very important to the functioning of any theatre and we are hoping that we can find a select group of young people who are sincerely interested in theatre. We will be holding special classes in the techniques of theatre and there will be many opportunities for practical learning through contact with such outstanding stars as Van Johnson, Arlene Francis, Cesar Romero and the others.

Dan Brunelle was fifteen years old when his mother talked him into trying an apprentice job at the playhouse:

Backstage at a theater is magical. Using every kind of process to create an illusion of setting that comes to life with actors is a fantastic education in the use of tools and techniques. I loved it right away. The people are brilliant, the pace is relentless, the actors and crew are multi-talented marvels of innovation who think on their feet with surprising results.

George Murphy was sixteen years old when he worked as an apprentice at the Mt. Tom Playhouse. A Holyoke native, he had gotten the acting bug as a school kid at the Joseph Metcalfe School where he debuted in *Scarecrow Dick* in the role of a tree. During a performance, he fell off the stage in the middle of dance routine (trees are not especially good dancers), and he got a laugh.

And I thought that was great. I don't know if I got hurt, but I just, "Wow!" That's what started it, Scarecrow Dick.

By the time he was a student at Holyoke High School and getting involved in more student plays and the debate team, his teacher got him in touch with the Mt. Tom Playhouse for a summer apprentice position, where he applied at "this magnificent house on [the corner of] Northampton Street that belonged to Jean and Carlton Guild." He does not believe he had any further contact with the Guilds.

Then they told me it would be thirty-five dollars a season that I would have to pay them to work for them. And I go home and I lay this on my father, and he thinks I'm a blithering idiot.

He says, "Who the hell works for someone and pays them to do it?" I don't think I ever wound up paying it. I think they just kind of waived it. And then I got up there and, "Do this, do that, build this." And I started building sets and building flats. I would wake up and get up in the morning and I would walk from Pleasant Street in Holyoke to the playhouse, every morning, seven days a week. I would walk there, and a lot of the times I'd hitchhike back, or some of the actors would bring me home.

I remember one night I was walking through the parking lot coming up from the theater. I'd usually go down to Route 5 and try and hitchhike, which was no big deal back then. And this car stops in the middle of the parking lot as I'm walking, and toot-toots on the horn. I look, and it's Cesar Romero in his brand-new Pontiac station wagon. And he said, "You work at the theater, right?"

I said, "Yes, Sir."

He said, "Where you going?"

I said, "I'm going home."

He said, "You live far?"

I said, "No, I live down in Holyoke, not real far." He thought it was far when he got there. So we talked a while, you know, and I mentioned his car. I said, "This is a beautiful car." And he said, "Yeah, I get one every year." He said, "Doesn't cost me anything."

I said, "You get it free?" Well, he said something to the effect of, "Yeah, I did a whole bunch of television ads for the Pontiac motor division, and as payment, every year they give me a new car." So he dropped me off in front of my house.

The next night when I saw him backstage after—Strictly Dishonorable was the show—after that he said, "Do you need a ride home tonight?" I don't think he ever called me by name.

I said, "Yes, Sir, I do."

He said, "Okay. I'll meet you in the parking lot." And for the rest of the week, he brought me right to my front door in Holyoke, every single night. I was telling my mother about him. And I was telling her about it, and she says, "Is there any chance I could meet him?" And I tried like hell, and he just didn't want to come in. You know, it was late at night. He just wanted to go about his business. Cesar Romero, he was just amazing. He said he had a friend, with my name. [Actor, later Senator George Murphy.] I don't think he ever called me by name, but he said, "I got a friend with your name."

The Mt. Tom Playhouse opening night made the front page of the *Holyoke Transcript-Telegram*, which called Mr. Romero and the play a triumph. It was an old chestnut comedy. "Romero dominated the show as the roguish opera star fanatically pursuing the virtue of a Southern belle..." Monica Lovett was the belle in question, and Dick Van Patten played a hapless romantic rival. The play was directed by Harold J. Kennedy, who also had a minor role in the show.

The overall feeling inspired by Mt. Tom's first show is hope for a season of true excellence. The fact that so much could be got out of such a vintage piece of drama is, in itself, an encouraging factor.

Prior to the opening curtain, Mt. Tom Producer Hugh Fordin made a brief speech, expressing his hopes for the company's future. If Monday night's entry is any indication, Hugh doesn't have any worries at all.

Theatre was back home on the mountain. The first review published in the *Holyoke Transcript-Telegram* was placed right beside a review for Storrowton. Afterwards, they were placed a few pages apart—a discreet effort not to make comparisons?

Harold J. Kennedy, originally from Holyoke,

where he grew up on Lincoln Avenue (the street where the Guilds had lived must have been a magnet for theatre folk), had traveled the country in stock companies as an actor, playwright, and director since the 1940s, as well as staging shows on Broadway. After he graduated from Holyoke High School, he left the area for Dartmouth College, and Broadway, where Orson Welles gave him his first job in theatre. He wrote a funny memoir of his career and the actors and actresses he worked with called *No Pickle, No Performance*, published in 1978. He recounted his work at the Amherst College summer theater, where he made his professional debut, as well as the summer theater operated at the Springfield Technical High School in the 1940s. Kennedy had worked extensively in summer theatre for several decades; it was truly a labor of love for him, and he felt that when it came to packaged shows…

…the biggest names in television and the biggest draws in summer stock are the people in the game and panel shows who use their own names and get a million dollars' worth of publicity every time they use them. You don't have to explain who Johnny Carson is. Or Steve Allen. Or Arlene Francis.

"We Call Everybody Darling" is a humorous chapter in his book about why some theatre people like Tallulah Bankhead, and as Kennedy admits, himself, call people "Darling": because they can't remember names. He recalls of the Mt. Tom Playhouse:

I suppose my worse personal experience was when I returned to my hometown of Holyoke, Massachusetts, to open a new theater in an amusement park there. I was directing and playing with Cesar Romero in Strictly Dishonorable. *Cesar and I had arrived in Holyoke at midnight the night before. We had a morning rehearsal at the Masonic Temple right next door to the telephone company on Maple Street.*

When we took our lunch break, Cesar and I headed for the local luncheonette and had to pass the phone company office. As we passed, windows flew open and heads appeared as all the switchboard girls recognized Cesar, and oohed and aahed and called out to him.

I was more interested in a sandwich and was forging on

ahead when a man came out of the main entrance and shouted, "Harold! Harold!"

"Hello, hello, darling," I said, and continued on.

Cesar caught me by the arm.

"Isn't that your brother?" he asked.

"Oh, my God," I said. "Hello. Hello, DARLING."

Young George Murphy gave a hand searching for an important prop for that play:

One day we needed a slot machine, or a couple slot machines for, I think it was Strictly Dishonorable. *And Chamberlain's, [Richard R. Chamberlain Jr., technical director] "How the hell are we going to get slot machines?"*

I said, "I think I know somebody." So I went down and I saw this cop that was friends with my father in Holyoke. And I told him what was going on, so he picks up the phone, he calls my father.

He says, "Your kid's down here, he wants some slot machines." Now, my father knows nothing about this.

"He wants what?!"

I told him what was going on. He said, "You're not going to play—," I said, "No, they don't work. They don't have to work, they just need them."

"All right."

So, I forget how the hell we got them up there, but there was two of them, old fashioned slot machines. They had been confiscated, you know, in gambling raids in bars around Holyoke, and they put them all in the jail downstairs, the cells they don't use anymore. It's full of stolen items and slot machines.

Dick Van Patten was also in the cast, and George Murphy recalled:

One heck of a nice guy…he was a really gentle guy. You know, when you get to see these people later on, you know, when you're growing up and you see them on television, some of them – I never looked at Peggy Cass the same way on those dumb quiz shows till I met her. But when you see someone like Dick Van Patten, absolute gentleman.

Mr. Murphy explains the layout of the playhouse:

[The dressing rooms] *they were downstairs behind the stage. Under the stage was like a storage area for whatever the hell we kept there. There's two big double doors in the front that you never really saw. Then there was a stairwell that went down on either side, and one side was the dressing rooms. There was one at the end on the left side that was, like, the star's dressing room. It was bigger than any of the other ones. And then there was a prop room and—God, I can't remember what the hell was in the other one. It might have just been muslin. I don't know, because we would make and paint the flats, you know, re-use a lot of stuff, on the side of the building every Sunday.*

Wrap night we'd have to strike the set…after the last show. There was a matinee in the afternoon and one at night. Strike the set, get everything off the stage, start setting up the new one. Chamberlain [Richard R. Chamberlain Jr., technical director] *always had plans for the new one because they got them in advance, mailed in or something. And we'd start setting things up, these huge flats. We'd put keystones in the corner and bolt them together, and paint the things before you even put them up. Then you have to get the furniture.*

Dan Brunelle, another apprentice, recalls the pace:

While one show was running we were building sets for the next, 12 to 16-hour days followed by 48 to 78 hours of striking the old set and putting up the next. We did this every week for the whole season and I don't remember if I ever got tired.

George's duties at the playhouse were varied:

It depended. Many times I would run the curtain. I figured out, because that curtain was gigantic and very heavy, and you had to have certain curtain speeds depending on the scene for whatever reason. And they would have a list of scene 1, end of bedroom, something, you know, there was something on the wall they put. So I'd have a cue knowing exactly when they were going to end and I'd jump up and grab the downside and just hang on it and let my body weight pull it down, and it would start rolling like crazy. And then, I mean, I got so good at it, then I'd grab the up rope and it would yank me up, but

slow the curtain down so it just touched the stage. And I'd let go and, you know, and drop down.

Hugh Fordin notes:

I remember for the first year, Arlene Francis was there, we sold out so much that we opened the fire doors and we had people sitting on bridge chairs in the passage way. If the fire department had come, they would have closed me down. We had another, oh, two hundred people that came for the Wednesday matinee, I remember. So it was bearable.

In his own program, a souvenir from *Kind Sir* in which Arlene Francis starred, sixteen-year-old George Murphy poignantly wrote in the margins, "Arlene's great, but not as pretty on stage than she is on TV. She kissed me. Got autograph. Great week. Best one all year. G.M., 7-9-64."

***

The Holyoke Transcript-Telegram headline in June crowed:

Another Giant: Tallulah Coming to Holyoke

The playhouse subscription drive was thriving at the news of the big star's impending arrival.

George Murphy recalls his encounter with Tallulah Bankhead in an essay published on his blog *Holyoke Mass Radio WREB*, used here by permission:

That week arrived and naturally all shows were sold out; the sets were up and ready. The producer, Mr. Hugh Fordin, was nervous, having heard that Ms. Bankhead was somewhat difficult. Everything must be as perfect as possible. She arrived at Holyoke on a Sunday, and went directly to her lodgings, a mere cabin hidden in the woods of Mt. Tom. It was en route to this cabin that my one on one with Bankhead transpired.

Producer Hugh Fordin, in his preparations for the megastar, recalled his own experience a few years previously with Tallulah Bankhead. This was at the Sacandaga Playhouse in Sacandaga Park, upstate New York when he was in college. He had worked one summer as a press agent for Anthony Brady Barrell, who operated the playhouse. It was also a star-a-week operation. When Tallulah came to town, Fordin was tasked with taking her to an Albany television station, about an hour away, to promote her show. Fordin was about eighteen or nineteen years old. He remembers:

During the technical rehearsal I went backstage and I introduced myself to her, and she was very pleasant. I said I had a show that was going to feature her on Tuesday morning and I would come and pick her up and we'd go to Albany. So she said, "Okay."

So I came by early Tuesday morning, and her maid came out of her room with her breakfast tray, and I said, "Is Miss Bankhead dressed?"

And she said, "What do you mean, dressed?"

"She's going with me to Albany."

She said, "I don't think she thinks so, but you're welcome to go in." So I went in and Tallulah was in bed naked.

She did have a blanket over her thighs, but she was naked from the waist up. And I said, "Miss Bankhead, I thought you were going to—you promised that you'd—."

She said, "I promised nothing."

I said, "Yes, you did."

She said, "I'm not going anywhere, darling."

I said, "Yes, you are. You're going with me. I cannot reneg." I think it was the second week or the third week. And so I went out and I went downstairs, and I told the producer, I said, "I don't think she's going to come, and as far as I'm concerned, she can rot in bed."

Her maid heard that, went upstairs, and came right downstairs and said, "Miss Bankhead is dressing. She'll be with you in five minutes." And sure enough, in five minutes she was down and I'm rushing, I'm going like 70 mph on the New York State Thruway, and she's babbling on about the election. She was working for Adlai Stevenson for president, and she said, "Tell me, darling, who are you voting for?"

And I kept skipping the subject. She said, "No, no, no, no. Tell me, who are you going to vote for?"

I said, "I'm not voting, Miss Bankhead."

She said, "What do you mean? Are you an alien?"

I said, "No, no, no, Miss Bankhead. I'm not old enough to vote."

At which point, she said, "Stop this goddamn car." And she opened the door to my car, which I was going 70 mph. She said, "I'm being told by this child…!" I had to stop the car to get her calming down. She was hysterical. We did make it in time for the program.

That whole week [when she performed at the Mt. Tom Playhouse], *boy. I don't think I ever reminded her when she worked for me at Mt. Tom of that story, because I don't think she would have been too happy. I think she did remember me. When she came to work for me at Mt. Tom, she did remember having known me before, but not that story or that I was seventeen, eighteen years old. So, that's my Tallulah Bankhead story.*

Another wrinkle with Miss Bankhead's appearance in Holyoke made it a memorable visit:

Well, with Tallulah we did it on television—not live— videotape. The show had been leased by Heywood Hale Broun, Jr., who had a television production company, and so I remember that Monday of the opening night, Monday night, the cameras had to come in and cables, and we had a big truck in front of the theater, in the parking lot.

Tallulah Bankhead reportedly gave a vaudevillian performance *off stage*. She was to stay at the Hotel Northampton, arriving in July after a jet flight to Logan in Boston from Miami where she had also played in *Glad Tidings*. Hugh Fordin met her at Logan with two limos to accommodate her fifty-seven pieces of luggage. Fordin had to hire yet another limo for all of it.

The headline:

Miss Bankhead Is Here; Tired from Long Night.

Tallulah Bankhead is in town and she's exhausted…she and her entourage and her cast got into Logan Airport in Boston at 5 this morning after a jet flight from Miami, Florida, where she closed a two week engagement in the same Glad Tidings *at the Coconut Grove Theater at Miami Beach.*

It took three hours to reach Holyoke from Boston. George Murphy recalls:

Mid-afternoon on Monday, July 13th, a limousine pulled up next to the theater. The driver got out and stood to the right rear of the car. I was watching from the outside rear of the theater…as he just stood there in the July heat. We watched and waited for about fifteen minutes; another car pulled up, some people got out, went to the limo with the driver, and they all just stood there together. Finally, the driver opened the door… And there she was!, dressed in a long flimsy/frilly sort of gown/lingerie looking thing, flowered if I remember correctly. My first impression was that she hadn't slept in two days or had been taking the Holy Water for most of that day. She had a sharp temper, and at times swore like a sailor, but she was Tallulah and she could and would do as she wished, when

and how she wished it. Hugh Fordin warned us that whatever she needed, whenever she needed it… we were to "JUST GET IT!"

Dan Brunelle remembers going down to the dressing rooms to give Miss Tallulah her five-minute "call":

She was in her altogether and I said, "Five minutes, Miss Bankhead." She said, "Thank you, darling," entirely unabashed, and I climbed back up the stairs, trying not to seem stunned. Five minutes later she was fully costumed, on stage, and I was somehow more sophisticated. I was fifteen.

In *Glad Tidings*, a comedy, Miss Bankhead played the role of a movie actress who complicates the coming wedding of one of her many former flames. Sixteen-year-old George Murphy had an adventure he would remember. We give him the spotlight:

…Although I watched it eight times, I cannot, for the life of me remember anything about it. The only other actor I remember in the production was Evelyn Russell, who was a real gem to most of us, and pushed us in the right direction when it came to performing services for La Bankhead. The show went very well that week, and she was loved by all who came to see her. Ticket prices had been raised from an average $3.50 to $4.50, but the audience had gladly paid even that exorbitant fee! There was the definite impression, and rightly so, that she was usually pretty much half in the bag all of the time, but this condition did not as I recall, affect her stage performance at all. There were many demands that week, and we adhered to them as much as possible. The theater was very hot and not air conditioned, a major bone of contention at all times! And, the one thing, above all else... she demanded to have her newspapers, as many different ones as possible, delivered to her cabin every morning.

As the week went on, we all toed the line. She had remarked several times that I had beautiful hair, somewhat of an embarrassment for me, as she would always muss up my then full head of red hair. On Sunday, July 19,1964: I arrived at the theater early that day; as this was strike day, after the final performance of the current show, the old set came down and the new one would be erected overnight. Van Johnson was scheduled to act in the play, A Thousand Clowns. I was with the others outside the *theater, busily painting flats, when a frantic Hugh Fordin came tearing down the hill, looking like a grizzly bear was after him. "Did anybody remember to get her papers?" Apparently, the answer was no, so Fordin handed me a $10.00 bill and yelled, "GO GO GO, hurry up and get 'em (before she wakes up and creates another row)!!"*

The theater car was a brand new Rambler convertible, white with a red interior, on loan from Konner Rambler in Holyoke. It had about 600 miles on it. Now I was Batman, jumping into the Batmobile, taking off to save the reputation of the Mt. Tom Playhouse and all of the people involved with it. With unequaled speed, I raced down the access road from the playhouse to Route 5 and into the city, to the little candy and soda shop on Hampden Street in Holyoke; leapt out of the car, raced to the door to find the shop "Closed. On Vacation," damn!! Back in the car, racing up to the drugstore at the other end of town, I stopped to take a sample of every newspaper, that city paper, this local paper, that other one, The Racing Sheet; I didn't even know what she wanted, so I took them all. The guy at the counter just stared at me as I ran out of the store with an armful of newspapers, jumped into the Batmobile, emblazoned with the words "CAR OF THE STARS" on either side, and sped off into the sun.

The bottom of the dirt access road that lead to her cabin had a sign planted there that read "SPEED LIMIT 5 mph." I had never seen a 5 mph sign before as a speed limit, but quickly found out the reason for this, as I tore up the road at 40mph, straight up on one side, straight down on the other, Galahad on his quest! I don't remember seeing the hill and the big dip right after it. But, I do remember being airborne and the nose of the new convertible smashing into the ground on the other side of the dip (and the brakes that didn't work while the car was airborne). The explosion I heard was the front right tire. I got out, muttered a few words like "Golly Gee!" or words to that effect, grabbed the newspapers, and like a marathon runner, raced another half-a-mile uphill in the July sun.

I remember distinctly knocking on that screen door, and peering inside for movement. A lone figure came to the door, and I thought, "Oh man, please don't let her yell at me." The woman who came to the door was a black heavyset lady, and I informed her I had Ms. Bankhead's newspapers, as I stood there, shaken, soaked, and out of breath. Then the unmistakable voice echoed from somewhere deep in the cabin, "Who's there, Molly?" Molly may not have been the name called out, but I will

use it here. Molly asked what happened to me, I told her, and she said please come in. I entered with the sweat-soaked papers, and Molly again asked, "Can I get you something?" And, before I could answer, I heard THE VOICE say, "How about a drink, Dahling?" (In the back of my mind I thought, wow, she really does say that.) At sixteen, I opted for ice water and was told to sit down, a few feet away from Tallulah Bankhead!! She was wearing a light blue colored nightgown and her hair was pulled back; she had a drink in one hand and may have had a cigarette (or ten) in the other. She looked at me while playing with her hair and said, "So, what do you do?"

"I work at the theater," I answered.

She said, "A MOOOVV-ieee theater?" I said: "No ma'am, the theater where you are performing." She put on her glasses and said, "Oh, I know you, you have beautiful red hair...," then followed with, "I HATE THAT GODDAMNED THEATER!"

I excused myself, announcing that I had to go back down the mountain and change the tire. She then abruptly asked me why I had come up there in the first place. I quickly said, "To deliver your papers, ma'am."

Miss Tallulah

Barbara Bernard interviews the stars on *The Barbara Bernard Show*, Channel 40, WHYN-TV, Springfield, Mass. Here with Van Johnson. Photo courtesy of *The Republican* (Springfield, Mass.)

She waved her hand, "Oh, that." I then did something I have never done again in my whole life, I impulsively reached to kiss her hand and thank her for the water, overhearing again the magical voice, dismissing me thistime: "Anytime, Dahling! Anytime." Molly asked if I wanted to call anybody for help, I said no and started trotting down the mountain to the car.

I fixed the flat, and then proceeded back up the mountain, as you can only go one way, and that is the one and only way to turn around, up at the cabin. When I got there, Tallulah was outside, sitting at a table under a yard umbrella; she looked up at me. I waved, and she yelled out, "Back already, are we?" I explained to her that I was just turning around, and she waved at me like I was one of the neighbors. I went back to the theater and told them of my accident; the damage to the car was passed off

as minor, as long as she had gotten her newspapers. The matinee and the evening performances that day went well ... And, then, it was a wrap! I made sure to stand at the actors exit when she was to leave. She approached me, smiled, and without a word, walked by as I mumbled good-bye. (At least, I think she may have smiled; I really don't remember, though I do recall the delicious scent of her obviously expensive perfume, like an exquisite blue cloud that wafted around and trailed after her). I watched the slight stagger in her walk as she approached the limo... crushed out a cigarette and got into the car; then, she was gone.

I picked up the cigarette butt and put it away in a small paper bag with a note on the bag so as not to forget. Stupid, I guess, and now long lost somewhere forever, but I will never forget the Lady nor the time a sixteen-year-old

kid had the distinct honor of sitting down (albeit, momentarily) with an immortal and hearing her call me: "DAHHHHHHHLING!!!!" Good old Tallulah. She was something. I never saw a woman so drunk all the time. And smoke? Oh, my God. Something like six packs a day, like John Wayne.

Outrageous Tallulah would die three years later.

Van Johnson, up next in *A Thousand Clowns*, must have been anti-climactic. Regarding the Rambler from Konner's car dealership that George mentioned, Van Johnson gamely appeared in an ad in the program and in the local newspaper posed by a Rambler from Konner's. Mr. Johnson was actually Hugh Fordin's neighbor in Manhattan.

"He was lovely," Barbara Bernard recalls of Johnson's appearance on her television show at the studio in Springfield, "Oh, what a nice person to interview."

In *A Thousand Clowns*, the *Holyoke Transcript-Telegram* reviewer declared star Van Johnson was only so-so, but the show was good. Donald Buka, who had some minor Hollywood experience, including a role as one of the youngsters in *Watch on the Rhine* (1943) with Paul Lukas and Bette Davis, was in the supporting cast, "gets some feeling out of the part of Miss Gladstone's...partner, and wins through as a sympathetic though ineffectual villain."

George Murphy wasn't charmed by every star:

Peggy Cass would see you burned at the stake before anybody hurt her dogs. She was miserable.

Marc Gonneville was a hair stylist downtown at

the Kay-Harvey beauty parlor on Maple Street, which had been contracted to do the hair of the visiting stars in the summer of 1964. He recalled likewise of Peggy Cass:

Peggy Cass came with that dog. That dog was running around the shop. Whether she liked it or not, jumping on people's laps, but that was her baby. She was very, very nice. I will say that.

Though not all of the stars who came to have their hair done left a good impression, Gonneville discreetly refrains from criticizing, but notes, "*Most* of them were all very nice."

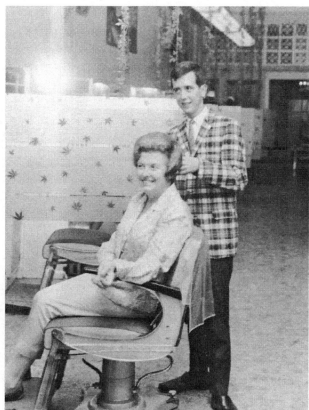

One of Marc Gonnevile's autographed programs.

The stars of the week would come every day for that evening's performance. Mr. Gonneville received a pair of complimentary tickets, and on his visits to the playhouse, would usually touch up the hair of the star at that point as well in the dressing room. Though the arrangement whereby the stars would drop by every day was more work for the salon, it was an interesting perspective to have access to these celebrities, to do their hair, and to come to know them, at least for a little while. Many gave Gonneville their autographs on play programs, or on their photos, which he kept in an album and generously shared for this project.

Peggy Cass and Marc Gonneville, photo credit Messenger Photos, courtesy Marc Gonneville

It was a lot of fun doing it, but I didn't get paid for that. It was all gratis. I just got, you know, my name is mentioned, and I used to get two tickets... some came in two, three times, but some came every day. You had to come do them when they were ready. They had rehearsals and stuff in between. But they were all very, very nice. I will say that. They were all very gracious people...I did Kathryn Crosby, Esther Williams. They walked around all over Holyoke, all of them.

Linda Seagrave, who was responsible for escorting the stars to various interview and TV appointments, shepherded them around sites in

Merv Griffin, stylist Marc Gonneville and cast members in the dressing room at the Mt. Tom Playhouse.
Photo courtesy Marc Gonneville.

the tri-city area. She noted in one program the delight of one star, Genevieve, who appeared with Donald Woods in *For Love or Money*, over her tour of an operations center on Westover Air Force Base.

George Murphy had mixed reviews of his encounters with the stars as a backstage apprentice. Of Merv Griffin, who appeared in the reviewed called *Broadway*:

After the show was over, he was sitting there playing the piano and whoever the hell the girl was in the show was standing there, I was on the stage and I just happened to stop and I'm watching him play the piano. I'm listening, and I look down. There's a dime on the floor. So I reached down and I picked it up. He had stopped playing,

they were just talking, and I said, "You might have dropped that, Mr. Griffin."

He says, "I don't want that."

I said, "I found it here on the floor."

And he was, [pretends to swipe the "dime" off the piano], *"I don't want the goddamn….!"*

"Okay." That was Merv Griffin.

He thought Lloyd Bridges was nicer.

I got to know Lloyd Bridges really well. I mean, we just were buddies. And he had a son up there, Jeff Bridges was up there. And Jeff and I at one time went up on the rides at Mountain Park and we palled around together and we hung out on the railing—I mean, who would have known? You know? Who would have known? We were both the same age. So I was downstairs where the dressing rooms and makeup and everything is and I just happened to pass by Lloyd's dressing room. You know, I said, "Hi, Mr. Bridges."

He said, "George, come here!" I went inside. He said, "Do you know where I can get a tape recorder?"

I said, "Yes, Sir, I can have one for you by tomorrow." Now, my cousin, Billy Fisher, had a tape recorder. So, I borrowed the thing and brought it up to the playhouse the next day, gave it to Lloyd Bridges and he had it for, like, two days. And did whatever he had to do, and I brought it back. And that's why he wrote [Mr. Bridges autographed George's program] what he wrote there, 'you've been very helpful,' or whatever it says, just because I brought him a tape recorder and hung around with his kid named Jeff. Who would have known?

Lloyd Bridges had his hair cut by Marc Gonneville and signed his photo to Gonneville: "Thanks for making my wife so pretty." He remembers Bridges as being very friendly. "He was great." His son, Jeff and his wife also came down to the salon.

That show also provided a little excitement. George Murphy remembers:

Oh, God, the fire scare. I was up at the concession stand again, and it's awfully quiet there, very quiet out front when the show's going on. You can kind of hear the stage show, but all of a sudden, you hear all this twittering coming through the doors, like something—you know, it's like people, you can hear them low talking, whispering.

So I go over to the door and I open up the door and peek in. And on both sides of the stage there's what appears to be smoke coming from the wings. And everybody, I guess, thought it was a fire. Well, I go out in front and I come running around to run down the side of the building, and I run into Richard Chamberlain [Richard R. Chamberlain Jr., technical director] or one of those guys, and I said, "What the hell's going on? Something on fire?"

And he said, "Nobody knows. Nobody knows." They called the fire department, or they're calling them, or whatever. He says, "Go on in and close the windows."

I said, "Are you serious?"

He says, "Go in and close the windows. We don't want to create a panic."

I said, "What the hell good is closing the windows going to do when it's 99 degrees out?"

He said, "The fire department's going to come in here. They're going to come in quiet, with no lights. Go close the goddamn windows!" So, okay.

So now the play's going on and this thing is huge, and I'm walking around, and my hands folded, and I get to one of the windows, which isn't a window. It's a gigantic piece of wood [gestures, arms spread] this wide, and probably as tall as the ceiling to the floor. It's held up by ropes, so when you open the window, it's got ropes and pulleys. You pull on this rope and it swings the wood in. I mean, you tie it off so the wood is open. And it leaves it open, so every night creature that flies, you know, comes through, mosquitoes and all kinds of stuff on the stage.

So I go over there and I'm doing just the south side because they're going to be coming that way. I lower this thing very nonchalant. I'm going—the people were, they're looking at the stage trying to figure out what's going on. The show is still going on, but this didn't look like smoke. It looked like fog. There was no smell to it. It just came out of nowhere out of both sides of the stage. I get all four or five of the windows closed. The fire department shows up, no headlights. No lights, no sirens. There was three of them, I think.

And they come pulling in, in front. Firemen get out. I was out there with a bunch of other people. They all go down, he said, "Is there any way to get into the theater without, you know, the stage?" whoever the hell this fireman was.

I said, "Yeah, you got to go around back. There's a walkway back there." So we go down through the dirt, up these stairs, down to the walkway. Now there's a second level where the dressing rooms are and prop rooms, and all that. And there's a little bit of this stuff down there, but nothing's burning. Nothing smells like smoke and nobody has any clue where the hell this stuff came from. We just don't know. They check the outside of the building, inside of the building, everything. Didn't find a single thing.

So now we go into the future. We go about maybe another month and a half or so and the show comes up and it might have been High Spirits. *I don't remember. But at one point they're trying to summon a genie, and whoever the hell was trying to summon him had a bottle, like, you know, things they use for genies. And put it in this potted plant thing that was there so you couldn't see it. And then he said the magic words, or whatever he did, and poof, there's this gigantic puff of what looks like smoke.*

It was flash powder.

When we saw it, it dawned on everybody that's what it had to be, and that canister, if it went off, I remember the canister was huge—they had to have somebody that was licensed or something to, you know, to set all that stuff up. But somehow, some of that ignited somewhere in the stage. That's the only thing we could think of, because it's odorless, it looks like smoke, but then again, it looks like

mist. So it had to be that.

In Anniversary Waltz, *Lloyd Bridges had to kick his foot through a TV screen. And the screen was facing away from the audience, and obviously, there wasn't a picture tube in it. So I was the guy with the hole in the flat backstage that made the sound of the TV, him kicking it—again, flash powder. That's what it was! It was the flash powder from the Lloyd Bridges show,* Anniversary Waltz. *That's where everybody put two and two together. It was* Anniversary Waltz.

George had to make the sound of Lloyd Bridges kicking through the TV:

We practiced before the show even started. Lloyd Bridges is on stage, and I'm backstage, and I had one of those big galvanized steel tubs with about thirty smashed bottles in it, broken. And I would look and watch him. I discovered that when he stood in front of the TV and he went to kick the TV, he'd lift his knee up and go like this [demonstrates] *in one fluid movement. And I—it took that long for the pan to fall. When his knee went up, I dropped it. He foot went forward, it hit the ground at the same time. The puff of smoke—and it sounded like he had put his foot through the TV set.*

Lloyd Bridges, photo courtesy Marc Gonneville

Fellow apprentice Dan Brunelle recalls another near mishap:

I don't remember the particular production, but I do remember being out in the house watching with another apprentice when a scene change was coming up requiring five people to pull one set upstage and another set to be flown from the wings. The set began to roll upstage but went out of alignment, at which point, the other apprentice and I remembered that we were two of the five people supposed to be pulling and weren't. We threw ourselves down the aisle and out to the stage entrance—to the great amusement of the audience—straightened things out and thankfully were not fired. The audience loved it. The curtain was up the whole time the entire kerfuffle displayed. These are the things that make live theatre unique to each audience and why it's so much fun.

In August Kathryn (Mrs. Bing, as she was billed) Crosby starred in *Sabrina*. Producer Hugh Fordin recalls:

She was always advertised as "Kathryn—indent—Mrs. Bing Crosby." Well, she didn't like that at all, and she came in at the Hartford airport, and I went to pick her up. She was the last person to get off the plane. And I said, "Mrs. Crosby, I'm Hugh Fordin, the producer."

She said, "Yes, I know."

I said, "Can I help you off?" She was very abrupt and rude.

She said, "No, I'll get off myself." Well, as it turned out, Bing Crosby came to Holyoke that week and he couldn't have been nicer.

Kathryn Crosby

George Murphy remembered:

One Sunday morning I was there when Kathryn Crosby was doing a show. Sabrina Fair, okay. And I was out in front. I was sweeping the apron out in front of the theater, and I heard a car coming. I turned around and here's this black limousine-looking thing pulls up with tinted windows right there where I'm standing with a broom. And the back window goes down and this face comes out. And he said, "Seen my wife, son?"

And it's Bing Crosby. I said, "No, Sir, I haven't...Merry Christmas." I really said that, "Merry..." and he laughed like hell. And then they went up to Hugh Fordin's office. At that time, I didn't know where the cabin was where I had that thing with Tallulah. I didn't know about that. Nobody knew about that. There's only a few people that knew where the cabin was off Route 5. It was up a dirt road up the mountain and, with dips and—boy. Who the hell would have thought that a dippy kid like me would be sweeping up a piece of asphalt and Bing Crosby would ask me where his wife is? You know, it sounds like stuff from a fairy tale, and I was impressionable then.

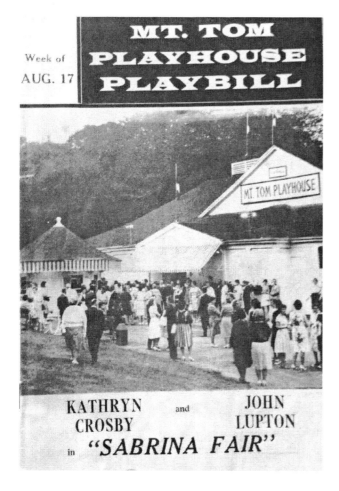

Week of
AUG. 17

MT. TOM
PLAYHOUSE
PLAYBILL

KATHRYN and JOHN
CROSBY LUPTON
in "SABRINA FAIR"

From the *Holyoke Transcript-Telegram:*

Bing Crosby and wife, Kathryn, gave superb performances Saturday night. Bing gave his to an appreciative audience of newsmen, while Kathryn performed before a capacity Mt. Tom Playhouse audience including Bing.

Bing spoke to journalists in the office of the Howard Johnson Motor Lodge on Northampton Street, where he and his wife were staying. He talked about his new TV show (*The Bing Crosby Show*), a family situation comedy that would air in September on local Channel 40, WHYN. (It lasted one season.) He flew from California, but was unable to land at Boston's Logan airport due to fog, so they landed instead at Hanscom Field in New Bedford and a chauffeured limousine took him to Holyoke. Mayor Daniel F. Dibble and the Holyoke Police met him at Exit 4 of the Massachusetts Turnpike. Mayor Dibble got into Bing's limo and drove to the hotel, arriving at 8:30 p.m. A large crowd in the meantime had also gathered at Barnes Airport in Westfield, expecting him to arrive there, as he was originally to have landed at Barnes from Logan.

Hugh Fordin recalls:

The press was there, and I said, "Mr. Crosby, would you mind if the press came into my office," and he did an interview, and he said, "No, not at all." He came in and did the interview.

Photos filled the paper of Bing and Kathryn standing outside the Howard Johnson Motor Lodge, and later of Kathryn checking out at the desk, and one of Kathryn and her mother, Mrs. Grandstaff, who had accompanied her. They arrived earlier for rehearsals. The newspapers gave more coverage to Bing Crosby's visit to the mountain than the play.

Sunday morning Big said he was a little upset about all of the security, but supposed it may have been necessary.

Mt. Park was jammed, despite the bad weather, with several thousand cars and people.

The *HT-T* noted that Crosby appeared relaxed and joking, and despite his being sixty years old,

Marc Gonneville in salon with Eloise Hardt (second from right) and Mrs. Lloyd Bridges families; Jeff Bridges on far right.
Photo courtesy Marc Gonneville.

was still going strong, "and gave a superb performance." He was taken to the playhouse and sat in the rear to enjoy the performance. He was finally able to greet his wife back at the Motor Lodge after the show. "Dinner, previously ordered from the Howard Johnson Motel, was sent to the room. It included champagne and barbecued chicken with all the works."

It was reported that Mayor Dibble and the Holyoke police, "spent considerable time with Crosby." The Crosbys left at 11:30 a.m. Sunday morning (Bing must have caught the last show), and were "gracious people" who requested that copies of the pictures and the *Transcript-Telegram* clippings be sent to them. A shot of Bill

Humphrey, the public relations representative for the playhouse, and Chester Swider, special services unit of the Holyoke Police flanked Crosby. *Sabrina Fair* enjoyed "capacity audiences."

In August 1964, Fernando Lamas directed as well as starred in *Once More with Feeling* with his soon-to-be wife, Esther Williams. The *Holyoke Transcript-Telegram* noted that Mr. Lamas, "...generally enlivened the evening with his discreet mugging. His portrayal of Victor Fabin is the best...and most convincing character on stage."

In a review by Timothy Dacey of the *Transcript*,

208

Esther Williams "managed to convey warmth and sympathy…"

The curtain became stuck as it rose for Act I and had to be disentangled by a stagehand in the snowiest white tennis shoes I have ever seen.

Fernando Lamas

Hugh Fordin remembers:

Fernando Lamas and Esther Williams came. They hadn't married yet and they really acted like teenagers, they were so sweet. I remember taking them to dinner. We went to the Yankee Pedlar.

George Murphy recalls the intermission music:

"The Pink Panther Theme," that and a tape by Michel Legrand. That and "The Pink Panther Theme" were the only two tapes they had for music when people were coming in and leaving. And so they'd put in the Pink Panther — da dum, dad um — the whole thing. The whole soundtrack. Then when that ended — that was another one of my jobs. Go to the tape recorder—I got to know every note of every one of those. And then Michel Legrand would go on, and then you had a problem. Then you had to rewind Michel Legrand, and then you put on the Pink

Esther Williams, photo courtesy Marc Gonneville

Panther, rewind that, and you start the Pink Panther over. Ba-dum, ba-dum….

I missed that so much I went out and bought the disc.

Hugh Fordin noted in his interview for this book that putting in air conditioning for the Mt. Tom Playhouse "would have been prohibitive. I mean, it was a huge theater. We had very big fans, and the door, the side panels would flip open. On each wall next to the doors, they had these big panels so that you could pull a pulley and they'd open up."

George Murphy notes:

The place was in pretty bad shape. We were constantly fixing something, especially leaks. I mean, there's nothing worse than having actors on the stage and there's water pouring down on them. That happened once — not pouring, but I mean, you know, just water dripping down. I don't think the audience even noticed, but we did. And the problem there is, you get an actor who doesn't know it's there and steps in it, and goes flying.

***

"Hugh Fordin is back." The *Holyoke Transcript-Telegram* crowed at the beginning of the 1965 season, "A simple declarative statement of fact that possesses a singular wealth of meaning for residents of Holyoke and the surrounding area."

A photo of the natty young man, arms crossed, leaning on a convertible, looking young, hip, and in control. He was theatre savvy despite his youth, packaged-show savvy, and by his second season surely knew he was playing toe-to-toe with the Storrowton Music Fair just south of Holyoke.

From *Transcript-Telegram*:

Last year, the old Casino on the mountain became, officially, the Mt. Tom Playhouse and, as such, joined the ranks of the major summer theatres in the East. Tradition-steeped playhouses such as Paramus...Paper Mill, Bucks County, Westport, Famous Artists, Dennis and Falmouth had to make room for a late-coming newcomer. And an era was begun.

Scheduled for the 1965 season:

Sheila Macrae in *Born Yesterday*.
Eve Arden in *Beekman Place*.
Tony Martin in his all-star review.
George Hamilton in *Gigi*.
Beatrice Lillie in *High Spirits*.
Arlene Francis in *Mrs. Dalley Has a Lover*.
Dana Andrews in *A Remedy for Winter*.
Alexis Smith and Craig Stevens in *Mary, Mary*.
Martha Raye in *Everybody Loves Opal*.
Walter Pidgeon in *The Happiest Millionaire*.

Imogene Coca was also scheduled, but cancelled the closing show and its replacement was *Stop the World, I Want to Get Off*, the Anthony Newley musical.

Born Yesterday had been done by The Valley Players in the 1950s when it was hot off Broadway. Star Sheila Macrae drew praise in her comic role. Just as the Mt. Tom Playhouse was banking on big names to make it thrive, so one could see that the big names were the most mentioned in the local press reviews. The star, rather than the play, was judged, though the supporting cast was still mentioned. Harry Brock

was played by Frank Campanella.

Gordon Macrae, the handsome baritone of 1940s and 1950s Hollywood musicals, visited his wife, like Bing Crosby of the previous year, staying at the Howard Johnson's Motor Lodge on Northampton Street. The newspaper ran a photo of them at pool, "eating fried chicken with their fingers and drinking coffee out of paper cups," and of them reading the *Transcript*.

Sheila had arrived at Westfield's Barnes Airport,

jokingly pretending to be her ditsy character, according to the article, "Right in character. She stepped off her chartered twin-engine airplane, she said, "So this is *Springfield!* I can't believe it!" She had flown in from Lake Tahoe, "including a short flight on Frank Sinatra's private jet."

A review by Michael McCartney gushed, Sheila Macrae, "makes play tingle." Sheila Macrae was a popular young current star, but a veteran movie star was next. The Mt. Tom Playhouse ran a display ad for *Born Yesterday* and to announce that Eve Arden was next to appear in *Beekman Place.*

Underneath, Storrowton ran an ad for their latest production: Ann Corio in *This Was Burlesque,* which had run for three years on Broadway. It would otherwise be only a footnote in the long span of Storrowton's guest entertainers, except that in two more years, Storrowton Music Fair founder Wally Beach would sell the enterprise to Ann Corio and her husband, Mike Innuncio. They would change the name to Storrowton Theatre, and would eventually show fewer stage musicals and more nightclub and concert-style acts.

Eve Arden co-starred with her husband, Brooks West, in *Beekman Place* by Samuel Taylor. The reviewer for the *Transcript-Telegram* said that she ran away with the show. No reviews of this period go into detail about the cast, not as much as the star. Most of the shows featured smaller casts, as would become the norm in regional theatre in the decades to come, to save money on salaries.

Eve Arden

George Murphy has very warm memories of Eve Arden:

She was gracious. She was Our Miss Brooks*; that was the same person. To me, it was the same person. And it's funny when you're young like that and you see somebody on TV and then you see them—you know, they're really like that. My brother, who was eight years my junior, he was up there this one evening. I think because he just wanted to meet that lady on television, and he just stood there, staring at her.*

And Eve went, "What's your name?"

"James."

"Hello, James, it's nice to meet you." And she bent down;

JUNE 28 thru July 3

MT. TOM PLAYHOUSE PLAYBILL

EVE ARDEN in **"Beekman Place"**

she kissed him on the cheek. And he talked about that ad infinitum, you know? He could not get over that Eve Arden kissed him on the cheek. She was gracious.

The *Transcript-Telegram* featured an article that week, "Cable TV – What is it?" What it was, was going to take over American popular culture in a few more decades, but nobody was predicting that now.

Anne Meara & Jerry Stiller,
George Murphy collection

Tony Martin brought his all-star review in July. One member of his troupe was Nancy Ames, known then for being the "TW3 Girl," the featured singer on the television comedy about current news events: *That Was the Week That Was.* She was billeted at the Schine Inn in Chicopee, having arrived with her husband, her manager, and her conductor. As the reporter for the *Holyoke Transcript-Telegram* interviewed her by the hotel pool noted:

One fan, a Westover AFB Captain, recognized her as the TW3 girl and politely requested Miss Ames to endorse the copy of a briefing he was about to give.

One assumes it was not a top-secret briefing.

Later in the interview, another Westover man, an NCO, asked her to autograph his conference schedule.

Star Tony Martin lost at least one fan in George Murphy, who remembers:

Tony Martin. Hated me. Hated me. He would go onstage—and he'd sing and the audience would go nuts. And there was one song—and again, I was always on stage left and I was always running the curtain. Somehow I got hornswoggled into bringing him a glass of gin with ice in it when this break, this certain song ended. They had a break and I would walk out on the stage and take this glass of gin and put it on the piano, and turn around and walk back. Then I'd stand there and watch him, you know, just waiting till I do my curtain thing.

So one night somebody in his entourage thought it'd be cute if they replaced it with water. Now, Tony Martin has no idea where this booze is coming from. There's just this short, red-haired, freckled face kid brings it out to him. For all he knows, I put it in there. So I'm standing there and he takes a sip and looks at the audience, and he— then he looks back and he glares at me. And I don't know what's wrong. I'm looking around, what the hell is this? When he got off stage, he went absolutely ballistic backstage.

He would have his drinking buddies come up and stay there till three, four, five o'clock in the morning getting toasted to the gills. They'd—nobody would say anything. So somebody would have to hang around there all night to lock up the theater till he and his cronies were all gone.

But he was livid because somebody put water in that glass, and I didn't find out till after the fact. They all thought it was hilarious.

While Howard Keel was wowing them in *South Pacific* at the Storrowton, George Hamilton brought the non-musical version of *Gigi* to the Mt. Tom Playhouse, a play that Hal Holbrook had starred in for The Valley Players when it was hot off Broadway. A few rocky moments were noted by the *Transcript-Telegram* reviewer, but the show was judged by the star, and not for its overall presentation.

George Murphy, like the newspaper, marveled at

the celebrities.

I sat out in the back there—there was a walkway that ran completely through the back of the theater and looked down into the woods. I sat out there one time with George Hamilton, and he hated Hugh Fordin with a passion. We sat out there and he just started talking about "blah, blah, son-of-a-bitch…" He was mad at—I don't know what happened between them. So I remember sitting there with him. We were both leaning in these chairs up against the back of the theater. And he said, "What goes on up there?"

I said, "Well, there's rides and games of chance, a regular amusement park."

He said, "You want to take a walk up?"

I said, "Sure." So he goes in the theater and he yells for his band manager, orchestra manager. He was doing Gigi *at the time. And all three of us go up there. Now, one of the drawbacks of me being at that theater most of my living life during the summer then is that I had a girlfriend who could care less about the theatre. And she was sick and tired of me, never seeing me, I'm always at the theater. So one day she said, "Bye."*

So now I'm walking down the midway on whatever day this was, and I got the bandleader on one side and George Hamilton's here and we're talking, all three of us. And I look up, and can you believe it, here comes Mary with her girlfriend. And we're walking down, and she looks at me and she recognized George Hamilton, I guess. Like, her jaw just dropped, [imitating], "Hi there!"

And I just kept walking with him. And I'm—[ignores her].

So those were the, you know, just some of the things that made it all worthwhile, because you never knew what was going to happen.

This season Beatrice Lillie was scheduled to appear in "the first full-scale Broadway musical comedy hit to ever appear in Holyoke."

George Murphy recalled:

She was in High Spirits. *And we actually built in one night a track, a steel track in the stage running from stage left to stage right that she would ride. She would ride—there's a song called "The Bicycle Song." And Bea Lillie as the medium—rides a bike across the stage…at that time she was eighty years old! And she would sit on this—it would be pulled across the stage. [Imitates her warbling voice] "Give me a bike, give me—" Oh, jeez, I'm telling you. You had to see it.*

Don Grigware recalls, "I remember her first entrance, riding a bicycle onstage and waving hello to everyone in that brusque, curt manner of hers, which was so terribly amusing."

Bea Lillie, photo George Murphy collection

Hugh Fordin:

I remember we even had to reinforce the rigging because the second year I brought in Bea Lillie in High Spirits *and she had to fly. And the fly gallery wasn't strong enough to support it, so we had to bring in steel beams to reinforce it.*

Curtain time was actually delayed opening night an hour and forty-three minutes while stagehands frantically adjusted the scenery that was meant for a larger stage. When the show finally went on, however, critics and audience felt the star was "magnificent." *High Spirits* had been touring for three months after a year on Broadway. The stage veteran who debuted in 1915 took it in stride, and apparently still enjoyed tinkering with the show. An ad-lib on opening night during one production number: Miss Lillie suddenly cried out to the audience, "Help! My living bra is dying!" In an interview with the *Holyoke Transcript-Telegram*, she confessed:

"I just threw that in for the cast, but the audience seemed to love it."

Also in that newspaper a column that regularly listed the events of "100 years ago…50 years ago…25 years ago…" In the "10 Years Ago" heading was listed a reprint of the obituary for Joseph Foley, who had died during the run of *The Caine Mutiny Court-Martial* in 1955.

10 YEARS AGO
July 23, 1955

Joseph Fitzgerald Foley, 45, a founder of the Valley Players and one of the best loved and most widely known members of the group, died suddenly at 9 this morning at the home of Mrs. Faith C. Jenks, 151 Locust St., where he had been staying this week. The show, "Caine Mutiny Court Martial," of which he was the star, has been cancelled.

A lot had changed in ten years. The stars were a sure attraction, but they didn't belong to Holyoke the way Joseph Foley did. They were just passing through. It was not so much a matter of what play was up next, but what star.

Television's Arlene Francis was next at bat. Hugh Fordin notes:

I remember two years in a row I had Arlene Francis because she did so well for me. What's My Line was still running on television, and I even bought a commercial for her show to go locally out of the Hartford station, CBS.

Don Grigware recalls, "My father just raved about how nice Arlene Francis was. I was thrilled as we watched her every week on *What's My Line* on TV."

Arlene had returned in *Mrs. Dalley Has a Lover,*

costarring with Ralph Meeker in this drama that was actually a Broadway try-out. Re-tooled as *Mrs. Dalley*, it did indeed open on Broadway that September, and ran for fifty-three performances, closing in November. It drew a great crowd at the Mt. Tom Playhouse, and though the star was clearly an audience favorite, the play itself drew mixed reviews.

Hollywood star Alexis Smith and her husband, Craig Stevens—known as television's *Peter Gunn*, appeared together in the comedy, *Mary, Mary*. Fordin recalls how he acquired the popular Hollywood couple:

My very first indoctrination into the professional theater happened the summer of '61—no, '59. I was going to the L'Eglise Française in New York to learn French because I was engaged to a French girl, and the woman sitting next to me in class was Flora Roberts, who was a very famous literary agent and the agent for Stephen Sondheim and Ira Levin. Ira Levin had just had a success on Broadway of a play called Critics Choice.

Flora and I became very friendly and she said, "Listen, Craig Stevens and Alexis Smith are going out on tour this summer in Critics Choice, and I'm not happy at all with the guy who's packaging the show. So most of the bookings are taken care of, but why don't you take it over?" because she had control over the play, and naturally, you know, no packager can assert his authority over the playwright's agent.

Alexis Smith

So I said, "Sure, I'd love to." And so I booked the rest of the tour and wanted to learn a little bit more about how packages were done, and I went along with the show and became very friendly with Craig Stevens and Alexis Smith.

The summer I had my—oh, and I bought a dog that summer and I named him Parker, which was the character that Craig played in Critics Choice. Now I have the theater on Mt. Tom and the second year Mary, Mary is being made available to certain summer theaters, but the royalty was very high. But I didn't mind it at all, because I could afford it in the size theater I had. And Crag and Alexis were going to be touring it, so, of course, I jumped on the bandwagon and I alienated a lot of producers,

summer stock producers, because they wanted me to boycott the show, and I didn't want to do that at all. So Craig and Alexis came and we, of course, reunited our friendship during opening night.

AUG. 9 thru AUG. 14

MT. TOM PLAYHOUSE PLAYBILL

CRAIG STEVENS   ALEXIS SMITH

in

"MARY, MARY"

Alexis and Craig prefaced their performance with a good will appearance at the Holyoke Stop & Shop supermarket on Lincoln and Hampden streets at 5 p.m. on Tuesday. The chain was celebrating its fiftieth anniversary, and were offering a drawing of free tickets to the show.

"Parker Ballantine", Fordin's little dog, (whose photo appeared in many programs along with the cast) had an unexpected starring role as well on opening night:

I never had him on a leash. He would just stay in—I had a little bungalow next to the playhouse, which was my office. *He usually either stayed there or he'd go out and just walk around. Sometimes he'd come in with some paint over his face because he went backstage and I knew that they were playing a trick, and the paint was water paint anyway.*

Craig Stevens

Opening night, I'm backstage with him, he walks on stage. During—and it was a scene in which Craig had his back momentarily to the audience, but Alexis was on stage and she saw the dog. And of course, she had to ad lib and she said, "Parker, what are you doing here? You're supposed to be offstage."

And I remember Craig turned around, white, because he thought, "My God, Alexis has blown it." Another play, entirely [Parker was Craig's character's name in Critic's Choice*]. So she picked up Parker and she said, "Parker's our dog, ladies and gentlemen." And she went offstage and she handed it to me.*

"She was beautiful," says Barbara Bernard, "She was absolutely gorgeous, and gracious. She was so good."

"What a class act!" Don Grigware recalls.

Her decade or so of touring in plays, with and without her husband turned out to be, of course, a prelude to her so-called "second act in life" triumph when she appeared on Broadway in 1971 and won a Tony Award for Stephen Sondheim's *Follies*. Fordin recalls:

Alexis and I remained very good friends. When she opened in Follies*, I was there opening night. Unbelievable. Nobody could imagine that she could do what she did. I mean, her dancing, and her singing, everything about it. It was just—it was tailor-made for her.*

I went backstage afterwards—and she used to kid to me about the days that she was at Warner Bros. and one movie in particular, called Night and Day*, with Cary Grant on Cole Porter. One scene, she said, where Cary Grant is at the piano trying to compose the song, "Night and Day." And she has to come in and say, "It's eleven o'clock, Lieutenant. Lights out." And she kept falling apart, she kept breaking up. They had to do that about twelve times. And she was an armed forces nurse at that point in the—*

So when I went backstage, went into her dressing room, and she said, "Well, what'd you think?"

I said, "I'm disappointed, Alexis, you didn't wear your army shoes." She broke up. She broke up. But I got so carried away with her. My friendship to Craig and Alexis remained from that playhouse days until shortly before her sudden death [in 1993 of brain cancer].

That was one of the high points of Mt. Tom, having them there, because it went full circle. You know, my first package and then my theater.

Hollywood veteran Dana Andrews performed in the romantic comedy, *A Remedy for Winter.* The play was still in development for a Broadway tryout, and Mr. Andrews as the aging lover had joined the cast only two weeks previously. The *Transcript-Telegram* thought he "fights the Mt. Tom acoustics a bit, but comes through to the audience as an individual, rather than the stereotype that often results from this kind of part."

Hugh Fordin recalls:

He was a recovering alcoholic. And I shouldn't say recovering, because he was still drinking, and it was not a successful week. The play was—the play never came into New York. But Leonard Spiegelgass wrote it. It wasn't a very successful play. He wasn't a very good stage actor. He was much better on film than he was—there are a lot of actors that are like that. They're very minimalist and—not that you have to be with large gestures, but he was really a close-up camera man.

Over at the Storrowton Music Fair, Lee Remick starred in *Annie Get Your Gun.* The Everly Brothers were scheduled to perform at Mountain Park on Friday, August 13th.

George Murphy recalled:

I'd be up at the concession stand. One night I was up there, hot summer night. And it's deathly quiet. You could hear the ambient noise from the Mountain Park and the rides. And here comes this guy running down the hill. I was leaning out the front of the theatre. This guy comes running down the hill and he runs up to me, and I look at him, and I recognize him. He said, "Is Mr. Fordin around?"

I said, "No, he's usually up the hill there in his little office."

"Yeah, but is he here now?" And this guy had a black eye. It was Phil Everly. He and his brother were up at

the Mountain Park doing a performance that Phil Dee was emceeing or something, and he came running down looking for Fordin.

How he got the black eye was not revealed.

The next star, Martha Raye, told Warren Craig of *Holyoke Transcript-Telegram:*

"New England people are so nice. The audiences are blunt, and if they like you, then you know you are really performing."

Raye starred in *Everybody Loves Opal.* One of the minor cast members was Gaylord Mason, as the *Transcript-Telegram* noted: "The one who used to play the young lead roles with The Valley Players, …handles the small role of a cop with aplomb." One wonders what kind of a homecoming it might have been for him.

Martha Raye, of course, was the whole show, with a spotlight so bright on her it didn't really shine on anybody else. Jon Klarfeild of the *Transcript-Telegram* wrote in his review:

But there's no play, really. The evening is actually Martha Raye doing what she does best, roaring, hamming, communicating with the audience, getting the audience to love her, ad libbing, double-talking and all that tried and true send-them-home-loving-you-to-death bit…If you want to enjoy this one, you'd better be certain you like Martha Raye and all that entails. Because you're not going to get an awful lot of Martha at her best, and precious little else.

George Murphy remembered:

I was chosen one night to sing "Happy Birthday" on stage in front of 1,500 people, whatever it was, to Martha Raye. And I stood up there, and I remember somebody had made up a phony dollar bill, a big one with her picture in the middle where Washington should be. And I stood up there, "Happy birthday…" And of course, the audience…

Singing "Happy Birthday" to Martha Raye. That was something else. We would sit out—she was just the same in person as she was on TV. She was that silly—she'd get up on the stage and they had go into intermission and she'd stand there and she'd go like this (pantomimes adjusting breasts) flip them over the shoulder and she was a riot. Very, very nice. You got both ends of the spectrum. You know? You got the people that, "I'm a star." The other ones that, "Eh, I'm just like you." You know. Those are the great ones. Those are the ones you remember that you wish that, you know, you had done more, or taken pictures, or done, kept in touch or whatever.

It was fun to see the stars up close. Peggy Bowe, who ushered for a few shows in the summer of 1965, notes an encounter in town:

There was an actress that had been on As the World Turns *forever, she was—at least to me at the time, an older woman. She was probably in her forties or fifties, again, and she had gone on a 'European vacation' on the soap. Most Sunday mornings my parents and I would go in to Howard Johnson's after church, and there she was having her breakfast. And I whispered to my mother, "That's—"*

But she didn't believe me. "No, it isn't."

I insisted, "Yeah, it is." And the actress obviously heard me, and she looked up and smiled and just said,

"Good morning, dear."

Martha Raye

Sheryl Mardeusz, who grew up in Chicopee, recalls being a child of twelve and leading her younger sister and brother on an outing to Newberry's on High Street across from city hall.

My sister and I took the bus from Willimansett to Holyoke…we don't remember the purpose, if it was just to walk around or whatever. But we did go to the soda fountain… they used to serve the sodas in these paper cones that were in these, like, silver bottom parts at the soda fountain. That's how they used to give you your soda.

So we were sitting there having our sodas, and a lot of the clerks were all a-twitter and all excited because a movie star had just walked into the store, and it was Walter Pidgeon. He was already an older man at the time, and he had, I remember, like a loose sweater and he had just pants and a shirt. He was very gracious, very nice. He was giving autographs to everyone. It was so cute the way all the little sales clerks were, like, ooh!, you know. And when once one girl or two got his autograph, they all came over, and he was gracious. He was happy to do it…In those days I was too young and bashful. But he was very gracious, he really was.

Young George Murphy had a different experience as Mr. Pidgeon's dresser:

Walter Pidgeon needed a valet every place he went to help him during his changes backstage. You'll never guess who they chose. Yeah. So, I had to be his valet. He was a miserable old curmudgeon, he was.

So I was told by his agent or his—somebody associated with him, he said, "Look," he says, "You're going to get paid for this. If he likes you, you get $50," which was a lot of money back then. "If he doesn't like you, you only get $20. That way you'll know if he liked you or didn't." Fifty if he does, twenty if he don't.

I said, "Okay, fine." So I helped him. He was just miserable.

"I don't want that! I said this thing over here!" And he'd sit there in his boxer shorts and I'm, "Oh, God, how do I get involved in this—?"

So I got through the week, and the company all packed up and they're ready to go, and this guy that was with them comes over and says, "Mr. Pidgeon wants to thank you. Take care. Bye." He left. I open it up. Ten bucks. He hated me. He hated me. Somebody wrote a story about that once in the newspaper. I got a clipping somewhere. He hated me.

Howard Johnson Motor Inn

Walter Pidgeon was another one of the stars who stayed at the Howard Johnson's, where he was interviewed poolside by the *Transcript*.

A bigger star Hugh Fordin's Mt. Tom Playhouse has not seen, yet a more affable star has yet to be encountered on the interview circuit.

As with most of the shows, this one had Broadway roots where Mr. Pidgeon opened the show in 1957, and since periodically toured with it. He remarked in his interview that sleep was a problem in Holyoke as, even during his interview, they could hear the sound of earthmovers clawing away at the hills nearby during construction of the future Route 91.

The review of the play was positive, his performance called a tour de force. Also in the play was young Nicholas Hammond, who had appeared in the 1965 film *The Sound of Music* as the older Von Trapp son, here playing one of the sons of Walter Pidgeon.

The final show at the Mt. Tom Playhouse was *Dear Me, the Sky is Falling*, with Gertrude Berg, stage, TV, and radio veteran probably best known for her role on the series *The Goldbergs*. The *Holyoke Transcript-Telegram* reporter interviewed her at the Howard Johnson Motor Lodge, where Mrs. Berg was staying. They chatted poolside, while young boys splashed in the water, and then asked for her autograph. The article was her life story, pearls of wisdom from a grandmotherly lady. There was no indication or hint of this being the last professional play on Mt. Tom.

Gertrude Berg with stylist Marc Gonneville at the Kay-Harvey salon, Maple Street, Holyoke.
Photo courtesy Marc Gonneville

A small display ad a few pages later advertised Jean Guild's new venture teaching voice, speech, and acting, "confidence through the spoken word."

A the beginning of that season under a half-page splashy display ad for Storrowton Music Fair, which was celebrating its sixth year of operation, there had been a small, plain display ad from the Mt. Tom Playhouse.

On behalf of our staff and casts, I would like to extend to

Storrowton Music Fair all Best Wishes for its sixth, singing, smash, successful season…Cordially, Hugh Fordin.

As Barbara Bernard acknowledges, "The thing that really hurt them was the Storrowton Music Tent. It was a different idea. They were trying to compete with Storrowton by bringing in big stars, but it was a smaller theater and it just couldn't—financially, it didn't work."

Paul Rohan, whose family were longtime Casino theater goers from The Valley Players through the Mt. Tom Playhouse area agrees:

The tent [Storrowton] *became kind of the place to go and, you know, if your budget was, as most people in Holyoke, a night of entertainment was—I mean, you made a choice. And I believe a lot of people made the choice of the musical with the well-known actor or company, as opposed to what was going on at Mountain Park. I would echo the sentiment that Storrowton probably did them in or played a significant role in doing them in. Also, Mountain Park itself had gotten to be kind of honky-tonky. I mean, not that an amusement park isn't honky-tonky, but when I was a kid it was a fine place to bring children. As I got older the crowd had changed, it was like it was just a rougher crowd.*

Don Grigware, at this writing senior editor for BWW Los Angeles, grew up in Holyoke where his father, Don Sr., ran the concession stand at the Casino through the 1950s until 1962. His link to Mountain Park and the Casino is both sweet and tragic: as a boy he was introduced to the magical world of theater, where:

I loved and cherished Jean Guild, Hal Holbrook and his wife, Ruby. My father used to work the concession stand and as a little boy, I delighted in sneaking into the theatre when the curtain went up and watched the actors from behind the seats. If caught, Carlton Guild could give a pretty nasty look and tell my father that I must stay out. But I found my way in.

Still a theatre professional, he muses, "To think my love of theatre all started with the Valley Players, as I watched all the shows as a little boy through my teen years." He notes, "It was summer stock, but boy, oh, boy, were they professional and never missed a beat."

Hugh Fordin remembers fondly:

It was a nice theater. I mean, I enjoyed those two years. Unfortunately, the second year the audiences were not as strong, even though I think the second year we had a bigger array of stars than we had the first year. There were only a few times that we really sold out for the whole week. Strange, because I would have thought people would have preferred proscenium to arena, which was what the music tent in West Springfield was.

Brad Russell, who later worked an actor in New York, worked at the Casino as a young man when he was known as Bob. He cleaned the theater and worked in the box office.

Jean and Carlton were very sweet to me and we remained friends for years. I can honestly say it was the happiest summer of my life.

Barbara Bernard:

Those were such good days. It just brought this whole community to be alive.

Marc Gonneville, who had styled the hair of the stars in the salon on Maple Street, later settled with his wife and family in Chicopee and at nearly seventy-four years of age at this writing still runs his own salon, the House of Marc, on Grattan Street. He remembers of the era:

It was a great time. I still remember the ladies with the long white gloves. Everybody would dress up to go to the theater. And then after the theater, everybody went to Gleason's Townhouse. Everybody would just gravitate down there...People came and got their hair done before going to the playhouse. It was a big social thing. And at the play, especially in Holyoke, it was like who's who in Holyoke would be at the play. That's the way it was. It was just part of the social life.

Mr. Gonneville also recalls the effect Storrowton had on the playhouse:

People were going there. They had bigger stars, maybe, I don't know. These weren't bad, they were all good.

Barbara Bernard notes:

It was tough to compete with Storrowton because, oh, the musicals were magnificent. And they were, of course, bigger stars—the Valley Players really was more of a repertory theater. It sold out every night—until Storrowton came. And then it was a matter of people having to make a decision. Can I afford this or that?

Paul Rohan of Holyoke, whose parents were avid theatergoers, affirms that when the Mt. Tom Playhouse closed, it was "a sign of the times."

So it was, "Well, we'll have to readjust and go to Storrowton." I went to a lot of the Storrowton productions.

Soon Mr. Rohan was off to college, and to the Army. His parents went to shows at Storrowton, to Williamstown, to Stockbridge, to dinner theatre in the area—another fad that, like the tent theaters, would burn hot for a while, and then fade away. There was still professional summer theatre around western Massachusetts, but not in Holyoke, never again on the mountain.

***

Author Marcia J. Moonbeau remarks on the state of summer theatre today, having written a history of *The Cape Playhouse of Dennis, Mass.* the famed summer theater on the Cape, that if its founder, Raymond Moore were alive at the time of publication of that book in 2001:

…he would have to deal with actors in an industry that has changed monumentally over the years. In 1927, performers worked primarily on the stage, mostly in New York, and usually in the winter. They were glad for the chance to earn money in the off-season and gladder to get out of the city. Today's actors may have more contracts, television deals or theatre opportunities anywhere in the country, year-round. Worse yet, salary demands often are such that they cannot be met by a summer playhouse. High maintenance costs, whopping production expenses and stiff competition have been the death of many seasonal theatres around the country.

That fall, when the Mt. Tom Playhouse, the old Casino, was shuttered for good and there was no indication it would never open again for a professional company—going "dark" is the theatre expression—in November, the biggest story was of the great Northeast Blackout where 30 million people were left without power for as much as thirteen hours in several northeast states, and Ontario, Canada. Holyoke, however, was one of a few communities with a municipal power company that was able to disconnect from the failed grid, and remained unaffected. Holyoke did not "go dark."

***

Hugh Fordin did not return in the spring:

After I left Mt. Tom, I didn't go back to working at all in summer stock. As a matter of fact, I went to work for a Broadway producer, David Merrick.

The year 1966 was first summer season since the war year of 1943 there had been no theatre on the

mountain. That year, Valley Players alumnus Hal Holbrook played his *Mark Twain Tonight!* on Broadway and won the Tony Award.® The following year, it was presented on television on CBS, and he won an Emmy.® He would also play the part in 1977 and in 2005 on Broadway. He has been Mark Twain longer than Samuel Langhorne Clemens had been Mark Twain. As of press time, Mr. Holbrook, approaching ninety-two years old, is still traveling across the country on a tour with his *Mark Twain Tonight!*

Peggy Bowe recalled being involved in a children's summer theatre camp to provide training in theatre to kids and present shows for children at the Casino/Mt. Tom Playhouse in the summer of 1968, rented for the event and run by Mary Lou Carroll, whose family owned Riverside Park in Agawam. The brief experiment was called The Mt. Tom Children's Playhouse.

We painted sets, collected and made props, we helped run the soundboard and did all the crew jobs. I was even in The Wizard of Oz. *I played Glinda and the Wicked Witch. I remember it was a fun summer because I finally got to really know the theater. I mean, I got to go into the bowels of the theater to the dressing rooms, which were in the back and underneath the stage. I got to see all the inner workings of the theater that I had never seen.*

The decade of the sixties ended with another break with the Casino's great past – the death of Mabel Griffith, who had been the leading lady, then a favorite character actress, through the teens and twenties. Her husband Willard Dashiell had acted and directed on Mt. Tom, and was the producer as well during the WPA years of the Great Depression. His last minor roles were with The Valley Players in their first two years. It is poignant that by the time his widow died, in an era where there were fewer summer repertory theaters and much less press about them, her passing on December 22, 1969 received a kind and gentle farewell in the *Springfield Union:*

In the mid 20s, the names of Mabel Griffith and William [sic] Dashiell held magnetic appeal for hundreds of residents of the area who for 52 weeks supported the stage company that played in the old Opera House on Dwight Street.

There were few in the theater field who came to this city [Holyoke] who cast a greater spell over local theatergoers than the Dashiells. The affection which the actress and director-actor held for this city was mutual. When the stock company disbanded after several years hence the Dashiells chose this city as their home.

There was no mention, however, of their tenure at the Casino on Mt. Tom.

Mountain Park continued to operate its midway rides and games of chance. A fire in the dance pavilion brought tragedy in June 1971 when the Holyoke High School Senior Prom was held in the Stardust Ballroom a short distance away from the empty theater. Propane canisters exploded as the result of a gas leak, and two park employees died of their injuries. One was Donald E. Grigware, father of Mr. Don Grigware who was interviewed for this book.

The other victim was eighteen-year-old David W. Griffin, who had graduated from Holyoke High School only the year before. They were treated first at Holyoke Hospital, then transported to Boston, were they died. The prom had been barely underway and fortunately only a small number of students had arrived at the time the fire broke out (some 300 were expected to attend). All the students on site escaped.

The Stardust ballroom and Tap Room were destroyed. It was seventy years old, built in 1901 and had seen the likes of the company picnics, parties, and Big Band music in the 1940s and 1950s—Duke Ellington played here, and Cab Calloway, Sammy Kaye, Guy Lombardo, Rudy Vallee, Xavier Cugat, Gene Krupa, Tommy Dorsey, and Harry James. In the 1960s, rock and roll echoed from the pavilion from Gene Pitney, Roy Orbison, the Everly Brothers, Jerry Lee Lewis, the Beach Boys, and the Lovin' Spoonful.

That week of the fire, Dan Dailey and Peggy Cass opened the season in *Plaza Suite* at the Storrowton. They received a good review from the *Springfield Daily News*.

In 1972, *Holyoke Transcript-Telegram* announced that the G. Fox chain of department stores planned to create a new mall in the highlands of Holyoke. It would be Holyoke's biggest attraction for out-of-towners. That year, the Casino playhouse was torn down. At the time, the boy who had grown up in that theater, William Guild, was directing his first full-length play at StageWest in nearby West Springfield. It was *Slow Dance on the Killing Fields* by William Hanley, starring the late Ron Glass and Guild's wife Hannah Brandon.

Mountain Park owner John J. Collins Jr. ordered the demolition of the theater, which by the end of its use had a seating capacity of 1,500, though its original capacity in at the turn of the century was 2,500 including outdoor seating. Being vacant, and with the nearby ballroom having been destroyed in the fire, it was deemed that the empty theater was also a likely a hazard and could be at the mercy of vandals.

Hugh Fordin remembers:

By and large, it was quite an experience for me. I don't have any bitter memories. I think I just went on. You know, summer theatre was starting to not be the kind of summer theatre as I remember growing up. About ten years later, I was on the Massachusetts Turnpike with

some friends, and I said, "Let's stop off in Holyoke. I want to show you the theater." And I didn't even know that they tore it down.

Don Grigware, who eventually became a teacher, an actor, and a writer notes:

My exposure to the Valley Players and to the Mt. Tom Playhouse was my introduction to the theatre. Somehow watching these actors made me realize that the work was not easy but so rewarding! It stimulated me to study acting and to perform. Years later when I studied with Stella Adler and Jose Quintero and they spoke of total commitment to the craft, my mind would always flash back to watching the Valley Players portray a myriad of characters week after week…whatever I have accomplished my acting and writing, however small, has made my life richer. What a background; I wouldn't trade it for anything.

George Murphy:

I had a lot of fun, a lot of good experiences up there—you never knew from week to week what was going to happen.

Holyoke celebrated its city centennial in 1973, the same year Westover Air Force Base was deactivated in Chicopee and became a reserve base. Downtown shopping changed in Holyoke and Springfield as stores, many family-owned such as Forbes & Wallace, went out of business and suburban malls replaced them. Steiger's, which had maintained decades of advertising for the theatre groups on Mt. Tom, finally went out of business in 1994.

Without newspapers, theatre can hardly exist— providing advertising as well as reviews. In 1983, the *Holyoke Transcript-Telegram* employed over one hundred people, with a circulation of about 30,000. Ten years later it went out of business, with a circulation of just 16,000.

The *Holyoke Transcript-Telegram* quoted one Holyoke resident in the 1980s when the park's days seemed numbered: "It was the perfect place for a family to go. There isn't a prettier setting in Holyoke. You are never going to find an amusement park with such beautiful wilderness all around. It was a great place to go to picnic.

When it was 90 degrees in the city, it seemed cooler there."

Mountain Park closed in 1987; reasons cited by Collins were increased insurance premiums. Twenty-eight of the amusement park rides were sold. The carousel was saved, restored with donated funds from citizens, and moved to downtown at the new Holyoke Heritage Park— built on the site of the old Skinner silk milk, which had been razed by fire. The carousel reopened December 7, 1993. It remains to delight children and remind the city of the amusement park that once sat on the mountain, with a theatre just beyond the midway.

The ski area on Mt. Tom, just above the amusement park, went out of business in 1998 and its equipment was sold. The lights of its ski trails had been a fixture and visible down the broad valley for miles. Most of land was sold to conservancy, and some 60 acres to a local developer. The mountain is dark now, a silent sentinel.

George Murphy:

It doesn't seem that long ago. It really doesn't. I mean, there's times I can picture myself walking up that hill and how I walked from my house on Pleasant Street. It's, like, oh, three, four miles. I didn't mind, though…and there were times I really didn't want to leave.

Community College with 850; these figures are dwarfed by the numbers of factory workers at the beginning of the century.

From author Tracy Kidder's essay:

As the city's population fell, from nearly seventy thousand at the peak to about forty thousand in the 1980s, the buildings of the Flats deteriorated. In the name of urban renewal—and partly in order to limit the size of the growing Puerto Rican population—City Hall presided over the demolition of many old apartment blocks. Most dramatically, the Flats burned. For years, flames lit the nighttime sky over Holyoke. Fires started in old wiring. Pyromaniacs and people bent on personal vendettas and professionals interested in insurance money set fires and several were fatal. The fires changed the landscape utterly.

Storrowton Theatre continued every summer on the fairgrounds of the Eastern States Exposition until 1978, when it was closed. According to Barbara Bernard, Storrowton suffered a lack of public support at the end in part:

I think because the ticket prices were getting a little too steep. That was a tough time economically around here. I just think that things change, you know? The summer theater at Mt. Holyoke was going then and, who knows? Maybe the summer theater took away some of the—one thing I remember from my own experience: on a hot summer evening it was uncomfortable being in that tent. And we still went to some of the shows, but it was uncomfortable.

Overlapping its last decade was a much smaller in-the-round tent theater founded in 1970 on the grounds of Mt. Holyoke College in South Hadley. The Mt. Holyoke College Summer Theater continued through 2001, when it closed. Must there always be a third act and then the final curtain for summer theaters?

The New Century Theatre was founded in 1991, located at Smith College in Northampton. It is currently in the process of vacating its theater at Smith, with the intention to relocate. It is the valley's only summer theater at this time.

The Majestic Theater in West Springfield, that small second-run movie house in the center of

CHAPTER 10

Encores

Journalist and outdoorsman Ben Bacham wrote of Holyoke in a collection of essays published as *The Pioneer Valley Reader:*

No other city in the Connecticut Valley gives so vivid a picture of nineteenth-century industrial America— Holyoke is pure New England mill town…Holyoke is vast, dense, and somber. Cold black water races through the canals. Smoke-stacks and church spires reach into the sky. There are bricks, millions upon millions of dark, sooty bricks, and a wealth of detail: granite windowsills, brass weathervanes, copper-sheathed cupolas, bell towers, ornamental ironwork, heavy wooden doors, cobblestone alleys, stone steps worn smooth by millworkers' feet. Holyoke was built for the ages.

The mills buildings, even in abandonment, are awesome. The architecture was meant to intimidate. The winter wind never blows colder than it does down these bleak streets lined with rusting cars, three-decker wooden houses, and brick tenement blocks. The bars fill up at eight in the morning. The unemployment officers are crowded.

In 1900 the biggest Holyoke employers were the Farr-Alpaca Company textile mill, the Skinner silk mill, the Lyman mills and the many paper mills. In 1999, the biggest employers in Holyoke were the City of Holyoke with 2,200 workers, Holyoke Hospital with 1,100 workers, and Holyoke town, was renovated and transformed into a playhouse for live professional winter stock Equity theatre in 1997, and continues to flourish.

In 1994 there was a proposal by Wally Beach, who had founded Storrowton, to start a music theater on Mt. Tom with partner David P. Boyle of Northampton. The Mountain Park Summer Theater project ran into delays on construction of a circus-style tent as was used for Beach's old Storrowton Music Fair tent in West Springfield. They were not able to establish their summer theater, and the project was abandoned.

George Murphy:

For many, many years after they razed the Casino, the ticket booth was still there. I went up one time, years ago, before it, you know, changed to what it is now. And I drove up and went down to that corner, and I looked at it. It was nothing but trees, you know, and I could picture that, you know, the road going in, the ticket booth, and the big rock that was out in front.

I got out of the car and I started walking down there, and I was looking for that rock, because I figured everything else would be gone. If I found that rock, I'd have my bearing. And I see through the woods — the ticket booth. There's a tree growing through it. I couldn't believe it. I went over and climbed through the window, and I was in that ticket booth again. From that perspective, I knew where the door was, I knew where the concession stand was. I knew where the road was. I knew where the path across the way was, just from being in that booth.

George Murphy does not think competition from Storrowton contributed to the demise of the Mt. Tom Playhouse, as it might have earlier for The Valley Players.

I think, first of all, ticket prices went crazy, and insurance prices went insane. That's one of the main reasons why the amusement park closed down, and I think the theater, with, you know, fire and—that place was so old and so dry and basically dilapidated.

Have people, the audience changed? From Monbleau's book, *The Cape Playhouse*, originally published in 1991:

Perhaps there are too many closet-like movie houses, televisions and VCRs. Perhaps there is an over-abundance of at-home, solitary, isolated activity. Maybe there is as much need for sociability now as there was in 1927. Maybe people are surfeited with canned, prepackaged and shrink-wrapped entertainment and long to watch living, breathing theatre.

Will younger generations succumb to the charm of live theatre?

George Murphy:

Well, we've got the one down here in West Springfield. [The Majestic.] Everybody twenty-five years ago had community theatre.

Nobody wants to go out anymore. You got television, you got music, you got videos. You got the computer. And it costs too much. It's a lot cheaper buying something online, or before if you liked that music, unless you had a record player or something and bought the album. Now, just turn on the computer and hear whatever you want. See whatever you want, watch movies whenever you want.

StageWest, a winter stock theater which began on the grounds of the Eastern States Exposition in West Springfield in 1967, housed in a theater that was a permanent building, and afterwards moved to downtown Springfield. William Guild, who had grown up in his parents' summer stock theater became a stage director. At StageWest (which would move to Springfield, and then later go out of business in 1998.), he directed his mother, Jean Guild. He remembers:

The last thing she did was a one-act play by Terence McNally called Next, *and it was two-character play. It was funny at the time, because it was about a 40-year-old man who's called up for the draft and he can't convince this dictatorial woman that this is all a mistake, and we had a ball doing it. It's about 45 minutes long. And that was the last thing she did.*

She played opposite Max Gulack. From a review by Francine Trevens in the *Springfield Daily News*:

Mrs. Guild managed the difficult feat of keeping her face straight without a sign of strain.

Her daughter-in-law, actress Hannah Brandon, who was married to William Guild, performed in the second-one-act play of this evening of three one-acts. The one-act play that December of 1970 was Jean Guild's last performance. "She was a very good actress," William Guild says of his mother. Of the 239 productions staged by the Valley Players, she had appeared in 181 of them, and it was reckoned that forty-nine of those appearances were in featured or starring roles.

Her remaining years were lost to her. William Guild relates:

She slipped into dementia, and in those days they didn't know what it was, of course. My father took care of her for a couple of years, but he was just too old to do it, and we got a caretaker in for a year and it just wasn't working. She no longer knew who he was or who I was, so we had to put her in a home where she could be supervised, because she tended to wander all the time.

Jean Guild

Jean Guild died in 1983 at Holyoke Hospital, having lived in Holyoke for more than forty years. She was eighty years old at the time of her death.

Peggy Bowe remarks:

I can remember she was the first person I knew that was against the Vietnam War. And she was adamantly against the war, and this was in '66 or '67 before it really became a big movement. She was a very well-read...I just feel bad that I didn't keep in touch with her as much as I probably should have. We used to exchange Christmas cards, occasional notes, but then life went on and you kind of lose track of those things.

Peggy tears up as she recalls:

When I heard that she passed, I'll admit it, I cried. You know, I don't come from a big family; I didn't have a lot of aunts and uncles. Jean Guild was more than a mentor and a friend, she was almost like family. The kind of family you choose for yourself.

It was requested at the time of her death that donations be made to the Actors Fund of America, for which The Valley Players had donated proceeds of tickets sales for twenty years. Carlton Guild died in July 1991, at eighty-two years of age, in Virginia where he had moved, and where his son William had relocated.

Peter Harris

Reunion 1993 Mary Kates, Library director, Peter Harris, Ruby Holbrook, Gaylord Mason, Holyoke Public Library

In August 1993, there was a reunion of The Valley Players at the Holyoke Public Library in the History Room, where much of the information for this book was obtained. Present were Peter Harris, who played for eight seasons; Ruby Holbrook; Gaylord Mason; Jean Burns; and Paul Graves. Ruby Holbrook, now divorced from Hal Holbrook, had appeared with The Valley Players over five seasons. It had been her first professional acting job.

The scrapbooks so meticulously kept by Carlton Guild were on display at the library gathering, and many of the production photos found in this book.

Peter Harris recalled going up the hill from the playhouse to the amusement park midway and taking a ride on the merry-go-round with some of

the other actors before opening night to ward off "the jitters." He donated to the Friends of the Holyoke Merry-Go-Round to restore the carousel, which was removed to downtown at the new Holyoke Heritage State Park; the park would officially open four months later, that December.

Others attending and signing the guest book were Molly Hosman of Chicopee, who had played bit roles; Barbara O'Leary Halpin, who had run the box office for so many years and also took bit parts; Jean Burns' daughter Maureen, who had taken a bit role as a child; Elsie Cappel, who had done choreography for the Players; Neil Doherty, local photographer who had taken so many production photos for the company; and Ralph Levy, who had played minor roles. Jean and Carlton Guild and most of the major players were gone by this time, but how they would have loved

Reunion 1993, Gaylord Mason on the left, Holyoke Public Library

to have been there.

And perhaps they would have raised a glass in fraternal spirit with another visitor to the occasion: Wally Beach, manager of the Storrowton Music Fair.

***

Curtain Calls…

Ellen Andrews died in 1982. She was an actress who appeared in some forty-five plays with the Valley Players and was a featured performer in twenty-three of them. "The Oracle" column of the *Holyoke Transcript-Telegram* used her obituary to comment on the passing as well of the Valley Players some twenty years earlier:

The Valley Players were an important part of the Holyoke area and it was sad when the plays ended. We can still remember how the audience gasped if a "Damn" or other such bit of profanity fell from the lips of the players who had no doubt already watered down, for Puritan

consumption, the dialogue that was acceptable in New York.

Simon Oakland died in California in 1983, only six days after Jean Guild passed. The wire press obituary was augmented in the *Holyoke Transcript-Telegram* with the remembrance that he had appeared with The Valley Players in the 1950s, and included comments by Carlton Guild. Guild recalled that Oakland had been, "very outgoing and a wonderful actor. Goodness oozed out of him. He always remembered people with cards and letters…He was a big bear of a man, like Stanley Kowalski in *A Streetcar Named Desire* [which Oakland had played on Mt. Tom], except he was as gentle as they come."

Hugh Franklin died in 1986, having enjoyed many years on television soap operas, such as *All My Children, As the World Turns, Love of Life*, and even *Dark Shadows*. He was still married to author Madeleine L'Engle at the time of his death.

In 1988, Ted Tiller died in New York City at

Reunion 1993 Ruby Holbrook, Jean Burns, unknown others Holyoke Public Library

seventy-five years of age. *The New York Times* obituary noted, among his other accomplishments, his eleven-year stint with The Valley Players of Holyoke, Massachusetts.

Hugh Franklin

Chalk it up to new editors and management at the *Holyoke Transcript-Telegram*, who were perhaps unaware of the history of theatre on Mt. Tom: Carlton Guild's passing in 1991 went unnoticed, and Jean Guild's passing rated only the family released obituary article that was also published in the Springfield newspaper. No such editorial love note was bestowed upon their memory as with Mabel Griffin by some astute theatre aficionado or valley historian.

Jean Burns died in November 2004 in Florida, at eighty-four years old. A director as well as an actress, she had performed also at the Mt. Holyoke College Summer Theatre, at StageWest in Springfield, as well as the Springfield community theatres The Callboard Theater and the Encore Players.

George Murphy went back to Holyoke High School when the Mt. Tom Playhouse closed.

After the Navy, he had a long career in local radio, community theatre, and television.

But I'd always dream of this place, you know? I went up there a couple years ago, just for the hell of it, and that, the house, it was a cabin that she [Tallulah Bankhead] was in is gone now. You could look down into the valley from that point, and now the trees are higher than, you know, the mountain itself. But I just wanted to see the house again. It's not there anymore.

Bertram Tanswell

Dan Brunelle later worked in a technical capacity for other theaters, but eventually left theatre work.

Long hours. No money. But an invaluable learning experience that I thoroughly enjoyed. You do the theatre because you love it, not because it pays a whole lot. Theatre gave me the foundation to succeed in a wide variety of building trades and was a great inspiration.

Peggy Bowe:

It was a wonderful experience. I'm just sorry I was a few years too young to really have been able to appreciate it.

William Guild relates his journey in, and out of, the theatre after he and his wife moved to New York:

We did theatre until 1977; summer of '77 was the last year we did it. We ran our own theater outside of Winston-Salem in North Carolina in Tanglewood State Park, and it was truly an old-fashioned barn theater: it had been a barn. But it got to the point where I was seeing a lot of actors that I knew growing up still living in the same walk-up apartments over grocery stores and things of that nature in New York and never getting anywhere financially at all. Working, like Gaylord Mason worked a lot, and several friends of ours had worked with him in other theaters. I just didn't want to keep on doing that. I saw the writing on the wall. I went into Real Estate and Hannah went into business.

Helen Harrelson

When he was still directing at StageWest in West Springfield, Guild reconnected with Ted Tiller from The Valley Players days:

Ted Tiller wrote Count Dracula. *We had scheduled* Dracula *for the season at StageWest, the 1971-72 season, and suddenly the Broadway rights were pulled, all the rights were pulled because of all things, somebody had optioned it for a musical. So we were left high and dry. We were supposed to start rehearsing it in two weeks, and we didn't know what to do. We were **thinking of** another substitute play, and I said to John Ulmer, "Wait* *a minute, wait a minute. Ted Tiller wrote for years for television and turned out a script every day for Arlene Francis when she had her morning show, and also a show called Mr. I. Magination. Why don't I call him and see if this is something that might be up his alley?"*

And I called him, and he said, "Let me read the book." Because it's got to be different than the play. So he called back, he was a very fast reader—he called back the next day and said, "I can do it." So that became Count Dracula *instead of* Dracula, *and he lived off of that for the rest of his life. The royalties just kept coming in, community theaters—when we were in Wales, we were walking down the street in Wye Valley and they had a community theater in there. It was "Count Dracula by Ted Tiller" on the marquee, it had just closed.*

Count Dracula, written by Ted Tiller, premiered December 10, 1971, with Guild's wife Hannah Brandon as Nina. John Ulmer directed, and William Guild was stage manager.

Hal Holbrook returned one last time to Holyoke. He performed his signature show *Mark Twain, Tonight!* on Saturday, November 18, 2011 at the Holyoke High School Auditorium on Beech Street. The day before, he spoke to kids in their classroom. Proceeds from the show benefited the ongoing renovation of the Victory Theatre on Suffolk Street. (Currently under a restoration project by its owners, the Massachusetts International Festival of the Arts.) Barbara Bernard came to see him and renew old acquaintance.

I met him after the show, and maybe it was a newspaper photographer, but they took a picture of the two of us facing each other. And I said to him, "Hal, I've lost track of Ruby. Is she still alive?" [Mr. Holbrook had been remarried at that time to actress Dixie Carter.] *And he said, 'Yes.' He looked me straight in the eye and he said, 'Ruby is still alive. She's in a nursing home in the Boston area.' And then he looked at me, he said, 'And I'm going to be seeing her when I leave here.'*

And then I started to cry. So that's the picture they've got.

For a moment, it was like old times.

As of this writing, Holbrook is still performing *Mark Twain Tonight!* across the country. He is approaching his ninety-second birthday.

***

Perhaps that larger-than-life rogue Tallulah Bankhead hit the nail on the head regarding the future of theatre. She is often quoted as saying:

If you really want to help the American theatre, don't be an actress, Da-a-a-h-ling—Be an audience.

For now, we won't say "the end," for in theatre there are always revivals—perhaps even one day for theatre on Mt. Tom—but in the tradition of the playwright's script we will simply "go dark" with…

FADE TO BLACK.

From 1952: Dorothy Crane, Mac Gress, Jean Guild, Lauren Gilbert, Tash Bozek, Nancy Wells, Vivian Marlowe, Bertram Tanswell, Jackson Perkins

Mt. Tom from the Holyoke Dam, photo by the author

SELECTED STAGE SHOWS AND PERFORMERS ON MT. TOM

1895 to 1900

May 21 1895 – the opening of the Pavilion Theatre, the first theatre on Mt. Tom. Vaudeville under manager Thomas F. Murray.

1896 season

Barker Family concerts, week of August 3rd.
Professor McGuire Wonderful Trained Horses.

Bucking Mule, week of August 11th.

American Band, instrumental concerts, week of August 21st.

The Aeolians – Musical Artists, week of August 24th.

1897 season (opened June 1st)

Adelina Orchestra, also vaudeville.

1898 season

Frank R Hay's American Entertainers, week of June 13th

Morris' Pony Circus, week of August 8th.
Southern Plantation Company, week of August 15th.
Knickerbocker Vaudeville Company and Forrest Tempest – the Greatest of All Educated Horses, week of August 22nd.

1899 season – vaudeville under manager William Burke

Hayes' Virginia Troubadours, week of June 12th.
Prof. Dunbar's Trained Goats, week of July 6th.
The Crane Bros. Mud Town Rubes, week of July 11th.

The rest of the season was devoted to vaudeville. The season ended September 9th.

1900 season – William Burke, manager. Jules Friquet musical manager for the season.

1901 to 1935

1901 season – the new theater, the Casino built. Among the famous vaudevillians who performed here was Eddie Foy, year unknown.

Grand opening week of May 27th – Hayes Virginia Troubadours.

Early June, vaudeville continued with George P. Guy's Minstrels, and the Migrani Family.

The Mt. Park Opera Company, under the direction of Robert Kane took over for the remainder of the season.

Said Pasha by Roland Stahl, first production, week of June 7th.

The Mascot, week of June 25th

Olivette, week of July 2nd.

Other productions this season included Gilbert & Sullivan's *HMS Pinafore, Boccaccio, The Chimes of Normandy*, and *Virginia*.

Girofle Girofla, Cavalleria Rusticana and *The Crimson Scarf* rounded out the season, which closed August 31st.

1902 –

The Barlow Brothers Minstrels with Eddie Leonard.

HMS Pinafore, June 5th, given by the Rise and Shine Club for the benefit of the Old People's Home.

Vaudeville with the George F. Hayes Troubadours week of June 10th.

The Two Thieves, begins the 2nd Mt. Park Opera Company season, company includes Emile Barringon and Florence Ackley, under management of Robert Kane, who also played some roles.

Said Pasha, July 4th, three performances

Rip Van Winkle, with Robert Kane in the title role.

Other productions this season included the *Black Hussar, Girofle Girofla, Fatinitza, The Beggar Student, Grand Duchess, Lily of Killarney, Nell Gwynne*, and *The Chimes of Normandy*.

The Bohemian Girl, week of August 3rd. Stars Nannie

Dodson as the Gypsy Queen, with other "dramatis personae" including Francis Carter, Charles Fulton, Mamie Scott, George Callahan, Victor DeLacey, Florence Ackley, and Florence Rother.

Fra Diavolo week of August 10th. The Mt. Park Opera Company under the management of Robert Kane.

1903 season:

Opened May 29, 1903 with Tom Brown's Troubadours in *A Foxy Coon*.

Lockhart's Famous Performing Elephants, week of June 6th.

The Opera Company began its season with *The Isle of Champagne* under the direction of Robert Kane, week of June 15th.

Dorothy, week of June 22nd.

Other productions were *The Mikado, The Pirates of Penzance, Carmen, Paul Jones, The Bohemian Girl, Fra Diavolo, Faust, the Lily of Killarney,* and *The Princess of Trebizande.*

1904 season:

The Mountain Park Stock Company took over the Casino with poplar "mellerdramers" including *Pink Dominoes*, which led off the season the week of June 20th, and *Turned Up, The Telephone Girl, Confusion, Uncle Tom's Cabin, Triss or Beyond the Rockies.* Movies and vaudeville finished out the season.

1905 season:

Vaudeville and Collins Moving Pictures, and the Casino Stock Company under the management of Robert Kane. Their shows included *The Red Hussar, The Gondoliers, The Telephone Girl, The Belle of New York, Jack and the Beanstalk, The Girl from Paris, The Mockery (?) Bird, Dorcas,* and *1492.*

1906 season:

The Casino operated a 12-week season under manager Robert Kane.

1907 season:

Vaudeville starts off the season with Libby Trayer in a musical and singing sketch, the DeMuths in a novelty "whirlwind dancing" sketch, Milt Wood (triple time shoe dancer), and special feature, Prof. Wormword's Animal Circus.

The Casino Opera Company featured prima donna Ada

Mead and W.H. Thompson, tenor.

When Johnny Comes Marching Home

Falke with DeWolf Hopper and Jeff DeAngels

Tar and Tartar.

The Chimes of Normandy – special amateur production with local talent from Holyoke and Springfield.

1908 season:

Professor Drake presents a magic lantern show The Passion Play of Obergammerau, May 30?

HMS Pinafore by the Bijou Opera Company, Emile Barringon, manager

The Cowboy and the Lady by the Mt. Park Musical Stock Company

Camille, with singing and dancing between acts.

1909 season:

Robin Hood, presented by the Mt. Park Opera Company under manager Robert Kane. Carrick Major and Grace Drew are the company's leads.

1910 season:

Miss Leigh DeLacy and Associate Players – six days a week, six matinees, vaudeville that changed the bill twice each week. This continued for three weeks then the Mt. Park Opera Company under manager Robert Kane finished the season.

1911-1912: Casino Stock Company. Stage plays.

1911 season:

Divarcon by Victor Sorda

The Man of the Hour

The Lottery Man

Clyde Fitch's The City
Sunday

Lulu's Husbands

The Fourth Estate

Charley's Aunt

Wildfire

Billy

The Penalty

Heir to the Hoorah

Specialties were given between acts.

1912 season: The Casino Musical Comedy Company, manager Lansing Ernest and treasurer L.P. Pellissier.

Coming Thru the Rye – cast of twenty-eight.

The Red Mill

The Little Host

The Flower of the Ranch

The Gingerbread Man

The Time, The Place, and the Girl

The All Star Vaudeville took over the season by July 22nd, featuring the Asahi Troupe of Japanese performers, also Jack Donahue and Alice Martin Stewart. *Temptation* featured Edwin Keough and Helen Nelson, and five other vaudeville acts.

Motion pictures were also on the bill.

From 1913 to 1924 no stage plays were regularly produced, instead vaudeville and motion pictures.

1913 season:

Vaudeville: Onaip – The World's Greatest Deceptionist; Kelly and Pollock; Mullen and Coogan; Al Fields & Lewis Jack; O'Brien, Hanel & Co.; W. Jeffrey, Jack Warner & Co.; Norine Carmen; Florence Ackley. Casino under the management of Lansing Ernest.

1914 season:

The Third Degree, presented by the Knights of Columbus Dramatic Club for a single performance. Directed by John J. Sheehen, nearly sold out.

Vaudeville takes over for the rest of the season, including Billy McDermott. A movie was shown on June 22nd – *The Dingbat Family*.

1915 season:

The Casino opened Memorial Day with the Ward Street Amateur Minstrels – fifty "all-star" performers for a single show.

Vaudeville ran for the rest of the season. Manager of the Casino is still J. Lansing Ernest.

1916 season:

Vaudeville opens the season with Thomas Egan Co., Delmore and Lee, Maurice Freeman & Co., and Tabor and Green. Prince Charles – The Monkey with Human Brains was also on the bill.

The Monrati Opera Company performed for one week.

1917 season:

Vaudeville opened the season again with the 5 Brossinis, Claude & Marion Cleveland, Fantelle & Stark, Armstrong & Ford, Bernardi and 16 Navassar – advertised as "Vaudeville's Highest Salaried Musical Act."

The Casino was renovated this season, the folding opera chairs were re-arranged.

1918 season:

The season opened with the Holyoke Dramatic Club presenting the comedy *Billy* as a benefit for the Red Cross, as the United States was now involved in World War I. It was a single performance, tickets went for 25, 50, and 75 cents. Special plaudits in the local press went to James N. Wells.

Then vaudeville took over. Fred J. Sarr was the manager, with Joseph Fahey in charge of the box office. Tickets could also be purchased in town down at the Riker Jaynes Drug Store.

The Casino Harmony Orchestra was the house band for the season. Vaudeville acts included Tabor & Green, Mabel McKinley, the Pauline Fielding Players, Ota Gygi – The Court Violinist to the King of Spain, the General Pisano & Company – Italian Sharpshooter, Mullen & Cogan comedians, the Ah-Ling-Foo Chinese magician, and Sterling & Chapman – Singers of Scotch Songs.

1919 season:

Vaudeville began with Henri Jacques Co. The season was filled by the B.F. Keith circuit vaudeville and also moving pictures. George E. Hammond was manager for the Casino this season.

Other acts included Ryan & Healy, the Dancing Doreens, Kharmua – Persian Pianist, Hemlin & Mack, and newsreels shown by the Gaumont company.

1920 season:

Vaudeville on the Keith circuit – with Mabel Berra – Comic Opera Prima Donna being the "hit of the season," as was Billy Gleason.

1921 season:

Vaudeville opened the summer with two performances by Virginia Pearson & Sheldon Lewis. The manager of the Casino is again George E. Hammond. An innovation this year was to employ "girl ushers."

Scenes From Famous Plays with the Richard Keane & Company ended the season.

1922 season:

J. Lansing Ernest returned as manager of the Casino. New scenery and lighting were featured, and again, vaudeville ruled the season.

1923 season

A crowd of over 1,000 opened another season of vaudeville, under the management of J. Lansing Ernest. Seats were 25 cents, with evening performances as high as 35 to 50 cents. Some acts including Sternad's Midgets, George Moran & Charles Mack – Two Black Crows.

1924 season:

Stage plays returned to the Casino this year as the Goldstein Brothers brought, or attempted to bring, New York stage companies for limited engagements. (In 1920, they had built the Victory Theatre in downtown Holyoke.)

The season led off with a benefit by the Holyoke Kiwanis Club in the musical comedy *Marcheta*.

Afterwards, the resident company, now the Mt. Park Players took over for half the season before the experiment failed. It started off with Nan Shannon who "Will render operatic selections." Irving Mitchell was leading man. Other members of the company included Mabel Griffith, Helen Lewis, Claire Maslin, Louis Walford, Jerry O'Day, Dillon Deasy, and Eugene Head.

Other shows included:

Playthings

Some Baby

Cappy Ricks

Slippy Joe McGee – which included a local boy in the cast, Dan Harrington

Gay Young Bride with Tommy Martelle

The Seventh Guest

Kempy

Sonny Boy

Smilin' Thru

Her Temporary Husband

Vaudeville took over. The experiment was interesting while it lasted.

1925 season:

The Goldstein Brothers Amusement Company returned with a company of actors headed by Helen Lewis and Jack McGrath as the leads, and included Mabel Griffith, Richard Polette, J. Arnold Daly, Miriam Hicks. Willard Dashiell was the director. After beginning the summer with a Kiwanis Club review, the company took over with:

In Love With Love

It's a Boy

The Hottentot

1926 season:

The Goldstein Brothers Amusement Company returned with a cast that included Dorothy Beardsley (who also directed a show), Mabel Griffith, Georgia Clark. Willard Dashiell returned as director, and Charles Shute was manager. The shows included:

The Whole Town's Talking with Dorothy Beardsley and King Calder as leads

Meet the Wife

Applesauce

Spooks

The Show Off

Mary by George M. Cohan

The Naughty Wife – directed by Dorothy Beardsley, the first time a woman directed a show in Holyoke.

Miss Marion Severance and Her Orchestra played between acts.

1927 season:

Lead off with the silent motion picture *The Black Pirate*, starring swashbuckling star Douglas Fairbanks, with musical accompaniment by the Victory Theatre orchestra.

The regular theatre season included:

Laff That Off - with Lillian Merchal and Merrill Matheny. Ralph Chambers was "second man" in the company, and Willard Dashiell returned as director.

The Patsy, July 6th.

One of the Family – Jack McGrath, a leading man in the 1925 season returns as a "jobber," or one-time performer for this show in June.

1928 season:

The Goldstein Brothers continued their management of the Casino summer season. James A. Bliss was director.

The company includes Helen Lewis and George Nolan (who would change his surname to Brent and become a leading Hollywood man in the next decade. He and Helen Lewis would shortly marry.)

Shows included *Sinner* and *Peg o' My Heart*.

1929 season:

The Goldstein Brothers, after leading off with Ray Walker's "Song and Dance Review," continued the rest of the season with Keith Circuit vaudeville, then switched to silent movies for the rest of the season.

1930 season:

Not so much growing pains as a split personality: The season started with the Mountain Park Players presenting musical comedy, but the venture was a failure. The shows *Tangerine*, and *The Gingham Girl* featured Frances Dumas and Charles Angle in the leads.

Next Willard Dashiell formed a dramatic stock company and presented a string of light comedies. Dashiell directed and Mabel Griffiths was on board as a character woman. Vera Loday was the ingénue. Kathryn Wylie began as the season's leading lady, but was followed by Peggy Coudray.

Shows included:

Your Uncle Dudley

Let Us Be Gay

Salt Water, starring Frank Craven. Leon Girard and His Orchestra offered selections during intermission.

This Thing Called Love

The Unknown Voice

The Alarm Clock

In the Wrong Bed

That Ferguson Family

1931 season:

RKO Keith's vaudeville, in a poor season, but brightened by the appearance of Holyoke native Eva Tanguay on the bill June 30th.

1932 and 1933 seasons: talking pictures.

1934 season:

Director Howard Hall brought a season of theatre back with the Mt. Tom Players.

The Curtain Rises with star/"jobber" Mabel Taliaferro, Grandon Rhodes, Richard Bishop, Ruth Lee, Katheryn March.

Big Hearted Herbert with Helen Carewe.

Pursuit of Happiness with Willard Dashiell, who, with Rose Burdick and Mabel Griffith, remained in the shows for the rest of the season.

Her Majesty the Widow

Laff That Off

Don't Wake the Wife

Thin Ice, which closed the season on September 4th.

1935 season:

The Mt. Park Casino Musical Comedy Players under manager George D'Andra and musical director Fred Hoff. This attempt to bring touring shows for limited productions fails after two shows, and the Casino is dark for the remainder of 1935.

Chins Up, with a cast of 30, including a ballet chorus from the Metropolitan Opera Company and Capitol Theatre in New York.

1936 to 1939

1936 – WPA shows

The Federal Theatre Players of Massachusetts took up residence at the Casino under the auspices of the Works Progress Administration. Willard Dashiell directed, and Grace O'Leary, a local actress, was among the cast.

All Star Vaudeville

Post Road

Wooden Kimona

The Campus Widow

Craig's Wife

Chalk Dust

Class of '29

Sepian Review

Russet Mantle with Lynn Riggs closed the season.

1937 season:

Directed by Willard Dashiell, who also performed.

Night of January 16th

The Perfect Alibi

Goose Hangs High

The Bishop Misbehaves

The Curtain Rises

1938 season:

Federal Theatre Players of the WPA returns, again under direction of Willard Dashiell

Ah, Wilderness, starring Wendell Corey

Left Bank by Elmer Rice

The Swanee Review, 60 member cast in blackface

The Black and White Review – vaudeville

American Wins (?) by Frank Charlton

Return to Death by an African American company of players

Boy Meets Girl

The Federal Theatre Orchestra plays between acts.

1939 season:

Federal Theatre of the WPA plays its third and last season, abbreviated due to Congress voting to discontinue funding. Willard Dashiell directs

Yes, My Darling Daughter

The Barton Mystery

Tons of Money, featuring Wendell Corey

1940 season:

The Pioneer Valley Drama Festival under co-producers Norman Thompson and David Perkins, and director Lewis Allen. The players were Arthur Treacher, Diana Barrymore, supported by Adrienne Ames, John Craven, Phyllis Brooks, Tommy Lewis, and Michael Whalen.

Up Pops the Devil with Michael Whalen.

June 24, 1940 – Arthur Treacher as Sam Harrington in *The Hottentot*. Also in the cast were Diana Barrymore as Peggy Fairfax, Colvil Dunn, Virginia Petrie, Richard Kendrick, Hazel Jones, Lee Parry, John McKee, William Balfour, and Anthony Weinberg.

Personal Appearance with Adrienne Ames, Phyllis Brooks, and John Craven.

July 8th was *Goodbye Again* (which would later be produced again by The Valley Players in 1954). Erik Rhodes, Phyllis Brooks and Marcy Westcott were featured, and the cast included Peggy French (who was the leading lady for the season), John Craven, Gordon Wilson, John McKee, Billy Wood, William Balfour, Lee Parry, and Blanche Hartman. Directed by Lewis Allen. The show was produced by Norman Earl Thomson and David F. Perkins.

On Borrowed Time, starring Taylor Holmes and Tommy Lewis, and directed by Lewis Allen.

Week of July 15th *I'd Rather be Right* (?) with Taylor Holmes, Mary Jane Walsh, Marcy Westcott

The Valley Players: 1941 to 1962

All shows directed by Dorothy M. Crane, except where noted.

1941 season:

Here Today, week of June 30, 1941, featuring Jackson Perkins as Mary Hilliard. Also in the cast were Kent Adams, Sonia Barclay, Walter Coy, Mary Elliott, Jean Guild, Lauren Gilbert, and Joseph F. Foley.

In the first program, Carlton Guild was listed as the business manager, E.C. Edsen, a press representative, Louise (Louie) Mudgett for community publicity, Wyman Holmes as stage manager. Talbot Peterson was in charge of the electrical department, and William Chalou, the property department. Set design was by Martin W. Fallon.

Night Must Fall, week of July 7, 1941, featuring Mr. Lauren Gilbert as Dan, with Mary Elliott as the cockney maid, and Jean Guild as Mrs. Bramson. Joseph Foley and Miss Louie Mudgett also in the cast. This was Miss Mudgett's first acting role with the Valley Players. Elsie Stevens, Jackson Perkins, and Walter Coy were also in the cast.

The Male Animal, with John O'Connor in the lead, the cast included Alberta Johnson, Jackson Perkins, Mary Elliott, James Anderson, Wyman Holmes, Kent Adams, Walter Coy, Norah Adamson, Joseph Foley Jean Guild, and Malcolm Alama.

The Cradle Song, week of July 21, 1941, featuring Carmen Matthews as Sister Joanna of the Cross, and Jean Guild as the Prioress. The cast also included Jackson Perkins, Louise Wallis, Gloria Humphreys, Genevieve Stevens, Phyllis Leon, Louie Mudgett as Sister Inez, Sonia Barclay, Doris Poland, Adele Lipkin, Mary Elliott, Joseph Foley, Kent Adams, and George Spelvin.

Mr. and Mrs. North, week of July 28, 1941, featuring Miss Jackson Perkins and Mr. Lauren Gilbert as Pamela and Gerald North. They were also married in real life. The cast included Charles Tagliavignt, Mary Elliott, Kent Adams, Kenneth Norton, Genevieve Stevens, John O'Connor, Walter Coy, Joseph Foley, Phyllis Leon, Malcolm Alama, James Anderson, George Spelvin, and Carlton Guild stepped out from his manager's position to play a minor role as a policeman.

One Sunday Afternoon, week of August 4, 1941, featuring Walter Coy as Biff Grimes, with Mary Elliott as Virginia. Also in the cast were Lauren Gilbert, Ann Lincoln as Amy Lind, Jean Guild, and Sonia Barclay, Norah Adamson, Adele Lipkin, Malcolm Alama, Kent Adams, James Anderson, George Spelvin, and Carlton Guild filled in as another policeman.

George Washington Slept Here, August 11, 1941, featuring Joseph Foley as Newton Fuller, with John O'Connor as Mr. Kimber. Cast included Jean Guild, Mary Elliott, Kent Adams, Louie Mudgett, Lauren Gilbert, Jackson Perkins, Norah Adamson, Brian Quinn as Raymond, Wyman Holmes, Harold Dumais, Malcolm Alama, Genevieve Stevens, Gloria Humphries, and Walter Coy.

John O'Connor

Petticoat Fever, August 18, 1941, featuring Mr. Lauren Gilbert as Dascom Dinsmore, with John O'Connor as the comic Englishman Sir James Fenton. The cast also included Kent Adams, Jackson Perkins, Phyllis Leon, Adele Lipkin, Joseph Foley, Russell E. Davis as Scotty, Gloria Humphries.

The Milky Way – August 25, 1941, a comedy featuring John O'Connor. Other members of the company appearing were Jackson Perkins, Lauren Gilbert, Joseph P. Foley, Kent Adams and Mary Elliott, Harold Dumais, Malcolm Alama, and John McQuade.

They closed the 1941 season with *The Vinegar Tree*, featuring Jean Guild as Laura Merrick. The rest of the cast included Lauren Gilbert, Joseph Foley, Jackson Perkins, Clifford Frazier, Jr. as Louis, Mary Elliott, Kent Adams, and Miss Bucket—a Holyoke kitty cat.

1942 season:

Theatre, with Joseph Foley as the Sergeant, and Willard Dashiell as the butler. The cast also included Alfred Paschall, Jean Guild, Lauren Gilbert, Gaylord Mason, Frank Rollinger, Ada McFarland, Ernest Woodward, and Ann Lee.

Love from a Stranger, July 6, 1942, featured Mr. Lauren Gilbert as Bruce Lovell in this melodrama adapted from a story by Agatha Christie. Jean Guild appeared, as well as Ann Lee, Jackson Perkins, Frank Rollinger, Joseph Foley, Norah Adamson, and Ernest Woodward.

Yes, My Darling Daughter, July 13, 1942, with Joseph Foley as Lewis Murray, featuring Jean Guild as Ann Whitman Murray. The cast included Lorraine Bate, Jackson Perkins, Elizabeth Sanders, Lauren Gilbert, and Gaylord Mason.

Out of the Frying Pan, July 20, 1942, featuring Gaylord Mason as Norman Reese. Bertram Tanswell makes his first appearance with the Valley Players as George Bodell. Also in the cast were Jean Guild, Frank Rollinger, Ann Lee, Jackson Perkins, James Bostick, Lorraine Bate, Ernest Woodward, Lauren Gilbert, Alfred Paschall and Joseph Foley.

Cuckoos on the Hearth, July 27, 1942, with Joseph Foley as Doc Ferriss. Also in the cast were Jean Guild, Dorothy Brackett, Ann Lee, Gaylord Mason, Ernest Woodward, Lauren Gilbert, Frank Rollinger, Alfred Paschall, Louie Mudgett, Jackson Perkins, and Francis Mayville.

Watch on the Rhine, week of August 3, 1942, featuring Mr. Lauren Gilbert as Kurt Müller. Lauren Gilbert, Norah Adamson, Ernest Woodward, Jean Guild, Frank Rollinger, Ann Lee, Maurice Wells, Jackson Perkins, Gaylord Mason, Harlan Stone, Marion Davis.

Three Men on a Horse, week of August 10, 1942, featuring Joseph Foley, with Ann Lee, Alfred Paschall, Willard Dashiell, Mr. Lauren Gilbert, Kenneth Andrew, John McQuade, Jackson Perkins, Jean Guild, Elizabeth Sanders, and Frank Rollinger.

Lauren Gilbert

Skylark, week of August 17, 1942, comedy with Jackson

Perkins in the lead, Kenneth Andrew, Alfred Paschall, Mr. Lauren Gilbert, Frank Rollinger, Kathryn Grill, Elizabeth Sanders, John McQuade, Ann Lee, and Joseph Foley.

Nothing But the Truth, week of August 24th, featuring Ralph Edwards "Master of Ceremonies on the Popular *Truth or Consequences* Radio Program" as Robert Bennett. John McQuade, Lauren Gilbert, Joseph Foley, Frank Rollinger, Jean Guild, Norah Adamson, Dorothea Jackson, Ann Lee, Jackson Perkins, and Elizabeth Sanders were in the cast.

Private Lives, the Noel Coward comedy played the week of August 31, 1942 – last show of the season at Valley Players. Jackson Perkins played Amanda, opposite her husband, Lauren Gilbert. Also featured Ann Lee and Joseph Foley. Jean Guild had a brief role as a French maid.

NO 1943 SEASON.

1944 season:

Claudia, week of June 27th to July 2nd, featuring Elaine Ellis as Claudia and Bruce Riley as David. Also in the cast: Beatrice Newport, Jean Guild, Roland Hogue, Steven Elliott, Grace Briscombe, and Helen Wagner.

Personal Appearance, week of July 4 through 9th, featuring Grace Briscombe as Carole Arlen. Also in the cast were Elaine Ellis, Jean Guild, Helen Wagner (who had performed on Broadway in Rogers & Hammerstein's *Sunny River*), Steven Elliott, Beatrice Newport, Gaylord Mason, Bruce Riley, Ken E. Andrew, Grace Briscombe, and Dorothy Griffin.

Penny Wise, July 4th through 16th. Gaylord Mason, Grace Briscombe, Beatrice Newport, Bruce Riley, Elaine Ellis, Helen Wagner, Ken E. Andrew.

Blind Alley, week of July 18th through 23rd, featuring Gaylord Mason as Hal Wilson and John O'Connor as Dr. Anthony Shelby, with Beatrice Newport, Steven Elliott, Helen Wagner, Gary Striker, Jean Guild, Elaine Ellis, Bruce Riley, and Ken E. Andrew.

Made in Heaven, week of July 25th through 30th, featuring Grace Briscombe as Jessica Starke Young, and Steven Elliott as William Hewitt Young, Sr. Also with Jean Guild, Peter Griffith, Bruce Riley, Grace Briscombe, Steven Elliott, Beatrice Newport, and Helen Wagner.

Hay Fever, August 1st through 6th, featuring Jean Guild as Judith Bliss. Also Helen Wagner, Gaylord Mason, Claudine Shannon, Roland Hogue, Steven Elliott, Beatrice Newport, Helen Harrelson, and Alfred Paschall.

Charley's Aunt, week of August 8th to 13th, featuring Bertram Tanswell as Lord Fancourt Babberley. Also with Gaylord Mason, Ken E. Andrew, Steven Elliott, Helen Wagner,

Beatrice Newport, Roland Hogue, Jean Guild, and Helen Harrelson.

Three's a Family, August 15th through 20th, featuring Jean Guild as Irma Dalrymple and John O'Connor as Sam Whitaker. Also with Louie Mudgett, Jacqueline Paige, Gaylord Mason, Helen Harrelson, Beatrice Newport, Steven Elliott, Ken E. Andrew, Claudine Shannon, Janet Fehm, Roland Hogue, Alfred Paschall, and Helen Wagner.

Broadway, August 22nd through 27th, August 22nd through 27th, featuring Gaylord Mason as Roy Lane and Helen Wagner as Billie Moore. The cast also included Ken E. Andrew, Jean Guild, Carlton Guild, Martha Jones, Helen Harrelson, Beatrice Newport, Estelle Lally, Janet Fehm, Helen Wagner, John O'Connor, Bertram Tanswell, Alfred Paschall, Steven Ellott, and Robert Emhardt.

Ladies in Retirement, week of August 29th through September 3rd, featuring Beatrice Newport as Ellen Creed. Directed by Bertram Tanswell. Helen Harrelson was in the cast, along with Helen Wagner, Steven Elliott, Martha Jones, Jean Guild, and Louie Mudgett.

1945 season:

Sets by Randall Brooks

Blythe Spirit, week of June 25th through 30th, featuring Martha Jones, Jackson Perkins as Ruth and Mr. Lauren Gilbert as Charles. Also in the cast were Helen Harrelson, Robert Emhardt, Eleanor Nichols Alderman, and Jean Guild.

Papa is All, week of July 2nd through 7th, featuring Robert Emhardt as Papa, and Jackson Perkins and Jean Guild, Gaylord Mason. The cast also included Hugh Franklin, in his Valley Players debut, Helen Harrelson, and Jean Guild.

Murder Without Crime, week of July 9th through 14th, featuring Gaylord Mason as Stephen and Hugh Franklin as Matthew, also with Helen Harrelson and Martha Jones.

Over 21, week of July 16th through 21st, featuring Jackson Perkins, with Robert Emhardt and Hugh Franklin, along with Helen Harrelson, Terry Little, Lynton Burr, Edward A. Wright making his first appearance with the Valley Players as Col. H. S. Foley; Jean Guild, Gaylord Mason, and Martha Jones.

Outward Bound, week of July 23rd through 28th, featuring Jean Guild as Mrs. Midget, Gaylord Mason as Mr. Prior, and Edward A. Wright as Scrubby. Also in the cast were Martha Jones, Terry Little, Jackson Perkins, Ronald Telfer, and Robert Ermhardt.

Kiss and Tell, week of July 30th through August 4th, featuring Jackson Perkins as Janet Archer, Robert Emhardt as Harry Archer, and Betsy Drake as Corliss Archer. Jean Guild,

Peter Griffith, Helen Harrelson, Jay Sawyer, Terry Little, Gaylord Mason, Martha Jones, Edward A. Wright, Dorothy M. Crane, Ronald Telfer, Hugh Franklin and Carlton Guild. The show was directed by Gaylord Mason.

Gaylord Mason

Arsenic and Old Lace, week of August 6th through 11th, featuring Jean Guild as Abby Brewster, Martha Jones as Martha Brewster, and Gaylord Mason as Mortimer Brewster. The cast also included Edward A. Wright (in two roles), Robert Emhardt as Teddy, Jay Sawyer, Helen Harrelson, Lynton Burr, Hugh Franklin as Jonathan, Ronald Telfer, Terry Little, and Carlton Guild as Lt. Rooney.

Snafu, week of August 13th through 18th, with Jackson Perkins and Terry Little. Also in the cast were Edith Leslie, Martha Jones, Hugh Franklin, Edward A. Wright, Helen Harrelson, Jean Guild, Ronald Telfer, Jay Sawyer, Louie Mudgett, Gaylord Mason, Lucille St. Peter, and Robert Emhardt.

The Torch Bearers, week of August 20th through 25th, with Hugh Franklin and Helen Harrelson, and Jean Guild. The cast also included Ronald Telfer, Robert Emhardt, Edward A. Wright, Arthur Stuart, Jackson Perkins, Carmen Matthews, Louie Mudgett, Carlton Guild and George Spelan as himself.

Tomorrow the World, week of August 27th through September 1st, featuring Hugh Franklin, Martha Jones, and young Paul Porter Jr. The cast also included little Phyllis DeBus, Jackson Perkins, Jean Guild, Ronald Telfer, Robert Sabin, Allen Knox, and Richard Williams.

244

1946 season:

The sets were by Donald F. Hermes.

Hope for the Best, week of June 24-29, featuring Hugh Franklin and Helen Harrelson, Jean Guild, Joseph Foley, Bertram Tanswell, Gaylord Mason.

Angel Street, week of July 1-6, featuring Ellen Andrews, Hugh Franklin, and Raymond Greenleaf. Directed by Bertram Tanswell.

The Hasty Heart, week of July 8-13, with Bertram Tanswell as Lachie, Gaylord Mason as Yank. Howard Ledig made his Valley Players debut in this play as Digger. Also in the cast were Jay Sawyer, William Brown, Joseph Foley, Helen Harrelson, Raymond Greenleaf, and Bertram Tanswell.

Donald F. Hermes

Ten Little Indians, week of July 15-20, with Raymond Greenleaf as Sir Lawrence Wargrave; Hugh Franklin as Dr. Armstrong; and Madeleine L'Engle making her debut with The Valley Players as Emily Brent. Also in the cast were Bertram Tanswell as Rogers the butler, Jean Guild as Mrs. Rogers, Roy Alexander as Fred Narracott, Ellen Andrews as Vera Claythorne, Howard Ledig as Phillip Lombard, Gaylord Mason as Anthony Marston, Joseph Foley as William Blore, Edward A. Wright as General Mackenzie.

What a Life, week of July 22-27, featuring Jay Sawyer (who was still in high school, visiting for the season from Virginia). Also in the cast were Randee Sanford, Hugh Franklin, Patricia Mowbray, Dorothy Sullivan, John Randall, Nancy Langdon Walsh, Edward A. Wright, Louie Mudgett,

Roy Alexander, Dorothy M. Crane, Grace Wright, Bertram Tanswell, Helen Harrelson, Ruth Elliot, Joseph Foley, Madeleine L'Engle, Gaylord Mason, and Howard Ledig. (Randee Sanford, John Randall, and Dorothy Sullivan were all young people from Holyoke.)

The Late George Apley, week of July 29-August 3rd, featuring Raymond Greenleaf and Beatrice Newport. Also with Louie Mudgett, Gaylord Mason, Helen Harrelson, Edward Wright, Jean Guild, Hugh Franklin, Alfred Paschall, Madeleine L'Engle, Randee Sanford, Howard Ledig, Ellen Andrews, Dorothy Crane, Bertram Tanswell.

The Man Who Came to Dinner, week of August 5-10. Alfred Paschall played Sheridan Whiteside, with Beatrice Newport, Jean Guild, Jay Sawyer, Helen Harrelson, Raymond Greenleaf, Louie Mudgett, Joseph Foley, Ellen Andrews, Hugh Franklin, Madeleine L'Engle as Harriet Stanley, Howard Ledig, Edward A. Wright, Roy Alexander, Marjory Miller (a local young actress from Longmeadow), George Alan Smith, and Gaylord Mason.

The Corn is Green, the week of August 12-17th, featured Jean Guild as Miss Moffat and Gaylord Mason as Morgan Evans. The cast also included Joseph Foley, Beatrice Newport, Jay Sawyer, Louie Mudgett, Raymond Greenleaf, Madeleine L'Engle, Helen Harrelson, James Anderson, Edward C. Purrington Jr., Robert L. Baker, Edward A. Wright, Ruth Elliot, Janet Herd, Cynthia Hill, Marian Herd, Lois Smith, and Stephen Cunniff, who was an usher for the playhouse. Directed by Bertram Tanswell.

Little Accident, week of August 19-24, featuring Gaylord Mason, Gloria Peterson, Joseph Foley, Howard Ledig, Doris Belack, George Alan Smith, Mel Roberts, Edward A. Wright, Beatrice Newport, Louie Mudgett, Helen Harrelson, Ruth Elliot, and Jean Guild.

But Not Goodbye, week of August 26-31, featuring Bertram Tanswell and John O'Connor. Also in the cast were Howard Ledig, Jean Guild, Helen Harrelson, Joseph Foley, Mel Roberts, Gaylord Mason, George Alan Smith, Edward A. Wright.

1947 season:

Dear Ruth, week of June 23-28, 1947, featuring Helen Harrelson, Gaylord Mason, and Joyce Van Patten as Miriam Wilkins. Also in the cast were Louie Mudgett, Jean Guild, Joseph Foley, Howard Ledig, Ruth Elliot, Bertram Tanswell, Robert S. Jeffers.

Uncle Harry, week of June 30-July 5, featuring Bertram Tanswell and Anne Follmann, with Ruth Elliot, Donald F. Hermes, Jean Guild, Helen Harrelson, Louie Mudgett (who also handled publicity for the Valley Players), Howard Ledig, John O'Connor, Joseph Foley, Ed Fuller, Gaylord Mason, George Alan Smith—and a couple of the technical staff doing acting chores in walk-on roles: manager Carlton Guild as The Governor, and Dorothy M. Crane (who also directed) as Matron. Anne Follmann and Ed Fuller were newcomers to the Valley Players with this production.

January Thaw, week of July 7-12 – "A Comedy with the Real New England Flavor" featuring Joseph Foley and John O'Connor. The cast also included Louie Mudgett, Phyllis DeBus, Jay Sawyer, Anne Follmann, Helen Harrelson, Gaylord Mason, Jean Guild, Ed Fuller, Bertram Tanswell, Howard Ledig, and George Allan Smith.

The Barretts of Wimpole Street, week of July 14-19th, featuring Beatrice Newport and Howard Ledig as Elizabeth Barrett Browning and Robert Browning. Also in the cast were Joseph Foley, Jean Guild as the maid, Wilson; Helen Harrelson, Ruth Elliot, Gaylord Mason, Clifford Lamont, Donald F. Hermes, John Randall, Ed Ford, Robert Jeffers, Eric Elliott, Miriam Stovall, John O'Connor, George Alan Smith, Ed Fuller, and the dog, Flush, was played by "Miss Hayes." Directed by Bertram Tanswell.

Our Town, week of July 21-26, featuring John O'Connor as the "Stage Manager" and Helen Harrelson as Emily Webb. Also in the cast were Ed Fuller, Herbert Lobl, Howard Ledig, Jean Guild as Mr. Gibb, Beatrice Newport as Mrs. Webb, Gaylord Mason as George Gibb, Emily Adelle Morrison as Rebecca, Malcolm Bertram Jr., Willard Cary, Joseph Foley as Mr. Web, Louie Mudgett as Woman in Audience, Donald Senecal as Man in Audience, Ruth Elliot, Bertram Tanswell, Miriam Stovall, J. Harris Melia as the Constable, Barclay Dwight, Donald F. Hermes, Carlton Guild as Joe Stoddard, and many others as townspeople and the church choir.

Miriam Stovall

First Lady, week of July 28-August 2nd, featuring Beatrice Newport and Ann Lee. The cast included Helen Harrelson,

J. Harris Melia, Miriam Stoval, John O'Connor, Jean Guild, Dorothy M. Crane as Mrs. Ives, Ruth Elliot, Louie Mudgett, Howard Ledig, Ed Fuller, Joseph Foley, Carlton Guild, Alfred Paschall, and Jay Sawyer. Three walk-on parts were taken by locals who also were drafted to be townspeople in *Our Town* the previous week: Priscilla Wells from Somers, Connecticut, and Byrde Merican and James Courtney, both of Holyoke.

The Little Foxes by Lillian Hellman, week of August 4-9, featuring Ann Lee. Also in the cast were Enid Raphael as Addy, Charles Benjamin as Cal, Miriam Stovall, Alfred Paschall as Oscar Hubbard, Gaylord Mason as Leo, Howard Ledig, Joseph Foley as Ben Hubbard, Helen Harrelson as Alexandra, John O'Connor as Horace Giddens.

Return Engagement, week of August 11-16, featuring Alfred Paschall and Beatrice Newport. The cast also included Jean Guild, Donald Senecal, Jay Sawyer, Helen Harrelson, Howard Ledig, Alice Mary O'Donnell, Miriam Stovall, Grace McTarnahan, Ruth Elliot, Gaylord Mason, Beatrice Newport, Alfred Paschall, Joseph Foley, John Randall, and Mary Landry. (Mr. Senecal, Miss O'Donnell, and Mr. Randall were all locals from Holyoke.)

Heaven Can Wait, week of August 18-23, featuring Gaylord Mason. Also in the cast were John O'Connor, James Courtney, John Randall, Edward R. Wright, Howard Ledig, Beatrice Newport, Alice Mary O'Donnell, Jean Guild, Marie Phillips, Joseph Foley, Ed Fuller, George Alan Smith, J. Harris Melia. Passenger were played by Peggy Griffin from South Hadley, stage manager Edward C. Purrington Jr., Robert Jeffers, Byrde Merican, and Louie Mudgett.

George and Margaret, week of August 25-30, featuring Jean Guild and Joseph Foley, with Ruth Elliot, Gaylord Mason, Helen Harrelson, Ed Fuller, Howard Ledig, Louie Mudgett, Beatrice Newport, and Carlton Guild as George.

Made in Heaven, week of September 1-6, featuring John O'Connor and Anne Follmann. The cast also included Helen Harrelson, Beatrice Newport, Howard Ledig, Gaylord Mason, Joseph Foley, Jean Guild, Ruth Elliot, Ed Fuller, Robert Jeffers, Jutta Wolf (replaced in at least one performance – noted in pencil – by Ruth Elliot).

1948 season:

Sets by Donald F. Hermes.

The Voice of the Turtle, week of June 21-26, featuring Helen Harrelson, John Bryant, and Jacqueline Paige.

Kind Lady, week of June 28-July 3, featuring Anne Follmann and Bertram Tanswell. The cast also included Barbara Webster, John O'Connor, Jacqueline Paige, Louie Mudgett, John Bryant, J. Harris Melia, Joseph Foley, Jean Guild, Ruth Elliot, Donald F. Hermes, and newcomer Betty June Oakes.

Edward Fuller

Years Ago, by Ruth Gordon, week of July 5-10, featuring Joseph Foley, Helen Harrelson and Jean Guild. Also in the cast were Ruth Elliot, Betty June Oaks, John Randall, John O'Connor William Dodds, Jacqueline Paige, and a cat. Directed by Bertram Tanswell.

Rain, week of July 12-17, featuring Jacqueline Paige as Sadie Thompson and John O'Connor. Also in the cast were Jean Guild, Richard Maxson, John Randall, John Bryant, Joseph Foley, Ed Fuller, Ruth Elliot, Anne Follmann, Bertram Tanswell, and Alice Mary O'Donnell, Jean Purrington, and Marie La Rochelle as native girls, and James Courtney as a native man.

John Loves Mary, week of July 19-24, featuring John Bryant and Helen Harrelson, with J. Harris Melia, Bertram Tanswell, Joseph Foley, Jacqueline Paige, Ed Fuller, William Dodds, Ruth Elliot, and John O'Connor.

Ghost Train, week of July 26-31. The cast included Ed Fuller, Jacqueline Paige, John O'Connor, John Bryant, Ruth Elliot, Jean Guild, Bertram Tanswell, Helen Harrelson, Carlton Guild as Herbert Price, Joseph Foley, William Dodds (who was the company's 2nd stage manager), James Courtney, and John Randall.

You Can't Take it With You, week of August 2-7 featuring John O'Connor as Grandpa Martin Vanderhof, Jean Guild as Penelope Sycamore, Pauline Meyers as Rheba, Bertram Tanswell as Mr. DePinna, Charles Benjamin as Donald, Cathy McDonald as Alice, John Randall as Ed, Ruth Elliot, Joseph Foley, J. Harris Melia, John Bryant as Tony Kirby, Ed Fuller as Boris Kolenkov, Jacqueline Paige, Carlton Guild as Mr. Kirby, Louie Mudgett as Mrs. Kirby, Westfield

native Anne Pitoniak as Olga, William Dodds, James Courtney, Richard Maxson.

Guest in the House, week of August 9-14, featuring Helen Harrelson, Ed Fuller, and Anne Pitoniak. The cast includes Betty Lou Keim, Pauline Myers, John O'Connor, Jean Guild, Florence Sundstrom, John Bryant, Ed Fuller, Charles Benjamin, Helen Harrelson, John Foley, Dorothy M. Crane as Mrs. Dow, Ruth Elliot, and Richard Maxson. Directed by Bertram Tanswell.

Pursuit of Happiness, week of August 16-21. The cast: John Bryant, Ruth Elliot, Charles Benjamin, John O'Connor, Ed Fuller, Helen Harrelson, Jean Guild, Bertram Tanswell, John Randall, Donald Senecal, and Joseph Foley.

All My Sons, week of August 23-28. The cast: John Foley, Jean Guild, John Bryant, Helen Harrelson, Bertram Tanswell, John O'Connor, Jacqueline Paige, Edward Fuller, Ruth Elliot.

Tons of Money, week of August 30 – September 4, featuring Bertram Tanswell and Mary Jackson, with Joseph Foley, Jacqueline Paige, Louie Mudgett, John O'Connor, Edward Fuller, Helen Harrelson, John Bryant, and William Dodds.

Accent on Youth, week of September 6-11, featuring John O'Connor and Helen Harrelson, with Jacqueline Paige, Bertram Tanswell, Joseph Foley, John Bryant, Jean Guild, James Courtney, and William Dodds.

1949 season:

Sets by Donald F. Hermes.

Jenny Kissed Me, week of June 20-25, featuring Joseph Foley, Miriam Stoval, and Tyler Carpenter. The cast also included Jean Guild, Louie Mudgett, Ruth Elliot, Jean Bellows, Mary-Elizabeth Donovan, Alice Mary O'Donnell, Betsy Smith, Stephen Reese, and John O'Connor.

George Washington Slept Here, June 27-July 2, 1949, featuring Jean Guild, Joseph Foley, and John O'Connor, with Miriam Stovall, Stephen Reese, Virginia Lewis, Louie Mudgett, William Dodds, Jean Bellows, Ruth Elliot, Dickie Simmons, Ed Fuller, Richard Maxson, Richard Erikson, Alice Mary O'Donnell, Nancy Carpenter, Robert Emhardt.

An Inspector Calls, week of July 4-9, featuring John O'Connor, with Jean Guild, Miriam Stovall, Stephen Reese, Edward Fuller, Ruth Elliot, and Joseph Foley.

Parlor Story, week of July 11-16, featuring Anne Pitoniak, and Edward Fuller. Others in the cast included Ruth Elliot, Miriam Stovall, Stephen Reese, J. Harris Melia, Joseph Hannigan, Jean Bellows, Leland Harris, and John O'Connor.

Dream Girl, week of July 18-23, featuring Miriam Stovall. Also in the cast were Jean Guild, Stephen Reese, Leland Harris (playing six roles), Anne Pitoniak, Edward Fuller, Jean Bellows, Louie Mudgett, Carlton Guild as A Doctor, Peter Harris, Walter Swift, Joseph Harrington, Albert Rossetti, and box office staff Alice Mary O'Donnell playing An Usher.

Apple of His Eye, week of July 25-30, featuring Anne Pitoniak and John O'Connor. The cast also included Jean Guild, Edward Fuller, Leland Harris, Alice Mary O'Donnell, nine-year-old Betty Lou Keim, Robert Emhardt, Jean Bellows, and Peter Harris.

The Heiress, week of August 1-6, featuring Miriam Stovall as Catherine Sloper, and Hugh Franklin as Dr. Austin Sloper. The cast included Jean Guild as Mrs. Lavinia Penniman, Louie Mudgett, Ruth Elliot, Stephen Reese, Peter Harris as Morris Townsend, Virginia Lewis, and Jean Bellows.

Boy Meets Girl, week of August 8-13. This farce featured Ruth Elliot, Hugh Franklin, Peter Harris, and Robert Emhardt, with Alice Mary O'Donnell, Jean Bellows, Stephen Reese, Betsy Smith, Carlton Guild playing a doctor for his second time this season, Norman Castonguay, and stage manager Edward C. Purrington Jr. as Young Man.

The Bat, week of August 15-20, a mystery thriller featuring Jean Guild and John O'Connor, with Miriam Stovall, Joseph Hannigan, Stephen Reese, Peter Harris, Edward Fuller, Norman Castonguay, and Robert Emhardt.

My Sister Eileen, August 22-27, by Joseph A. Fields and Jerome Chodorov, based on the stories of Ruth McKenney, featuring Ruth Elliot as Eileen and Jean Bellows as Ruth. Also in the cast were Joseph Foley as Mr. Appopolous, David Bates, the Guild's son William in a walk-on role, Daniel Burke and Stephen Burke, Joseph Hannigan and Richard Erickson as a couple of drunks, J. Harris Melia, Edward Fuller as The Wreck, William Dodds, Miriam Stovall, Stephen Reese as Frank Lippincott, John O'Connor as Chic Clark, and Carlton Guild as Ruth and Eileen's father, Mr. Sherwood. Also in the large group of crowd passersby and the Brazilian Navy were Mona Stevens, Virginia Lewis, Peter Harris, Albert Rosetti, Paul Schrade, George Allen, Richard Maxson, Louie Mudgett, set designer Donald F. Hermes, and box office staff Mary O'Donnell and Edward C. Purrington Jr.

Fresh Fields, with August 29-September 3, featuring Jean Guild, Miriam Stovall, Edward Fuller, and Madeleine L'Engle. Also in the cast were Ruth Elliot, Stephen Reese, Jean Bellows, Joseph Foley, and Louie Mudgett.

The Late Christopher Bean, week of September 5-10, featuring John O'Connor and Jean Guild, with Ruth Elliot, Jean Bellows, Miriam Stovall, Stephen Reese, Joseph Foley, Walter Kohler and Edward Fuller.

1950 season:

Sets this season by Gerald Freedman.

For Love or Money, week of June 19-24, 1950, featuring Miriam Stovall and Tyler Carpenter, with Jean Guild, Ralph Longley, Edward Fuller, Louie Mudgett, Joseph Foley, and Judy Somerside.

Peg O' My Heart, week of June 26-July 1, featuring Betty June Oakes as Peg, with Jean Guild, Joseph Foley, Miriam Stovall, Archie Smith, Tyler Carpenter, Edward Fuller, Alice Mary O'Donnell as a maid, and Ralph Longley.

Life with Mother, week of July 3-8, featuring Miriam Stovall as Vinnie, Joseph Foley as Father, and Robert Emhardt. Cast also includes Louie Mudgett, Ralph Longley, John O'Connor, Steven Burke and Herbert Lobl, Clifford Tatum Jr., a 12-year old veteran of TV, radio and movies, who had toured with Mady Christians in *I Remember Mama*. Also Marian Hatfield, Jean Guild, Louise Wallis (of the Mt. Holyoke College faculty), Jean Bellows, Mary-Elizabeth Donovan of Longmeadow, and Rosalie Trombowski, a recent graduate of Emerson College brought in by Louie Mudgett. She played the Irish maid, Bridget.

The Traitor, week of July 10-15, featuring John O'Connor, Joseph Foley, and Phil Arthur. Cast also includes Miriam Stovall, Louie Mudgett, Jean Bellows, Edward Fuller, Carlton Guild, Water Swift, J. Harris Melia, Edward C. Purrington Jr., Albert Rosetti, Richard Erickson, Walter Dobbs, and Robert Emhardt.

The Royal Family, week of July 17-22, featuring Jackson Perkins, Phil Arthur, and Nina Probette. The cast included Jean Bellows, J. Harris Melia, Walter Swift, George Kyron, Edward Fuller, Jean Guild, Miriam Stovall, Ralph Longley, Joseph Foley, John O'Connor, Rosalie Trombowski, and Albert Rosetti.

Harvey, week of July 24-29, featuring Joseph Foley and Jean Guild. The cast included Jean Bellows, Peggy Towne, Louie Mudgett, Miriam Stovall, Edward Fuller, Ralph Longley, John O'Connor, Rosalie Trombowski, Arthur Bell, and George Kyron.

The Winslow Boy, week of July 31 – August 5, featuring Hugh Franklin and John O'Connor. The cast included Barry Truex, Virginia Lewis, Jean Guild, Helen Harrelson, Ralph Longley, Louie Mudgett, and William Dodds.

Jacqueline Paige

The Philadelphia Story, week of August 7-12, featuring Helen Harrelson as Tracy Lord, with Jean Guild as Margaret Lord, Mary-Elizabeth Donovan as Dinah, Ralph Longley, Carlton Guild, Joseph Foley as Uncle Willie, Rhodelle Heller as Liz Imbrie, Tyler Carpenter as Mike Connor, Edward Fuller as George Kittredge, Hugh Franklin as C.K. Dexter-Haven, Peggy Towne, and William Dodds.

Love Rides the Rails, Or, Will the Mail Train Run Tonight? week of August 14-19, with Ruth Elliot, Edward Fuller, Ted Tiller, Tyler Carpenter, Bertram Tanswell, Jean Guild as the widow mother, Ralph Longley, Rhodelle Heller, Marian Hatfield, Joseph Foley, J. Harris Melia, William Guild, Judy Barger, and William Dodds. John Marion at the piano accompanying the musical numbers. Choreography by Elsie Cappel.

Light Up the Sky, week of August 21-26, featuring Nan McFarland, Jean Guild, Ruth Elliot, Bertram Tanswell, with Rosalie Trombowski, Tyler Carpenter, Ralph Longley, Salem Ludwig, Edward Fuller, William Dodds, Joseph Foley, and Edward C. Purrington Jr.

The Damask Cheek, week of August 28-September 2, featuring Miriam Stovall and Ruth Elliot, with Hildegarde Halliday, Jean Guild, Ralph Longley, Marian Hatfield, Henry Garrard, and Tyler Carpenter.

The Happiest Years, week of September 4-9, featuring Jean Guild and Ralph Longley. The cast also included Marian Hatfield, Hildegarde Halliday, John O'Connor, Edward C. Purrington Jr., Ruth Elliot, Jacqueline Paige, and Edward Fuller.

1951 – 10th season:

Sets by Hal Shafer

Good Housekeeping, week of June 18-23, featuring Jean Guild and John O'Connor, with Nancy Wells, Gaylord Mason, Joyce Van Patten, Mac Gress, Donald Somers, Louie Mudgett, Sophia Klosek, and cheerleaders played by Ann Dowling, Vivia Epstein, and Sandra Stockser.

The Man, week of June 25-30 featuring Gaylord Mason and Pamela Simpson. The cast included Nancy Wells, Donald Somers, Carlton Guild, Mac Gress, William Dodds, and "Miss Hayes" the cat returned for her role as Sarah the cat.

Born Yesterday, week of July 2-7, with Si Oakland as Harry Brock and Nancy Wells as Billie Dawn. This was The Valley Players' 100th show. The cast included Vivian   , Gaylord Mason, Archie Smith, Richard Erikson, Ronald Hannah, Carlton Guild as the Assistant Manager, John O'Connor, J. Harris Melia, Judy Barger, Mac Gress, Donald Somers, Jean Guild, and William Dodds.

The Firebrand, week of July 9-14, featuring Phil Arthur, Archie Smith, and Jacqueline Paige. This was the company debut of Hal and Ruby Holbrook. The cast also included Nancy Wells, Mac Gress, Jean Guild, John O'Connor, Gaylord Mason, Carlton Guild and William Dodds as two soldiers, James Courtney as a hangman, and ladies of the court played by Vivian Marlowe and Sandra Stockser.

Goodbye, My Fancy, week of July 16-21, featuring Jackson Perkins with Joyce Van Patten, Ann Dowling Vivian Marlowe, Nancy Wells, Louie Mudgett, William Dodds, Bernard Spencer, Mac Gress, Marian Hatfield, Jean Guild, Jacqueline Paige, Ruby Holbrook, Archie Smith, Hal Holbrook, Phil Arthur, Si Oakland, and two juniors at Holyoke High School: Joan Cappel and Mary Lou Mayer.

Because Their Hearts Were Pure, week of July 23-28, featuring Hal Holbrook, Nancy Wells, and Phil Arthur, with John Marion at the piano, and Jean Guild, Louie Mudgett, Jacqueline Paige, Si Oakland, John O'Connor, Bertram Tanswell, Gaylord Mason, Ruby Holbrook, Claire Bessette, Jeanne Courchesne, Rita Mitchell, Janet Mungall, Hilda Scott, Jane Senecal, Judy Barger, Mac Gress, William Guild, and Ronald Hannah.

Two Blind Mice, week of July 30-August 4, featuring Gaylord Mason, Louie Mudgett, and Jean Guild. Also in the cast were Carlton Guild, Jacqueline Paige, William Dodds, Ann Dowling, Charles Benjamin, Ruby Holbrook, Bertram Tanswell, John O'Connor, James Courtney, George Kyron, Glen C. Gordon, Ronald Hannah, Hal Holbrook, Mac Gress, Si Oakland, and choir members played by Beulah May Daniels, Irene Gray, and Margie Pete.

The Joyous Season, week of August 6 – 11, featuring Jean Guild as Mother Superior. The cast also included John O'Connor, Si Oakland, Gaylord Mason, Mac Gress, Ruby

Holbrook, Nancy Wells, Jacqueline Paige, Hal Holbrook, Ann Dowling, Bertram Tanswell, Louie Mudgett.

See How They Run, week of August 13-18, featuring Gaylord Mason, Ruby Holbrook as Penelope Toop, with Hal Holbrook, who played the Reverend Lionel Toop, Nancy Wells, Jean Guild, James Courtney, John O'Connor, Bertram Tanswell, and William Dodds. This was Ruby Holbrook's first featured role.

Come Back, Little Sheba, week of August 20-25, featuring John O'Connor and Jacqueline Paige, with Nancy Wells, Gaylord Mason, Tom Lennon, Jean Guild, James Courtney, Hal Holbrook, Carlton Guild, William Dodds.

Candlelight, week of August 27-September 1, featuring Gaylord Mason, Hal Holbrook, and Miriam Stovall, with William Dodds, Nancy Wells, John O'Connor, Ronald Hannah, and Jacqueline Paige.

The Fatal Weakness, week of September 3-8, featuring Jean Guild, Jacqueline Paige, with Louie Mudgett, Nancy Wells, John O'Connor, and Gaylord Mason.

1952 season:

O Mistress Mine, week of June 16-21, featuring Lauren Gilbert and Jackson Perkins, with Jean Guild, Tash Bozek, Mac Gress, Nancy Wells, and Vivian Marlowe.

Second Threshold, week of June 23-28, featuring John O'Connor and Gloria Hoye, with Hal Holbrook, Bertram Tanswell, Nancy Wells, and Mac Gress.

Gramercy Ghost, week of June 30-July 5 featuring Hal Holbrook, Ruby Holbrook (in their first featured pairing), Bertram Tanswell, and Edward Fuller, with Jean Guild, Warren Humes, John O'Connor, Mac Gress, Michael O'Brien, Jacqueline Paige, and locals from Springfield and Holyoke: Paul Clifford and Lynne Zimmerman.

The Silver Whistle, week of July 7-12, featuring John O'Connor, Jacqueline Paige, Nancy Wells, Edward Fuller, with Bertram Tanswell, Jean Guild, Ruby Holbrook, Hal Holbrook, Mary Farrell, Si Oakland, James Van Wart, Carlton Guild, Michael O'Brien, and George L. Cobleigh of Springfield.

A Streetcar Named Desire, week of July 14-19, featuring Miriam Stovall as Blanche and Si Oakland as Stanley. The cast also included Lucille Deans, Nancy Wells as Stella, Edward Fuller as Mitch, Jacqueline Paige, John O'Connor, Hal Holbrook as Pablo Gonzales, Paul Clifford, Jeanne Kenworthy, Jean Guild and Carlton Guild as A Single Woman and A Single Man. The show was directed by Robert Emhardt.

Season in the Sun, week of July 21-26, featuring Hal and Ruby Holbrook, with Gregor Rowland, Jean Guild, Edward

Fuller, Nancy Wells, Si Oakland, Jacqueline Paige, Bertram Tanswell, John O'Connor, with roles taken by locals: Joan Cappel and Stephen Burke of Holyoke, and Paul Clifford, Jean Burns and her daughter, Maureen Burns, of Springfield.

The Luck of Caesar, week of July 28-August 2, a new play written by former company George Alan Smith, a former stage manager for The Valley Players, and a native of Holyoke, about a New England factory town, featuring Si Oakland and Ellen Andrews. The cast included Stanley Greene, Jean Guild, Nancy Wells, Hal Holbrook, John O'Connor, Edward Fuller, Carlton Guild, James Van Wart, J. Harris Melia, and young Thomas J. Finn of Holyoke as "Young Man."

The Happy Time, week of August 4-9, featuring John O'Connor, Jacqueline Paige, Nancy Wells, Marto Santamaria, with Bertram Tanswell, Hal Holbrook, Paul Lipson, Jean Guild, Nancy Wells, Patricia Drodz (a first-timer noted to be from the Willimansett neighborhood of Chicopee), Tom Lennon, Mitchell Erikson, and Carlton Guild.

Room Service, week of August 11-16, featuring Hal Holbrook, Bertram Tanswell, Mitchell Erickson, and Ted Tiller. Also in the cast were Gene D'Arcy, John O'Connor, Nancy Wells, Mary-Elizabeth Donovan, Paul Lipson, J. Harris Melia, Warren Humes, Carlton Guild, Thomas J. Finn, and James Van Wart.

Glad Tiding, week of August 18-23, featuring Jackson Perkins, Tyler Carpenter, with Jacqueline Paige, Jean Guild, Robert Colson, Mary-Elizabeth Donovan, Nancy Wells, Ted Tiller, Mac Gress.

The High Ground, August 25-30, featuring Jean Guild as Sr. Mary Bonaventure, and Jackson Perkins as Sarat Carn, with Ruby Holbrook as Nurse Phillips, Nancy Wells, Eleanor Farnese, Bertram Tanswell as Willy, Hal Holbrook, Jeanne Shelby as Mother Superior, John O'Connor, Lee Firestone, and Jacqueline Paige.

I Like It Here, week of September 1-6, featuring Bertram Tanswell and John O'Connor, with Nancy Wells, Carlton Gould, Jean Gould, Robert Colson, Hal Holbrook, Mitchell Erikson, and Jeanne Kenworthy.

The Sun Looks Down, week of September 8-13, a production in association with Fred F. Finklehoff and James S. Elliott, directed by James J. Elliott, featuring Victor Varconi, Paula Morgan, and Julean Compton, with Daryl Raymond, Bunny Warner, Teddy Roberts, Ludmilla Taretska, Henry Sharp, Victor Millan, Felicia Grey, Edward Groag.

1953 season:

The sets for this season were by Hal Shafer.

Nina, week of June 15-30, featuring Lauren Gilbert, Jackson Perkins, and Joseph Foley also with John O'Connor. This four-person play (rare among the usual plays of large casts The Valley Players chose), was directed by Jacqueline Paige in her first time directing.

Affairs of State, week of June 22-27, featured Helen Harrelson, John O'Connor, Hal Holbrook, with Don Thomas, Jacqueline Paige, Joseph Foley.

The Velvet Glove, week of June 29 – July 4th, featuring Anne Follmann, John O'Connor, Bertram Tanswell, and Mary Jane Kersey. Also in the cast were Jacqueline Paige, Anne-Marie Gayer, J. Harris Melia, Hal Holbrook, Jean Guild, Mac Gress, and Bertram Tanswell.

The Shop at Sly Corner, week of July 6-11, featuring John O'Connor and Mac Gress, with Mary Jane Kersey, Jean Guild, Jacqueline Paige, Hal Holbrook, Bertram Tanswell, Edward Fuller, and Francis Donovan, Jr.

Sight Unseen, week of July 13-18, a ghostly comedy featuring Helen Harrelson, Jean Guild, Edward Fuller, and Hal Holbrook, with Jean Jones, Jean Burns, Bertram Tanswell, Jacqueline Paige, John O'Connor, Anne-Marie Gayer, and J. Harris Melia.

Happy Birthday, week of July 20-25, featuring Helen Harrelson, Edward Fuller, with Jean Guild, Lucille Gibbs, Bertram Tanswell, Hal Holbrook, Jean Burns, Joseph Foley, Lily Marr, Virginia Low, Ann-Marie Gayer, Peter Harris, Don Thomas, Edward Fuller, J. Harris Melia, Jacqueline Paige, Sylvia Meredith, and Mac Gress.

See My Lawyer, week of July 27-August 1, with Ed Fuller, Hal Holbrook, Ted Tiller, Bertram Tanswell in the featured roles, and Virginia Low, Peter Harris, Mac Gress, George Abbott, Jacqueline Paige Robert Colson, Roger Landry, Anne-Marie Gayer, Dorothy Johnson, Joan Cappel, James Van Wart, and John Gaffney.

There Shall Be No Night, week of August 3-8, with John O'Connor and Jean Guild in the featured roles, and with Henry Sharp, Jerry Melo of Springfield playing son Erik, and Anne-Marie Gayer. Hal Holbrook as radio announcer, James Van Wart, Peter Harris, Mac Gress, Edward Fuller, Ted Tiller, Carlton Guild, Robert Colson, John Gaffney of Springfield, Dorothy Johnson of South Hadley Falls, Joan Cappel of Holyoke.

Happiest Days of Your Life, week of August 10-15, featuring Ted Tiller as headmaster of an English boys' school, Jean Guild as the headmistress of a girls' school in this comedy-farce. Also featured Edward Fuller, Jacqueline Paige, with Hal Holbrook, Anne-Marie Gayer, Bertram Tanswell, Sally Donovan of Longmeadow, and Douglas Cummings as pupils. Jean Jones, and Jean Burns of Springfield, Don Thomas of West Springfield and Carlton Guild were cast in minor roles as parents.

The Country Girl, week of August 17 -22, with John O'Connor and Jacqueline Paige, and Si Oakland played Bernie Dodd. The cast also included Ted Tiller, Edward Fuller, Mac Gress, newcomer Claire Kirby.

Father of the Bride, week of August 24-29, featuring Edward Fuller, Claire Kirby and Anne Pitoniak. Also in the cast were Francis Donovan Jr., Mac Gress, John Martone, Lucile Gibbs, Jean Guild, Gerald Hellerman, Sally Donovan, Ted Tiller, and Carlton Guild, J. Harris Melia, James Van Wart, Robert Colson, Chrisanthe Carozi.

Bell, Book and Candle, week of August 31-September 5, with Hal Holbrook and Miriam Stovall. Also starring Jean Guild, Mac Gress, and Ted Tiller. Pyewacket the cat was played by Yum Yum.

Gigi, week of September 7-12, last show of the season. Claire Kirby as Gigi. Hal Holbrook as Gaston, with Jean Guild as Mme. Alvarez, Jacqueline Paige, Ted Tiller, Eleanor Farnese, Chrisanthe Carozi.

1954 season:

Sets this season by Don Swanagan, joined by his wife, Virginia, also a set designer.

The Moon is Blue, week of June 21-26, 1954, featuring Nancy Wells, Stephen Pluta, and Edward Fuller, with Don Thomas, in a four-person play that was unusual for the large-cast shows normally staged by The Valley Players.

Gently Does It, week of June 28-July 3, featuring Si Oakland, Ellen Andrews, Jacqueline Paige, Jean Guild. Cast also included Anne Ives and Edward Fuller.

Goodbye Again, week of July 5-10, featuring Ted Tiller and Virginia Low. Also in the cast, Robert Colson, Enid Schwartzwald, Jacqueline Paige, James Daggitt, Nancy Wells, Mac Gress, John O'Connor, Carlton Guild, Robin Jones.

Holiday, week of July 12-17, featuring Ellen Andrews as Linda and Si Oakland as Johnny Case, Nancy Wells as Julia, and Mac Gress as Ned. Also in the cast were Virginia Low, Ted Tiller, John O'Connor, Jean Burns, Edward Fuller, James Daggitt, and Enid Schwartzwald. Directed by Jacqueline Paige.

My Three Angels, week of July 19-24, featuring Michael Enserro, Howard Ledig, Edward Fuller, and Nancy Wells, with John O'Connor, Jean Guild, Jacqueline Paige, Edward Fuller, Ted Tiller, Peter Harris, and Jerry Melo.

Here We Come Gathering, week of July 26-31, featuring Jean Guild, Ted Tiller, Peter Harris, Nancy Wells, with Howard Ledig, Ruth Elliot, Lynn Thatcher, and Carlton Guild.

The Magnificent Yankee, week of August 2-7, featuring John

O'Connor and Ann Driscoll, with J. Harris Melia, Ted Tiller, Jerry Melo, Walter Case, Jean Guild, Carlton Guild, Edward Fuller, Mac Gress, Manuel Duque, Howard Ledig, James Daggitt, Robert Colson, and Peter Harris. Secretaries were played by William Brooks, Harry Crane, Robert Furey, Vern Jones, and Arthur Trudeau.

The Girl from Wyoming, week of August 9-14, an old-time musical "mellerdramer" featuring Edward Fuller, Ruth Elliot, and Ted Tiller. Cast also features John Marion, Jean Guild, Don Thomas, Howard Ledig, Jerry Melo, John O'Connor, Judith Love, Mac Gress, Carlton Guild as the silent Bartender in the old west saloon, and his son played by his real-life son, William Guild. Other chorus-type roles, Cowboys and Boston Boys played by James Daggitt, Peter Harris, Walter Case, and Manuel Duque. Cowgirls and Boston Girls played by Jacqueline Paige, Nancy Wells, Judith Carlberg, Jo Ann Rothmyer, Marilyn Courchesne, Christine Thompson. Peter Harris also doubled as the stagecoach driver, and Jacqueline Paige doubled as the Indian Squaw.

Chicken Every Sunday, featuring Jacqueline Paige, John O'Connor, including Nancy Wells, Jean Guild, Judith Love, Ruth Elliot, Ted Tiller, Mac Gress, Edward Fuller, and Howard Ledig, Jean Jones, Peter Harris, Don Thomas, Lucille Gibbs, Jerry Melo, Curtis Bayer, Manuel Duque, Robert Colson, J. Harris Melia, Jean Burns, and her young daughter, Janice Burns.

Ruth Elliot 1949 photo by Lucas and Monroe Studio

Three Men on a Horse, week of August 23-28, featuring Ted Tiller, Howard Ledig, Ruth Elliot, and Edward Fuller, with Nancy Wells, Robert Colson, J. Harris Melia, Peter Harris, Mac Gress, and Carlton and Jean Guild, James Daggitt, Elaine Levine, and John O'Connor.

Time of the Cuckoo, week of August 30-September 4, featuring Jacqueline Paige, Howard Ledig, and Stephen Pluta, with Ellen Love, Nancy Wells, Enid Schwartzwald, Jean Guild, John O'Connor, Michael Atkin, and Mac Gress.

Late Love, September 6-11, featuring Edward Fuller, Ellen Andrews, Jean Guild, with Ted Tiller, Peter Harris, Sylvia Meredith, and Nancy Wells.

1955 season:

Sets this season by Don Swanagan.

The Four Poster, week of June 20-25, 1955, featuring Helen Harrelson, Howard Ledig in a rare two-person play.

The Southwest Corner, week of June 27-July 2, featuring Jean Guild, Jacqueline Paige, and John O'Connor, with Jerry Melo, Edward Fuller, and Jean Burns. New to the company was Constance Simons from Chicopee, who had first been taken by her parents to the Casino to see The Valley Players when she was a child.

Dial M for Murder, week of July 4-9, featuring Howard Ledig as Tony Wendice, Ellen Andrews as Margot, and Frank Wolff as Max, with Edward Fuller as Captain Lesgate, John O'Connor as Inspector Hubbard, and Jerry Melo as Thompson. Directed by Jacqueline Paige.

Sabrina Fair, July 11-16, featuring Virginia Low as Sabrina, Frank Wolff as Linus, and Jerry Melo as David, with Jean Guild as Mrs. Larrabbee, John O'Connor as Mr. Larrabbee, Jean Burns as Margaret the maid, Lynn Katz, Edward Fuller as Fairchild, Joan Cappel, Walter Swift, Enid Schwartzwald, Harry Crane, and Howard Ledig.

The Caine Mutiny Court-Martial,* week of July 18-23, featuring Joseph Foley as Captain Queeg, Howard Ledig, Frank Wolff, with Michael Enserro, Carlton Guild, Robert Colson, Richard H. Pervonga, Walter Swift, and members of the court were Joseph Connolly, James Boyle, Milton Hayward, Paul Giblin, Thomas "Tom" Lennon, and John Gaffney.

*Lead actor Joseph Foley died of a heart attack the morning of Friday, July 22nd. The final two performances on Friday and Saturday evening were canceled.

Reclining Figure, week of July 25-30, featuring Howard Ledig, Michael Enserro, Virginia Low, and John O'Connor, with Stanley Greene, John Gaffney, Edward Fuller, Jerry Melo, Carlton Guild, and Robert Colson.

Time Out for Ginger, August 1-6, featuring Edward Fuller, Nancy Devlin, Julie Christy, with Jean Guild, Constance Simons, Jerry Melo, Mac Gress, Carlton Guild, and Michael Enserro.

The Remarkable Mr. Pennypacker, week of August 8-13, featuring John O'Connor in the title role, with Jacqueline

Paige as Ma Pennypacker, with Nancy Devlin, Jacqueline Geoffrey, Karen Marie Buchanan, Guy Lescault, Thomas Taylor, Pierre Hayward, Joy Ann Renjilian, Jean Guild, Jerry Melo, Virginia Low, Harry Crane, Jeffrey Thomas, Michael Enserro, Robert Colson, Mac Gress, Howard Ledig, Carlton Guild, and Walter Swift.

The Bishop Misbehaves, week of August 15-20, featuring Ted Tiller (Michael Enserro, originally, cast, was stricken with laryngitis, so Mr. Tiller stepped into the role), Jean Guild, Howard Ledig, Virginia Low, John Oliver, Jacqueline Paige, Robert Colson, Jerry Melo, Mac Gress, Edward Fuller, John O'Connor.

Lo and Behold, week of August 22-27, featuring Ted Tiller, Virginia Low, Edward Fuller, Jacqueline Paige, with Jerry Melo, Mac Gress, Judith Love, and Howard Ledig.

The First Mrs. Fraser, week of August 29-September 3, featuring Jean Guild, John O'Connor, Mac Gress, and Judith Love. Cast also includes Jacqueline Paige, Edward Fuller, Jerry Melo, Virginia Low.

Kind Sir, week of September 5 -10, final show of the season. Featuring Judith Love and Howard Ledig, Edward Fuller, Jacqueline Paige, and John O'Connor.

1956 season:

Sets by Richard E. Bianchi.

The Tender Trap, week of June 18-23, 1956, featuring Howard Ledig, Edward Fuller, Virginia Low, and Nancy Devlin, with Constance Simons, Molly Hosman, Jerry Melo, and Robert Colson.

A Roomful of Roses, week of June 25-30, featuring Ruby Holbrook and Nancy Devlin, with Jean Guild, Jacqueline Paige, Sarah Hardy, Richard Baublitz, Edward Fuller, Howard Ledig, and eight-year-old TV actor Dickie Nevins.

The Seven Year Itch, week of July 2-7, featuring John O'Connor and Constance Simons, with Kevin Burns, Ellen Andrews, Jacqueline Paige, Virginia Low, Ted Tiller, Howard Ledig, Jerry Melo, Jean Burns, and Debra Koff.

Anastasia, week of July 9-14, featuring Jean Guild as the Dowager Empress, Ellen Andrews as Anastasia, and Howard Ledig as her Svengali, Prince Bounine, with Ted Tiller, Constance Simons, Ralph Levy, John O'Connor, Robert Colson, Jean Burns as a charwoman, Sam Banham, Jacqueline Paige as Baroness Livenbaum, and Jerry Melo.

Strange Bedfellows, week of July 16-21, featuring Virginia Low, Howard Ledig, John O'Connor, Anne Ives, with Ted Tiller, Barbara O'Leary, Jacqueline Paige, Constance Simons, Guy Lescault, Ellen Andrews, Louise Wallis, Edward Fuller, Jerry Melo, Jean Guild, Sam Banham, Christine Thompson, Jacqueline Geoffrey, and Priscilla Gingras.

The Solid Gold Cadillac, week of July 23-28th - featuring Jean Guild. Also in the cast were Sam Banham, Ted Tiller, Edward Fuller, Howard Ledig, Virginia Low, Jerry Melo, Molly Hosman, Stephen R. Ellsworth, Patricia Maier, Carlton Guild, Milton Hayward, Robert Colson, Ellen Andrews, Milton Hayward, Carlton Guild. Directed by Jacqueline Paige.

Bad Seed, week of July 3-August 4th, featuring Ellen Andrews as the distraught mother and Claudia Crawford as the wicked girl. The cast also included Howard Ledig, Jean Guild, Edward Fuller, Stephen R. Ellsworth, Virginia Low, Jerry Melo, Jacqueline Paige, Carlton Guild, Robert Colson, and John O'Connor.

Three's a Family, week of August 6-11th, featuring Jean Guild, John O'Connor, and Jacqueline Paige. Also in the cast were Jean Burns, Virginia Low, Jerry Melo, Joan Cappel, Richard Jenkins, Norman Twain, Ellen Andrews, Patricia Maier, Robert Colson, Edward Fuller, Lynn Kratz, and Harry Crane and Carlton Guild.

The Male Animal, week of August 13-18th, featuring Howard Ledig, Ellen Andrews, Edward Fuller, and Jerry Melo. Also in the cast: Evelyn Davis, Constance Simons, Norman Twain, Ted Tiller, Jean Guild, John O'Connor, Jacqueline Paige, Harry Crane, Robert Colson.

The Rainmaker, week of August 20-25th, featuring Virginia Low and Howard Ledig. Cast includes John O'Connor, Edward Fuller, Norman Twain, Jerry Melo, and Ted Tiller.

King of Hearts, week of August 27-September 1st, featuring Ted Tiller, Lucille Pierlot, and Jerry Melo. The cast also included Jean Guild, Harry Crane, Edward Fuller, Schuyler Larsen, Robert Colson, David Black (11 years old from Springfield), and Ralph Levy.

Laburnum Grove, week of September 3-8, featuring John O'Connor, Jacqueline Paige, and Edward Fuller, with Virginia Low, Jerry Melo, Ted Tiller, Jean Guild, Howard Ledig, and Carlton Guild.

The 1957 season:

Sets by Paul Rodgers.

Mark Twain Tonight!, week of June 10-15, 1957, a one-man play conceived and performed by Hal Holbrook in this, the premiere of the play in its first full-length form.

The Loud Red Patrick, June 17-22, featuring John O'Connor, Ted Tiller, with Rennie Jarrett, Jan Jarrett, Constance Simons, Lee Graham, Ellen Andrews, Jerry Melo, and William Guild.

Speaking of Murder, week of June 24-29, featuring Ellen Andrews, Constance Simons, Jean Guild, Phil Arthur, with Daphne Andrews, Edmund Gaynes, Jody Cutler, Lee

Graham, Ted Tiller.

Reluctant Debutante, week of July 1-6, featuring Lee Graham, Jean Guild, and John O'Connor, with Barbara O'Leary, Ellen Andrews, Constance Simons, Robert Pinney, and Jerry Melo. The show was directed by Ted Tiller.

Desk Set, week of July 8-13, featuring Jacqueline Paige, with Constance Simons, Jean Guild, Lee Graham, Jerry Melo, Phil Arthur, Dorothy M. Crane (doubling as director) as The Lady in the Blue Suit, William Guild, Carlton Guild, Molly Hosman, Kathleen Sullivan, Ralph Levy, Ellen Andrews, Robert Colson, and Harry Crane.

Witness for the Prosecution, week of July 15-20, featuring Dean Lyman Almquist, Peter Harris, Ellen Andrews, with Constance Simons, Carlton Guild, Jerry Melo, Ralph Levy, George Koshores, Don Thomas, John O'Connor, John Gaffney, Ronald Irving, Richard Pervonga, Robert McEntire, Robijane Crane, Royal Wells, Marilyn Lettis, Marino Grimaldi, Martin Heyman, Regina Sobolewski, Harry Crane, Paul Wiley, Jean Guild, Robert Colson, and Peggy McKenna. The show was directed by Ted Tiller.
When We are Married, week of July 22-27, featuring The Company and Anne Ives, with Peggy Lang, Frank Wolff, Constance Simons, Ralph Levy, Robert Colson, John O'Connor, Ellen Love, Peter Harris, Ellen Andrews, Ted Tiller, Jean Guild, Peggy McKenna, Carlton Guild.

The Great Big Doorstep, week of July 29-August 3, a folk play featuring Ellen Andrews, George Mitchell, with Peggy Lang, Constance Simons, Arelene Ross, Mac Gress, Jerry Melo, Jean Guild, Frank Wolff, John O'Connor, and Ted Tiller.

Great Sebastians, week of August 5-10, featuring Jacqueline Paige, John O'Connor, Frank Wolff, Paul Lilly, with Lynn Katz, Marino Grimaldi, Robert Colson, George Koshores, Richard Pervonga, Constance Simons, Jean Guild, John Gaffney, Jerry Melo, Ted Tiller, Mac Gress, Nancy Dreikorn, Ralph Levy, and Harry Crane.

Vinegar Tree, August 12-17, featuring Jean Guild, with Sam Banham, Ted Tiller, Ellen Andrews, Frank Wolff, Constance Simons, and Jerry Melo.

Home of the Brave, week of August 19-24, featuring Frank Wolff, Henry Barnard, Jerry Melo, with John O'Connor, Pat Patterson, and Peter Harris.

There Goes the Bride, week of August 26-31, featuring Ellen Andrews, Ted Tiller, Frank Wolff, with Jerry Melo, Barbara O'Leary, Constance Simons, Jean Guild, and Peter Harris.

1958

Sets this season by Paul Rogers.

Visit to a Small Planet, week of June 9-14, featuring Ted Tiller and David C. Jones, with Arthur Tell, Jean Guild,

Anne Baker, Jerry Melo, Charles Laundra, Marino Grimaldi, Robert Colson, Ralph Levy, Ronald Irving. The dog, Rosemary, was played by Cuddles, a Holyoke native. The director of the show was Peter Harris.

Miranda, week of June 16-21, featuring Anne Baker as the mermaid Miranda, Henry Barnard, and Ellen Andrews, with Wini Haslam, Patricia Devon, Charles F Laundra, Jean Guild, Jerry Melo.

Night Must Fall, week of June 23-28, featuring Henry Barnard as Dan, Jean Guild as the invalid who is charmed by the new handyman, and then murdered by him and Ellen Andrews. The cast also included Ted Tiller, Debra K. Freedman, Jean Burns as Mrs. Terence, Anne Baker, John O'Connor.

Petticoat Fever, week of June 30-July 5, featuring Jerry Melo, John O'Connor, Anne Baker, with Marino Grimaldi, Joy Renjillian, Joyce Renjillian, Ted Tiller, Carlton Guild, Robert Colson, and Debra K. Freedman.

The Mousetrap, week of July 7-12, featuring The Company, with Ellen Andrews, Peter Harris Robert Pinney, Louise Wallis, John O'Connor, Anne Baker, Ted Tiller and Jerry Melo.

The Matchmaker, week of July 14-19, featuring Ellen Andrews as Mrs. Levi, John O'Connor as Horace Vandergelder, and Ruby Holbrook as Mrs. Molloy, with Robert Pinney, Ralph Levy, Dorothy M. Crane (doubling as director), Jerry Melo, Katherine Henryk, Ted Tiller, Peter Blaxill, Anne Baker, Tom Lennon, young William Guild as August, Catherine Payne, and Barbara A. O'Leary.

The Happiest Millionaire, week of July 21-26, featuring Martin Ashe and Anne Baker, with Barbara A. O'Leary, Peter Harris, Peter Blaxill, Marino Grimaldi, Robert Pinney, John Davis, Martin Ashe, Ellen Andrews, Louise Wallis, Katherine Henryk, Jerry Melo, Edward J. Reidy, Jean Guild. The show was directed by Ted Tiller.

Whistling in the Dark, week of July 28-August 2, featuring Michael Keep, with Jean Guild, Jerry Melo, Robert Pinney, Ralph Levy, Peter Harris, Edward J. Reidy, Richard Pervonga, Ted Tiller, Katherine Henryk, and Marino Grimaldi.

Separate Tables, by Terrence Rattigan, week of August 4-9, featuring John O'Connor as Major Pollock, Ellen Andrews as Mrs. Shankland and Miss Railston-Bell, with Marilyn Lettis, Catherine Payne, Jean Guild as Mrs. Railston-Bell, Jean Burns as Miss Meecham, Peggy Belcher, Ted Tiller, Pauline Flanagan, Jerry Melo, and Katherine Henryk.

Bus Stop, week of August 11-16, featuring Harry Holsten, Anne Baker, and Ellen Andrews, with Katherine Henryk, Michael Keep, Ted Tiller, John O'Connor, Peter Harris.

Ring Around Elizabeth, week of August 18-23, featuring Ellen

Andrews, with Jean Guild, Ted Tiller, Katherine Henryk, Edith Leslie, Anne Baker, Dorothy M. Crane (doubling on directing), Michael Keep, Jerry Melo, Ralph Levy, and Robert Colson.

Holiday for Lovers, week of August 25-30, featuring Jean Guild, John O'Connor, with Katherine Henryk, Ted Tiller, Ellen Andrews, Molly Hosman, Anne Baker, Jerry Melo, and Michael Keep.

1959

Sets by Leon L. Munier, Jr., and by

Janus, week of June 15-20, featuring Ellen Andrews, Bertram Tanswell, and Ray Gandolf, with Jean Guild, and Ted Tiller. The show was directed by Peter Harris.

Howie, week of June 22-27, featuring Franklin E. Cover, Jean Guild, David C. Jones, with Katherine Henryk, Blanche Cholet, Ray Gandolf, Ellen Andrews, Ted Tiller, Barbara O'Leary, Robert Colson, William Guild, Peter Harris, Marino Grimaldi, Molly Hosman, Bertram Tanswell, and Carlton Guild.

Dear Delinquent, June 29-July 4, featuring Katherine Henryk, Ray Gandolf, with Robert B. Pinney, Peter Harris, Bertram Tanswell, Jean Guild, Blanche Cholet, and David C. Jones.

Dracula, week of July 6-11, featuring David C. Jones in the title role, with Ellen Andrews, Ray Gandolf as Jonathan Harker, Ted Tiller, Bertram Tanswell as Van Helsing, Robert B. Pinney, and Katherine Henryk.

Third Best Sport, week of July 13-18, featuring Ellen Andrews and Ray Gandolf, with Marino Grimaldi, Peter Harris, Ted Tiller, Jean Burns, Katherine Henryk, David C. Jones, Robert Pinney, Jean Guild, and Walter L. Boughton.

Teahouse of the August Moon, 200th show, week of July 20-25, featuring Marino Grimaldi and Ray Gandolf, with Ralph Levy, David C. Jones, Dorothy M. Crane, Judith Rothstein, John F. Alves Jr., Frank Alves, Robert B. Pinney, Walter L. Boughton, Richard Gabel, Richard Pervonga, James P. Boyle, Peter Harris, Ellen Andrews, Robert C. Colson, Bertram Tanswell, Katherine Henryk, Ted Tiller, Judy August, David Black, Patricia Hohol, Denis Perron, Joyce Remjillian, and Joy Ann Remjillian. The part of Lady Astor the goat was played by a Holyoke native, loaned for the occasion. The show was directed by Bertram Tanswell.

Spider's Webb, week of July 27-August 1, featuring Ruby Holbrook, with Bertram Tanswell, Ted Tiller, Robert B. Pinney, Sidney Sloane, Jean Guild, Robert C. Colson, Ray Gandolf, Gordon Diver, Walter L. Boughton, and Peter Harris.

Will Any Gentleman?, week of August 3-8, featuring Ted Tiller, Bertram Tanswell, with Robert B. Pinney, Carlton

Guild, Katherine Henryk, Ellen Andrews, Robert C. Colson, Jean Burns, Ray Gandolf, Peter Harris, Molly Hosman, Jean Guild, and Walter L. Boughton. Dancers: Karen Marie Buchanan and Jacqueline Geoffrey.

Anniversary Waltz, week of August 10-15, featuring Ray Gandolf, Ellen Andrews, with Jean Burns, Bill Galarno, Sidney Sloane, Walter L. Boughton, Katherine Henryk, Marino Grimaldi, Carlton Guild, Ted Tiller, Jean Guild, and Frederick E. Purches.

Diary of Anne Frank, week of August 17-22, featuring Hugh Franklin and Mr. Frank and Katherine Henryk as Anne, with Jean Burns as Miep, Jean Guild as Mrs. Van Daan, Walter L. Boughton, Bill Galarno as Peter Van Daan, Ellen Andrews as Mrs. Frank, Debra K. Freedman as Margot, Peter Harris, and Ted Tiller as Mr. Dussell. The show was directed by Bertram Tanswell.

Once More with Feeling, week of August 24-29, featuring Ellen Andrews, Ray Gandolf, and Ted Tiller, with Bill Galarno, Robert C. Colson, Marino Grimaldi, Bertram Tanswell, and Peter Harris.

Cat on a Hot Tin Roof by Tennessee Williams, week of August 31-September 5, featuring Katherine Henryk as Margaret, Ray Gandolf as Brick, and Walter L. Boughton as Big Daddy, with Ellen Andrews, Peter Harris, Jean Guild as Big Mama, Pamela Morgan, John F. Alves Jr., Ted Tiller, and Robert C. Colson.

1960 season:

Sets by Robert T. Williams.

Auntie Mame, week of June 20-25, featuring Sue Ann Gilfillan in the title role, with Carolyn Brenner, Ted Tiller as Ito, Barry Keating as young Patrick, Judith Love as Vera Charles, John B. Davis Jr., Jack Gianino, John Gaffney, Peter Harris, Carlton Guild, David C. Jones as Mr. Babcock, Peter Duryea, Edward J. Reidy, Marsha Pettit, Walter L. Boughton as the butler and as Claude Epson, John Ulmer, R. H. Pervonga, Wendy Goodwin, Clarice Tatman, Sam Lloyd, Lynn Katz, Jean Guild as Doris Upson and as Mother Burnside, James B. Creane, James Secrest, Jean Burns as Agnes Gooch, Nuella Dierking, Jacqueline Evans.

Picnic, week of June 27-July 2, featuring Jack Gianino and Jacqueline Evans, with Sue Ann Gilfillan, Nuella Dierking, Jean Burns, with James Secrest, John Ulmer, Barbara O'Leary, Doris Drozdal, and David C. Jones. The show was directed by Walter L. Boughton.

No Time for Sergeants, week of July 4-9, featuring James Bernard, David C. Jones, and James Secrest, with Robert Colson, Ted Tiller, Walter L. Boughton, John Ulmer, Jack Gianino, Nuella Dierking, Robert Jundelin, Denis Donahue, Peter Duryea, John Davis, Robert Googins, Peter Harris, Carlton Guild as a psychiatrist, William Guild as an infantryman and general's aide, Joy Ann Remijilian, and Ralph Levy.

Life with Father, week of July 11-16, featuring Walter L. Boughton as Father, and Shirley Bryan as Vinnie, with Marsha Pettit, James Secrest as Clarence Jr., David Black, Barry Keating as Whitney, Richard Holmes as Harlan, Dorothy M. Crane (doubling as director) as Margaret the maid, Jean Burns as Clara, Nuella Dierking as Mary Skinner, Ted Tiller as Reverend Dr. Lloyd, Donna Gabel, Jean Guild as Nora, Peter Harris, David C. Jones, Beverly Driver, and John Ulmer.

Mister Roberts, week of July 18-23, featuring John Ulmer in the title role, and Bill McDonald as Ensign Pulver, with Carlton Guild as Chief Johnson, Walter L. Boughton, Peter Harris, David C. Jones Cedric Jordan, Robert Jundelin, John Davis, Peter Strauss, Peter Duryea, Denis Donahue, James Secrest, Paul Giblin, Robert Googins, Nuella Dierking, William Guild as a shore patrolman, Francis Shea, Ted Tiller, and David Black.

The Golden Fleecing, week of July 25-30, featuring Jim Oyster, with John Ulmer and Nuella Dierking, and David Black, James Secrest, John Davis, Peter Strauss, Katherine Lurker, Peter Harris, Walter L. Boughton, Robert Colson, Denis Donahue, and Peter Duryea.

Sunrise at Campobello, week of August 1-6, featuring Franklin E. Cover as Franklin Delano Roosevelt, with Mary Holland as Eleanor Roosevelt, Jean Guild as Sara Delano Roosevelt, and Robert Colson, with Nuella Dierking, Barry Keating, James Secrest, John Davis, Douglas Black, Joy Remijilian, Jean Burns as Miss Marguerite (Missy) LeHand, Ted Tiller, Carlton Guild, Peter Duryea, James Creane, Robert Jundelin, Walter L. Boughton, and David C. Jones.

Arsenic and Old Lace, week of August 8-13, featuring Jean Guild as Abby Brewster and Jean Burns as Martha Brewster, with Franklin E. Cover as Mortimer, David C. Jones as Jonathan, Walter C. Boughton as Teddy, with Carlton Guild as Reverend Dr. Harper, Peter Duryea, Nuella Dierking, Ted Tiller (doubling as director), Peter Harris, Peter Strauss, Edward J. Reidy, Robert Colson. The show was directed by Ted Tiller.

The Desperate Hours, week of August 15-20, featuring Walter L. Boughton as Dan Hillard, and Jack Gianino as Glen Griffin, with Peter Harris, John Ulmer, David C. Jones, Jean Burns as Eleanor Hilliard, Peter Holmes as Ralphie Hilliard, Nuella Dierking as Cindy Hillard, James Secret as Hank Griffin, Franklin C. Cover, Peter Duryea, Ted Tiller, Ralph Levy, and Jean Guild.

The Gazebo, week of August 22-27, featuring Ted Tiller and Polly Campbell, with David C. Jones, Jean Burns, Franklin E. Cover, Peter Harris, John Davis, John Ulmer, Robert Colson, Peter Duryea, and Robert Jundelin.

Tea and Sympathy, week of August 29-September 3, featuring

Polly Campbell and James Secrest, with Franklin E. Cover, and Jean Burns as Lilly Sears, John Ulmer, Robert Jundelin, Peter Duryea, Franklin E. Cover, Denis Donahue, and Walter L. Boughton. The show was directed as John Ulmer.

1961 season:

Sets by Joe Gerson, Charles Gazer, and Alan Ulick.

The Marriage Go-Round, week of June 19-24, 1961, featuring Richard Kronold, Polly Campbell, with Gretchen Kanne and Peter Harris. The show was directed by Ted Tiller.

Ah, Wilderness, week of June 26-July 1, featuring James Secrest, Walter L. Boughton, and James Coco, with Jean Guild, Bret Prentiss, Ellen Leef, Barry Keating, Sue Ann Gilfillan, Ted Tiller, Sai Springwell, Ian Brown, Polly Campbell, Barbara O'Leary, Carlton Guild, and Peter Harris.

Five Finger Exercise, week of July 3-8, featuring Sue Ann Gilfillan, Walther L. Boughton, James Secrest, Ray Girardin, Sai Springwell.

Invitation to a March, week of July10-15, featuring Polly Campbell, Sue Ann Gilfillan, James Secrest, and Sai Springwell, with Judith Love, Richard Holmes, Ray Girardin, and Richard Kronold. Directed by Ted Tiller.

Inherit the Wind, week of July 17-22, featuring Walter L. Boughton as Henry Drummond, James Coco as Matthew Harrison Brady, and Peter Harris as E.K. Kornbeck, with Dorothy Brewer, Carlton Guild, James Secrest, Martin Fallon, Polly Campbell, Richard Kronold, Louise Hesse, Patrick Bowler, Harry Boyle Jr., Jody Cutler, Barry Keating, Sue Ann Gilfillan, David Black, Dolores Stein, Barbara O'Leary, John Davis, Robert Zygmunt, Walter Halpin, Jean Guild as Mrs. Brady, Ray Girardin, Ted Tiller as the judge, James Pike, Bret Prentiss, Robin Barnes, Richard Lagmonter, Peter Beck, Denis Donahue, John Davis, Francis Shea, David Black, Valentine Doyle, Geraldine Cullen, and Carol Ann Brisset.

Rebecca, week of July 24-29, featuring Richard Kronold as Max deWinter, Sai Springwell as the new young Mrs. de Winter, and Jean Guild as the sinister Mrs. Danvers, with Carlton Guild as butler Frith, Poly Campbell, David C. Jones, Peter Harris, Ronni Bloom, Ray Girardin, Ted Tiller, John Davis, and Nadene Oxman.

The Boy Friend, week of July 31-August 5, featuring Irene Dean, John Baylis, Judith Love, Susanne Cansino, and James Pompeii, with James Secrest, Sue Ann Gilfillan, Susan Lane, Louise Magee, Ellen Leef, Peter Harris, Ian Brown, Denis Donahue, Barbara Gingris, Patricia Hohol, Eloyce Bujnicki, Linda Jorczak, Diane Mroz, Louise Hesse, Ronni Bloom, Valentine Doyle, David Black, Robin Barnes, John Davis, Ted Tiller (doubling as director), Jean Guild, Ed

Todd, George Coppez, Al Rehbein, and local television personality Barbara Bernard as "Miss Riveria of 1926." The show was directed by Ted Tiller and Peter Harris, with choreography by Elsie Cappel.

The Pleasure of His Company, week of August 7-12, featuring Peter Pagan, Sue Ann Gilfillan, Ted Tiller, Patricia O'Morran, with Peter Harris, David C. Jones, Ted Tiller, and Ray Girardin.

A Majority of One, week of August 14-19, featuring Jean Guild as Mrs. Jacoby, and Ted Tiller as Koichi Ansano, with Muriel Teitel, Polly Campbell, Peter Harris, Louise Magee, Geraldine Cullen, Peter Beck, James Secrest, Barbara Gingras, David Black, Dorothy Brewer, Ellen Leef, Valentine Doyle, Ray Girardin, and James Pike.

Sound of Murder, week of August 21-26, featuring Polly Campbell, David C. Jones, Vincent B. Carroll, Sue Ann Gilfillan, with Ted Tiller and Peter Harris.

Under the Yum-Yum Tree, week of August 28-September 2, featuring Vincent B. Carroll, Susanne Cansino, James Secrest, Bret Prentiss, and Peter Harris. The show was directed by Ted Tiller.

1962 season:

Sets this season by Joseph S. Morton [sp], and Anne Gibson.

Critic's Choice, week of June 18-23, 1962 featuring Bruce Brighton and Patricia Tyler, with Jean Guild and Sue Ann Gilfillan. The show was directed by Ted Tiller.

Blood, Sweat, and Stanley Poole, week of June 25-30, featuring James Coco and Clark Warren, with Ray Girardin, James Van Wart, Sue Ann Gilfillan, Ted Tiller, David C. Jones, Marino Grimaldi, Bret Prentiss, Carlton Guild, Walter L. Boughton, and Debra Koff Freedman.

The Best Man, week of July 2-7, featuring Walter L. Boughton, Edward Claymore, and Ted Tiller, with Susan Ann Gilfillan, Patricia Tyler, and James Van Wart, Ray Giardin, Elizabeth Webb, Susan Dibble, Bret Prentiss, Lynne Goodwin, D. Britton MacLaughlin, George Weir, Barry Keating, Jean Guild, Ted Tiller, Marino Grimaldi, Carlton Guild, Clark Warren, and David C. Jones.

Dark of the Moon, week of July 9-14, featuring Richard Manual, Sonia Torgeson, with James Van Wart, and Ted Tiller, Sue Ann Gilfillan, Marjorie Mascha, Jean Guild, Clark Warren, Deborah Donnelly, Edward Claymore, Debra Koff Freedman, Barbara O'Leary, D. Britton MacLaughlin, Marty Lorin, Barry Keating, Carlton Guild, Elizabeth Webb, Marino Grimaldi, Suzanne Johnson, Olive Warner, George Weir, Susan Dibble, Raymond Jahus, Ray Girardin, Jean Burns, and David C. Jones. Choreography by Marjorie Mascha.

Death of a Salesman, week of July 16-21, featuring Walther L. Boughton as Willy Loman, Jean Guild as Linda, with Edward Claymore and Ray Girardin, with William Guild as Bernard, Sue Ann Gilfillan, James Van Wart, Ted Tiller, Clark Warren, Deborah Donnelly, D. Britton MacLaughlin, Marjorie Mascha, and Olive Warner.

Roman Candle, week of July 23-28, featuring Ray Girardin, Sonia Torgeson and Marino Grimaldi, with Bret Prentiss, Marjorie Mascha, Jean Guild, Ted Tiller, Walter L. Boughton, James Van Wart, Clark Warren, William Guild, Carlton Guild, D. Britton MacLaughlin and George Weir.

The Miracle Worker, week of July 30-August 4, featuring Sue Ann Gilfillan as Annie Sullivan, Linda Gale as Helen Keller, with Judith Love as Kate Keller, and Ted Tiller, Walter L. Boughton as Captain Keller, Wannetta McCoy as Martha, Gary Nelson as Percy, Jean Guild as Aunt Ev, Ray Girardin as James, Marino Grimaldi, Gertrude Jeannette as Viney, and Deborah Donnelly, Olive Warner, Judy Vile, Suzanne Johnson, Jody Cutler, and Jonnie Mae Owens.

Write Me a Murder, by Frederick Knott, week of August 8-11, featuring Clark Warren and Judith Love, with James Van Wart and William Martel, Jean Guild, George Weir, Marino Grimaldi, D. Britton MacLaughlin, and Bret Prentiss. The show was directed by Ted Tiller.

The Pursuit of Happiness, week of August 13-18, featuring Ray Girardin and Marilyn Cunningham, with Ted Tiller and Jean Guild, Marjorie Mascha, Marino Grimaldi, James Van Wart, Bret Prentiss, Barry Keating, D. Britton MacLaughlin, and Clark Warren.

Little Mary Sunshine, week of August 20-25, featuring Margaret Hall, with Richard Marshall, Susanne Cansino, Ted Tiller, Joel Warfield, Floria Mari, and James Van Wart. Chorus was played by Jacquee Dean, Deborah Donnelly, Susan Lane, Marilyn Cunningham, Marjorie Mascha, Patrick Smith, Clark Warren, Nicholas Paulik, Bret Prentiss, Marino Grimaldi, George Weir. Dancing staged by Susanne Cansino. "The Bearcats" musical combo: Ed Todd, Russell Falvey, and George Coppez. Richard Marshall was musical director. Dorothy L. Crane, production coordinator.

The Glass Menagerie, week of August 27-September 1. Broadway and television actress Grace Carney starred as Amanda. Ray Girardin played Tom, with Marilyn Cunningham as the sensitive daughter, Laura. Clark Warren as the Gentleman Caller. Directed by Ted Tiller. This was the last show of The Valley Players.

Casino-in-the-Park – 1963

A Thurber Carnival, June 28-July 6, 1963.

Pygmalion, July 9-13. Linda Seff as Eliza, Anthony Zerbe as

Professor Higgins, and George Ebeling played Colonel Pickering. The staff also included: James Kenny, Janet Sarno, Victoria Ryan, Vala Clifton, Robert Klein, Dolce Alviani, Kevin Courtney, John Robb, Dale Skillicorn, and local community theatre player and future WREB Holyoke radio personality, Barbara Heisler as Mrs. Eynsford-Hill.

J.B., July 16-20. Archibald MacLeish's Pulitzer Prize-winning play was presented with George Ebeling in the title role. Also featuring James Kenny, Walter Rhodes, Janet Sarno as J.B.'s wife Sarah. Directed by Keith Fowler.

Period of Adjustment, July 23-27. Cast includes Walter Rhodes, John Robb, Victoria Ryan, James Kenny, Loli Little, Ellen Rocklin, Elizabeth MacRae, and David Cronin.

Threepenny Opera ran July 30 to August 10th, and featured Stephen Elliott as Mack the Knife, with Anthony Zerbe as the street singer, James Kenny, Louise Shaffer, Janet Sarno, Ruth Hunt, Keith Fowler, Dale Skillicorn, Tom Neumiller, and Walter Rhodes. The ensemble playing the Ladies and the Gang were Bob Klein, David Nancarrow, John Robb, Barry Keating, Robert Mathews, Dolce Alviani, Eileen Hall, Ellen Rocklin, Victoria Ryan, Vala Clifton. The constables were Jim Brick, Douglass-Scott Beheen and Tom Neumiller.

A Far Country, August 13-17, Anthony Zerbe as Sigmund Freud; Janet Sarno as patient; supporting cast includes Victoria Ryan, James Kenny, John Robb, Barbara Heisler as a maid, and Ellen Rocklin. Directed by Keith Fowler.

Fashion, August 20-24, with Louise Shaffer as the show stealer in this comedy/old-time mellerdramer spoof. Others in the cast were company members Janet Fowler, John Robb, Robert Klein, Keith Fowler, Eileen Hall, Walter Rhodes, Joseph Nassif, Thomas Neumiller, Dale Skillikorn, Victoria Ryan, Vala Clifton, Dolce Alviani, Fred Sliter, and Candy Voegel.

Romeo and Juliet, August 27-31, with Nicholas Pryor and Margaret Cowles, as well as Bernard Drabek, Dale Skillicorn, Walter Rhodes, Robert Klein, John Robb, James Kenny, Victoria Ryan, Janet Sarno, David Cronin, Thomas Neumiller, Barry Keating, and Fran Goddu.

The Mt. Tom Playhouse: 1964-1965

1964 season:

June 22-27: Cesar Romero in *Strictly Dishonorable*, with Monica Lovett, directed by Holyoke native Harold J. Kennedy, who also played a role, Leopold Badia, Walter Flanagan, Milt Rubin, Fran Godu, and Dick Van Patten.

June 29 – July 4: Genevieve and Donald Woods in *For Love or Money*.

July 6-11: Arlene Francis in *Kind Sir*, with Peter Adams

July 13-18: Tallulah Bankhead in *Glad Tidings*.

July 20-25: Van Johnson in *A Thousand Clowns*.

July 27 – August 1: Peggy Cass in *Bachelor's Wife*, with Edith King, Ramon Bieri, and Denis Berube. Directed by Holyoke native Harold J. Kennedy.

August 3-8: Merv Griffin in *Broadway*, with Jackie Bertell, William Cain, Lloyd Hubbard, Rik Colitti, Michael Fairman, Karl Fredericks, Dermot McNamara, Cele McLaughlin, Maureen Reynolds, Rhoda B. Carrol, Barbara Lucas, Leta Anderson, Kay Frazier, Bert Siebert, Chuck Kittredge, and Vernon Agen. Directed by Francis Ballard.

August 10-15: Lloyd Bridges in *Anniversary Waltz*, with Eloise Hardt; the star's fourteen-year-old son, Jeff Bridges; Zamah Cunningham; David Kerman; Helen Martin; Merle Albertson; Felix Munso; Marina Habe; Rick Chamberlain; and Jack Perry. Directed Robert Livingston.

August 17-22: Kathryn Crosby ("Mrs. Bing") in *Sabrina Fair*, with John Lupton, Nancy Cushman, Helen Noyes, William Blackard, Richard Bowler, John D. Irving, Katherine Raht, Debra K. Freedman, Suzanne Johnson, Denis K. Berube, Dick King, and Harold J. Kennedy. Directed by James Monos. Production manager Len Bedsow. Mrs. Crosby's wardrobe by Jean Louis.

August 24-29: Fernando Lamas and Esther Williams in *Once More with Feeling*, with William Macy, Tom Connolly, Richard Durham, Jack Washburn, Ralston Hill, Walter Bouton, Darlene Johnson, Bobie Schwartz, Francis Godu, Karen Wickstrom, Bob Lear, Gloria Mador, and Dolores Stein. Directed by star Fernando Lamas.

August 31 – September 5: Martha Raye in *The Solid Gold Cadillac*, with Lew Prentiss, Mervyn Williams, Robert Fitzsimmons, Donald Marye, Thomas Ruisinger, Lynn Wood, and Will Gregory. Staged by John Allen.

September 7 – *Stop the World, I Want to Get Off* –starring Kenneth Nelson and Joan Eastman, Kay Cole, Jill Choder, Karen Lynn Reed, Diana Corto, Carol Guilford, Julie Anderson, Stephanie Winters, and Virginia Mason. Directed by Ben Strobach.

1965 season:

June 19-26: Sheila Macrae in *Born Yesterday*.

June 28-July 3: Eve Arden in *Beekman Place*.

July 5-10: Tony Martin in his all-star review, including Nancy Ames.

July 12-17: George Hamilton in *Gigi*, with Jan McArt, Dorothy Sands, Janet Fox, Jon Richards, and also starring

Anna Russell, directed by William Francisco.

July 19-24: Beatrice Lillie in *High Spirits*, with John Michael King, Ann Mitchell, Karen Jensen, Tom Avera, Gloria Warner, and Carol Arthur. Directed by Franklin Lacy. Choreographer Al Lanti, Musical Director was Don Jennings.

July 26-July 31: Arlene Francis in *Mrs. Dally Has a Lover*, with Ralph Meeker and Robert Forster.

Alexis Smith and Craig Stevens in *Mary, Mary*, with Joe Campanella, Barnard Hughes, and Diana Walker. Directed by Fred Baker.

Dana Andrews in *A Remedy for Winter*, with Susan Oliver, Polly Rowles, Michael Baseleon, Walter Reilly.

August 30-September 4: Martha Raye in *Everybody Loves Opal*. Also featuring Gaylord Mason (former Valley Players member), Sarajane Levey, Lewis Prentiss, Art Kassul, Donald Marye.

August 23-August 28: Walter Pidgeon in *The Happiest Millionaire*, with Bruce Brighton, Eileen Bennett, Nicholas Hammond, Clyde Venture, Christopher Wynkoop, Steve Scheffer, Susan Carr, Muriel Williams, Katherine Raht, Yolande Childress, Richard Lundin, Phillip Kenneally, and Louise Hoff.

August 30 – September 4: Gertrude Berg in *Dear Me, the Sky is Falling*, with Roger Dekoven.

SELECTED LIST OF SOME NOTED PERFOMERS ON MT. TOM:

Some Casino actors who went on to fame in Hollywood films, TV, or the stage:

Eddie Foy
Sarah Bernhardt
John Craven
Taylor Holmes
George Brent (George Nolan)
Wendell Corey
Betsy Drake
Ralph Edwards
Raymond O. Greenleaf
Simon Oakland
Barbara Bernard – local TV personality – WHYN
    Channel 40 for some twenty years, later
    newspaper columnist with the *Springfield Republican*.
Ray Gandolf
James Coco
Hal Holbrook
Mary Jackson

Eva Tanguay – one of the highest paid
    performers in vaudeville and Holyoke native
Madeleine L'Engle – novelist

Mt. Tom Playhouse (1964-1965)

All the featured stars had some claim to fame in films or television :

Walter Pidgeon
Alexis Smith
Craig Stevens
Van Johnson
Kathryn Grant Crosby
George Hamilton
Dana Andrews
Tallulah Bankhead
Arlene Francis
Eve Arden
Lloyd Bridges
Beatrice Lillie
Nicholas Hammond

SOME FAMOUS VISITORS TO THE CASINO/MT. TOM PLAYHOUSE

Leo Carillo, Hollywood character man and TV star in *Cisco Kid* to see *The Reluctant Debutante* performance accompanied by Pat Casey, July 1957.
Bing Crosby to see his wife Kathryn Crosby in *Sabrina Fair* in 1964.
Helen Hayes attended *The Magnificent Yankee* in 1954
Hal Holbrook – to see his wife, Ruby Holbrook perform in *A Roomful of Roses* in 1956.
Gordon MacRae –came with his wife Sheila, who starred in *Born Yesterday*

NOTES

Chapter 1

"A view of the valley from a book of essays by local writers called *The Pioneer Valley Reader*.

The themes that have emerged in the Pioneer Valley are big ones…" O'Connell, James C., ed. *The Pioneer Valley Reader – Prose and Poetry of New England's Heartland*. (Stockbridge, Mass.: Berkshire House Publishers, 1995), p. xii.

"The immigrant mill-hands found in Holyoke…" The *Catholic Observer* – Centennial Issue 1870-1970, article by Peter G. Loughran, p. 2.

"Author and Pulitzer Prize winner Tracy Kidder, who wrote of Holyoke…" Kidder, Tracy. "Among Schoolchildren," essay in *The Pioneer Valley Reader – Prose and Poetry from New England's Heartland*. James C. O'Connell, ed. (Stockbridge, MA: Berkshire House Publishers, 1995), p. 232.

"Author Edwin M. Bacon described the canals..." Bacon, Edwin M. *The Connecticut River and the Valley of the Connecticut – Three Hundred and Fifty Miles from Mountain to Sea*. (NY: G.P. Putnam's Sons, The Knickerbocker Press, 1906), p. 422.

"In 1890, Springfield had a population of 44,179..." DiCarlo, Ella Merkel. *Holyoke-Chicopee: A Perspective* (Holyoke, Mass.: Transcript-Telegram) 1982, p. 231.

"A 1906 viewpoint of Mount Tom was expressed by Edwin M. Bacon in his book, *The Connecticut River of the Pioneer Valley of the Connecticut – Three Hundred and Fifty Miles from Mountain to Sea:...*", p. 418.

Chapter 2

"From Ella Merkel DiCarlo's book on the history of Holyoke, *Holyoke-Chicopee, A Perspective*:

The stranded minstrels finally arrived..." DiCarlo, p. 218.

"Touring in these days was still rugged, as this editorial in *Byrnes' Dramatic Times* of November 1884 attests:

There are some managers who have really had the decency..." Byrnes' *Dramatic Times*, November 22, 1884, p. 4.

"Her act is described in author Trav S.D.'s history of vaudeville, *No Applause—Just Throw Money*:

If anyone embodies the spirit of vaudevillianism..." Trav S.D. *No Applause – Just Throw Money – The Book that Made Vaudeville Famous.* (NY: Faber and Faber, Inc., 2005), p. 199.

"Vaudeville historian Trav. S. D. notes in his book, *No Applause—Just Throw Money* that this art form was...

...the first major American institution..." Trav S.D., p. 10.

"Mt. Tom is now the beacon of Western Massachusetts ..." Holyoke newspaper, June 28, 1889. The Valley Players Collection, Holyoke History Room, Holyoke Public Library.

"From July 1898, a Holyoke newspaper reported:

Denno and Langway, acrobatic wonders..." Holyoke newspaper, July 26, 1898. The Valley Players Collection, Holyoke History Room and Archives.

"John Drew, the popular song and dancing comedian..." Holyoke

newspaper clipping dated June 27, 1898. The Valley Players Collection, Holyoke History Room and Archives.

"The crowd was large last night at Mountain Park..." Holyoke newspaper, August 16, 1898. The Valley Players Collection, Holyoke History Room and Archives.

"Enormous crowds witnessed the two performances..." Holyoke newspaper, September 6, 1898. The Valley Players Collection, Holyoke History Room and Archives.

"The great herd of ponderous performing kings..." Unpublished typescript, The Valley Players Collection, Series 4, Holyoke History Room and Archives, Holyoke Public Library.

Last night every one of 2,000 seats at the Mt. Park Casino were sold out with 200 people turned away." Unpublished typescript, The Valley Players Collection, Series 4, Holyoke History Room, Holyoke Public Library.

'Mabel Griffith is very pretty, sort of an emotional actress and won many laurels for her acting..." Unpublished typescript, The Valley Players Collection, Series 4, Holyoke History Room and Archives, Holyoke Public Library.

"Slim audience at The Fourth Estate *due to uncertain weather. Two things noticeable lately—late of applause and tardiness of a number of patrons...."* Unpublished typescript, The Valley Players Collection, Series 4, Holyoke History Room, Holyoke Public Library.

Chapter 3

"The Goldstein Brothers punched up the publicity for the shows..." *History of Mt. Park Casino*, unpublished typescript July 1966 in the Holyoke History Room and Archives, Holyoke Public Library.

"The Playhouse Players has established themselves as one of the best stock companies to be found anywhere..." Playhouse Players Programs folder 1928 – Holyoke History Room, Holyoke Public Library.

"Another special event of the season was when a radio transmission of a Gene Tunney fight..." *History of Mt. Park Casino*, unpublished typescript July 1966 in the Holyoke History Room and Archives, Holyoke Public Library.

"Valley Arena, which according to local historian and journalist Ella Merkel DiCarlo, "Offered boxing..." DiCarlo, Ella Merkel, p. 316.

"Black entertainers who came to Holyoke..." DiCarlo, Ella Merkel, p. 295.

"Black performers also stayed with a Jennings family...." DiCarlo, Ella Merkel, p. 321.

"The American Thread Company and the Skinner Silk Company..." WPA *Guide to Massachusetts,* Federal Writer's Project. (1937, rpt. NY: Pantheon Books, 1983) p. 248

"Back in those best-forgotten days of depression, in 1932..." The Valley Players program, *Goodbye Again,* week of July 5-10, 1954, p. 8, author's collection.

"Things close to home are never appreciated. Holyoke lags in support of a group that ranks..." Local newspaper article, History of Mt. Park Casino, unpublished typescript July 1966 in the Holyoke History Room and Archives.

"In 1935 there was an extensive renovation..." Unpublished manuscript – Holyoke History Room, Holyoke Public Library.

*"*Holyoke population in 1938 was 56,139 (already dropping). It's railroad station was on Mosher Street..." WPA *Guide to Massachusetts,* Federal Writer's Project. (1937, rpt. NY: Pantheon Books, 1983) p. 248.

One factor in creating this prosperous atmosphere is the skilled type of worker employed by the numerous paper mills that manufacture high-grade writing paper, the principal support of the town.

"...an extensive wooded area through which winds a fine road past heavy growth of laurel..." WPA *Guide to Massachusetts,* Federal Writer's Project. (1937, rpt. NY: Pantheon Books, 1983) p. 250.

"History in the making has a way of sneaking up on us. Frequently it is an established and often fairly startling fact before we really are aware of it...." Burns Mantle syndicated column, *Springfield Sunday Union and Republican,* August 29, 1937, p. 4C.

"For the first time in the reviewer's experience the members of the audience..." History of Mt. Park Casino, unpublished typescript July 1966 in the Holyoke History Room, Holyoke Public Library.

"The reviewer noted the troupe was popular with the audience, but he felt that they should have eliminated the "political propaganda" in several lines." *History of Mt. Park Casino,* unpublished typescript July 1966 in the Holyoke History Room, Holyoke Public Library.

"The government is now the largest theatre producer in the country..." History of Mt. Park Casino, unpublished typescript July 1966 in the Holyoke History Room, Holyoke Public Library.

"In Massachusetts there were twenty-six WPA theatre companies employing eighty performers..." *History of Mt. Park Casino,* unpublished typescript July 1966 in the Holyoke History Room, Holyoke Public Library.

"Unlike many parks during the Depression, Mountain Park continued to survive..." Ducharme, Jay. *Mountain Park.* (Charleston, SC: Arcadia Publishing, 2008), pp. 7-8.

"According to Ella Merkel DiCarlo, there was an acting group called The Suitcase Theater..." DiCarlo, Ella Merkel, pp. 324-325.

Hartwig wrote in an article for the *New York Times,* published August 4, 1935:

"The continued growth and spread of the Summer Theatres that now function through New England..." Walter Hartwig, *New York Times,* August 4 1935.

Chapter 4

"As the summer theatre has gradually grown into an institution..." Walter Hartwig, *New York Times,* August 4 1935.

"By October 1942 the *Springfield Daily Republican* would be canceling home delivery of newspapers..." *Springfield Daily News,* October 17, 1942, p. 1.

"The *Holyoke Daily Transcript* crowed, "Diana Barrymore Arrives Here For Rehearsal". She traveled with her maid and stayed at the Roger Smith Hotel..." *Holyoke Daily Transcript,* June 20, 1940, p. 6.

"They closed after six performances with heavy losses." Unpublished typescript, The Valley Players Collection, Series 4, Holyoke History Room, Holyoke Public Library.

"We are happy to announce that by special arrangement with the Holyoke Street Railway Company..." Mountain Park Casino-Pioneer Valley Drama Festival program week of June 24, 1040, producer's note.

"Mr. and Mrs. Guild have already made several trips to Holyoke and have discussed plans..." Holyoke *Transcript-Telegram,* February 7, 1941, "Mountain Park to Have Summer Stock Season." Valley Players Scrapbook 1941, Valley Players Collection, Holyoke History Room, Holyoke Public Library.

"Amherst College president Stanley King announced the decision to close Kirby for the 1941 season..." *Holyoke Transcript-Telegram,* February 10, 1941, "Kirby Theatre Not to Operate This Summer." Valley Players Scrapbook 1941, Valley Players Collection, Holyoke History Room, Holyoke Public Library.

"If you have a problem and you don't know what to do, ask Jean Guild..." *Springfield Union,* August 26, 1983. "Jean Guild, 80, retired actress; co-founder of Valley Players," p. 20S.

"On her rests a major share of the responsibility for choosing the plays to be produced each season..." Valley Players program George and Margaret, August 25-30, 1947, p. 14, Valley Players Collection, Series 3, Vol. 2, Holyoke Public Library.

"Miss Crane, a quiet-spoken woman with a low, pleasing voice..."

Holyoke Transcript-Telegram, July 28, 1949, "Miss Crane 'Behind-The-Scenes' Celebrity of the Valley Players." Valley Players Scrapbook 1949.

"Last night's audience at Mountain Park Casino enjoyed every line and situation…" WMAS radio copy, review by Milton Hale, July 1, 1941 5:15 p.m., Hotel Charles, Springfield, Mass. Valley Players Scrapbook 1941.

Night Must Fall starred Mr. Lauren Gilbert and Jean Guild…" Valley Players program – *Uncle Harry* week of June 30-July 5 1947, production notes. Author's collection.

"Every time I mention Jackson Perkins the word "versatile" comes out of the typewriter almost of its own volition…" *Springfield Daily News*, August 13, 1941, "Doings in the Theaters" column by W. Harley Rudkin. Valley Players Scrapbook 1941, Holyoke Public Library.

"There was a good-sized audience present at last night's performance and it responded…" *Daily Hampshire Gazette*, September 2, 1941, "'Vinegar Tree' is Ably Presented by The Valley Players'", review by R.M.H. Valley Players Scrapbook 1941. Holyoke Public Library.

"For the first two weeks at the Casino, finances were not too rosy…" *Springfield Union*, September 8, 1941, "Valley Player Urged by Theatergoers to Return," by A. L. S. Wood. Valley Players Scrapbook 1941, Holyoke Public Library.

"After a winter and summer of stage productions in this city, the question of whether or not…" *Springfield Daily News*, September 19, 1941, "Is Legitimate Theater Wanted Here?" editorial. Valley Players Scrapbook 1941, Holyoke Public Library.

"Even though the Trade High School plays starred well-known names like Francis Lederer, as well as Kitty Carlisle and Tallulah Bankhead, they were not well attended…" *Springfield Daily News*, September 19, 1941, "Is Legitimate Theater Wanted Here?" editorial. Valley Players Scrapbook 1941, Holyoke Public Library.

"In one short season The Valley Players became a tradition, both in personnel and in good theater…" *Springfield Daily News*, undated newspaper 1942, "Doings in the Theaters" by column by W. Harley Rudkin. Valley Players Scrapbook 1942. Holyoke Public Library.

"I would be unhappy to see this revival of the summer theater wilt and die just as it is getting nicely started once again…" *Springfield Daily News*, May 2, 1942, "Emergency Should Week Out Much Indifferent Theater," by W. Harley Rudkin. Valley Players Scrapbook 1942. Holyoke Public Library.

"My weekly salaam to Jackson Perkins, an actress of fine talent and keen understanding…" *Springfield Daily News*, July 7, 1942, "Doings in the Theaters" column by W. Harley Rudkin. Valley Players Scrapbook 1942. Holyoke Public Library.

They're doing everything but swinging from the chandeliers at the

Mountain Park Casino this week…" Springfield Daily News, July 7, 1942, "Doings in the Theaters" column by W. Harley Rudkin. Valley Players Scrapbook 1942. Holyoke Public Library.

"Dolly Crane knows exactly how many steps it will take the girl who has a walk-on part to get on and off the stage…" *Holyoke Transcript-Telegram*, May 22, 1961, "Dolly Crane to Direct 189th Play For Valley Player Here on June 26th," p. 18. Valley Player Scrapbook, Valley Players Collection, Holyoke Public Library.

"…he hadn't seen the part until Thursday of rehearsal week…and that meant a terrific amount of work…" *Springfield Daily News*, August 8, 1942, "Gas Rationing Can't Keep Local Theater Enthusiasts at Home." Valley Players Scrapbook 1942. Holyoke Public Library.

"I found Jackson Perkins more believable than Mady Christians, who originated the character.…" *Springfield Daily News*, August 4, 1942, "Doings in the Theaters" column by W. Harley Rudkin. Valley Players Scrapbook 1942. Holyoke Public Library.

"The Valley Players had a very definite plan, when they came here last year that they would give this bewildered Valley relaxing plays…: *Holyoke Daily Transcript*, August 6, 1942, review of Watch on the Rhine. Valley Players Scrapbook 1942. Holyoke Public Library.

"War or no war; rationing, Western Massachusetts theater lovers will still patronize something they like—even if they have to get there…" *Springfield Daily News*, August 8, 1942, "Gas Rationing Can't Keep Local Theater Enthusiasts at Home." Valley Players Scrapbook 1942. Holyoke Public Library.

"In spite of gas and tire curtailments, The Valley Players, now halfway through their second summer at the Mountain Park Casino, Holyoke, are breaking all records for that theatre…" *Variety*, August 12, 1942, "Mass. Strawhat's Record." Valley Players Scrapbook 1942. Holyoke Public Library.

"The only legitimate company operating this summer in Western Massachusetts, the Valley Players are…" *Variety*, August 12, 1942, "Mass. Strawhat's Record." Valley Players Scrapbook 1942. Holyoke Public Library.

"In spite of gas and tire curtailments, The Valley Players, now halfway through their second…" *Variety*, August 12, 1942, "Mass. Strawhat's Record." Valley Players Scrapbook 1942. Holyoke Public Library.
"So engrossed was the audience in the tomfoolery of Three Men on a Horse *that Dorothy Crane's announcement from the stage that a blackout was in effect …"* *Springfield Daily News*, August 15, 1942, "Footlights Down but Not Out as Actors Cope with Blackout."

"The snugging of the wooden shutters at the Casino Saturday night…" *Springfield Daily News*, September 1, 1942, p. 5.

"We are not going to say goodbye, for we are already thinking about and planning for next summer…" Valley Players program *Private Lives*, August 31, 1942, Valley Players Collection, Series 3, Vol. 1, Holyoke Public Library.

"This particular group of players has given us cheer and something that we could…" Holyoke Daily Transcript, September 3, 1942. Editorial. Valley Players Scrapbook 1942. Holyoke Public Library.

"The Harrison Hall Players in Fitchburg, the Cape Playhouse in Dennis, the Peterborough Players in New Hampshire, the Monomoy Theater in Chatham among them…" *The Billboard*, "Cowbarns Get 382 Weeks," September 12, 1942, p. 9.

"Holyoke greets the Valley Players. They give us the sign that we are past the peak of our war limitations. The program for the season is rich with promise…" Holyoke Transcript-Telegram, June 27, 1944. Valley Players Scrapbook 1944-1945. The Valley Players Collection. Holyoke Public Library.

"We are very glad to be back. It was a great disappointment to us not to be able to return in 1943…" Valley Players program *Return Engagement*, July 11-16, 1947, p. 11, Valley Players Collection, Series 3, Vol. 2, Holyoke Public Library.

"This summer stock company is the only one…available on anything approaching a convenient public transportation schedule for Hartford…" The Hartford Times, August 1, 1944. "Fan Fare" column. Valley Players Scrapbook 1944-1945. The Valley Players Collection. Holyoke Public Library.

"…the players take their bows in fixed position suggestive of the old Daguerreotypes, with the exception of …" Daily Hampshire Gazette, August 9, 1944. "Charley's Aunt Make Vacation Visit to Park". Valley Players Scrapbook 1944-1945. The Valley Players Collection. Holyoke Public Library.

"Jean Guild still has nightmares about her experience of coming on stage for the third act on opening night and discovering that the all-important wall telephone…" Valley Players program, *Uncle Harry*, week of June 30 – July 5, 1947, production notes. Author's collection.

"The present summer stock is more than a mere financial enterprise. It is almost a school of the theater, where young people do a lot of studying and get a great deal of experience for not much more than good board and room…" Belchertown Sentinel, July 13, 1945, "Old Steeple Soliloquies" column, page 2. Valley Players Scrapbook 1944-1945. The Valley Players Collection. Holyoke Public Library.

"During the run of *Arsenic and Old Lace*, the reporter Olive Pearson Rice of the *Springfield Republican* spent the day with The Valley Players…" *Springfield Republican*, August 9, 1945, "Valley Players Eat, Play, Act Together in Joint Living Plan" by Olive Pearson Rice, p. 10.

"It was one grand mix-up. We never did get the Tuesday night tickets all straightened out…" Valley Players program *Return Engagement*, August 11-16, 1947, Valley Players Collection, Holyoke Public Library.

Chapter 5

"Springfield theatergoers will not have to travel far for their summer stage fare. The nearest spot is the Mountain Park Casino…" Springfield Daily News, "Off Stage" column by W. Harley Rudkin, 1945, Valley Players Scrapbook 1946-1947. The Valley Players Collection. Holyoke Public Library.

"The local paper eagerly followed them as they took up residence again in their usual digs: the summer home of Albert Steiger, the founder of the local department store chain…" *Holyoke Transcript-Telegram*, undated article, 1946, "Valley Players Start Moving in for Fifth Season at Mountain Park." Valley Players Scrapbook 1946-1947. The Valley Players Collection. Holyoke Public Library.

"The cast had just finished an evening performance of Hope for the Best, and most of them were then rehearsing Angel Street…." *Springfield Daily News* undated 1946, "Off Stage" column by W. Harley Rudkin. Valley Players Scrapbook 1946-1947. The Valley Players Collection. Holyoke Public Library.

"If the Valley Players were a baseball team, their score this season could not be a more enviable one. It seems to be just one hit after another…" Holyoke Transcript-Telegram, July 30, 1946, "Valley Players Register Another Hit," review by M.T.F. Valley Players Scrapbook, 1946-1947. The Valley Players Collection. Holyoke Public Library.

"The *Springfield Union* visited the Steiger estate up in the Highlands that summer, noting that the winding driveway was a bit rocky…" *Springfield Union*, August 10, 1946, "Life for Valley Players Frequently Hectic, But Somehow the Play Manages to Go On," by Francis Merrigan, p. 5. Valley Players Scrapbook 1946-1947. The Valley Players Collection. Holyoke Public Library.

"Actors and crew were in positions in the wings. They all waited tensely for that second…" Springfield Sunday Republican, August 4, 1946, "Major Portion of the Valley Players' Backstage Staff Grew Up in the Valley, Which They Left for Stage Careers," by Olive Pearson Rice, p. D1. Valley Players Scrapbook 1946-1947. The Valley Players Collection. Holyoke Public Library.

"Curtains in summer theaters went down with a happy, hope-filled thud last night, resounding contrast…" Springfield Republican-Union, September 1, 1946, "Here and There in Theater" by Louise Mace. Valley Players Scrapbook 1946-1947. The Valley Players Collection. Holyoke Public Library.

"Before the war the summer theater was gaining sway in other parts of the country, but naturally war activities, shortages, and gas rationing restricted most group's programs…" Holyoke Transcript-Telegram,

July 12, 1947, editorial. Valley Players Scrapbook 1946-1947. The Valley Players Collection. Holyoke Public Library.

"*During the war lots of Americans had time to sit in far-off places and think about the life they wanted to live. Up at the Casino, the Valley Players are presenting...*" *Holyoke Transcript-Telegram,* July 21, 1947, "Former Newspaperman With Valley Players Expert on Sound Effects," by Mary Clayton, p. 3. Valley Players Scrapbook 1946-1947. The Valley Players Collection. Holyoke Public Library.

"*If you have in your attic unwanted furniture, dishes, silverware, draperies, or other things that you would be willing to give...*" *Valley Players* program Heaven Can Wait, August 18-23, 1947, p. 9, Valley Players Collection, Series 3, Vol. 2, Holyoke Public Library.

"It was noted in a *Boston Post Magazine* article by theatre critic dean Elliot Norton, that of all the nation's summer theatres open for business this season, nearly half of them were in New England..." *Boston Post Magazine,* June 13, 1948, "The Circuit – New England to Have Lion's Share of Nation's Summer Theatres," by Elliot Norton, p. 3. Valley Players Scrapbook, 1948. The Valley Players Collection. Holyoke Public Library.

"*...without a doubt one of the best actresses that ever graced the footlights at the Casino. Not affected, a voice that is soothing, and a grace in acting that is just natural...*" *Holyoke Saturday Democrat,* July 3, 1948, "Notes from Valley Players." Valley Players Scrapbook 1948. The Valley Players Collection. Holyoke Public Library

"*It's not good for the nerves! Great credit must be given to the Valley Players the way they stood up in the first and second acts. Most of them must have had sore throats the next day. It's quite a job to try to drown out thunder and rain...*" *Holyoke Saturday Democrat,* July 10, 1948, "Notes from Valley Players." Valley Players Scrapbook 1948. The Valley Players Collection. Holyoke Public Library.

"*Favored with hot, humid weather, the Monday night opening found the atmosphere of* Rain *extending from the superb stage set with its hibiscus and bougainvillea-draped terrace...*" *Hampshire Gazette,* July 13, 1948, "Valley Players Make Hot Night Even Warmer." Valley Players Scrapbook 1948. The Valley Players Collection. Holyoke Public Library.

"*Many of the plays written in the 1920s or early 1930s have lost their original appeal. They "date" in subject matter...*" Valley Players program for Little Accident, August 19-24, 1946, author's collection.

"Barbara Halpin of Holyoke, interviewed by the *Holyoke Transcript-Telegram* in the 1980s in a retrospective article on Mountain Park, recalled her days as a teen taking the bus to the Casino..." *Holyoke Transcript-Telegram,* February 1, 1988, "Park Gave Holyoke Theater, Thrills," by Bill Zajac.

"*You Can Take it With You* was the profitability champ in the 1948 season, grossing $5,287.40 total receipts and an attendance that week..." The Valley Players Financial Accounts 1941-1962, Valley Players Collection, Series 4, Administration 1941-19842, Box 1, Holyoke Public Library.

"*Miss Jacqueline Paige is demonstrating, and without an alibi, that she is a great actress. Her work...*" *Holyoke Saturday Democrat,* July 17, 1948, "Notes from Valley Players." Valley Players Scrapbook 1948. The Valley Players Collection. Holyoke Public Library.

"*The local company could have been satisfied just to rollick through this old-fashioned melodrama. Instead they have given painstaking care to reproduce set, costumes, makeup, and acting styles as they were in the '20s...*" *Springfield Union,* July 27, 1948, "Players put 'The Ghost Train' Back On the Tracks in Superb Manner" review by A.B.M. Valley Players Scrapbook 1948. The Valley Players Collection. Holyoke Public Library.

"*As always, we shall hope to do at least one play, as we say, "For ourselves," because we think it is a fine play...*" Valley Players program *Accent on Youth,* week of September 6-11, 1948, p. 13. Valley Players Collection, Series 3, Vol. 2, The Valley Players Collection. Holyoke Public Library.

"*Laughter is probably still echoing around the Mt. Tom Range after last night's opening of* Apple of His Eye *at Mountain Park Casino. John O'Connor and Anne Pitoniak...*" *Springfield Daily News,* July 26, 1949, "Robust Comedy Production at Mountain Park Casino," review by R.C.G.

"*Miss Stovall is remarkably effective as the girl, impressing her portrayal with delicacy of speech...*" *Springfield Union,* August 2, 1949, "'The Heiress Occupies The Stage at Mountain Park," by Louise Mace. Valley Players Scrapbook 1949. Holyoke Public Library.

Chapter 6

"Insurance fees in 1950 amounted to $571, and came in at $738 by the end of the decade. FICA and Unemployment amounted..." The Valley Players Financial Accounts 1941-1962, Valley Players Collection, Series 4, Administration 1941-19842, Box 1, Holyoke Public Library.

"Total payroll for actors—regulars and guess actors, or "jobbers" was $10,612 in 1950. By 1959, the actors' salaries came in..." The Valley Players Financial Accounts 1941-1962, Valley Players Collection, Series 4, Administration 1941-19842, Box 1, Holyoke Public Library.

"Gross ticket sales, however, did not keep pace with costs, despite the popularity..." The Valley Players Financial Accounts 1941-1962, Valley Players Collection, Series 4, Administration 1941-19842, Box 1, Holyoke Public Library.

"The profit for the 1950 season was $5,400. The lowest

profit level was…" The Valley Players Financial Accounts 1941-1962, Valley Players Collection, Series 4, Administration 1941-19842, Box 1, Holyoke Public Library.

"*Valley Players are more generously supported than they were at the start…They have earned that….*" Holyoke Transcript-Telegram, June 10, 1950, "Our Valley Players," editorial. Valley Players Scrapbook 1950. Holyoke Public Library.

"*Without depriving it of durable essence or affronting it with an air of condescension they play it straight…*" Springfield Union, June 27, 1950, "Peg O' My Heart" Shows its Age With Heart of Gold," by Louise Mace. Valley Players Scrapbook 1950.

"*Why more people don't read plays we don't know, but we do know that they are missing…*" Valley Players program *The Philadelphia Story*, week of August 7-12, 1950, p. 9. Valley Players Collection, Series 3, Vol. 2, Holyoke Public Library.

"*…Joe couldn't repress a little smile when he said that and the audience was quick to pick it up…*" Undated newspaper clipping 1950, Valley Players Scrapbook 1950. The Valley Players Collection. Holyoke Public Library.

"*It is difficult to determine at times who is enjoying the whole thing more, the audience or the actors…*" Daily Hampshire Gazette, August 15, 1950, "'Love Rides the Rails' Hilarious Affair at Mt. Park Casino," review by G.N. Valley Players Scrapbook 1950. Holyoke Public Library.

"*…the Valley Players were coming over to eat frankfurts and cold meats and baked beans…*" Holyoke Transcript-Telegram, August 25, 1950, "A Week at a Time" editorial. Valley Players Scrapbook 1950. The Valley Players Collection. Holyoke Public Library.

"The champ in both box office receipts and attendance for 1951 was the comedy *Born Yesterday*, at $5,087.58 and 6,182 attendance. The lowest…" The Valley Players Financial Accounts 1941-1962, Valley Players Collection, Series 4, Administration 1941-19842, Box 1, The Valley Players Collection. Holyoke Public Library.

"*You had to learn all new lines. A new play…I can't even believe today what we did. You'd stay up till 2 o'clock ..*" Mountain Park Memories, documentary produced by David Fraser, WGBY-Springfield, Massachusetts, A Division of the WGBH Educational Foundation, c. 2002.

"*Mr. and Mrs. Guild are citizens of Holyoke. They and their splendid corps, and that includes…*" Holyoke Transcript-Telegram, June 19, 1951, editorial, "Welcome Valley Players At Age Ten." Valley Players Scrapbook 1951. The Valley Players Collection. Holyoke Public Library.

"*The company took a chance, a gambling chance to try and revive the Casino. Holyoke, as you know is pretty hard to please when it comes to stage shows…*" Holyoke Saturday Democrat, June 28, 1951, editorial "Our Valley Players". Valley Players Scrapbook 1951. The Valley Players Collection. Holyoke Public Library.

"*One dignified elderly lady was last night heard yelling to the villain* [played by Hal Holbrook] *in a soprano voice…*" Daily Hampshire Gazette, July 24, 1951, "Fun Aplenty In Valley Players' Show This Week." Valley Players Scrapbook 1951. The Valley Players Collection. Holyoke Public Library.

"*It's pleasant here. The response of the community is encouraging, and it gives the actors…*" Holyoke Transcript-Telegram, August 17, 2951, "The O'Connors Look Forward to Drama Tour For Two." Valley Players Scrapbook 1951. The Valley Players Collection. Holyoke Public Library.

"*One of the few actors in existence who know what they will be doing in future months, Mr. Holbrook and his wife will take their 'Theatre of Great Personalities' on tour…*" Valley Players program *Candlelight*, August 27-September 1, 1951, p. 13. Valley Players Collection, Series 3, Vol. 3, Holyoke Public Library.

"*Not all the summer Play Houses can look forward to the next season as we in this community…*" Holyoke Transcript-Telegram, undated (September 1951), Oracle column. Valley Players Scrapbook 1951. The Valley Players Collection. Holyoke Public Library.

"*The situation in Dennis as in all summer theaters is getting more difficult every season…*" Holyoke Transcript-Telegram, undated (September 1951), Oracle column. Valley Players Scrapbook 1951. The Valley Players Collection. Holyoke Public Library.

"*…the company made good, but the "angel" that protected them; made the patrons like the cast and the company…*" Holyoke Saturday Democrat, March 22, 1952, editorial "Good Scout Louie Mudgett." Valley Players Scrapbook 1952. The Valley Players Collection. Holyoke Public Library.

"*…We are a theater-loving people…The Valley Players are strictly of a high order. They are prosperous enough now to provide beautiful settings for their plays. The educational and cultural values…*" Holyoke Transcript-Telegram, June 13, 1952, "Meet Holyoke's Valley Players" editorial, p. 11. Valley Players Scrapbook 1952. The Valley Players Collection. Holyoke Public Library.

"*Judging from audience reaction and the prolonged applause as the curtain fell, the Valley Players…*" Valley Players program, *Goodbye Again*, week of July 5-10, 1954, producer's notes, p. 9. Valley Players Collection, Holyoke Public Library.
"*…had audiences rocking back and forth so much with laughter that seats broke right, left, and center…*" Valley Players program, *Goodbye Again*, week of July 5-10, 1954, producer's notes, p. 9. The Valley Players Collection. Holyoke Public Library.

"*Ted Tiller makes an enormously funny hen-pecked husband who breaks his bonds and puts his wife in her place…while Jean Guild makes an excellent domineering wife…*" Unknown paper, July 23, 1957, "Valley Players Produce Many Guffaws," clipping, Valley Players Collection. Holyoke Public Library.

"*Unlike last week's production,* The Country Girl *is theater, not a show...*" *Springfield Union,* August 18, 1953, "Odet's *Country Girl* Presented at Casino," by Louise Mace.

"*Every summer company should have the chance to relax at this point from the rigors of steady stock production...*" *Springfield Sunday Republican,* August 9, 1953.

"Holbrook's wife Ruby was absent from the roster this year, and as one program explained..." The Valley Players program, *See My Lawyer,* week of July 27-August 1, 1953, Valley Players Collection, Holyoke Public Library.

"*Ted Tiller is priceless as the somewhat more than eccentric Robert Carlin...His entrances bring joy to the audience...*" Undated newspaper clipping, The Valley Players Collection, Holyoke Public Library.

"*Admirable actor as he was from the outset in 1951, his work has broadened and deepened...*" The Valley Players program, *Bell, Book & Candle,* week of August 31-September 5, 1953, p. 15. The Valley Players Collection, Holyoke Public Library.

"Expenses for the 1954 season included operating the Dodge truck and the 1934 Ford Panel truck..." The Valley Players Financial Accounts 1941-1962, Valley Players Collection, Series 4, Administration 1941-19842, Box 1, Holyoke Public Library.

"*She told members...that she was impressed with the entire establishment at the Casino...*" *Holyoke Transcript-Telegram,* August 5, 1954. "Helen Hayes Moves to Tears In Watching Valley Players." Valley Players Scrapbook 1954. Valley Players Collection. Holyoke Public Library.

"*The specialty numbers were marvelous. The Players have shown that they are all very versatile...*" *Holyoke Saturday Democrat,* August 14, 1954. "Don't Miss 'The Girl From Wyoming.'" Valley Players Scrapbook 1954. Valley Players Collection. Holyoke Public Library.

"*Let's remember that a reviewer is a contentious person doing a difficult task with really remarkable accuracy...* Valley Players program, *My Three Angels,* week of July 19-24, 1954, producer's notes, p. 15. Valley Players Collection. Holyoke Public Library.

"*The highways are well-moteled. Around midnight their "No Vacancies" signs glare at you in the dark...*" *Brockton Enterprise,* as quoted in the *Holyoke Transcript-Telegram,* August 31, 1954. "Brockton Visitor Writes Of Trip To See Valley Players, Paper City." Valley Players Scrapbook 1954. Valley Players Collection. Holyoke Public Library.

"*Ted Tiller and Jean Guild, as usual, were two of the funniest people on stage...*" *Daily Hampshire Gazette,* August 17, 1954. "'Chicken Every Sunday' Gives Many Laughs at Mt. Park," review by B. D. Valley Players Scrapbook 1954. Valley Players Collection. Holyoke Public Library.

"*Miss Guild has the uncanny ability to make each and every performance a tour de force of her dynamic personality...*" *Holyoke Transcript-Telegram,* August 1955, review of *The Bishop Misbehaves* – Valley Players Collection clipping. Holyoke Public Library.

"*Even the Fourth of July fireworks display between the second and last acts couldn't break the tension...*" *Springfield Daily News,* July 5, 1955. "Dial M' Gets Crisp Showing At The Casino," review by R.C.G. Valley Players Scrapbook 1955. Valley Players Collection. Holyoke Public Library.

"They insured the macaw for $50." *Holyoke Transcript-Telegram,* July 13, 1955. "Macaw Subsitute For Cockatoo In Players Show". Valley Players Scrapbook 1955. Valley Players Collection. Holyoke Public Library.

"*Sabrina Fair* was the highest grossing show of 1955 at $5,812.51, with a top attendance of 5,736..." The Valley Players Financial Accounts 1941-1962, Valley Players Collection, Series 4, Administration 1941-19842, Box 1, Holyoke Public Library.

"*This very much loved player, for so many years with the Valley folks, does something more than one of the best roles he has ever given his admirers...*" *Holyoke Transcript-Telegram,* July 19, 1955, The Oracle column, p. 22. Valley Players Scrapbook 1955. Valley Players Collection. Holyoke Public Library.

"The *Springfield Union* called the play "one of the most significant dramas of our time," and found Foley's work equal to others who played the role on Broadway and the screen." *Springfield Union,* July 19, 1955. "Court Martial Episode is Strongly Performed," by Louise Mace. Valley Players Scrapbook 1955. Valley Players Collection. Holyoke Pubic Library.

"*Joseph Foley outdoes himself in the taxing role of Queeg...*" *Holyoke Transcript-Telegram,* July 19, 1955. "Valley Players Do Outstanding Job in 'The Caine Mutiny.' Valley Players Scrapbook 1955. Valley Players Collection. Holyoke Public Library.

"*It was something of an omen that, for his last appearance on his home stage...*" *Holyoke Transcript-Telegram,* July 23, 1955. "The Great Play Goes On," editorial, p. 6. Valley Players Scrapbook 1955. Valley Players Collection. Holyoke Public Library.

"*The stage where Joseph Foley spoke his last lines as an actor will be dark...*" *Springfield Union,* July 23, 1955, article by "L.M.", p. 14.

"*Although our actual productions are a seasonal adventure limited to twelve weeks, a vast amount of our time during the other forty weeks...*" Valley Player program, The First Mrs. Fraser, week of August 29-September 3, 1955, p. 6. Author's collection.

"*Of course Holyoke is a better place in which to live summers than it would be were it not for our friends, the Valley Players. Let's make the most of them…"* Holyoke Transcript-Telegram, June 6, 1956. "Year Fifteen For Our Valley Players" editorial. Valley Players Scrapbook 1956. Valley Players Collection. Holyoke Public Library.

"From chuckles to uproarious laughter evidenced at the Valley Players production…during the opening night performance Monday, the play was a popular one with the audience." Holyoke Transcript-Telegram, July 3, 1956, p. 9.

"The top play from a business perspective in the 1956 season was *The Solid Gold Cadillac*, grossing $7,289.44 with an attendance of 6,104…" The Valley Players Financial Accounts 1941-1962, Valley Players Collection, Series 4, Administration 1941-19842, Box 1, Holyoke Public Library.

"In a portent of the future, Carlton Guild remarked to the *Holyoke Transcript-Telegram* at season's end that he did not feel big name guest stars…" Letter to the editor from Carlton Guild, August 3, 1957.

"His portrayal is both a science and an art. He has paid scrupulous attention to detail…" Daily Hampshire Gazette, June 11, 1957. "Holbrook Brings Mark Twain Back To Life In Fine Opener," review by V.Z.G. Valley Players Scrapbook 1957. Valley Players Collection. Holyoke Public Library.

"The *Holyoke Transcript-Telegram* called it 'a fascinating artistic masterpiece…'" Holyoke Transcript-Telegram, June 11, 1957, "Hal Holbrook Does Remarkable Job in 'Mark Twain Tonight'" review by A.B.M. Valley Players Scrapbook 1957. Valley Players Collection. Holyoke Public Library.

"…a unique and rewarding program…in all life, so it seemed, there was Samuel Langhorne Clemens himself…" Springfield Union, April 9, 1959, "Hal Holbrook's 'Twain' Big Hit, quoting earlier review of Valley Players *Mark Twain Tonight!* production.

"Unfortunately, possibly as lead show of the season, (typically a slow spot in the season rotation) possibly because of its experimental nature, *Mark Twain Tonight!* was the lowest earner…" The Valley Players Financial Accounts 1941-1962, Valley Players Collection, Series 4, Administration 1941-19842, Box 1, Holyoke Public Library.

Springfield Union, brought down the house. Also, Jacqueline Paige as lead Bunny Watson and Jean Guild as Peg:

"…are grandly funny in a Christmas Eve bout with the bottle, and in the course of a romp Molly Hosman does a standout bit of characterization…" Springfield Union, July 9, 1957. 'The Desk Set' Entertaining Comedy on Casino Stage" by Louise Mace. Valley Players Scrapbook 1957. Valley Players Collection. Holyoke Public Library.

"There is always one place where Holyoke gets on the front page so that our town looks like the Capitol of Massachusetts…" Holyoke Transcript-Telegram, July 2, 1957, Oracle column. Valley Scrapbook 1957. Valley Players Collection. Holyoke Public

Library.

"The attendance was lower this season, a drop of nearly 5 percent from 1956. Carlton Guild noted that most summer theaters…" *Holyoke Transcript-Telegram*, September 4, 1957, "Valley Players' Attendance Off Slightly This Year." Valley Players Scrapbook 1957. Valley Players Collection. Holyoke Public Library.

"The owners of Mt. Park have agreed to let you park on the grass…" The Valley Players program, *Visit to a Small Planet*, June 9-14, 1958, Valley Players Collection, Series 3, Holyoke Public Library, p. 7.

"I am especially glad about one angle of this success—it surely is a wonderful vindication…" Letter Hal Holbrook to Carlton and Jean Guild, April 14, 1959, quoted in *Holyoke Transcript-Telegram*, April 21, 1959, "'Mark Twain Tonight!' Which Is Getting Steady Rave Notices Had Its First Theater Audience Here". Valley Players Scrapbook 1959. Valley Players Collection. Holyoke Public Library.

"Over a period of years a resident company, which is basically unchanged in management and varies in acting talent…" Springfield Republican, April 19, 1959, "Here and There in the Theater" column by Louise Mace. Valley Players Scrapbook 1959. Valley Players Collection. Holyoke Public Library.

"We have to plan a 12-week season very carefully in advance," Mrs. Guild explained, *"in order to provide variety for our audiences…"* Springfield Union, April 9, 1959, "'Janus to Open Casino Season," p. 38.

"Every one of the metropolitan reviewers wrote of Mr. Holbrook's portrayal in glowing terms…" Springfield Union, April 9, 1959, "Hal Holbrook's 'Twain' Big Hit.

"A new and refreshing era of theater came to this area last evening with the gala opening of the Storrowton Music Fair's presentation of The King and I…" Springfield Daily News, June 16, 1959, "Storrowton Music Fair Off to Colorful Start" by W. Harley Rudkin. Valley Players Scrapbook 1959. Valley Players Collection. Holyoke Public Library.

"A new theater era broke over Springfield Monday night with the opening of the spacious and colorful Music Fair at Storrowton…" Springfield Union, June 16, 1959, "Music Fair Brings New Theater Era to City," by Louise Mace. Valley Players Scrapbook 1959. Valley Players Collection. Holyoke Public Library.

"A Storrowton play later that month, *Say Darling*, was the last review published by *Springfield Union…" Springfield Union*, June 30, 1959, "'That's All There Is'…Louise Mace Ends 42-Year Theater News Career." Valley Players Scrapbook 1959. Valley Players Collection. Holyoke Public Library

"At the end of the season, it was reckoned that The Valley Players might not open in 1960. .." *Springfield Union*, September 2, 1959. "Valley Players May Not Answer '60 Cue; Other Summer Stages' View Brighter." Valley Players

Scrapbook 1959. Valley Players Collection. Holyoke Public Library.

"Over at the Storrowton Music Fair, their highest weekly attendance was for *Oklahoma!*, a sellout at 14,000 people…" *Springfield Union*, September 2, 1959. "Valley Players May Not Answer '60 Cue; Other Summer Stages' View Brighter." Valley Players Scrapbook 1959. Valley Players Collection. Holyoke Public Library.

Chapter 7

"A Holyoke newspaper, undated, rejoiced that the Valley Players 'have almost signed a lease for their Casino home…'" *Holyoke Transcript-Telegram*, undated 1953, "Come Back, Ye Valley Players", Valley Players Collection clipping. Holyoke Public Library.

"Carlton Guild spread the advertising dollar as far as he could to all local papers.." The Valley Players Financial Accounts 1941-1962, Valley Players Collection, Series 4, Administration 1941-19842, Box 1, Holyoke Public Library.

"The top grossing show of the 1960 season was *Auntie Mame*, at $6,388.44, with an attendance of 4,088. Lowest receipts…" The Valley Players Financial Accounts 1941-1962, Valley Players Collection, Series 4, Administration 1941-19842, Box 1, Holyoke Public Library.

"*Why, then, it is reasonable to ask, does anyone get involved in the producing of plays?...*" Valley Players program, *Gently Does It*, week of June 28-July 3, 1954, p. 10. Author's collection.

"The actors never saw the set until a few hours before opening curtain…" *Holyoke Transcript-Telegram*, May 22, 1961, "Dolly Crane to Direct 189th Play For Valley Player Here on June 26th," p. 18. Valley Player Scrapbook, Valley Players Collection, Holyoke Public Library.

"*…did not meet the challenge of the play, despite the admirable efforts of the two principals James Coco and Walter Boughton…*" *Holyoke Transcript-Telegram*, July 18 1961 "Challenge of a Fine Play Not Met But: Stars Boughton, Coco Splendid in Valley Players "Inherit the Wind" by Robert Levey. Valley Players Scrapbook 1961. Valley Players Collection. Holyoke Public Library.

"The *Agawam News* remarked, 'Those two don't even have to try!'" *Agawam News*, July 27, 1961, "On Stage at the Casino" column by Florence Moreno, Valley Players Scrapbook 1961. Valley Players Collection. Holyoke Public Library.

"*Audiences at the Mountain Park Casino this week are being pleasurably treated to an annual experience—that of seeing a bright, fresh, new star rising on the horizon…*" *West Springfield Record*, "Miss Springwell Scores Triumph in Casino Drama," July

27, 2961. Valley Players Scrapbook 1961. Valley Players Collection. Holyoke Public Library.
"Reviewer Florence Moreno of the *Agawam News* advised her readers…" *Agawam News*, August 3, 1961, "On Stage at the Casino" column by Florence Moreno. Valley Players Scrapbook 1961. Valley Players Collection. Holyoke Public Library.

"The *Springfield Union* noted of Susanne that she 'is a block buster in her own way…'" *Springfield Union*, "Mt. Park Musical Spoof is 'What Doctor Ordered'" review by R.E.B, August 1, 1961. Valley Players Scrapbook 1961. Valley Players Collection. Holyoke Public Library.

"*Had the cast taken a deep, deep breath following last night's final curtain and started the show once more…*" *Holyoke Transcript-Telegram*, "The Boy Friend Wonderful", review by Bob Levey, August 1, 1961. Valley Players Scrapbook. Holyoke Public Library.

"*Perhaps the most surprising about this production is the apparent ease with which the resident company turns to musical comedy…*" *Daily Hampshire Gazette*, August 2, 1961, "Musical Comedy Taken in Stride by Valley Team" review by R.J.L. Valley Players Scrapbook 1961. Valley Players Collection. Holyoke Public Library.

"*It would appear as though, finally, this reborn organization is shaking free of its growing pains and realizing that its patrons have come to join in the fun of …*" *Chicopee Herald*, August 3, 1961, "The Play's the Thing" review by W. Manta. Valley Players Scrapbook, 1961. Valley Players Collection. Holyoke Public Library.

"It was the highest grossing show of the season at a soaring $9,394.11, with a grand attendance of 5,246." The Valley Players Financial Accounts 1941-1962, Valley Players Collection, Series 4, Administration 1941-19842, Box 1, Holyoke Public Library.

"*The production was plagued with a variety of opening night mishaps…*" *Holyoke Transcript-Telegram*, August 22, 1961, "Valley Players Have Uphill Fight Opening Night with Uneven Script". Valley Players Scrapbook 1961. Valley Players Collection. Holyoke Public Library.

"*If the Valley Players are going to try as hard to improve themselves next season as that have raised their standards this season, then we would say bravo!!..*" *Chicopee Herald*, August 31, 1961, "The Play's the Thing" by W. Manta. Valley Players Scrapbook 1961. Valley Players Collection. Holyoke Public Library.

"*The response at the box office has been disappointing. Nearly all of us go to see a Valley Players production once in a while..*" *Holyoke Transcript-Telegram*, July 27, 1962, "An Empty Stage, Unless…" p. 8. Valley Players Scrapbook 1962. Valley Players Collection. Holyoke Public Library.

"*Everyone is glad to see that the Valley Players are all ready for another season at the Mountain Park Casino…*" *Holyoke*

Transcript-Telegram, May 26, 1962, "They Can't Live on Kind Words", p. 6. Valley Players Scrapbook 1961-1962. Valley Players Collection. Holyoke Public Library.

"…a 'very super-duper production…too, we would like to add a bravos on the choral work of the players…'" *West Springfield Record*, July 12, 1962, "'Dark of the Moon' Given Fine Interpretation By Augmented Cat of Casino's Valley Players," review by R. W. Valley Players Scrapbook 1961-1962. Valley Players Collection. Holyoke Public Library.

"John Gordon, new theatre critic for the *Springfield Union*, broke the rumor that the end was near for The Valley Players…" *Springfield Union*, August 17, 1962 "Valley Players May Be Near Final Curtain," p. 1.

"The Valley Players paid ten payments of $400 each for rental of the Casino from the Mt. Tom Amusement Co., Inc.…" The Valley Players Financial Accounts 1941-1962, Valley Players Collection, Series 4, Administration 1941-19842, Box 1, Holyoke Public Library.

"Holyoke Ice and Fuel, bought lumber from the Street Lumber Corp…" The Valley Players Financial Accounts 1941-1962, Valley Players Collection, Series 4, Administration 1941-19842, Box 1, Valley Players Collection. Holyoke Public Library.

"The headline in the *Springfield Sunday Republican* was like a death-watch: "Theater-Lovers Pulling for Survival of Casino." *Springfield Sunday Republican*, August 26, 1962, "Theater-Lovers Pulling for Survival of Casino" by John M. Gordon, p. 8C.

Chapter 8

"*Local theater-goers learned today that the Holyoke Chamber of Commerce is sparking an area-wide effort…*" *Holyoke Transcript-Telegram*, December 7, 1962, "Area-Wide Effort is Planned for a Summer Theater at Mt. Park."

"*J.B.*, however, 'was stupendous. It was a superior artistic achievement that could stand comparison with the very best." *Holyoke Transcript-Telegram*, August 3, 1963, p. 1.

The *Daily Hampshire Gazette* remarked that the company, "…showed its talents were abundant in *A Thurber Carnival* and *Pygmalion*, but this latest production [*J.B*] removes all doubt of its ability…the finesse of the Casino players deserves the widest possible audience."

"However, the opening night audience had only 150 to 200 people." *Springfield Sunday Republican*, "On Stage and Screen" column by John M. Gordon, July 14, 1963, p. 8C.

"…*put the Casino in the Park back in the company of the angels. It is top quality…*" *Holyoke Transcript-Telegram*, August 2, 1963, "Quality Shows Should Draw Greater Attendance at The

Casino in the Park" by Anabel B. Murphy, p. 1

"*For these complimentary aims to be realized, the project has to break even financially…*" *Holyoke Transcript-Telegram*, August 2, 1963, "Quality Shows Should Draw Greater Attendance at The Casino in the Park" by Anabel B. Murphy, p. 1

"*Nobody knows how many people there are who would be sorry to see the theater go under, but who have not yet attended any shows…*" *Holyoke Transcript-Telegram*, August 2, 1963, "Quality Shows Should Draw Greater Attendance at The Casino in the Park" by Anabel B. Murphy, p. 1

"*We feel sure the Pioneer Valley Foundation will try again. They have learned a lot …*" *Springfield Union*, Wednesday, August 28, 1963, "Mountain Park Presenting 'Romeo and Juliet' in Finale,' review by R. E. B., p. 12.

Chapter 9

"Hugh Fordin, described by the *Holyoke Transcript-Telegram* in 1964 as a 'young, personable and energetic man,' entered…" *Holyoke Transcript-Telegram*, June 17, 1964.

"Evening shows started at 8:30 Monday through Friday, and Saturday's evening show started at 9 p.m. Matinees were Wednesdays and Saturdays." Mt. Tom Playhouse programs, The Valley Players Collection, Holyoke Public Library.

"Prices for matinees were $3 for the front orchestra and side divans…" Mt. Tom Playhouse programs, The Valley Players Collection, Holyoke Public Library.

"*Every summer theatre needs apprentices…*" Unknown paper, May 7, 1964, The Valley Players Collection, Holyoke Public Library.

"*Tallulah Bankhead is in town and she's exhausted…she and her entourage and her cast got into Logan Airport in Boston at 5 this morning after a jet flight from Miami…*" Unknown newspaper clipping dated July 8, 1964, The Valley Players Collection, Holyoke History Public Library.

"*Bing Crosby and wife, Kathryn, gave superb performances Saturday night. Bing gave…*" *Holyoke Transcript-Telegram*, August 24, 1964. "Kathryn Crosby's Performance Superb as Husband Bing Watched", p.1.

"The *Holyoke Transcript-Telegram* noted that Mr. Lamas, '…generally enlivened the evening with his discreet mugging.'" Holyoke Transcript-Telegram, August 25, 1964. The Valley Players Collection, Holyoke Public Library.

"*Last year, the old Casino on the mountain became, officially, the Mt. Tom Playhouse…*" *Holyoke Transcript-Telegram* clipping, June 17, 1965. The Valley Players Collection, Holyoke Public Library.

"The newspaper ran a photo of them at pool…" *Holyoke Transcript-Telegram* clipping June 25, 1965. The Valley Players Collection, Holyoke Public Library.

"Sheila had arrived at Westfield's Barnes Airport, jokingly pretending to be her ditsy character…" Unknown newspaper, June 19, 1964, "Shelia Arrives & Stars Tonight in First Mt. Tom Playhouse Show." The Valley Players Collection, Holyoke Public Library.

"A review by Michael McCartney gushed, Sheila Macrae…" *Holyoke Transcript-Telegram* clipping, review by Michael McCartney, June 21, 1965. The Valley Players Collection, Holyoke Public Library.

"An ad-lib on opening night during one production number: Lille suddenly…" *Holyoke Transcript-Telegram*, July 23, 1965. "'High Spirits' Star Is Happy Woman," by Tim Dacey.

"The *Transcript-Telegram* thought he "fights the Mt. Tom acoustics a bit, but comes through…"" *Holyoke Transcript-Telegram*, August 3, 1965, "'A Remedy for Winter' Shows Hit Potential at Mt. Tom Playhouse," p. 8.

"New England people are so nice. The audiences are blunt, and if they like you, then you know you are really…" *Holyoke Transcript-Telegram*, September 3, 1964. The Valley Players Collection, Holyoke Public Library.

*"*Martha Raye, of course, was the whole show, with a spotlight so bright on her it …" *Holyoke Transcript-Telegram*, August 17, 1965, "If Martha's Your Cup of Tea Get Up To The Playhouse Quick," review by Jon Klarfeld, p. 5.

"On behalf of our staff and casts, I would like to extend to Storrowton Music Fair all Best Wishes for its sixth, singing, smash, successful season…Cordially, Hugh Fordin." *Holyoke Transcript-Telegram*, June 1, 2016, ad, p. 5.

"In the mid 20s, the names of Mabel Griffith and William [sic] *Dashiell held magnetic appeal…"* *Springfield Union*, December 24, 1969, p. 23.

"In 1983, the *Holyoke Transcript-Telegram* employed over one hundred people, with a circulation…" *Springfield Republican*, July 22, 2015, "Dwight Family Delivered 'Great Little Newspaper', by Stephen Jendrysik, p. P6.

"The *Holyoke Transcript-Telegram* quoted one Holyoke resident in the 1980s when the park's days seemed numbered…" *Holyoke Transcript-Telegram*, February 1, 1988, "Park Gave Holyoke Theater, Thrills," by Bill Zajac.

"In 1900 the biggest Holyoke employers were the Farr-Alpaca Company textile mill, the Skinner silk mill…" *Springfield Sunday Republican*, January 3, 1999, "Goodbye to the 20th Century" by Marla A. Goldberg, p. G8.

"As the city's population fell, from nearly seventy thousand at the peak

to about forty thousand in the 1980s, the buildings of the Flats deteriorated…" Kidder, Tracy. "Among Schoolchildren," essay in *The Pioneer Valley Reader – Prose and Poetry from New England's Heartland.* James C. O'Connell, ed. (Stockbridge, MA: Berkshire House Publishers, 1995), p. 232.

"Mrs. Guild managed the difficult feat of keeping her face straight without a sign of strain." *Springfield Daily News,* December 8, 1970.

"The Valley Players were an important part of the Holyoke area and it was sad when the plays ended. We can still remember how the audience gasped…" *Holyoke Transcript-Telegram,* June 3, 1982, obit of Ellen Andrews.

"Simon Oakland died in California in 1983, only six days after Jean Guild passed. The wire press obituary was augmented in the *Holyoke Transcript-Telegram…*" *Holyoke Transcript-Telegram,* August 31, 1983.

BIBLIOGRAPHY

BOOKS:

Bacon, Edwin M. *The Connecticut River and the Valley of the Connecticut – Three Hundred and Fifty Miles from Mountain to Sea.* (NY: G.P. Putnam's Sons, The Knickerbocker Press, 1906)

Brown, Richard D. "Ingenuity and Enterprise in Springfield – The Urbanization of a Country Town 1790-1840," in *Springfield 1636-1986.* Michael F. Koenig and Martin Kaufman, eds. (Springfield: Institute for Massachusetts Studies. 1987)

Carroll, Carole Lee; Bunny Hart, and Susan Day Meffert. *The Ogunquit Playhouse: 75 Years – America's Foremost Summer Theatre.* (Portsmouth, NH: Back Channel Press. C. 2007)

DiCarlo, Ella Merkel. *Holyoke-Chicopee: A Perspective* (Holyoke, Mass.: Transcript-Telegram) 1982

Ducharme, Jay. *Mountain Park.* (Arcadia Publishing), 2008.

Erdman, Andrew L. *Queen of Vaudeville – The Story of Eva Tanguay.* (Ithaca: Cornell University Press, 2012)

Graci, David. *Mt. Holyoke-An Enduring Prospect – A History of New England's Most Historic Mountain.* (Holyoke, MA: Calem Publishing Co. 1985)

Holbrook, Hal. *Harold.* (NY: Farrar, Straus and Giroux, NY, 2011)

Holyoke Transcript-Telegram – The Last 100 Years (Historical Briefs, Inc., 1991)

Kennedy, Harold J. *No Pickle, No Performance.* (NY:

Doubleday and Company, Inc. 1978)

Kidder, Tracy. "Among Schoolchildren," essay in *The Pioneer Valley Reader – Prose and Poetry from New England's Heartland.* James C. O'Connell, ed. (Stockbridge, MA: Berkshire House Publishers, 1995)

Laurie, Joe Jr. *Vaudeville: From the Honky-Tonks to the Palace.* (NY: Henry Holt and Company, 1953)

Monbleau, Marcia J. *The Cape Playhouse.* (Dennis, Mass: The Raymond Moore Foundation, 1991, rpt. 2001)

O'Connell, James C., ed. *The Pioneer Valley Reader – Prose and Poetry of New England's Heartland.* (Stockbridge, Mass.: Berkshire House Publishers, 1995)

Ozieblo, Barbara, ed. *The Provincetown Players—A Choice of the Shorter Works.* (Sheffield, England: Sheffield Academic Press. 1994)

Slide, Anthony. *The Encyclopedia of Vaudeville.* (University Press of Mississippi; Reprint edition, 2012)

Thibodeau, Kate Navarra. *The Skinner Family and Wistariahurst.* (Charleston, SC: Arcadia Publishing, 2005)

Thomas, Peter A. "Springfield's Indian Neighbors" essay in *Springfield 1636-1986.* Michael F. Koenig and Martin Kaufman, eds. (Springfield: Institute for Massachusetts Studies. 1987)

Trav S.D. *No Applause – Just Throw Money – The Book that Made Vaudeville Famous.* (NY: Faber and Faber, Inc., 2005)

WPA Guidebook to Massachusetts. Federal Writers Project, 1937, (rept. NY: Pantheon Books, 1983)

NEWSPAPERS AND PERIODICALS:

Agawam News (Agawam, Massachusetts)
Amherst Journal Record (Amherst, Massachusetts)
Belchertown Sentinel (Belchertown, Massachusetts)
The Billboard
Boston Daily Globe
Boston Post Magazine
Brockton Enterprise
Byrnes Dramatic Times (New York City)
The Catholic Observer
Chickuppy and Friends Magazine (Chicopee, Massachusetts),
Chicopee Herald.
Daily Hampshire Gazette (Northampton, Massachusetts)
The Hartford Times
Holyoke-A Weekly Union-News Magazine (Springfield, Massachusetts)
Holyoke Daily Transcript (Holyoke, Massachusetts)
Holyoke Daily Transcript and Telegram
Holyoke Saturday Democrat

New York Herald Tribune
New York Times
Springfield Daily News (Springfield, Massachusetts)
Springfield Daily Republican
Springfield Republican. MassLive website
Springfield Sunday Republican
Springfield Union
Springfield Union-News
Springfield Sunday Union and Republican.
Valley Shopper
Variety
West Springfield Record (West Springfield, Massachusetts)
The Westover Flyer (Westover AFB, Chicopee, Massachusetts)

INTERVIEWS AND CORRESPONDENCE

Barbara Bernard
Margaret "Peggy" Bowe
Dan Brunelle
Hugh Fordin
Marc Gonneville
Don Grigware
William Guild
Sheryl Mardeusz
George Murphy
Jim Othuse
Paul Rohan
Brad"Bob" Russell

COLLECTIONS AND ARCHIVES

The Valley Players Collection, Holyoke Public Library History Room and Archives. Mt. Tom Playhouse programs, most also from The Valley Players Collection, Holyoke History Room and Archives, as well as the *Holyoke Transcript-Telegram* on microfilm.

Letter Carlton Guild to Mrs. Mary Kates, Holyoke Public Library - The Valley Players Correspondence 1983-1984, Valley Players Collection, Series 4, Holyoke Public Library, Holyoke, Massachusetts.

Letter to the public from the Guilds, May 8, 1961. Valley Players Scrapbook 1961, Valley Players Collection, Holyoke Public Library.

Letter Hal Holbrook to Carlton and Jean Guild, April 14, 1959, quoted in *Holyoke Transcript-Telegram*, April 21, 1959, "'Mark Twain Tonight!' Which Is Getting Steady Rave Notices Had Its First Theater Audience Here". Valley Players Scrapbook 1959.

Springfield newspapers on microfilm in the Springfield City Library collection, Springfield, Massachusetts.

UNPUBLISHED MANUSCRIPTS

History of Mt. Park Casino, unpublished typescript July 1966 in the Holyoke History Room and Archives.

Mountain Park Casino-Pioneer Valley Drama Festival program

VALLEY PLAYERS/MT TOM PLAYHOUSE PROGRAMS

From the author's collection, and in the collections of Paul Rohan; Marc Gonneville; and in The Valley Players Collection, Holyoke History Room and Archives – Holyoke Public Library, Holyoke, Massachusetts.

FILM, VIDEO and RADIO

Fifty Years at Westover, a video documentary, producer/director John Gordon, c. 1990.

Mountain Park Memories, television documentary produced by David Fraser, WGBY-Springfield, Massachusetts, A Division of the WGBH Educational Foundation, c. 2002.

WMAS radio copy transcript of a review by Milton Hale, July 1, 1941 5:15 p.m., Hotel Charles, Springfield, Mass. Valley Players Scrapbook 1941.

INTERNET WEBSITES

Image Museum (https://imagemuseum.smugmug.com)

Library of Congress Prints and Photographs Online (http://www.loc.gov/pictures)

Murphy, George. "Tallulah and Me," essay on Mr. Murphy's *Holyoke Mass. Radio WREB* blog, March 26, 2007, used by permission.

PHOTO CREDITS:

Front and rear cover photos: from the Valley Players Collection of the Holyoke History Room, Holyoke Public Library, used by permission. Mt. Tom Playhouse photo from the *Holyoke Transcript-Telegram.* Most of the Valley Players photos were taken by Neil Doherty, but are noted as such in captions only when that can be verified; however unless otherwise noted, it is most likely that Mr. Doherty is the photographer.

Introduction:

P. xiii – Photo of the actors peeking through the flats, Neil Doherty presumed photographer.

P. xiv – 1887 map of the Holyoke-Chicopee-Springfield area.

Chapter 1: The various photos of Mt. Tom, Holyoke, and Springfield are all either from the author's collection, local libraries, or found online; all are pre-1920 and are in the public domain.

P. 10 – Holyoke 1906

Chapter 2

P. 24 – Mt. Park Opera Company cast 1901 – Holyoke History Room, Holyoke Public Library, used by permission.

Chapter 3

P. 40: Federal Theatre posters – Library of Congress

P. 42 – Mountain Park poster – Holyoke Public Library

P. 43: Federal Theatre poster, library of Congress

Chapter 4

Pioneer Valley Drama Festival program – Holyoke Public Library

All Valley Players photos are from the Valley Players Collection, Holyoke History Room, Holyoke Public Library. Used by permission. Photographer is Neil Doherty, except where noted by Raymond D'Addario.

P. 50 Carmen Matthews, Jean Guild, Gloria Humphries, Doris Poland, and Brightside kids on roller coaster; photo by Raymond D'Addario.

Chapter 5

All Valley Players photos are from the Valley Players Collection, Holyoke History Room, Holyoke Public Library. Used by permission. Photographer is Neil Doherty, except where noted.

P. 75 Ellen Andrews and Helen Harrelson 1946, in the dressing room, *Holyoke Transcript-Telegram* photo.

P. 82 Toto's on Route 5, Holyoke. Holyoke History Room, Holyoke Public Library. Used by permission.

Chapter 6

All Valley Players photos are from the Valley Players Collection, Holyoke History Room, Holyoke Public Library. Used by permission. Photographer is Neil Doherty, except where noted.

P. 118 Smith residence Lincoln Street, Hal Holbrook, possibly Ruth Elliot, and Simon Oakland, with unidentified boy. Valley Players Collection, Holyoke Public Library, used by permission. Photographer unknown.

P. 119 Hal Holbrook, Ruby Holbrook, baby Victoria Holbrook, possibly Guild residence on Lincoln Street. Valley Players Collection, Holyoke Public Library, used by permission. Photographer unknown.

Lincoln Street picnic, Hal Holbrook, Ruby Holbrook across facing camera, Valley Players company. Valley Players Collection, Holyoke Public Library, used by permission. Photographer unknown.

P.120 Lincoln Smith residence on Northampton Street: Simon Oakland and Bertram Tanswell. Valley Players Collection, Holyoke Public Library, used by permission. Photographer unknown.

Lincoln Street picnic, Jacqueline Paige, Dorothy Crane, unknown, John O'Connor, unknown. Valley Players Collection, Holyoke Public Library, used by permission. Photographer unknown.

P. 127 Rehearsal in the Lincoln Smith barn on Northampton Street, Jean Guild and Hal Holbrook are among the cast. Valley Players Collection, Holyoke Public Library, used by permission. Photographer unknown.

P. 129 JFK, Mrs. Kennedy holding baby Caroline ride on a float in the St. Pat's Parade, Holyoke, 1958.
Photo by Ann Lynch Beebe, author's collection.

P. 145 *The Reluctant Debutante* 1957, Lee Graham, modeling fur for Langley furrier fashion shot, Neil Doherty photo.

P.170 Jacob and Adeline Barowsky, and Holyoke Mayor Samuel Resnic.. Holyoke History Room, Holyoke Public Library, used by permission.

Chapter 7

All Valley Players photos are from the Valley Players Collection, Holyoke History Room, Holyoke Public Library, used by permission.

Chapter 8

Images taken from Casino-in-the-Park programs, Holyoke History Room, Holyoke Public Library, and ads from the *Holyoke Transcript-Telegram.*

Chapter 9

P. 196 Arlene Francis publicity photo from Kind Sir program

P. 200 Barbara Bernard interviews Van Johnson on *The Barbara Bernard Show,* Channel 40, WHYN-TV, Springfield, Mass. Photo courtesy of *The Republican.*

P. 202 Peggy Cass and Marc Gonneville, photo by Messenger Photos, courtesy Marc Gonneville.

P. 203 Merv Griffin, stylist Marc Gonneville and cast members in the dressing room at the Mt. Tom Playhouse. Photo courtesy Marc Gonneville.

P. 206 Lloyd Bridges publicity photo, courtesy Marc Gonneville

P. 208 Marc Gonneville in salon with Eloise Hardt and Mrs. Lloyd Bridges families; Jeff Bridges on far right.
Photo courtesy Marc Gonneville.

P. 209 Esther Williams, photo courtesy Marc Gonneville

P. 212 Anne Meara & Jerry Stiller, George Murphy collection

P. 213 Bea Lille, photo George Murphy collection

P. 220 Gertrude Berg with stylist Marc Gonneville at the Kay-Harvey salon, Maple Street, Holyoke. Photo courtesy Marc Gonneville.

Chapter 10

P. 229 Reunion 1993 Mary Kates, Library director, Peter Harris, Ruby Holbrook, Gaylord Mason, Holyoke Public Library collection, used by permission.

P. 230 Reunion 1993, Gaylord Mason on the left, Holyoke Public Library collection, used by permission.

P. 231 Reunion 1993, Ruby Holbrook, Jean Burns, unknown others, Holyoke Public Library collection, used by permission.

P. 234 From 1952: Dorothy Crane, Mac Gress, Jean Guild, Lauren Gilbert, Tash Bozek, Nancy Wells,
Vivian Marlowe, Bertram Tanswell, Jackson Perkins. Holyoke Public Library

P. 235 Mt. Tom from the Holyoke Dam, photo by the author.

P. 252 Ruth Elliot 1949 photo by Lucas and Monroe Studio, Valley Players Collection, Holyoke Public Library, used by permission.

INDEX:

Also by the author:

ABOUT THE AUTHOR

Non-fiction:

Jacqueline T. Lynch's novels, short stories, and non-fiction books on New England history and film criticism are available from many online shops as eBooks, audiobooks, and paperback. She is also a playwright whose plays have been produced around the United States and in Europe, and has published articles and short fiction in regional and national publications. She writes *Another Old Movie Blog* on classic films.

Ann Blyth: Actress. Singer. Star.
Movies in Our Time: Hollywood Mirrors and
    Mimics the 20ᵗʰ Century
States of Mind: New England
The Ames Manufacturing Company of Chicopee,
    Massachusetts
Calamity Jane in the Movies

Fiction:

The Double V Mystery Series:

Cadmium Yellow, Blood Red
Speak Out Before You Die
Dismount and Murder
Whitewash in the Berkshires

Beside the Still Waters
Meet Me in Nuthatch
Myths of the Modern Man
The Current Rate of Exchange
Collected Shorts

Website: *www.JacquelineTLynch.com*